PHILOSOPHICAL AND LITERARY
PIECES

PHILOSOPHICAL AND LITERARY PIECES

BY

SAMUEL ALEXANDER

EDITED, WITH A MEMOIR,
BY HIS LITERARY EXECUTOR

Essay Index Reprint Series

 BOOKS FOR LIBRARIES PRESS
FREEPORT, NEW YORK

First Published 1940
Reprinted 1969

STANDARD BOOK NUMBER:
8369-1269-1

LIBRARY OF CONGRESS CATALOG CARD NUMBER:
70-93313

PRINTED IN THE UNITED STATES OF AMERICA

PREFACE

PROFESSOR ALEXANDER gave me entire discretion regarding the publication or republication of all his writings; but I am happy to know that my judgment as respects this volume was in entire agreement with his. And we had many talks about what the book was to be. It will be sufficient, I think, if I now explain, firstly, that he published during his lifetime everything that he wanted to publish; secondly, that we agreed not to republish anything that he wrote last century; thirdly, that we both thought it would be a mistake to republish anything that was superseded by *Space, Time, and Deity*. These principles of omission implied the absence of some very good work; but the list of published work printed in the present volume should enable Alexander scholars and/or thesis-writers to find what they want, if with some little difficulty.

I have the pleasant duty of expressing my gratitude to the various responsible persons who showed their appreciation of what Mr. Alexander had done and had been by courteously permitting the republication of these pieces. I have, I hope, made correct formal acknowledgment by printing the source of obligation in each instance with sufficient accuracy and plainness. But in a more personal way I should like to thank each and all for the promptness and kindliness with which they did what I hoped they would do.

Many of Alexander's best and closest friends have helped, to an extent I cannot compute, by sending me his letters, and, often at personal inconvenience, by supplying me with recollections and with other material for the Memoir. I have pieced these things together as smoothly as I could; and they have made the Memoir. But I have also omitted much that was sent me, thinking I had to be

PREFACE

ruthless in avoiding repetition. It is harder for me to thank those whom I have not quoted extensively than to thank the others. Still, all who wrote to me did so from a pious and tender attachment to Alexander's memory. We therefore worked together, and although I alone must take the blame for the faults that disfigure the Memoir I hope that the skilful and willing assistance I have had may redeem many of these defects and allow an indulgent public to forgive me.

Having received permission to repeat myself, I wrote a much shorter version of this Memoir for the British Academy; but there was little verbal repetition.

J. L.

UNIVERSITY OF ABERDEEN
January 1939

CONTENTS

Professor S. Alexander, *aetat.* 68 . . *Frontispiece*
(From a photograph by F. W. Schmidt, Manchester.)

                                                        PAGE

Memoir 1

PHILOSOPHICAL AND LITERARY PIECES

I. The Mind of a Dog 97
(Reprinted from *The Cornhill Magazine*, July 1906.)

II. Dr. Johnson as a Philosopher . . . 116
(Reprinted from *The Cornhill Magazine*, October–November 1923.)

III. The Art of Jane Austen . . . 138
(Reprinted from the *Bulletin of the John Rylands Library*, July 1928.)

IV. Molière and Life 164
(Reprinted from the *Bulletin of the John Rylands Library*, July 1926.)

V. Pascal the Writer 188
(Reprinted from the *Bulletin of the John Rylands Library*, July 1931.)

VI. Art and the Material 211
(Manchester University Lectures, No. XXIII.)

VII. Art and Instinct 233
(The Herbert Spencer Lecture, delivered at Oxford, May 23, 1927. Published by the Clarendon Press.)

VIII. Artistic Creation and Cosmic Creation . 256
(Reprinted from the *Proceedings of the British Academy*, vol. xiii.)

CONTENTS

	PAGE
IX. NATURALISM AND VALUE	279

(Reprinted from *The Personalist*, October 1928.)

X. VALUE 287

(Reprinted from the *Bulletin of the John Rylands Library*, July 1933.)

XI. NATURAL PIETY 299

(Reprinted from *The Hibbert Journal*, July 1922.)

XII. THEISM AND PANTHEISM 316

(Reprinted from *The Hibbert Journal*, January 1927.)

XIII. SPINOZA 332

(Manchester University Lectures, No. XXIX.)

XIV. SPINOZA AND TIME 349

(The Fourth Arthur Davis Memorial Lecture, delivered before the Jewish Historical Society at University College, May 1, 1921. Published by George Allen & Unwin for the Arthur Davis Memorial Trust.)

ELENCHUS OPERUM 387

MEMOIR

I. Schoolboy and Undergraduate

FORTUNATELY this narrative may begin with Alexander's own words :

Recollections

18 *Ap*. 1928.—I am moved by a suggestion of my friend and colleague Powicke to set down some recollections, mainly about various interesting people I have met. I do not propose to write an autobiography and still less a confession, for I have no mind to talk about my faults, and I am not proud of my virtues, such as they are. These are notes which may possibly amuse my friends or be useful to myself when I am older (I am 69 now) and begin to forget. I have never kept a diary, and the letters I have kept are so disorderly that I had best confine myself to what I can remember now without their help.

I was born in Sydney,[1] N.S.W., on 6 Jan. 1859 and I never knew my father, who died just before my birth. He died of consumption, but none of his children inherited it. My mother removed to Melbourne when I was 4 or 5, living in St. Kilda. My earliest recollections are of 3 things, only one of which is pleasant — of being petted by my grandmother who used to dip toast or bread into her coffee and give it to me. (I seem to recollect her death ; I must have been in the room, for I have a picture of a figure rising at full height from the bed and then falling back supported in the arms of my mother or my aunts.) My other recollections are (1) of Darlinghurst Gaol, near which we lived but never any of us inhabited, and I am

[1] At 436 George Street. Alexander was brought into the 'Covenant of Abraham' on January 13, 1859.

sorry to say, (2) of having gone to my aunt's near by, coming away early, and, I am sorry to say, when asked why, inventing a lie.

At St. Kilda, we first had governesses and private tutors, but the last of these tutors, a Mr. Atkinson, set up a private school to which my 2 brothers and I went (I was the youngest) and a few other boys. He was, I am afraid, quite mad. For he issued a great poster to advertise the school in which he said that he had a boy (meaning me) who wrote like the Muses and did other wonderful things like that. He had some phrases which he said, if you knew, you knew all French and all Italian. His wife, who, he said, was a sister (or daughter) of F. A. Paley, the classical scholar at Cambridge, he was very proud of because she had a gift for solving arithmetical problems in her head; and she used to do these in our presence, and I daresay had a remarkable gift of that kind. After the advertisement my mother distrusted our teacher, and so did other people, and the school came to an end.

When I was about 12 or 13 I went to Wesley College,[1] the head of which was M. H. Irving, a remarkable man. He was the son of Edward Irving, and is the baby in the arms of Irving's wife whom Carlyle refers to in his *Reminiscences*. Martin Irving had been at Balliol and a pupil of Jowett (I suppose when Jowett was tutor), and after being a schoolmaster at, I think, Bluecoat School, had gone out to Melbourne as Professor of Classics at the University, having got married or wishing to do so. He gave up his chair to be headmaster of the School. Later in life he had a school of his own and then became Minister of Education of Victoria for a time in the Berry administration, I believe. The school (Wesley College) was a very good one, giving us a broad education in Classics, Mathematics, English (which was made a point of), French, and some science. I have always felt grateful to it, for its efficiency and many-sidedness — Irving was a man of character, rather stern but very kind. His lessons to the

[1] In 1871, to be precise.

MEMOIR

VIth Form were always a delight to us. He used for a time to take the VIth every week to see some interesting manufacture, say bootmaking, the Mint, and we had to write an essay on what we had seen. I once saw him cane a boy; he went white in the face as he did it. Many years later he came to see me in Manchester (about 1896 or 7) and stayed in the house. He was 66 and a distinguished-looking man and very well preserved. He lived the remainder of his life at Albury in Surrey among a settlement of Irvingites, in which church he held high office.

Two of my fellow-schoolboys I have seen since in England, J. W. Springthorpe, who was head of the Australian Medical Service in the War, and Felix Meyer, a gynaecologist in large practice at Melbourne.

My mathematical teacher at Wesley College was H. M. Andrew, who succeeded Irving as head — a Cambridge man, afterwards Professor of Physics.

After 2 years at the University where I had done well, I came to England [1] and have not returned to Australia since. My mother was persuaded to let me come and made the sacrifice of money necessary to support me, even if I got [sic] a scholarship at Oxford or Cambridge. What I should have done without such a scholarship I don't know, but I supposed she was advised that my chances were good. I was greatly perplexed whether I should go to Oxford or Cambridge, Irving advocating the first and Andrew the second. I have never had a character of decision and for a long time I remained uncertain and perplexed, and bored others as well as myself in England. One person whom I consulted was Todhunter the mathematician, whom I went to Cambridge to see. Even after my first 2 terms at Oxford I was a prey to the doubt whether I should not exchange to Cambridge, and went to coach with Routh at Cambridge who told me that I was not certain of doing very well in

---

[1] Round the Horn. 'Sam left by the *Renown* on the 12th May 1877 and arrived in London after a voyage of 108 days.' Comment from Australia.

Mathematics. That quieted my mind and I returned comfortably to Oxford where I already had a scholarship at Balliol [I still sometimes wonder whether Cambridge would not have suited me better].

I came to Oxford after arriving in England and coached for Balliol with Arthur Higgs, an excellent scholar and a very odd man who lived by taking pupils for pass Greats. He assured me I was not good enough to be taken at Balliol and sent me in at Lincoln where they would not have me as a scholar, though afterwards they took me as a Fellow. But I went on and sat at Balliol. One of the candidates was George Curzon, who gave me my first experience of how rude an Eton boy can be. I sat at the same table as he and some other Eton boys, and I suppose he was unfavourably impressed by my air. At any rate one day when I went out, having finished the paper before the time, Curzon said quite loud, ' I don't think Mr. Alexander is going to get a scholarship '. I daresay that I agreed with him after my experience at Lincoln. Well, I got a scholarship and he didn't. But I don't think I was elected for my Latin and Greek but on the strength of an essay (and, I fancy, a Greek essay) and of flooring the rather easy mathematical paper which was then set in the classical scholarships. (I also sat for the mathematical scholarship and was placed *prox. access.*) There was a distinguished-looking young man sitting near me who seemed to do his papers with great ease and rapidity. He was J. W. Mackail who was first. (I came next.) I never knew Curzon when we were undergraduates. But curiously enough when I had taken my degree in the summer of 1881 he came to me to be coached for Greats and was my first pupil. Very pleasant too I found him. Neither of us remembered that little incident of 1877. I saw him from time to time and always had a regard for him. Considering his *hautain* manner, he seemed to me an affectionate man. I saw a good deal of Jowett, who asked me several times to breakfast or after dinner, when I met many distinguished people. I will put down what I remember of them. Just after my election J. introduced me to Lyulph Stanley (later Lord Sheffield) as a scholar, and said, 'I forget, Stanley, if you were a scholar of Balliol'. S. said, 'No. I was a fellow but never a scholar'. J. said, 'Ah, it's a better thing to be a scholar of Balliol than a fellow of Balliol'. At one party I met Huxley, who talked with Alfred Marshall (who was then at Balliol) about Ireland. M. spoke of the difference of race between the English and the Irish, but Huxley was contemptuous. One morning Sir George Jessel, the Master of the Rolls, said he had made an experiment to see if you really saw double when you were drunk and that he found he really did see double, but afterwards (I suppose as the intoxicant went on) saw single again. Jessel's blotched face looked as if intoxication were not a matter of a single experiment with him. Lady Jessel, whom I sat next to, said of D. S. Margoliouth,[1] who was then a famous undergraduate and whom she had met or also may have been at the breakfast, that 'he was very plain' (M.'s face is remarkable but very ugly). At one breakfast Dean Stanley (who was wearing an order with red ribbon round his neck) told us stories of Gladstone and Disraeli which are given, I think, in Stanley's *Life*. One was that Disraeli had gone round the pictures at the R. Academy and said to R. Browning, 'Very poor stuff this, Mr. Browning'. At the banquet Disraeli praised the exhibition to the skies, and Browning, who was sitting next Gladstone, told him what D. had said to him. Gladstone said, 'It's bad enough to hear this sort of thing in the House of Commons where one has to listen to it every day, but to have to listen to it here is absolutely hellish'. The other was that when Gladstone was in retirement D. strolled down to him at a public dinner where G. was sitting next the Dean and said to him, 'You really must come back to the House, Mr. Gladstone, we can't do without you'. And G. said, 'There are things possible and there are things impossible. What you ask me to do is a thing impossible.' D. turned to Stanley

[1] Who magnanimously permits publication.

MEMOIR

and said, ' Behold the inexorable wrath of Achilles '. — At this same or another breakfast was present John Stuart Blackie, who got very excited and, I think, put his foot on a chair, and Jowett had to cool him down. I don't know whether it was on this visit or another that Blackie came to a gathering of undergraduates and talked, I forget about what. At one moment he said, ' I have kissed many lassies in my life ; aye, and many lads too. Now there's a lad I should like to kiss.' And he marched to the end of the room where was Leonard Huxley who was extremely good-looking and threw his arms about him and kissed him, to Huxley's dismay and our delight. — Other people I remember seeing were Jebb, and Andrew Lang, and Lewis Campbell.

We used to take essays to Jowett. Once he told me, ' Your style is too flowery. The Chinese like a flowery style. We don't.' A. C. Clark once wrote an essay which was too full of examples, and J. got down his Plato from a shelf and read the passage from the *Theaetetus*, ' Too much, Theaetetus, too much. I ask you for one and you give me many.' He said very little on these occasions. Several times I went in my last year or afterwards to stay with him at Malvern or at Boar's Hill. He went on with his work and talked to us at meals. He would take us singly for walks. On one of these he asked me how old I was, and when I said ' 22 ', he said, ' You have 30 or 40 years before you of reading and writing '. He did me the great kindness of doing essays with me after I had taken my schools, by way of preparing for a fellowship. After one of these on Metaphysics, when I had been very enthusiastic, he said, ' It's extraordinary what a fascination metaphysics seems to possess for certain minds — it's like falling in love ; but you get over it after a time '. Once on returning from a Long Vacation I told him I had read all Hegel. He said, ' It's a great thing to have read the whole of Hegel ; but now that you have read him, I advise you to forget him again '. I fear I took this advice, but these sayings of his were not intended as discouragement or as

MEMOIR

sceptical but to advocate moderation — I wish I had taken his advice to read for Mathematical Greats. I had got a first in Mathematical Mods. but after Greats [1] I was tired of being examined, and also wanted to do what my friends were doing. But I have always regretted it. The result was that I broke off my mathematical work, and though I don't suppose I should have become a mathematician, the higher work would have been of great advantage to me in philosophy.

I have written something about Jowett in an article on Johnson in the *Cornhill*.

Here the narrative breaks off, never to be resumed. It was written at great speed (very illegibly and without revision) on the unruled side of a used examination script. The typescript of *Space, Time, and Deity* and of much else had the same humble material for its art. That was one of the quaint economies of an amazingly generous man.

I shall make a few rather desultory comments upon the narrative.

Alexander's surviving brother, Maurice, tells me that the father's name was Samuel, that he was about thirty-eight when he died, and that (Mr. Maurice believes) he had emigrated from somewhere in England. The mother's maiden name was Eliza Sloman. She came from Cape Town and of a family that had settled in South Africa about 1820 after emigrating from Chatham, I suppose under the plantation scheme of the Regency parliament. Samuel Alexander, the father, was a saddler in a good way of business (which he owned and ran himself.)

In 1930 when Alexander received the Order of Merit, Australia woke up to his renown, and made a search after biographical material. In one of the articles that appeared at the time, entitled 'Australia's New Headline to Fame', it was said that Alexander's first teacher (I suppose [2] the

---

[1] Alexander had firsts in Mathematical and in Classical Mods. and in Classical Greats.

[2] If the information is accurate.

first after Atkinson) was 'a wonderful old man named Walter Thomas Pegus who kept a collegiate academy in the marine suburb [of St. Kilda] '. The article went on to say that Alexander, when he entered the University of Melbourne, 'got all three exhibitions of the college, a thing never done before or since'. There was mention, also, of Irving, whose chair at the University (before he took to school-mastering) had the pleasant title of 'Professor of Classical Comparisons and Philosophical Logic '.

The Registrar of the University of Melbourne writes : 'Samuel Alexander matriculated on the 22nd March 1875 and entered upon the Arts Course. At the Honour examination of the first year, he was placed in the first class and was awarded the Classical and Mathematical Exhibitions : at the Honour examination of the second year he was again placed in the first class and awarded exhibitions in Greek, Latin, and English ; Mathematics and Natural Philosophy ; and Natural Science.'

Alexander kept several letters from Springthorpe (certain of them metaphysical) and some from Meyer. During his last years some other Australian schoolfellows wrote him from their vicarages and from other such addresses.

Meyer kept some early letters from Alexander. The first, written a month or so after Alexander's arrival, is signed D.S. (Dejected Samuel) : ' I'm not going to get the Balliol. Haven't the ghost of a chance for it. Higgs says so. So does Mr. Abbott. I don't know whether I'll go in for it at all ; perhaps I'll go for the Balliol Mathl. Schol., which is as much tin.' The second, written on 18th January 1878, might well have been signed E.S. (Elated Samuel) : ' For myself, I am myself . . . I had done my best to make myself as miserable up to Nov. 29 as I could. I am happy now. In sheer despair and utter inability to see my way I came to Oxford . . . and the result of it all is that I'm a howling swell. I thought I had done miserably in the Classical exam. and often was inclined to knock off. . . . My Latin prose, which is my weakest point, was

MEMOIR

the very best done. My essay (on the Political and Public duties of Private Individuals — just fancy! what a hideous subject) was very swell and was, I believe, the best. I made a great point out of something Elkington told us one day in lecture. . . . You will think I have grown conceited, but I haven't. I look upon the affair with becoming humility and cannot yet make out how ever I got the scholarship.'

Alexander kept two letters from Irving written from the Grammar School, Hawthorn, about the Balliol scholarship. These letters have an undertone of sadness because of a bitter private sorrow of the writer's. But of course they were jubilant. ' I told nobody about your Lincoln absurdity, O you and Higgs of little faith ! ! ' ' *Macte* (I can't say *novâ*) *virtute puer* — for the *Virtus* has been there ever since I knew you.' ' I am really grateful to you for having persevered in spite of Strong [1] and Higgs.' ' If you were here just now I think Mr. Berry would give you a statue.' [2] ' You will tell me a little about the fight and the victory, won't you ? and beg a set of papers for me ? . . . You have made me a very happy man.'

A photograph taken just before Alexander left Australia shows a sensitive face, neither very striking nor beautiful. The hair is brushed straight back, making the brow rather impressive. Alexander had then an incipient moustache but no beard. Nobody seems to remember when the beard began, but he did not restrain it for long. I think it must always have been an improvement.

But let us pass to England.

I found two letters from Todhunter among Alexander's papers. They were written in 1877, the first just before and the second just after the award of the Balliol Scholarship. The writer did not know, or said he did not know, enough about Alexander's mathematical powers to advise him at all confidently. They show what Alexander feared, and the sort of career to which he aspired even then. Alexander's trouble at the time was the strength of the

---

[1] In Melbourne.   [2] ' Statute ' is what is written.

opposition he would have to face in the Scholarship competition at Balliol. He had clearly made up his mind to aim at an academic post either in classics or in mathematics, and was anxious to know whether an Oxford degree in mathematics and physics would be as likely to lead to advancement as a Cambridge degree in these subjects. On that point Todhunter was very frank. 'You must remember that I am a Cambridge man. . . . The honour to be gained, in such subjects, by Oxford undergraduates, is, I think, very small.'

In the obituary notice of Alexander in the *Manchester Guardian* (which was written, as I surmise, with knowledge) it is stated that Alexander's 'official tutors' at Balliol were Forbes, Strachan Davidson, and A. C. Bradley, and that T. H. Green and R. L. Nettleship were also tutors of Balliol at the time. I shall later have something to say about Green and A. C. Bradley. Regarding Nettleship I shall anticipate and refer to a review that Alexander wrote in later life of Nettleship's *Philosophical Remains*. He there expressed his admiration for Nettleship's determination 'to live his theories and beliefs', like a very Greek philosopher of old. 'The secret of his character and thinking', Alexander wrote, 'we gather to have been his simplicity and sincerity and directness of contact with whatever he did and thought. Those qualities gave singleness to a nature which was full of contrasts ; modest and independent, no stranger to passion and yet respectful ; gay at times and genial, and at the same time austere and even pathetically stoical.'

Dr. Mackail tells me that Alexander, the undergraduate, although very much liked by all who knew him, was not prominent in the general life and activities of the College. He adds that Alexander 'did not appear in *The Masque of Balliol*', verses so often quoted and misquoted in later days.

Alexander conscientiously visited Australian undergraduates. 'There has been a perpetual flux of Australians into this place ;' he wrote to Meyer in Nov. 1881, just after

MEMOIR

'a trouble got over', viz. his First in Greats, 'I am doing my duty manfully this term. Am going to call on one at Magdalen in a quarter of an hour. Keep of the W[esley] College is here, I find, at Corpus and the Lord only knows who beside. Springy [*i.e.* Springthorpe] I have of course seen [in London], but he was then in arms against English radicalism, Bradlaugh, and other monsters of the imagination, and was despairing of improvement in English politics and altogether disposed to exalt Mr. Berry at their expense.'

Alexander never had any interest in ball games even as a boy. At Oxford he was a rather uncomfortable Volunteer. He used to tell of a peremptory order to get his hair cut before the next parade, and (I am told) of 'the resentment of two privates, of whom he was one, at having to sleep in a barn and watch next morning the officers' adieus to the ladies of the house'.

Anticipating again, I may remark that Alexander kept two of Curzon's letters written to him in 1888. In the first of them Curzon regretted that, having been abroad, he had been unable to participate 'in the agreeable composition you suggest'. This was plainly a pupil's testimonial to Alexander's capacity to teach philosophy. Curzon added that he feared 'that anything related to Philosophy and signed by me would not have improved your chances'. The next letter has more general interest and gives an indication of Alexander's attitude in social and political affairs. Here it is:

'7 ST. JAMES'S PLACE S. 10
Feb. 21, 88

'MY DEAR ALEXANDER,

'As you say controversy is a bore and I will not enter upon it. One word only in answer to your points. (I wish Home Rule were always advocated on such high and respectable grounds.)

'I don't want to begin to Federate the Empire by untying the United Kingdom. Otherwise you may find no Empire left to federate. I don't think you appreciate the effect which the granting of Home Rule to Ireland would have upon our colonies and upon India. So far from fostering the movement for Federation it would give the *coup de grâce* at once. Secondly the constitution proposed to be given to Ireland by Mr. Gladstone was in no respect a Federal Constitution.

' If it were, why begin to Federate in the one case where Federation will not be accepted by all the people and is certain to mean Civil War ?

'Yours ever [1]

'GEORGE CURZON'

II. FELLOW OF LINCOLN

The *Jewish Chronicle* of May 5, 1882, contained the following paragraph: 'A Jew has been elected to a Fellowship of one of the colleges of the two Universities for the first time since the passing of the Test Act of 1870. Numa Hartog would doubtless have obtained a Fellowship at Trinity College, Cambridge, if ruthless disease had not carried him away before he could possess that crowning honour. It has been reserved for Mr. Samuel Alexander, of Balliol College, to earn the honourable distinction of being the first Jew to obtain a Fellowship. . . . Mr. Alexander intends, we believe, to remain in England [there had been a reference to his Australian origin] and should now be welcomed among us as an honour to the whole Community.' The last sentence is not altogether happy and (perhaps from perplexity) there is no mention of the circumstance that Alexander's Fellowship was at Lincoln College.

Alexander gave an account of his career from this date onwards to the electors at Owens College, Manchester, in 1893 — or, at any rate, he signed the statement, and I assume that he wrote it. (Odd things have occurred in matters of this kind, but they are not relevant here.) I shall quote the greater part of the statement verbatim :

---

[1] The ' ever ' is not easily legible.

MEMOIR

'In 1882 I was elected to a Fellowship at Lincoln College, my tenure of which expired a few days ago [June 6, 1893]. After a year's absence, during part of which I acquired some knowledge of German University life, I returned to Oxford, and took part in the philosophical teaching at Lincoln and at Oriel College, and also temporarily at Worcester College. Since taking my degree I have devoted myself to studying and teaching philosophy. My lectures at Oxford were mainly on subjects connected with Metaphysics and Ethics, but I also lectured on Greek Logic, and as tutor I taught all the subjects required for the Philosophical school, which includes Logic, Moral Philosophy, and Politics.

'In 1885 I was appointed Examiner for the full term of three years in the Honour School of *Literae Humaniores*, one portion of which consists of Philosophy. Two years ago I was honoured by reappointment to this office for a like term. I have also examined on several occasions in Logic and Mental Philosophy, as well as in Moral Philosophy for the Home and Indian Civil Services.

'In 1887 I was awarded the Green Moral Philosophy Prize for a dissertation in Ethics. This was made the foundation for a systematic work on Ethics, published in 1889 under the title of *Moral Order and Progress*. Besides this work, I have contributed various articles on philosophical subjects in *Mind*, the *Proceedings of the Aristotelian Society*, the *International Journal of Ethics*, and elsewhere.

'Wishing to obtain for a time more freedom for private study, I left Oxford at the end of 1888. During part of my time of absence I taught Elementary Psychology to a small class at Toynbee Hall, and presided over the meetings of a Philosophical Society at the same place, the members of both class and society being for the most part untrained students. But I gave up the greater part of my leisure during this time to studying Psychology, and in order to make myself well acquainted with the latest or experimental development of that science, I spent the winter of 1890–91 in Germany, working in the psychological laboratory of Professor Münsterberg at Freiburg i. B. Since that time I have also endeavoured by practical work and study in Physiology and Biology, here and at London, to qualify myself for further study in this department of the subject, and I have also exercised myself in the proper practical work of Psychology.

'From June of 1891 I have been again resident in Oxford. Besides my work as Examiner I have, during the last two years, given a course of lectures on Psychology, and I have taught private pupils in all the usual subjects of the philosophical school. I may mention that both these pupils and my old college pupils, though reading for Honours, have been of all degrees of merit. On several occasions I have lectured to popular audiences at Toynbee Hall and at the London and Cambridge Ethical Societies.'

As before, I shall make a commentary on this statement, but this time my commentary will be longer than its text.

The period of reading and of waiting for a Fellowship was rather trying. In witness I quote part of a letter from A. C. Bradley when the Fellowship was won.

'I am most unfeignedly and unmixedly glad. . . . I know how happy you must be feeling, not only because of the honour, but because now you will be able to follow your bent, instead of being driven to think of £ s d and such abominations as the Bar. I speak as a philosopher: the Bar may be a fine enough thing to a Barman, and no doubt it has its place in the scheme of things — said scheme including murders and frauds. But it is a mere $\dot{a}\nu a\gamma\kappa a\hat{i}o\nu$. I am heartily glad you are free from it.'

The newly appointed don acquired a part of his knowledge of German university life at Berlin. As I write I have before me a Berlin photographer's picture of a group of young men with Alexander seated in the centre and C. G. Montefiore beside him. Its date is November of 1882. Alexander has a full beard (it was reddish-brown and in the photograph is trimmer than usual). The face is striking rather than handsome, not at all austere, and alert rather than grave. It is unsmiling. The figure is also alert, and neither slim nor stout. The hand is delicate with, it would seem, rather long fingers.

Alexander has recorded some of his recollections of Lincoln College in a speech he made about Warde Fowler, then the sub-rector of the College. 'I remained in College', he said, 'with an interval of a year or two till 1893 and during that time saw a good deal of Fowler. During the first years we were almost the only Fellows in College and often dined together in Hall, for Merry, who soon after became Rector when Mark Pattison died, was then living in the Parks, Washburn West was irregular in his residence, and both Andrew Clark and the Senior Fellow Metcalfe lived outside. Later there came into residence F. J. Ashley (Sir F. J. A.) and Baldwin Spencer (afterwards Sir W. B. S.) and J. E. King.

'. . . We were a fairly happy family, and on terms of great personal kindness with one another. Fowler was exceedingly gentle, but he was subject to irritation, sometimes because he misheard what was said, but sometimes he lost his temper over trifles. We instituted breakfast in Common Room and I can remember much interesting discussion of Gladstone's first Home Rule Bill. . . . These breakfasts came to an end because one morning, something having displeased him, I think the food, Fowler took up a small loaf and flung it at the other end of our dignified Common Room, and we felt that the experiment had lasted long enough.

'The porter at College, the excellent John Hammond, was devoted to him, and so was his Swiss guide André, whom I met when I was on a walking tour with Fowler about the region of Engelberg and the Rhône-gletscher. — A simple-minded man this who, when Fowler was in want of a toothbrush, offered to lend him his own. Fowler often went expeditions in Switzerland, not climbing ones I think, but in search of birds and flowers. The most constant friend of all was Billy [his dog] about whom he wrote at least one article in *Macmillan's Magazine* telling of how he met his end in a drain-pipe in pursuit of a rabbit. . . . He introduced me to Courthope's *Paradise of Birds*, for which I have not ceased to be grateful.'

Mr. J. E. King tells me that the omission of Alexander's name from Warde Fowler's published reminiscences is due to the fact that they were compiled from diaries that had 'dried up' in Fowler's later years. In 1893, just after Alexander had gone to Manchester, Fowler wrote, ' What shall I do without you and Billy, the two friends who knew my weak points best ? ' He went on to say that Alexander would be mentioned in the ' little memoir of old Billy ' that was to appear in *Macmillan's* of December. The last letter Alexander had from Fowler, in 1918, begins, ' Yes it was my doing, but every one agreed joyfully at once '. ' It ' was Alexander's election to an Honorary Fellowship at Lincoln.

During the 'eighties Alexander made several visits to Switzerland and also to Tuscany and Touraine. He was often one of an Oxford group ; *e.g.* he had a holiday with F. H. Bradley at Mürren in 1887. That was his pleasure ; but he also thought of his health. He found the climate of Oxford rather unkind to him, and in the later years of his fellowship lived out of College a good deal, chiefly at Headington.

Alexander was not wholly satisfied with Oxford's intellectual climate. Towards the end of the period we are now considering he wrote to Stanley Hall's *American Journal of Psychology* about it, contributing to a series of open letters upon education. He had much to praise ; but he complained, firstly, of ' the tendency for the undergraduates to rely on lectures to a greater extent than even the vanity of the lecturers themselves would think desirable ', and secondly, of the ' most glaring weakness in the Oxford teaching ', the extrusion of psychology ' except as a part of logic '. Alexander said that William Blunt of

Christ Church had lectured on the subject and that he himself ' hoped to extend activity in this direction '.

That was in 1892, but it was an old opinion of Alexander's. In general it is plain that Alexander, while conforming like other lecturers to the system, was anxious to rejuvenate it.[1] That, for him, meant mixing philosophy with biology, with experimental psychology, in a word, with science. A fuller idea of his attitude may be inferred from some other things that he said in this open letter to Hall. ' The spell of Green's personality removed ', he wrote, ' the idealistic German philosophy by which Oxford has been so deeply influenced has lost much of its potency,[2] must I say, for evil or for good ? ' He found the times more favourable to criticism than to construction ; but he himself always longed for construction of a gradual and ' plodding ' kind.

In the matter of psychology he had rather gratifying success. Many of his old students, for example, Mr. Stephen Gwynn, retained for life (or said they did) something of the stimulus that Alexander had given them in this direction, and wrote him about it long years afterwards. Alexander's letter of application to Manchester contains a rather stilted but obviously sincere testimonial from a group of his psychological students (including a lady, one Fellow of a College, and a future University Vice-Chancellor). That may be a dubious type of testimonium, but it is interesting to a biographer. Legends grew up about this bearded and enthusiastic psychologist-philosopher. It was said that he had invented a pleasure-thermometer, and there were earnest enquiries about how it worked. A rumour says that Alexander tried to measure fear, he himself, in war paint, being the affrighting stimulus,

---

[1] At Lincoln he prepared an elaborate plan for college reform. It dropped.

[2] Cf. one of Alexander's earliest reviews (of Lotze, 1884) : ' Philosophy was then, and even after Lotze, is still, in a state of anarchy. The purely idealistic philosophy seems to have overreached itself, and especially in its view of nature it shocks the scientific habits of the time ; it has dropped out of mind, and as an " ueberwundener Standpunkt " is sometimes considered worthy of a compassionate historical interest.'

and that the experimenter was surprised at the immoderate hilarity he aroused.

I shall have a little more to say about experimental psychology; but, of course, it was not Alexander's exclusive or even his main occupation in these Oxford days. As his letter of application stated, he lectured on varied subjects, and he read the inevitable papers to senior societies. He has marked ' the first paper I wrote, I think ' on the (professional) typescript of a piece that he called ' Finger-Posts to Religion '. Probably it was not the first, for the date is November 14, 1886. It was read before the Religious Union Society at Oxford, James Bryce being in the chair. The paper was tentative and rather slight, but it attempted, like all Alexander's later work on this theme, to start from the emotion of reverence and give it a metaphysical status. A course on *Elementary Ideas in Philosophy* given in 1891–92 received a degree of finish that bespeaks ulterior designs.

Something should also be said about what seems very arid, Alexander's activities as an examiner in Greats, and in its long-drawn-out *vivâ voce* tests. Merry, the Rector of Lincoln, remarked in his Manchester testimonium that Alexander ' possessed a physical power that enabled him to conduct a long and complicated examination without flagging '; and some of the candidates were grateful to Alexander for the rest of their lives. I quote from a letter from a distinguished civil servant written many years afterwards : ' I have still a lively and grateful recollection of an occasion when I was being viva'd in Greats by your co-examiner who was very little in sympathy with the precepts I had imbibed from my tutor. I thought he was being unfair, and you intervened with an adroitness which my nervousness even then allowed me to admire.'

Alexander's abandonment of Oxford for London (and later for Freiburg) in 1888 was meant to be a more serious step than it was in the event (for he returned to Oxford). A letter from A. C. Bradley shows this. ' I have no doubt at all you are right ', Bradley wrote, ' and it is the brave thing to do. And I have no doubt you are right about psychology.'

I have very little detailed information about Alexander's activities at Toynbee Hall, but have enough to demonstrate that he lectured on a prodigious variety of subjects, and that he thoroughly enjoyed the zest of a rawer and townier intellectual atmosphere than Oxford's. A quotation from a letter written to Alexander in 1888 has some bearing on the point: ' It would be just like you to say that the Simpering Associates were the most clever and charming women you had met with the glorious exception of the pudding-makers of Berlin. I know *they* hold the 1st place.' The draft of a letter from Alexander to Ramsay MacDonald in 1930 refers to the same period: ' When you and I some forty years ago went together up Leith Hill along with the Mathesons I could not have imagined, and perhaps you could not, that the day would come when you would be Prime Minister and I receiving at your suggestion the highest honour open to me '.

During the later 'eighties Alexander employed some of his time in reviewing, and much in connection with the Aristotelian Society.[1] He joined the Society in April 1885 and soon became one of its Vice-presidents. He read several papers (some of them published) and took part in symposia with coming men like Stout and Ritchie and Muirhead, but also with eminent persons like Henry Sidgwick and G. J. Romanes. A very interesting point in connection with his later philosophy is that he boldly affirmed, despite what the redoubtable Sidgwick had said, that ' ought ' could be reduced (in a subtle way) to ' is '. That was his lifelong conviction. When, forty years later, he reviewed Westermarck's *Ethical Relativity* he wrote: ' In these days when ethical works pour out from Oxford and Cambridge in a brilliant reactionary flood to prove that no account can be given of good or right, it is a refresh-

---

[1] In the *Oxford Magazine* of November 25, 1891, there is a skit on philosophy entitled ' The External World on the Aristotelian Society '. Alexander is represented as *pro* psychology and *anti* Oxford Idealism.

ment to have a writer who attempts to throw light upon right and wrong by tracing them back to their origin '.

But Alexander debated many other things, and Shadworth Hodgson (who, to use the vernacular, *was* the Aristotelian Society at that time) had much to say, in letters as well as in discussion, about Alexander's views concerning self and substance and activity. ' I object to that fundamental fallacy ', he said, ' which is fundamental and common to all Idealists — to the varieties of Idealism represented by yourself and Bosanquet and Ritchie [1] — though you are all at variance on other points among yourselves. What is this common fundamental fallacy ? This : — you identify knowing with the knower.'

But let me turn to ethics, for that was the subject of Alexander's first book, *Moral Order and Progress*.

Alexander gained the Green Prize Essay in 1887, and the book (which was based upon the prize essay) was published in 1889 by the firm then known as Trübner and Co. of Ludgate Hill.

The book was very well received and had a vigorous existence for many years. Indeed it went into three editions, or, as we should now say, ' impressions ' — for no change was made. By 1912 Alexander had altered his views so considerably that he wanted the book to die, and he said so in what may be called an official letter. He retained that attitude. He thought that the volume had served its turn both in its author's development and in the development of British ethical theory. It had developed what may be called the Anglo-Aristotelian-Hegelian movement in British ethics in the direction of a sophisticated evolutionary theory with some boldness, and with much painstaking attention. In doing so it had advanced and had helped to consolidate something that was strong enough to outlive its youth. But the work, in another way, was ' dated ' and therefore, he thought, ephemeral.

This verdict, on the whole, would seem to be just.

[1] Fellow-symposiasts on the subject in Alexander's first symposium at the Aristotelian Society.

MEMOIR

Whatever may be thought about 'evolutionary ethics' — and Alexander remained an evolutionist in ethics to his last sagacious breath — the last and most interesting part of the book (*i.e.* Book III, which deals with 'moral dynamics' and with 'progress') has less analytical perspicuity than the earlier part, which, dealing with 'moral statics', gave the lecturer and prize-essayist an opportunity to review the traditional moral conceptions. This comparative analytical failure was natural because 'static' conceptions (puzzling although they remain) have had centuries of first-rate thinking devoted to them. Alexander's views about progress, about the place of ethics in a social bioplasm, about the sufficiency of Natural Selection, about a moving equilibrium as the arbiter of all value, could not satisfy his later self or a later age in the form in which he stated them in his first book.

The success of the book, it is true (and also a great part of its merit), depended upon the careful work that he put into his account of moral 'statics', that is to say into his account of 'the moral order' and of 'moral predicates' with the general design of showing how goodness and rightness and virtue and perfection should be included in an 'equilibrium of conduct'. That made the book useful as a textbook — with a distinctive 'modern' point of view at a time when Green was not modern enough. The volume, however, had the defects as well as the merits of this prize-essayist virtue. Regarded as a continuous argument it has a fault that, later, Alexander was quick to detect in others (as I know to my chagrin, although also, I hope, to my advantage). It is too episodic, too fond of pursuing distinctions for their own sakes without sufficient attention to their place in the general argument. For the rest it may suffice here to say that Alexander's style [1] at this period was just what he thought his later style was — workmanlike and no more. (But it was *very* workmanlike, especially in the freer treatment, and more generous range

[1] He made a point of avoiding what he called O.S., *i.e.* Oxford Style, *i.e.* too many quotations from the Greek.

of illustrations of Book III.) It is difficult to discern either in its style or in its contents the promise of what was later so abundantly plain, the passion and the mastery of a speculative philosopher of genius.

In this matter, there are at least two regions where biography and philosophy intermingle. The first has to do with origins and the second with results.

The book was dedicated to A. C. Bradley, ' whose teaching inspired me to pursue the study of ethics '. Bradley valued the compliment highly and began to help with the proofs. (But he was too busy to persist. It was his brother, F. H. Bradley, who made the time to read them through.) The situation, however, was delicate. Alexander was afraid that A. C. Bradley might want to dissociate himself altogether from a book which, while it owed much to Green and was invariably respectful towards that author, was also an attack on his views, particularly with regard to the metaphysical part of his ethics. A. C. Bradley reassured Alexander about that. He denied that he should be presumed to follow Green's doctrine because he had edited Green's manuscripts. But he was troubled. ' The public ', he said, ' is always careless about ideas, and greedy about the persons who write.' It might seem to the public that Oxford idealism had become very sick, and the lay mind was too easily misled about the patient's condition.

The book had some interesting results. Among other things it led to a long and close friendship between Alexander and Lloyd Morgan (who reviewed it for *Nature*. It is odd to come upon a letter from Lloyd Morgan addressing Alexander as ' Dear Sir '). Herbert Spencer wrote a long and rather grumpy letter. There was correspondence, and later a friendship, between Alexander and Leslie Stephen. Indeed Alexander accompanied Stephen in at least one of his walking tours ' in the North '.

Alexander had plainly thought, and had plainly said in the book, that Stephen was the best of the evolutionary moralists. The correspondence, accordingly, was very amicable from the outset; but Stephen was a valuable and valued critic. 'I should like', he said in his first letter, 'to see you next time take a rather more limited field and treat it as thoroughly as you please.' In the next letter he hoped that Alexander's next book would not be 'too much intended for beginners'. In subsequent correspondence the *Dictionary of National Biography* stood in the way of serious philosophical discussion on Stephen's part, and the letters were mostly about testimonials, the most judicious way in which Stephen and R. B. Haldane could assist Alexander, and such-like things; but it is clear that Stephen read Alexander's occasional papers as well as his book. There was, for instance, an interesting comment upon what Alexander thought about the Argument from Design:

'If you mean by God a particular being, a Jupiter or Jehovah, the explanation is at least relevant. If there be such a being of whose character and purposes we know something, the fact that he made a sphere might throw some light on the case and on future probabilities. But as we get towards Spinoza's God, the explanation becomes a mere set of words. God = the Universal Cause. Then you only tell me in a roundabout way that the thing is caused, which I knew before, and as it is caused by a being of whose purposes and character I can know nothing except from the facts which he is supposed to cause, I have made a circuit back to the facts. It is a mere roundabout leading nowhere. David Hume spoke more to the point about this than any English writer.'

I append some notes on Alexander's other writings about this time. He sent his paper on 'Hegel's Conception of Nature' (published in *Mind* of October 1886) to the best people for their criticism, as was his wont, and received *inter alia* two letters in reply from J. H. Stirling clearly showing what those who had wrestled with the secret of Hegel thought about all attempts to Darwinise that philosopher: 'You are always modest', Stirling wrote, 'and both in good temper and taste too. You are

very gentle with these " Modern Theories " in the end.'
But ' I never hesitate to call the Darwinian proposition a proposition of dementia '.

Alexander's winter semester of study in experimental psychology in Münsterberg's laboratory at Freiburg [1] led him to support Münsterberg (with reservations) against Titchener regarding one of Alexander's lifelong interests, the correct analysis of will and of activity. Alexander's discussion appeared in the April *Mind* of 1892, and Alexander and Münsterberg exchanged many letters. I cannot resist the temptation of quoting what Münsterberg said about Titchener after Münsterberg had gone to Harvard a little later, and before he had fully mastered the English language. ' I don't read any line what he writes ; he came to see me here in my house, we were both very polite, he invited me to live in his rooms when I come to Cornell, but notwithstanding that his last article must be as ignoble as the first and I don't read any line from it.'

Although Alexander returned to teach in Oxford in 1891, he had made up his mind at least a couple of years earlier to apply for a professorship somewhere else.[2] A. C. Bradley's advice about this decision is of great interest in itself even apart from its bearing upon Alexander's state of mind. I shall therefore quote Bradley's letter rather fully, remarking that it was written from Liverpool (where Bradley then had a chair) and that it did not refer to Manchester :

' [My main impression] is this : that if you are thinking mainly of teaching philosophy and wish mainly to interest people in the subject, it is a very doubtful step. The numbers must (I imagine) be small and of them the majority would be ill-educated. . . .

' On the other hand there is great interest in the work of pushing forward the Colleges and in spreading education. And if you care much about that, or think you would care,

---

[1] To be ' advanced ' in Oxford in those days was to cast eyes on Germany.
[2] Incidentally, there was some talk about going to America, perhaps to California.

and are pretty fit for this kind of work, I think you would be happy in it, and would feel you were doing good. I cannot help feeling that this is really the decisive question. It is vain to expect students of the kind I had at Balliol or near it (with very rare chance exceptions), and therefore vain to look for sympathy in any forward movement of your own mind. But there are great compensations of the kind I have mentioned. I should feel therefore that it depends on your own consciousness of yourself.

'There is the question of health. I do not know how good yours is. . . . Weak health is a terrible drawback in work in these places, where a man should be able to bustle a bit. On the other hand there is a deal of stimulus — much more than at Oxford — no atmosphere of everything being known and nothing mattering, and a constant feeling that you can be of use by very middling work. *Per contra*, a feeling that a strong man with no particular fineness of intellect could do more — but this, I think, is to some extent a delusion. Certainly you have to do your best in order to succeed — but it is your best in shaping your mind to meet ill-educated ones, and trying to get ideas into a striking shape. You must learn to be a trifle brazen, and intellectual fastidiousness is fatal, and modesty not wholly an advantage. I have got rid of all mine.

' Reading this over, I think it is a little too gloomy about philosophy — in this way : people in these places are ignorant, and they do not like thinking, but they are very ready to be *inspired*, often when they only partly understand. They will regard you as an apostle to some extent — which is embarrassing but also stimulating.

' One other thing occurs to me. I don't know if you have any definite ideas of the future : but I think I ought to mention my opinion — that a man is a good deal lost in these places, unless he can write as well as teach. It does not matter to a Scotchman who is known of old to his College mates : but I should doubt if success as a teacher in one of these Colleges would be any help to promotion at Oxford. . . .

MEMOIR

' I certainly think it does one good in many ways to be in places like these — shakes one up, interests one in unintellectual people, and gives one more idea of life than Oxford can. The ugliness and philistinism are hard to bear for some people : others don't seem to mind. It depends a good deal how much you depend on externally. If it is or would be a pleasure to you to feel you were shaping things more than a young man commonly can in Oxford, you have lots of that in these places.

'. . . Excuse hurry. I shall be anxious to know your decision. I can't help a great regret at the thought of your leaving Oxford — philosophy there being in such a bad way. I have never been sure I was not to blame in going. But you will have considered that.'

Alexander made three unsuccessful applications for a chair before he succeeded at Manchester. I do not know how much his testimonials had to do with his selection, but I can imagine an elector making a very good case from them. Such an elector could show that the writers of the testimonials were of the highest distinction — Jowett, Wallace, Cook Wilson, R. L. Nettleship (an earlier testimonial, since R. L. Nettleship was dead), A. C. and F. H. Bradley, Leslie Stephen, Bosanquet — that they all spoke with affection as well as with esteem, and that they had a book as well as slighter pieces on which to base their opinion of Alexander's powers and promise. Cook Wilson said : ' He is one of the very few who have real metaphysical power. I doubt if there is anyone of more promise [in Oxford] than Mr. Alexander.' ' He is one of the few men ', R. L. Nettleship said, ' whom I have known at Oxford with a genuine love of speculation and a natural gift for it.' ' I do not think that the electors could do better,' said Bosanquet. ' I can only say ', Mr. Gilbert Murray wrote from Glasgow, ' that for my own part when I was reading philosophy with him I was so absorbingly interested that I could scarcely think of other studies.' A laconic elector need not have quoted more, but it would have been very relevant to add that the Waynflete Professor of

MEMOIR

Physiology testified to the completeness of Alexander's knowledge of the nervous system. He had known Alexander, he said, for eight years; the later ones largely spent in his laboratory.

Alexander used to tell a story about his election at Manchester, and he had decided to tell it in public in 1925 in his reply at the presentation of his bust by Epstein. He did not do so because the subject of the story, Professor Stout, had a cold, and so, in the end, was unable to be present. But I have permission to tell it now. What Alexander was to have said was this :

' She [the University of Manchester] took me in when, either by hopefulness or by wilfulness, I had cut my moorings to Oxford at Lincoln College, and had made the discovery that it might be easier for a vessel to leave her harbour than to return. That entry into this University was a fortunate event for me, all the more that if they had judged by our merits as philosophers, their choice, had it not been for an accident which I will narrate, should have fallen on my dear and eminent friend, Mr. Stout, from whom I have learnt so much, who with Mrs. Stout has braved the long journey from St. Andrews and the waiting at Leuchars Junction, the windiest station in Europe, in order to be present to-day. Now Mr. Stout, in the days before he came under the control of Mrs. Stout, was negligent of his appearance, and he came to the final interview with the Council with his neck-tie riding half-way up his collar. I told him he would never be taken in that condition, and set his neck-tie right ; but apparently thinking it unfair to take advantage of the offices of a rival, he deliberately tore it back to its old place, and this act cost him the election. The Council rightly decided that its professor of philosophy should set an example in a well-dressed university.'

Mrs. Stout's comment is said to have been, ' The impudence of *him* talking about well-dressed men '. I shall not say more about that topic now, except to remark that I understood from Alexander, when he told me the story, that he and Stout were arrayed for the occasion, like black tulips, in the unaccustomed glory of frock-coats. At any rate Mrs. Mary Tout, widow of the distinguished historian, tells me that her husband persuaded Alexander to buy a silk hat for the occasion and that Alexander never wore it again. I learn, however, from another quarter, that Alexander has been known to crush his silk hat at a synagogue door.

Alexander made more than one attempt to return to Oxford as Professor. A letter from F. H. Bradley refers to one of these efforts: ' Of course if I am asked my real view I shall have to say that, since the University has gone out of its way to make Lloyd George a Doctor (I forget whether it was of Law or Theology), they (if they want to be consistent) are bound now to elect ——.'

It is fitting here to quote what the Public Orator said at Oxford when Alexander received its honorary doctorate at the Encaenia of June 1924 : ' Et quid est gratius quam ea studia quae praecipue nostra sunt eo quoque pervenire ubi plerique se negotiis potius quam Musis deditos esse profitentur ? '

III. Professor at Manchester

Manchester, despite the hesitating softness of its climate, seemed to suit Alexander much better than Oxford. True, he was subject, constitutionally, to recurrent dolefulness, and he complained at various times of eye-strain, colds, indigestion, and such-like ailments. He also suffered from the depression, although he conquered the irritableness that is usual among the deaf. He had an ear operation early in the century, but there was no permanent improvement. In the main, however, Alexander had a very serviceable physical constitution.

For convenience' sake, although rather arbitrarily, I shall divide what I have to say about the period of his active professorship at Manchester into three sections, and

MEMOIR

treat firstly of the man, secondly of the professor, and thirdly of the writer.

I

At first he lived in rooms in Withington or in Fallowfield, at one time in the same house as Edward Fiddes in Fallowfield, and at another time in the same house as P. J. Hartog (now Sir P. J.) at Mauldeth Road in Withington. Later he shared a house with S. J. (now Sir S. J.) Chapman.

Early in the century there was a very important change in his way of living, for his family came over from Australia in 1902. From 1903 onwards Alexander was head of this entire household under the same roof. The household consisted of his mother and her sister, Miss Nancy Sloman — two bent old ladies, the mother full of shrewdness and vitality, the sister by this time very much less vigorous; two elder brothers, Henry and Maurice, and the elder sister Rosetta. Henry Alexander died in 1903, Miss Nancy Sloman in 1908, the mother in 1917, and Miss Rosetta Alexander in 1923. Mr. Maurice Alexander, who was a teacher of music, is now the sole survivor of the family. I need hardly say that Alexander was an affectionate son, but I should like, in common with all his friends, to mention here how much he owed to his sister's devoted efficiency, and, as a guest, to be grateful to her memory as a hostess. Her sudden death from angina was a heavy blow to both her brothers.

So radical a domestic change for a man over forty who had not seen his new house-fellows for nearly a quarter of a century might well have been a very difficult experiment. One of the first things that I heard about Alexander (and my informant thought it very notable) was that the change made no difference to him at all. He was just as accessible as before, the same companionable being that he had always been whether in his house or outside it. It was pleasantest, perhaps, to be alone with him at his fireside. Then the hours sped as he talked (but never one-sidedly), and was gentle, gay, witty, and shrewd, all in the most effortless way that could be imagined. But if there were a large company he was still the perfect host, and his Wednesday evenings were a beneficent institution. Of a Wednesday he would usually invite someone to dinner, a stranger who might be lonely, a new colleague, a former student, or the like. Later in the evening a dozen people, or twice that number, would drop in, colleagues, schoolmistresses (principally young) from the Withington Girls' School (of which he was a Governor), perhaps a young author or two. There used to be cakes and coffee and what Alexander called 'pop' (*i.e.* ginger-beer). Later there was no 'pop'. With these simple aids Alexander made the evening memorable, moving his guests about, and moving among them with seraphic impartiality, delighted to hear an argument starting, and melting all possible asperities without himself being soft in the slightest degree.

'His Wednesday evening parties', a lady writes me, 'were an established feature of the University life. Young dons, a few advanced students, an occasional professor, crowded every seat in his study, and I and a good many more knelt or crouched on cushions, talking until midnight in the way young academic people do. Sometimes he would enthrall us with anecdotes of Jowett or other high lights at Oxford; sometimes we would discuss, not always without malice, current events. He would suddenly flash across the room something to stimulate or aggravate me and in my hot-headed way I would fly in retaliation.'

Sir Sydney Chapman has given my narrative a worth it could not otherwise hope to attain by sending me an account of his friendship with Alexander and by allowing me to quote from it at my discretion. I shall now avail myself of the privilege

'It was not until I joined the staff of the Owens College', he says, 'that our really intimate friendship began. From the outset I was with him frequently. It was not long before he invited me to join him in a small house he had taken in Booth Avenue, Withington, and I naturally jumped at the offer. Here we held our weekly evenings, on Wednesdays, when anyone could drop in — or rather Alexander did, for he was a figure in Manchester. We had an ideal housekeeper, Mary, who could not do enough for Alexander — and that indeed was the attitude of all who served him.

'When I came to live with Alexander I found he was subject to occasional fits of depression. It was not unhappiness about anything in particular, but just a cloud of melancholy which enveloped him and made him miserable before it lifted, as it did as a rule in two or three days. He was quite philosophical about these attacks in his normal state, but could not throw them off. Nor did he try to disguise his low spirits at such times — with his transparent nature I expect it would have been impossible for him to do so successfully — and I doubt whether his friends would have liked him to pretend to be cheerful when he was feeling gloomy. But whether he could have fought down his depression by arguing with himself is another matter. I think not. A man so gifted both in his emotional and intellectual sides was almost bound to be subject to moods. But in none of his moods can I ever remember his having lost his temper apart from fretfulness now and then, which is a different thing. It was not, I should say, so much that he controlled it, as that his temper was not of the explosive type. He was rather sorry than angry when others would have been angry. Yet he was human enough to confess afterwards to having felt irritation when anyone in his company had been exceptionally wrong-headed or pretentious. And sometimes confession afterwards was uncalled for, as he had shown his feelings by his deprecating look and by a withdrawal into himself after a few brief expostulatory remarks.

'In his occasional moodiness Alexander resembled the great Dr. Samuel Johnson, and it was not the only point in which there was resemblance. His appearance helped it, his full figure, his somewhat lumbering gait, his attitude when he sat, and his pondering expression which lighted up, however, when he was amused or about to say something witty. Of course his views were of a different complexion, and he was not pontifical nor did he bludgeon in argument; but there was often the same pointedness in his remarks so that they stuck in one's mind, and he was equally all against shams. Curiously enough — or perhaps one ought to say "significantly" — Alexander was a regular reader of Boswell, and knew it so well that he was constantly quoting the doctor.

' Our *ménage* at Booth Avenue was bound to be broken up when Alexander's mother and sister and two brothers came from Australia to live with him or when I married. This reunion with his family necessitated a larger house. Alexander felt very strongly the binding force of family ties. Nevertheless he must have profited considerably from having left Australia alone and from his cloistered life at Oxford. It is not unlikely that this isolation from his home fostered that self-reliance which was so essential to the fruition of his innate originality. But however that may be, he had, I believe, an uncomfortable feeling that separation from his family was unnatural, and therefore welcomed reunion as the restoration of what he regarded as a perfectly balanced human existence. Home life is of course made by the women, and nobody could have done more to create the surroundings needed for his life than his fond mother and his capable and devoted sister.'

' The Wednesday evenings grew into a *salon* after the removal to Brunswick Road. My wife and I seldom missed attending. All sorts of people came, not merely the University set, though they usually predominated. If we went in good time, we were first received in the drawing-room with a welcoming smile by Mrs. Alexander, a small and rather frail-looking old lady, who had little to say but was a good listener and seldom forgot a face. We then climbed the narrow stairs to the study, the largest room in the house, where there was already a buzz of talk if others had arrived before us. Alexander was far from being just the mechanically efficient host. He thoroughly enjoyed himself and threw himself into the topics that came up. If he was suffering from one of his depressions, for that evening at any rate it would almost pass away. The conversation was generally very much alive, and people would move freely from one group to another as fancy dictated. Alexander seemed to pervade them all. When you joined on to any set he had just left you would generally find the talk he had started or stimulated still carrying on.

' The secret of the popularity of Alexander's Wednesday evenings was his power of getting quickly at the personalities of people, whether men or women or old or young or of occupations quite different from his, and of discovering their tastes and finding an interest in them even when he knew little about them. His mind had a remarkable sweep. But he never pretended or posed, and there was never any question, even on subjects of which he was a master, of deferring to him as a much older and wiser man, though of course he was held in deep and admiring respect.

'. . . He played a part in a certain small discussion society called " Us ", and later among a group mainly of scientists when the talk, in being confined to fundamental things, was meat and drink to him.'

I shall try to say something in my own way about the character and personality of this remarkable man.

There is a quality that the early Chinese philosopher, Mo Tzŭ, called *jen*. It is usually translated ' human-heartedness ', which includes, I suppose, human-headedness as well as large-heartedness. If that be what *jen* means, Alexander had *jen* and had it to overflowing.

He loved his kind so unaffectedly, so gladly, and so sincerely that few of his kind could resist loving him, or ever did resist. That was why he was the best-loved man in Manchester, in all circles of that city. Women adored him — there is no other word — but the affection of the men was as deep as the women's. He spoke and acted as if he was unconscious of the delight that it was to be with him, but one of the riddles in him was that he was *not* unconscious of it. He never set out to please, but he knew very well that he did please, and that he did more than merely please. His charm in a private company was unstudied and unsought. In public it was studied and even earned. But whether he sought it or did not seek it, he knew it was there and, I should say, he acquiesced in his social magnetism. For him it was as natural to charm as to breathe.

This *jen* in his character had its fruits in a grave courtesy, a winning smile, a gaiety that suited what was gay, and a gravity that suited what was deep. Indeed when I think of him I am irresistibly reminded of what he himself said of his friend L. T. Hobhouse, namely that he was ' deep but gay '.

Alexander's depth was indisputable, but gaiety, I admit, is scarcely an accurate term to describe the other aspect of his character. ' He was *almost* frivolous when he felt lighthearted ', one of his oldest friends tells me. ' I can see him now ', another writes, ' singing in chorus in my rooms " Old King Cole was a merry old soul " and slapping his knees as the chorus came ' — but this was remarked as something strange. His genius for friendship did not spring from gaiety. It arose, to quote Sir Sydney Chapman, from the circumstance that ' you were quite sure that he was as he seemed to be, and that you were really face to face with a personality almost unbelievably free from egotism or littleness '. Again, Sir Sydney (who was the first I mentioned above) says very definitely that ' he was happy in a sober way — it was not in his nature to be joyous though every now and then there was a certain gaiety in his talk ', and that the nearest approach to the truth is to say that sometimes he *glowed*. Nevertheless I am reluctant to think that there was not a certain gaiety in his depth, a jocund quality that was lived and not assumed, something sunny and radiant and even debonair in this great sagacious child.

When I speak of his human-heartedness I do not mean

to suggest that he was just a mass of benevolence in a $17\frac{1}{2}$-inch collar. It is true that he could and would suffer fools benignly, not from hypocrisy but from inveterate courtesy. But his judgments of men and of women could be very sharp, and even (I used to think) just a little cruel although never malevolent. In particular I thought him much too hard upon what he took to be idleness, and rather too insensitive to unvivacious merit (I am speaking, now, of serious things and not of the elfin malice in which he delighted). I may add that although he was a just man, I do not think he had a passion for abstract justice or over-much admiration for righteousness as such.

His affection for the young of the human species was very great. He would teach little boys of ten to wrestle, and persuade them of the simple truth that his mind could be as boyish as theirs. He would make friends with a tiny girl at a children's party by giving her an enormous hand-kerchief and inviting her to dust his shoes or pretend to her elder sister that he was Bottom the weaver who had to waggle asinine ears. I suppose, on the whole, that he preferred little girls to little boys, though not indiscriminately, with the same sort of preference that he felt about their elders. At any rate he liked little girls very much indeed. I have seen a series of letters that he wrote every Christmas to a little girl, the series continuing until she grew up; and although they were written at a different period from that to which I am referring now, I shall quote from a few of them here, preserving the sequence, in order to show the changes in their manner and phrasing. 'Ever since Nov. 2 I have had nobody to pet me and so I have been rather unhappy and missing you.' 'Are you very wise and learned now? And are you very old?' 'I quite agree with you that you are 13 till you are 14, and I should insist on it.' 'I add these particulars lest the curious postman should have time to read this and think that it is rather public for me to send you heaps of love on a postcard. *But I do.* So I shall conceal my name.' 'Do write and tell me about your dear self, what you are doing and what you mean to do. It will cheer up a very dull old dog. For the old dog loves you as much as ever.'

And here is a letter that he wrote in 1914 to a young lady who had sent him her photograph:

' The picture which arrived to-day is charming in itself, but though it gives an excellent idea of your hat, it does not, I think, of you. Now 51 young women could be found to look, with the hat, much like this picture. But there is only one who would be found to look like you; and that is the photograph I should like to have. When you are taken next, spurn the equalising decoration, and be taken as your unique self independent of unnecessary decoration. And send me that one, though I'll keep this, please, meanwhile. If this does not flatter your vanity, it must be boundless, as I believe it is.'

Alexander's human-heartedness extended beyond the human species to other companionable animals. Here his Irish terrier Griff was the main object of his affectionate regard, and it is to be feared that Alexander's attempts to read Griff's mind with the aid of the psychology of the day (*i.e.* Mr. Thorndike's) were not rigidly impartial. Indeed, by all accounts Griff was a thoroughly stupid animal, who failed disastrously in his intelligence tests in the psychological laboratory and, in the home, was as likely as not to try to jump out of a first-floor window when he was made to hunt the slipper. But Alexander (like Warde Fowler with his Billy) wrote about Griff to *Cornhill*, and (as the reader will see) ended with a parable about theism, when, after saying what he thought about Griff, he began to surmise what Griff thought about him.

The name ' Griff ' was short for ' Begriff '. In other words, the dog was a philosopher's dog, an Irish-Hegelian terrier. But Alexander on holiday could pet every cur in the village and he was also interested in quite un-Hegelian animals, especially if, by a stretch of language, they could be called domestic. For many years he would visit the Manchester Zoo every Sunday morning. Once, on a walk with Sir Sydney Chapman, Alexander stopped at a farm for wayside refreshment and strolled towards a fine bull that was lying in the farmyard. The farmer's wife stopped him. ' If you want to pat something ', she told him, ' you'd better pat a cow that's tied up.'

Here is a true story about Griff. Alexander was on a three-days cycling holiday with Professor and Mrs. Tout, but was anxious concerning Griff's health and advised by frequent telegrams about the animal's condition. A telegram on the second day was not reassuring. Alexander found it awaiting him just before dinner at the close of a long day's journey. Dinnerless he rode a hard nine miles for the nearest station, Manchester, and Griff.

Many wondered why Alexander never married. I don't know the answer and any conjectures I may have formed have a very slight foundation. But I shall quote what a very close friend of Alexander's has written to me : ' To my mind — though of course I may be wrong — there is no mystery at all. The simple fact has seemed to me to be that Alexander, being what he was, was not a marrying man ; and with his psychological make-up he was complete without being the father of a family. It never struck me that there was something lacking in him through his *not* having that side to his life. Anyway, if he had married and had had a family his personality would necessarily have been, in some suble ways, different from that of the Alexander we knew.'

Alexander's generosity was a marked feature of his character, and, like the rest of him, had its paradoxical side. He was not, in the ordinary sense, open-handed. On the contrary he was ineradicably frugal in his personal expenditure. He could not be mean ; but he could and did economise. He would never engage a porter unless he had more than two bags to carry.

In early and in middle life this economy may have been dictated by circumstances. In particular the Australian crash of 1893 had left him with liabilities that he had to meet and did meet. But his frugal personal habits remained when he was in easier circumstances. He did not alter them in any way towards the close of his life when he had few pensioners, a pension himself, and a certain capital. (He died worth £16,000.) This frugality extended to all unusual expenditure such as a holiday or even a journey unless the journey were a matter of duty, say to attend the funeral of a friend.

On the other hand his usual expenditure, whether he were in straitened or in easy circumstances, included generous help, out of all proportion to his means, to distressed compatriots, to students and former students whose luck was out, to the families of a friend who had died or of someone who had enriched letters, but not his widow or children. In all such cases, and during all his life, he never fumbled with the purse-strings. He cut the purse. It was the same with less stealthy and more open benefactions. Where others would think of five guineas and give two, he would think of twenty-five and give them with apologies for not giving more. I mention such figures to indicate the order of his ideas of this kind. Returning to his private benefactions, I should add that in all such matters he was prodigal of his time, and resolute with his memory.

His own account of this matter (I quote from Mrs. MacCunn) was this: 'Oh yes, I am avaricious. You see I could not *give* to things if I were not.' The occasion was the loss of a briar pipe that had once cost half a crown.

The only recreation that he mentioned in *Who's Who* was cycling, but of course his chief recreations were conversation and companionableness and reading, the last very catholic and often modern but with a recurrent bias towards Fanny Burney and other writers of George III's reign.

He liked to play a pre-emptive game of bridge, but was in no danger of becoming an addict even if he had been encouraged. When the standards of play were low, he may not have had a very accurate idea of what his rating would have been at the Portland Club. When the Culbertson Age had dawned he had no illusions at all in this vital matter. ' I am worse than ever before, if you can imagine it ', he wrote to a former opponent; and again : ' Very little bridge, alas, since you went. The ——s have been kind, but I played wildly the last time so that I expect they'll wait for a time before they ask me again.' But he enjoyed the game. In another letter he wrote, ' It was good, very good, to play bridge even at the cost of sleep.'

When he played cut-throat bridge his calling, I am told, ' was founded on his high expectations from the undisclosed hand '. *Aliter*, he *would* play it.

Alexander the professor allowed himself much less foreign travel than Alexander the don. He did, however, have three months in Italy during the session 1912–13, and a part of a letter that he wrote to Wildon Carr throws some light upon his tastes. (The rest of the letter, being all about technical philosophy, and very full, is a proof that he carried his master passion about with him wherever he might happen to be.)

'Assisi, 6.2.13

' I have been roaming so that I either couldn't or wouldn't sit down to write. Now after 3 quiet but full days at this most beautiful place I have got to possess my soul in peace. To-morrow I go to Perugia ; but this place, where I intended to stay only 2 days, has tempted me to stay 4. Naples I was very glad to see tho' I had to represent to myself that I might not get the chance again before I could make up my mind to go. I spent 5 days and saw only 2 things, Pompeii (twice) and the Museum the most of the time. The first I found profoundly interesting even on the second visit when the day was wet. As for the Museum I found it enchanting. The Farnese part is great enough, but the bronzes including most of all the household ornaments, like lamps, enthralled one. It was bad weather mostly, and Naples is a beastly place when it is wet, and isn't very good, I should think, when it is fine— But it is a relief to be away from the town and in this exquisite countryside. Though I have got a cold and am sorry for myself, Assisi has been one delight to me. It has been glorious weather and the place would be delicious were there no St. Francis, and no churches or frescoes.'

II

The first business of a professor is to teach, and Alexander had plenty of teaching to do. Until psychology achieved its independence in the University he had to teach (and he loved to teach) that subject, including its experimental branches, as well as the considerable range of (shall I say ?) more philosophical themes. He was also in charge of pupils from the Day Training Colleges. It is true that he had assistance,[1] and very effective assistance, since he chose his man with the utmost skill and pains, searching always for ability and refusing to be a respecter of places. Nevertheless he could not escape being something of an academic drudge.

(I should add that his skill in selecting assistants had the sort of reward that is customary in human things. Some of his assistants, indeed a high proportion, achieved eminence. Others, and again rather a high proportion, became the victims of fortune, or of themselves.)

Philosophy is not one of the big subjects in the Manchester curriculum and there were very few 'advanced' students. Consequently Alexander's direct influence as a teacher was rather small, although, in the course of years, it spread to many parts of these islands, and, indeed, of the world. That was a source of regret to the student body. For although, as a students' magazine said in 1905, ' he was to be seen at every College function from the dance to the charwomen's supper ', and of course was a public figure on his bicycle, it was felt that a man so

---

[1] ' I worked for two years with Alexander just before the war ', Professor G. C. Field writes, ' and I have always felt the deepest affection and respect for him then and since. In all personal matters he was kindness and consideration itself, always ready to spare his juniors in every way it could be done, always accessible and easy to approach, never interfering or making demands. He would always be ready to take a great deal of trouble to give help and advice in matters concerning one's career.'

like an angel, for all the shabbiness and shagginess of his magnificence, should have had a wider professional influence. ' Sammy ' should really have taught a less exotic subject.

I have had the luck to receive first-hand recollections from some of his old students and am particularly grateful to Miss Hindshaw, to Mrs. Forrester, to Mrs. Baer, and to some others.

An interesting point (which is capable, in fact, of alternative explanation) is that Alexander, when he went to Manchester, did not seem to have learned to use his voice very well. Sometimes he whispered and at other times startled the class with a sudden unpremeditated shout. A students' magazine spoke of ' lectures being muffled through a yawn ' and another of mannerisms with a waistcoat button. Unintended mannerisms had disappeared from Alexander's later perfection in the lecturer's art, and the expressive movements of his hands were an asset to his oratory and conversation.

' As we were a small group, 3 or 4 men and 2 women ', one correspondent tells me, ' he could do his diagrams very informally, sometimes on his waistcoat, sometimes on the soles of his boots.' It does seem rather informal.

He — er —, hum'd and haw'd a good deal, and the decrepitude of his cap and gown distressed all the women. In 1905, however, they seized their opportunity and established his dignity on ceremonial occasions. In that year St. Andrews made him its honorary doctor *utriusque juris*, and his feminine admirers (that is to say, all University women in Manchester) presented him with his red gown, to the reciprocal and high gratification of all the parties concerned.

His interest in psychology was very keen. He expatiated (although without practical demonstrations) upon hypnotism. (He had been to the clinic at Nancy.) The subject of imagery fascinated him, as various papers and his great book were later to show. He had a plethysmograph to measure pleasure and vanity. But it didn't always work, and many of the other instruments, being held together by bootlaces or the like, suffered some abatement of their precision. One of them was supported by two library books in place of missing screws. When a new psychologist was appointed and the books went back to the library, Alexander was very happy. He had been assuring the librarian for seven years, he said, that he had never had any such books.

According to one of my informants, ' He was uniformly good in the eyes of women students and lecturers. I say " uniformly " advisedly, as I can hardly remember any jealousy among his *women* friends and students. On the other hand, I have often seen signs of acute jealousy among the young men followers, where one was being specially listened to.' I set this down without malice.

But let me return to the topic of his methods and appearance in the classroom.

Dr. Marie C. Stopes, the first woman lecturer on the scientific staff of the University, sends me a vivid impression, the result of a scientific plan she had formed. Being herself inexperienced in lecturing at the time, she went the round of the various professors hoping, by elimination, to gain a rudimentary idea of the lecturer's art.

' I shall never forget Professor Alexander's lecture ', she says. ' I slipped in at the back of a small class of advanced philosophy students. His shiny, greeny-black mackintosh was slung on a chair near him. The writing on the blackboard was entirely illegible, and when he wanted to replace it with some more hieroglyphics he took the mackintosh and cleaned the board with it more than once. His deep mellow voice and a sort of jovian assumption of humility to his audience was very similar to the atmosphere he created for a large and important audience. All students listened with rapt attention but none of them had the sense either to provide him with a duster to clean the blackboard or to shake the chalk off his mackintosh, and I saw him snatch it up at the conclusion of his lecture and slip it on, chalk and all, as he left the room.'

MEMOIR

At this point I should like to interpolate a pair of observations, the first concerning the matter of handwriting, the second about the Great Clothes Question.

Sir Philip Hartog tells me that, in the 'nineties, a reference to the illegibility of his handwriting was almost the only thing that really annoyed Alexander. He denied the alleged fact, sometimes hotly. A few years after the new century began he took to using his typewriter for correspondence. The change was not wholly successful, partly because the ribbon never seemed to be fresh. 'What a warning is your type-written, hand-bitten [1] letter of the 13th inst', Shadworth Hodgson wrote him in 1912, 'against ever learning the art of typewriting.' Later Alexander reverted to the pen except for the printer's benefit. His reason may have been the deterioration of an ageing instrument. More probably it was his belief in his own legibility; for in a letter of 1936 he protested that he *could* be read, pleading *res ipsa loquitur*. That was true, except for proper names, but the difficulties were considerable. I suppose he could read his own jottings; but I don't see how he could.

The Great Clothes Question has become a matter of notoriety. 'He was the most unconventional object in the Order of Merit', says Sir Michael Sadler in *Time and Tide*. The obituary in the *Daily Telegraph* says that he used to ride through the streets of Manchester on his bicycle 'in undistinguished clothes and a cloth cap'. His clothes, if undistinguished, were not undistinctive. He must, it is true, have had some tidy clothes; for he often had his photograph taken, and then he was tidy. It is also true that what may be called his London suit was quite passably tidy, that his sister made him rather smarter, and that he has been known to ask for approbation of a new suit. In the main, however, he must have been the despair of his hatter (he wore wide-awake hats, choosing between several old ones. During the Boer War the small boys shouted 'Krug-ger'). He cannot have thought that an overcoat

[1] Or 'hard-bitten'?

was an instrument for suggesting superficial opulence, and his tailor must have been one of the few men who did not really love him. (But he once had a holiday suit made to special orders with a pocket on either side to carry a duodecimo volume.)

I have only insufficient confirmation of the story that, cycling to Liverpool to give a lecture (clothed, one may say, as a cyclist should be clothed), he said ' Underneath ' when his host asked him where his dress-clothes were, and gave the same answer, later in the evening, when he was asked where his pyjamas were.

Here, however, is an authentic anecdote. Alexander was cycling to the South and had arranged to spend a night at Oxford with the Sidney Balls. He arrived, very dusty, in the afternoon when they were out, and (without telling the maid that he was the expected guest) asked if he could have a bath. ' Certainly not ', said she.

Mrs. Tout has told me something similar. She and her husband were spending August on a farm in Derbyshire, and were out for the afternoon. Returning, they were waylaid by the farmer's daughter, who with finger on lip and a mysterious air told them there was a man waiting for them who said he had cycled a long way to see them and wouldn't go away. ' So I showed him into the little back sitting-room and locked the door quietly.' They found Alexander reading a volume of verse and quite unaware of his captivity. On another occasion, when invited by a colleague to dinner, Alexander had to tap on the window and show his smiling face to the dining company because the maid had refused him admittance.

These important digressions are leading me away from my present subject, Alexander the teacher. So I shall abandon them.

Alexander was a great teacher. As a very perspicacious correspondent tells me, ' He managed to convey to his pupils that what he was lecturing about mattered a great deal, that it was of importance to find out what other philosophers had thought about it, and to concentrate upon thinking it out for oneself. I call this the top of University achievement. That he was not particularly systematic in his courses is certain. He could be almost casual, following the closely reasoned lecture of one day with apparently disjointed and not wholly coherent thinking aloud another day. He was by no means the orator whom students flocked to hear as congregations flock to hear the stirring words of eloquent preachers. On the contrary, his enunciation [and now begins the alternative explanation I suggested some pages back] was somewhat slow and in parts halting, and it was not at once realised how suited it was to the subject matter. The hesitations frequently meant that he was seeking the right word, convinced that nothing but exactly the right word would do justice to the right thought. On running the lectures over in their minds afterwards, and conning what they had jotted down in their notebooks, his students would awake to the fact that what they had previously taken for granted was no longer so obvious and at the same time that a pattern, which it seemed important to get right, was coming out of what had previously presented itself as a hopelessly confused tangle. In the smaller advanced classes the backbone of his exposition, like that of Socrates, was discussion. I never knew a teacher who managed to create a greater respect for his subject and reverence for himself.

'With audiences for the most part academically uninstructed, for example at the University Settlement, Alexander could be at the same time profound and simple without patronisingly talking down to people. I should add that when he gave a public lecture there was nothing go-as-you-please about it. It was always a masterpiece in language arrangement and delivery, with the interest artistically preserved throughout. He took great pains over the preparation of these discourses, as he did in all his writings.'

Mrs. Baer, Alexander's first honours student at Manchester, has given me a valuable account of his methods of teaching. Whereas Robert Adamson, his predecessor, had (very nearly) dictated his lectures, Alexander deliberately repudiated that method and seemed, in effect, to be conducting a sort of conversation with himself, or, less frequently, with his class. He would begin a sentence, and begin again, and begin yet again. He was also very willing to explore side tracks if they were at all promising, or if they seemed so to him on the spur of the moment. The docile type of student groaned, the adventurous type rejoiced. The adventurers learned to wander hopefully with a justified hope, and to discern how they might arrive.

In short, as I have said, Alexander was a great teacher. The phrase, however, may be construed in several ways, some of which would not be applicable to him. He was not one of those (I believe) who finds either inspiration or delight in the routine of pedagogy, whose interest in the progress of each several student is a daily and hourly obsession, who has a passion for altering the curriculum. In that sense, teaching was not one of Alexander's major interests, and some who worked with him were even disappointed. I quote a very frank statement from Alexander's friend, admirer, and former colleague in the Philosophy Department at Manchester, Professor G. C. Field. ' I should not have called him a stimulating head of a department. For one thing he always gave me the impression that he was not really interested in the teaching side of the work. He was conscientious about it and knew the students, often making shrewd remarks about them. But he did not want to take more trouble about it than necessary. I was left entirely free to conduct my own classes in my own way within the limits of the prescribed curriculum. But any suggestions for altering or adding to the curriculum were not welcomed. They weren't exactly snubbed, but the general attitude was like Lord Melbourne, "Why can't you let it alone ".' This comment refers to the years just before the war when Alexander was enthralled with his own adventures in speculative philosophy. Therefore they may not apply with accuracy to other periods; but I do not think they would be definitely inaccurate at any period.

Professors have other duties than the duties of teaching. They have, for instance, to administer, and they usually find that their profession requires them to bestir themselves about causes that originate in the university but have to be aired before the public.

Dr. Fiddes, before his retirement the distinguished Registrar of the University of Manchester and in due time one of its Pro-Vice-Chancellors, tells me that 'Alexander was not at his best in dealing with business details'. He adds that Alexander's judgment in Senate and Committee 'was usually sound, except when he allowed it to be biassed by sympathy for the weaker party. But he never had any axe of his own to grind, and he had a very good eye for the right man for an appointment — the most essential part of academic administration.'

There speaks the administrator by profession, a being whose expert judgment I invariably accept. I learn from other sources that Alexander could never bring himself to grind philosophy's axe, a defect in a community where each exponent of a subject is supposed, as a matter of course, to defend that subject with readiness and pertinacity. I also learn that Alexander was a successful Dean of the Arts Faculty, and was accepted as the sage of the faculty. (He was seldom surprised and never hurt when his views did not prevail.) It need hardly be added that he was one of the most companionable of colleagues. His chairmanship of the Library Committee (for many years) was a privilege to himself and to all. His conversation in the Common Room (I am speaking now of the early years of George V's reign) was less robust than Rutherford's, less inundating than Elliot Smith's; and his charm was different from Horace Lamb's; but he brought distinction to a distinguished company. From the day of his arrival at Manchester he set himself, like F. E. Weiss and T. F. Tout, to show the lecturers and assistants that they were fellows of a corporate body, like an Oxford College, and not, as in the Scottish universities of those days, persons of a lower caste than the professors. If I had not read what Alexander said about Curzon in his reminiscences, I should have said that there were *no* traces of snobbery in his composition. Having read the reminiscences, I shall amend the statement by saying that I never expect to meet a man who has fainter traces of it. He was quite indifferent to class distinctions academic or other, and no one could be less of an intellectual or of a moral snob.

Sir Sydney Chapman tells me about Alexander's speeches in the Senate of the University. ' His utterance was deliberate with characteristic pauses to get the right word, so that one seemed to see or feel his thought unfolding itself at its own pace behind his sentences. He seldom carried the Senate away, but more often than not got his way in the end. The leaven did its work, and members would say to themselves before deciding, ' Well, though it mayn't have been convincing at the moment, there was a lot in what Alexander said '.

Alexander was prominent in several of the more public aspects of the University's policy, always acting as one would expect of a left-wing radical who sat loose to party politics.

One such aspect was pioneer work in connection with the Day Training Colleges. The Men's College had been established in Manchester in 1890 and the Women's in 1892. Here Alexander worked in collaboration with Miss C. I. Dodd, the Mistress of Method in the Women's College, and gave her very effective help in her vigorous and successful efforts to found a ' Herbartian ' elementary demonstration school for girls. This school was later united with the boys' demonstration school opened under a scheme prepared by Professor Findlay and is called the Fielden School.

Alexander believed, like another J. S. Mill, in the emancipation of women and was prepared to further the feminist movement in the ways that its advocates had chosen. He took the chair and spoke at a crowded Women's Suffrage meeting in Alexandra Park in 1908, he walked behind a banner in their processions, and when he could, he helped the agitators in their troubles with the police. Rumour, it is true, somewhat exaggerated his attitude here. ' At the time of the suffragettes' violence ', he wrote in a later letter, ' I was asked whether it was true that I had said publicly that they would be justified in throwing vitriol at Asquith. To which I replied that if I could be so wicked I could not be so foolish.' He did, however, believe in the policy of ' continuous pestering ', and that meant a good deal in a university in which Miss Christabel Pankhurst was a student of law. The leaders of the movement among the University women (as one of them informs me) believed that he was with them heart and soul, although, or perhaps because, they knew that he advocated a certain restraint that they were not always willing to exercise, and made close enquiry into the facts when ' conduct contrary to the practice of decent people ' was alleged. To the end of his life Alexander was an ardent feminist, never a foolish although perhaps sometimes a fond one. He shared the feminist belief that women, even in novel-writing, were not allowed to compete with men on equal terms.

This enthusiasm with Women's Suffrage was connected (although not, perhaps, by a strictly logical consecution) with Alexander's peculiar position in the University, where, as it was said, he was ' a sort of godfather of the women's side. Nobody would have dreamt of taking any important step in that connection without first consulting him.' It was helped (again perhaps without very strict logic) by the eagerness of some of the best of his women pupils to have the vote.

More generally the number of women students in the University encouraged Alexander's firm belief that they must be put on a perfectly equal footing with the men. Here there was some leeway to overcome.

Women had been excluded from Owens College under John Owens' will, and were not admitted till 1883 although their disability had been removed by statute in the early 'seventies. When Alexander went to Manchester there were no residences for the University women although there were two for the men. Alexander, along with C. P. Scott of the *Manchester Guardian* and some others, set himself to change all that. (Of Scott he said in a letter to a quite impartial spectator, ' I am glad to have known at any rate one really great man. I've known a good many big ones but that's not the same thing.') A Hall of Residence for Women was opened in 1900. It is now Ashburne Hall. Alexander was an honorary secretary and, as his papers show, was not in the least like a *fainéant* secretary. Dr. Fiddes tells me that he believes Alexander was the only man who was admitted to honorary membership of the Old Ashburnian Association.

If it be asked, not why Alexander was willing to be the godfather of the University women but why they wanted to be his godchildren, some observers at least have no doubt at all. I quote from Sir Sydney Chapman :

' The reason, no doubt, was that Alexander had an amazing understanding of women. I have never observed it in the same degree in anybody else. It was an intuitive and appreciative understanding and I think most women recognized it at once. Some people — and women too — said he had an illusion about women — that he put many of them on higher pedestals than they were entitled to — and I think there was some truth in this. Probably he was more easily taken in by women than by men but that was an amiable weakness and in our mixed community helped to make up for the fact that so many were apt to underrate women.'

' Moreover it was in character. Alexander certainly tended to overrate everybody male or female. It was once said and not altogether without foundation that all Alexander's geese were swans. It might have been added that before he had done with them many of Alexander's geese had become swans, because he had classed them and treated them as swans from the first though they had started as geese, as everybody else knew. It was ingrained in him to think the best of people. Another aspect of the same trait was his unqualified delight in the successes of his friends — a far rarer virtue than sympathy with people in misfortune. Can it be wondered that he was held in an affectionate regard far beyond the measure which is the lot of most ? '

Another movement in which Alexander took a very prominent part was the evolution of Owens College into the independent University of Manchester. Of the three federal colleges in Manchester, Liverpool, and Leeds, Liverpool favoured independence, Leeds favoured the continuance of the federal system, and Manchester, after some hesitation, took Liverpool's view. There was much zealotry and some bitterness, especially among the graduates. Alexander gave a reasoned defence of the case for separation in *The Speaker* of March 1, 1902, and repeated his contention in a letter to the *Manchester Guardian* of June 11 of the same year, the letter being published as a separate pamphlet with the title ' A Plea for an Independent University in Manchester '. He believed in civic universities, ' the crown of the educational system of the district '. He thought that ' the mantle of the Victoria University hides the defects of the individual Colleges ' and that the change would ' represent a stage onwards from the dreary Chinese ideal which identifies the University with an apparatus for examination '.

I shall speak later of the way in which Alexander presented for honorary degrees.

III

For many years after his appointment to Manchester, Alexander the professor almost silenced Alexander the writer. Except for a brilliant little essay on Locke, no book came from his pen until *Space, Time, and Deity* appeared in 1920. I shall say something about the little book on Locke now, in order to clear the decks for the main action.

Alexander always used to say that he preferred an ounce of original speculation to tons of commentary on other people, and he used to represent himself (I dare say he used to think of himself) as one who was not a scholar. His 20,000 words on Locke [1] (a volume in Constable's series of ' Philosophies Ancient and Modern ' then — 1908 — published at a shilling) give a complete refutation of the second of these opinions. Alexander had all the qualities that were required, and in an eminent degree — the power of composing a vivid, brief biography, mastery in exposition, sympathy with the author's problems, indulgence for what was excusable, clarity concerning what was less excusable. The level of Locke scholarship in this country has risen very greatly since Alexander wrote; but Mr. Gibson who began the good work, and Mr. Aaron who continued it, have the highest praise for Alexander's book, for all the brevity of it. At the time when it appeared the best judges (such as Stout and Pringle Pattison) were rightly emphatic in their commendation, and so was the aged Campbell Fraser who had done so much for the history of British philosophy in his time, and was still engaged on that business in 1908 in his ninetieth year. After several letters to Alexander he summed up, ' I do not know of any exposition so luminous and reasonable '.

But let us turn from this delectable parergon to the preparation of Alexander's great achievement.

[1] In his own copy Alexander has marked for deletion the passage from ' It is characteristic . . .' (penultimate line of p. 35) to the conclusion of the paragraph (p. 36).
He composed a new paragraph showing the growth of his own theory of mental ' acts ' and of our ' enjoyment ' of them (which we are about to see). The new paragraph ran : ' Retention or memory, discrimination, comparison, abstraction (which puts a limit between man and brutes) are other examples of such " acts which we may take notice of in our mind ". One word of caution is here not unneeded. The idea of reflection is the mental process itself, as contemplated by us; it is not the idea with which the mental act is concerned. Thus in remembering we have an idea of a past event before our minds. But the " idea of reflection " is that of the act of remembering, not that of the past event. It is in fact the idea of the mind's act in reviving a former perception, along with the consciousness that it had that perception before. Problems are raised by this statement which are not considered by Locke, doubtless because he was satisfied with the simple description of the facts.' The date is 1911.

MEMOIR

When the present century was in its infancy many of his friends thought that Alexander would never write another big book. ' For years ', one of them tells me, ' he must have been in the same position as Newman before he finally cut himself adrift from the Church of England, for his philosophical faith was of the fibre of his being. Only in Alexander's case it was not a matter of changing sides but of cutting himself adrift and then being really adrift without anything to anchor himself to. For years he had not more than fitful gleams of what he thought might eventually prove to be a delusive dream.' The thing was apparent even on a walking holiday. ' I can see him now in one of his meditative moods ', the same friend writes, ' following about twenty yards behind in his old mackintosh (for there was much rain and wet mist on the hills) with his hands clasped behind him, dragging his stick. It was not that he was tired but his body moved slowly when his mind moved fast.'

Later when his mind began to move with a purpose, as well as swiftly, he would talk very freely about his ideas, although his increasing absorption in his own thoughts became very noticeable. ' He lagged more and more behind in our walks at Alstonfield, and hung for longer intervals over gates, swinging his stick.' [I am told that Alexander was usually a ' less indomitable ' walker than many of his friends.]

Alexander said himself that it was not till 1907 or thereabouts that he really began to have anything to say. Of that he was the best judge, but it would appear from his correspondence that some of his friends thought that a process of very active fermentation had begun in his mind a little but not much earlier. One or two of them were rather shocked. They thought he had ' surrendered to Moore ', that is to say, had wolfed Moore's ' Refutation of Idealism ' (in *Mind*, 1903) rather too voraciously. That opinion, right or wrong, may conveniently introduce this part of our story. Moore had held that the act of knowing was a distinct existence from the object known, and that all idealists somehow tried to amalgamate the two with apparent plausibility but ultimately to their ruin. Much of Alexander's 'realism' had a similar basis, metaphysically elaborated. The act, he held, was physically a nerve movement, psychologically 'enjoyed' but not contemplated, and it formed part of a continuum of acts which *were* the 'subject' (or the mind). A mind was 'together' or 'compresent' with the object that it contemplated, and the general relation of 'compresence' was universal in nature. In human knowing, the 'object' was non-mental; and the analysis held of every species of knowing and of the objects appropriate to each.

Alexander used to take it for granted that anyone who meditated the writing of a serious book on philosophy would first release certain *ballons d'essai* in the philosophical journals and in such-like skies. Indeed I am afraid he often judged an author more by these tentative flights than by the subsequent book. He himself was very faithful to the method, and welcomed all the technical correspondence to which (in his case at least) it immediately led.

Alexander was elected President of the Aristotelian Society for three successive years from 1908 onwards, and gave presidential addresses on 'Mental Activity in Willing and in Ideas', on 'Sensations and Images', and on 'Self as Subject and as Person' in these years. That was his first platform in the new enterprise, and he was immersed in private controversy with eminent philosophers for many years afterwards. If he had been at Oxford he might have talked these matters over (although he could never have talked them *out*) with his friends. Being at Manchester, and in a philosophical sense rather solitary, he had to use the post. There cannot be many philosophers after the sixteenth century who submitted to so long and so protracted an ordeal of this kind as Alexander.

It would take me too long to analyse this correspondence, and so I shall give but a single set of specimens, viz. a part of what he had to answer from F. H. Bradley. In doing so

MEMOIR

I intend to gratify the technical reader, and I beg the indulgence of the others.

Alexander seems to have been turning towards realism in 1904, for in that year Bradley wrote, ' You will be amused to hear that I never read a page of Reid. I suppose he puts things frankly. You will, I hope, go on with your proposed essay and finish it.'

After Alexander's first two presidential addresses had appeared, the correspondence became much more strenuous. There were five letters of criticism from Bradley between February 5, 1909, and April 12, 1910. I shall try to indicate the pith of their contents by sufficient quotations from them.

From Bradley's first letter :

' Your point of view is new to me . . . and I am sure it is worth working out fully. . . . Naturally I find at once insuperable difficulties. Being myself perhaps really more of a " sensualist " than of an " intellectualist ", I can make nothing of " activity ", " direction ", etc., etc., without something which is active. . . . I feel the same difficulty when I am asked to think of merely external relations [*e.g.* between act and object]. . . . Another point is that I don't think you meet the case of those who deny reality outside of experience. I do not understand this to be a postulate. The point is this : that we contend that no such reality is given and that it is reached by an indefensible abstraction. I do not think that you defend the abstraction. I think you assert that independent reality is given. That is what we deny. It is not a matter of postulation, I presume, on either side, but of observation. The presence of sensations, given apart, is to me unverifiable. I for myself reach them only by an abstraction which I regard as vicious. I do not think you meet my case at all. But this is probably because I have not understood you.'

Bradley's second letter was no nearer agreement :

' I am decidedly at issue with you as to the foundation from which you start. Your fundamental fact I take to be no fact at all but an untenable fiction. The idea of an act (over against an object) which act is the act of nothing given at all is to me unthinkable, as are " directions " where there are no given points. This is in principle the thing I have been urging against Ward and other Kantians or pseudo-Kantians all along. . . . In other words, no matter of fact, no experience.

'Again, your " together " is a fiction. In the feeling there is *always more* and *often less* than " together ".

'If, in short, I do *not* experience myself as sensuous matter I don't experience myself *at all*.

'I have so far not understood how you conceive the real world. But as regards its relation to the world of imagination, dream, etc., your difficulty seems to me to be very great. . . . The course you take lands you (so far as I can see) in this difficulty, that the explanation you give of your *unreal* world as subjective applies also just as well to your *real* world.'

Bradley's third letter is similar :

'I don't know *what* your view is. . . . First as to the relation [between act and object]. This I *think* you say is given. Is it mental or not ? . . . You see the troubles that will come and I need not develop them ? . . .

'Then as to the mind. . . . An activity of *nothing* to me is senseless. My mind is once for all " debauched " and I am past argument here. Then your troubles as to feeling and conation are great. . . .

'Another point I notice is as to our knowledge of the subject. You say ' It is only felt '. But how can you speak of it if it is not an object ever ? Here you are in the same hopeless dilemma, I think, in which Ward is. In fact, in principle you both follow Kant to your ruin. You don't, I presume, mean to say " I can only feel myself and when I do it becomes my brain ". . . . I fail *if I go low enough* to find that *any* activity is given *at all* with a perceived object. . . .

'Another point which you seem to ignore is the *practical* side of Idealism — the experience of the satisfied will which has carried *itself* out into the object. . . . I suppose

(I can only suppose) that on your view the will is either an illusion or that it alters simply myself and not the object at all. I have no doubt that this is ridiculously foreign to what you hold — but how can I tell what that is when you don't tell the reader ? Or do you tell him and I have not noticed it ? Perhaps.'

Bradley's other letters repeated these criticisms. I quote a passage from the fourth :

' You tell your audience at Glasgow to observe a perceiving act. By all means. Next week a man will come and tell them to observe their own passivity as against the activity of a perceived object. They will find this very plausible. The week after you will return and tell them — what ? I have no idea.'

From Bradley's fifth letter :

' I understand *nothing* of what you say, literally *nothing* [about acts and activity] except that, as to pleasure and pain you are apparently in Ward's position — whatever that may be.'

Alexander's affinities to Ward's (Kantian) position in psychology were sufficiently shown in a long and careful paper that he wrote for the *British Journal of Psychology* (December 1911) entitled ' Foundations and Sketch Plan of a Conational Psychology '. Bradley's reference to Glasgow had to do with another characteristic phase of Alexander's activities at the time.

Alexander had become a propagandist. He went up and down the universities in a missionary spirit, and had high hopes of Scotland because Scotland had once had its Reid. The editor of the *Glasgow Herald* invited a contribution upon ' Knowledge and Reality ' which duly appeared, in about two columns, on March 12, 1910. These two columns give one of the best accounts (for all their simplicity) that Alexander ever gave of his philosophy at this stage of its progress. He was firm but very confident. ' The difficulty in the case is due to our prejudice that things which we know must somehow be dependent upon us. We will still be intruding our dear minds into the objects. Whereas if we describe faithfully what happens when we perceive, we recognise that the object is . . . entirely distinct from us and that consciousness is only another thing along with it and, let us add, excited by it.' The true philosophical method consisted ' in recognising that you yourself are but a thing among other things ', and in accepting the fact that in perception, imagery, and ideation a physical object is ' revealed '.

The first time I met Alexander was during this propagandist period, and I remember enough about the occasion to indicate something of the manner of man that Alexander was at that time. The year, I think, was 1911; the place Cambridge. Alexander told us that he wanted converts, and that he was resolved to look for them among the young.

He gave his address in a largish and very uncomfortable lecture room — I think in Caius. After the speech the young were invited to ask questions, but as the questioner (owing to Alexander's deafness) had to advance to the platform and shout within a few feet of the lecturer's ear, the invitation led to small response. All the self-conscious among the young — that is to say, all the young — doubted whether their questions could really be worth such vociferous publicity.

The brunt of the discussion fell upon Miss Jones, the Mistress of Girton, who was not among the potential converts. She was meek, perplexed, and inaudible.

Alexander was aware that the majority of his audience might already be converted. What he may not have understood quite so well was that most of his younger auditors in Cambridge regarded him as a person who had stolen from Moore's armoury but was not very expert in the use of the weapons he had purloined. They chose to regard all that was individual in Alexander's view (although that, in reality, was most of it except for a part of its start) as a piece of rather whimsical maladroitness. I fear I disclosed as much to Alexander after the meeting; but Alexander made no obvious distinctions between the arrogant and the others. That was always his way. If he said anything severe, the inference, nearly always, was that he respected the collocutor. He said nothing severe to me on this occasion, although I am happy to recall that on later occasions he was frequently quite decidedly severe.

By 1912 Alexander was engaged with questions concerning the 'tertiary' qualities of goodness and value, or, in other words, with an advanced stage of his philosophy, and he sketched his views in some articles in *Mind*. In 1913 he was immensely heartened, and indeed elated, by his election to the British Academy. To the end of his life he would say that this was the only honour that he really prized. Here is what he wrote to an old friend at the time :

7.7.13

'*Erubesco referens* the terms of the recommendation (which I suppose I ought not to have seen). So I send them as they reached me. Only return them for my private solace on wintry days. Well, I am very glad anyhow : thank you warmly for your congratulations. What they say about not having time to write is rot — I hadn't anything to say till 5 or 6 years ago. And the statement about my " knowledge " is fearful exaggeration. I am, as I told you, a damned amateur. But I humbly accept the general substance of the statement and I am delighted to think that they thought the general quality of my stuff good enough.'

Alexander read a paper on ' The Basis of Realism ' (meaning contemporary realism ' and for the most part my own form of it ') to the Academy in January of 1914. The paper (which is long but the best account he ever gave of the epistemological realism with which he began) was in some sort a reply to Bosanquet, who in his Adamson Lecture at Manchester in 1913 on ' The Distinction between Mind and its Objects ' had attacked Alexander's new realism, braving the prejudices of an audience that he supposed to be steeped in the learning of the Egyptians,

and expounding the view that what was meant by the
'world' was reality's self-unification, that the straining
after such a unity was 'mind', and that 'objects' are the
fragments in such a mind-world. Alexander replied that
the temper of realism was ' to de-anthropomorphise ', that
is, ' to order man and mind to their proper place among
finite things ', restated his philosophy of the 'compresence'
of enjoyed mental acts with the non-mental things they
contemplated, vindicated the artfulness as well as the
strenuous *naïveté* of his realism, and found a place for the
'riches' of mind. 'The windows of things', he said, 'are
variously glazed. Though each thing is in active relation
with the whole universe it only sees the universe in those
characters of things which it is able to see, which its glass
transmits.' Here the tertiary qualities (and the 'values')
had their place. An appendix followed on 'the wider
issues'.

At this stage of his career Alexander had become a
famous philosopher, and the little world of philosophy was
eager to hear what he might say in a big book. Hence his
appointment (in 1915) to be Gifford Lecturer in Glasgow
was regarded by all knowledgeable people as a peculiarly
happy choice.

He gave the lectures in the war years 1917 and 1918, in
winter, when railway travel was scarcely commodious;
but he had a good audience, despite political and seasonal
inclemency, and he charmed it. At the end of the first
series he wrote :

5.3.17

' I finished my Glasgow lectures for this year a fortnight
ago, and have been trying to sleep them off since. They
went off, on the whole, well. The audience was very
attentive, to me touchingly so, and much larger than I had
anticipated in war-time, with the place depleted of students.
I think there were a steady 50–70 who came throughout,
and in the first 4 or 5 lectures there were more. They
began at 200 and shrank in the middle to the faithfuls who
were very faithful.'

MEMOIR

The title of the lectures was 'Space, Time, and Deity' (the initials corresponding to Sanctae Theologiae Doctrina[1] but the substance not altogether). The order of treatment corresponded closely to the later book, and need not be separately considered here.

Alexander did some work for his country as a 'half-timer'. (That was in 1917, in the Intelligence Department of a Government service,[2] and concerned the geographical and historical distribution of the Jews.) The war over, he set to work with sedulous patience to make the Gifford Lectures into a book that should be worthy of him. He was cheered the while by the interest that so many philosophers took in its progress. (In 1918, for example, the Aristotelian Society discussed an abstract of his views, with which he supplied them, for four of its meetings; a most singular event in its history.) In Alexander's own study, however, the going was hard, and the author faltered for some months, just when the proofs had begun to come in. He was overwhelmed by a sense of his littleness in comparison with the task to which he was tied. That mood passed, and *Space, Time, and Deity* appeared in the autumn of 1920.

The book was metaphysical in the grand manner; and I should say (I hope after due reflection) that it is the boldest adventure in detailed speculative metaphysics attempted in so grand a manner by any English writer between 1655 (when Hobbes very nearly completed his trilogy by the publication of *De Corpore*) and 1920.[3]

---

[1] In 1938 there was a public announcement of the death of the author of 'Space, Time and *Dietary*'.

[2] I am told that Alexander, at the beginning of the war, canvassed for recruits in the Withington district, and that his persuasive tongue had a good deal of success, not to the entire content of the mothers of some of the recruits. He actively assisted the Belgian refugees.

He had a wide and sympathetic correspondence with young men at the Front, including T. E. Hulme, who discussed realism with him from an artillery garrison. Alexander was himself too much of a realist to exaggerate the importance of these rays of humanity in a grim sky; but he also knew that the small thing was worth doing well.

[3] I am not forgetting Locke, Hume, and F. H. Bradley, and I am not saying that either Hobbes or Alexander was of the stature of the first two of

Magnificent in its conception, it is skilful and very thorough in its execution. It builds on (and with) space-time and comes to deity, beyond which human conjecture is dumb. It reviews the pervasive (or 'categorial') features of reality. It describes the evolution of the grander and more novel complexities of movement (for all is movement, it says) when life and mind 'emerge'. It attempts an understanding of the mysteries of illusion and error — perhaps the hardest of all philosophical problems — with a faithful and, as Alexander would say, a 'plodding' thoroughness, that, whatever its success, can scarcely be over-praised. It grapples with the problems of 'value'. It blossoms into theology. It is 'naturalism' if you will, but a 'naturalism' that, like Spinoza's (but with the attribute of *tempus* replacing the attribute of *cogitatio*), is not only a theory of 'Deus *sive Natura*', but also, and more integrally, of 'Natura *sive Deus*'.

Because of the scale of the argument it would be useless on my part (and even impertinent) to try to present an adequate epitome. Instead I shall offer a few comments that are, in effect, recollections of conversations I had with Alexander; and I have misgivings about attempting so much. I think Alexander exaggerated the extent to which I understood him; but he knew that, very often, I did not agree. Our discussions were apt to drop very suddenly. Still, they were frequent.

What I shall say is this:

(1) In what I have said about Alexander's 'realism' up to the present I have been chiefly concerned with his epistemological realism, a theory of knowledge. That was the first thing he tackled when he 'felt he had something to say' about 1906, and for long years afterwards. This epistemological theory was also what was commonly meant by 'the new realism' in England at the time. But Alexander's philosophy always had ontology, the theory of

these. I am talking about the nature of his enterprise. I may also remark that M'Taggart's *The Nature of Existence* (Vol. I) appeared in 1921 and Whitehead's *Process and Reality* in 1929.

existence, for its goal, and he believed from the first (unlike many others among the new realists) that the epistemological theory of realism had a clear ontological message. In *Space, Time, and Deity* epistemology (although it came in rather bulkily) was included almost apologetically. As Alexander later said (1927), ' theory of knowledge is not the foundation of metaphysics but only a chapter of it which it takes in its stride '. Alexander continued to believe that epistemological realism was true, and that his metaphysics required its truth, but his endeavour in *Space, Time, and Deity* was to ' de-anthropomorphise ' philosophy, not by epistemological analysis, but by showing how an ontological realism, properly understood, took men's minds in its stride.

(2) Alexander always said that his doctrine of space-time — *i.e.* of a matrix in which space, interpreted as space-stuff like Descartes's *extensio* but never timelessly (since it was motion and time was its ' mind ') — had been reached *metaphysically*, that is to say, by intellectual experiments with the ' ultimates '. He was delighted, and surprised, to find that he came so near to Minkowski's position ; but that was an uncovenanted mercy, and quite unpremeditated. Although his sympathies were with the left wing of modern physics, he deliberately abjured the support of any scientific theory.

(3) It was Plato's *Timaeus* and Kant's ' Analytic ' that were his favourite fountains in the past. The resemblance of his philosophy to Spinoza's was another uncovenanted mercy, and all the more welcome on that account.

(4) Alexander held that the categories, *i.e.* the pervasive complexities of motion in the ocean of reality, were the primary subject matter of philosophy. In comparison with them all empirical things (including minds) were only ' whirlpools in the ocean '. Therefore Book II of *Space, Time, and Deity* was the heart of it. His system (he said) ought to be judged by its account of the categories — universal and particular, substance, causality, quantity,

and motion. He thought that none of his critics had sufficiently grasped the point.

(5) It is often asked whether his views on theism should be taken very seriously, the more particularly because he is reputed to have told his friends in Manchester, with a beaming smile, that he had 'found a place for God at last'. It is easy to describe 'natural piety' as 'philosophic jam', to say that nature looks as if it were going to the devil rather than going to the good, to wonder how anyone could *reverence* the nature of things: and so forth. It is also notorious that many Gifford lecturers have treated theism rather perfunctorily as an appendix to what they were saying about something else. Alexander (it is said) *had* to speak about God; and he did so.

In my opinion Alexander's theism was an integral part of his philosophy, and a part as serious as any other part. I never asked him the question directly, but it is answered in much that he said in many of his writings. He believed that all the great human instincts were satisfied 'objectively' not simply as a matter of private capricious gratification: that such satisfaction, while it 'mixed' men's minds with the rest of nature, revealed nature's properties: that there *was* an 'instinct' of natural reverence and that this instinct revealed a 'growing God'.

In his British Academy Lecture printed in the present volume (*infra*, p. 275), Alexander said, very explicitly: 'For my own part I believe that, in the end, a theistic conception of God's deity is demanded by the facts of nature'. There is no reason at all to doubt the sincerity of this statement, although honest men may plague themselves without end about the sufficiency of Alexander's theism.

The book received wide and full attention abroad as well as at home, and the quality of the reviewers was high. True, there were some incompetents who talked about 'the philosopher's dumpling' and so forth; but there were not very many of these. Full agreement, of course, was neither to be expected nor desired, but there was little hostility. I think, it is true, that M'Taggart did not mean to be kind when he wrote a very curt notice for the *Cambridge Review*, and remarked that ' in every chapter we come across some view which no philosopher, except Professor Alexander, has ever maintained '. I doubt whether Alexander can have relished a criticism from the Cape in which his style, remarkably enough, was described as ' colourless and pedestrian '; and I know that he was always grieved, and always surprised when any one suggested that he wrote badly. But Alexander's reviewers, in general, were profoundly and gratefully impressed — if they were seldom convinced. Even the theologians, with very few exceptions, were respectful, the best of them holding, with Dean Inge in the *Guardian*, that ' this philosophy seems to be entangled in a subtle materialism which must prevent it from coming to terms with any genuine Christian philosophy '.

The earlier and necessarily rather hurried reviews included the opinions of such men as Lord Haldane (in *Nature*) or Mr. Joseph (in the *Oxford Magazine*), but the level of reviewing among lesser and anonymous writers was high, and, in view of the difficulty of their theme, gives a very pleasing impression of British competence in philosophy at the time. The foreign reviews — Italian, French, and Belgian — also attained a high standard and showed the keenest interest. Some may have betrayed a tendencious aim. The neo-scholastics in Belgium and elsewhere find neo-realism in harmony with neo-Thomism. But there were dissentients from the Netherlands, one of them complaining of uncritical assumptions (' onbevooroordeelde wetenschap ') in a reasoned and reasonable criticism.

When the technical journals, with their more leisurely methods, had had their say there could be no doubt that Alexander had reached the public that he wanted to reach, and that he had held the attention of the learned world over a long and intricate course. The reviewer in *Mind* was Professor Broad, in two articles. Alexander replied in an article ' Some Explanations ' in October 1921, principally concerning the points on which he and Broad had failed to agree after ' a long and amicable correspondence '. He also met a challenge from Stout (regarding sense-perception) at a philosophical congress in Manchester in the subsequent summer. On the whole, however, he refrained from public controversy so far as he could, and he meant his preface to the second impression of *Space, Time, and Deity* (1927) to be his last word about the book. He had a vast private correspondence to deal with, however, lasting for many years and conducted by members of the intellectually lower middle classes as well as by reputed aristocrats. Among the aristocrats in later years were eminent men of science as well as professional philosophers.

Having said so much about F. H. Bradley's criticisms while Alexander's philosophy was in the making, I should add what he said about the book itself in a letter of April 28, 1922 :

' First I think that the book is really a great book. The thoroughness with which the questions are faced and the detail is worked out — especially in all the part which concerns the theory of knowledge with its subordinate psychological detail — won my sincere admiration. It is, so far as my knowledge goes, far away the best thing that has been done in the way of a systematic realism.

'. . . Of course I don't agree with your whole position. . . . Your book (I find in my notes) seems to start with something like materialism and to end in something like a voluntaristic Pantheism.

' As to the start — Space, Time, and Motion are to my mind abstractions quite unthinkable as real apart from quality. Apart from qualities there can be no real " complexes ", " configurations ", " directions ", etc. But the qualities in your work when they *do* come, and are added, seem to me (according to you) to come for no reason and to be really accidental. On the other hand they really seem (according to you *in practice*) to qualify Reality not as *mere* facts but essentially. And, further, Reality (as Space-time) contains a " nisus " and seems essentially to be a progress — though you hardly attempt to justify this. A " forward movement " of time is one thing and a progressive " nisus " is surely another.

' You seem to end by practically making the world an unconscious Will for complete qualification, which Will becomes gradually conscious of itself and of its own nature and end. You refuse on the other side to allow this consciousness at any stage to *react* — which in fact it seems to do — though you do make God in some sense responsive.

' *If* you are further led to hold that this " nisus " to an end is also actually realized and accomplished and is not merely " in progress " you have on your hands apparently all the difficulties of Absolutism.

' I think further that you both fail at the beginning to get rid of the inherent contradictions of space-time as finite and infinite, but at the end when you introduce a quality higher than " mind " you fall into contradiction of another kind. I know what " Mind " means, and I know what a " higher something else " means — but, for myself, I cannot without becoming meaningless or self-contradictory combine these two ideas. If the " something else " or " something more " really still falls within Mind there is self-contradiction. If not, to me there is meaninglessness. The result therefore seems to be something like Absolute " Idealism " — to me at least.

' Of course on this point I myself have had trouble and have been criticised — but not, I think, rightly. I do not think that there is anything self-contradictory or meaningless in holding that there is " a higher form of mind " which makes good the defects and carries out the aims of finite minds. I think that this idea has a positive sense, and that, if, for any reason, it cannot be real, the onus of showing this falls on the objector. It is for him, I think, to show that such a Mind is so different from any mind we know, and different also in such a way that we can fairly say that it is either contradictory [1] or else meaningless.

[1] ' Contrary ' is in the text.

And I do not say that the objector here has no case — but I, myself, think that he is wrong. . . .

'I will say a few words in conclusion on the Proofs of God's existence. On the Ontological Proof I differ since I am quite clear that there *is* an *idea* of the Ultimate Reality which is distinct from the Ultimate Reality *as real*. But it is the *practical* proof on which I wish here to say something. If we take God to be something like (*e.g.*) the Jewish Jehovah, then surely you would only have to provoke ruin (in certain ways) in order to find out that he was " all there " — and *perhaps* to be convinced of the same by " serving him ".

'And now, in the religious experience of so many devout persons, the presence and action in prayer of a responsive Power may, I think, be taken as an experienced fact. And I think that this " proof " of God's existence is good — *as far as it goes*. The difficulty of course lies in fixing the extent (as to the nature of this Power) to which we can thus go.

'Am I wrong in thinking that your general doctrine as to the *non-reaction* of the higher stage of development upon the lower is what stands in your way here ? '

I have spoken about reviewers, partly because I have a lot of information about them that I would like to share ; but Alexander's work was precisely what he wanted it to be — ' an ingredient in the philosophical ferment of the day ' — for at least a decade ; and there is force in it now. Its vivifying influence was seen in all the philosophical journals, both directly and indirectly, and in a rather ample vintage of philosophical books. Among the earliest of such books was Bosanquet's *The Meeting of Extremes in Contemporary Philosophy* (1921). Bosanquet may have been a little too ready to believe that the rebel provinces in philosophy ought to be content with a plain explanation of the intentions of the central government, but his delight in the ' truly speculative attitude ' of contemporary philosophy as he saw it — ' free, concrete, penetrating, and widely appreciative' — revealed a temper that his opponents were eager to reciprocate.

Partly in consequence of Bosanquet's book, it became the fashion to explain that Alexander really belonged to 'the great idealistic tradition in philosophy', *philosophia perennis*. That might be a defensible statement — if there were any such thing as *the* great idealistic tradition. But I do not think Alexander would have accepted the statement, not because he was overfond of being called a 'realist' — that phase had passed — but because he thought to the end that idealism was something that should be outgrown. Towards the end of his life he thought that nobody read him; he was surprised that anybody bought him; and he was sure that Whitehead had excelled him. I shall say nothing here about the third of these opinions. As to the first, it is false, despite the fact that philosophy's present drift towards an anti-metaphysical logistical positivism makes Alexander's work just a little unfashionable. But metaphysics will last as long as the human race, and if British metaphysics in the present century has any enduring influence, Alexander's book cannot but be reckoned among its greater achievements. The serious pursuit of metaphysics needs system as well as inspired sketch-work; and any one who thinks he has little to learn from Alexander's genius for the architecture of metaphysics is only an amateurish philosopher.

Alexander thought his essay on *Spinoza and Time* (1921) an important appendage to his metaphysics. Its publication also led to much correspondence, this time exclusively among the intellectual upper classes. In this connection a long letter from Joachim has peculiar interest, the more particularly because Joachim took the view that if a Spinozist had to choose between admitting an insoluble contradiction in the master's conception of an infinity of attributes, on the one hand, and, on the other, admitting (like Alexander) a confusion in his conception of 'ideas', it was the former alternative, although hard, that should be accepted.

MEMOIR

IV. Retirement

Alexander was glad to retire. ' I'm quite sure I want to go and cultivate my soul in peace without being obliged to teach half-truths to students ', he wrote me as early as 1921. He might have consented to remain had the complicated machinery required at Manchester for continuing a professor in office after sixty-five been set in motion. But it was not, and he rejoiced to be free.

Here is a letter he wrote about the matter (Christmas 1923):

' Yes, I retire at the end of this session, and I sigh for my release. I wish I had had the energy to resign last spring when I lost my sister (angina). But it would have hurried them also and, another " also ", I thought another year's savings would be useful. Think of having your days free to do the things you like best; and I propose to go on for 20 years, my mother having lasted on before me to 86. Time for many philosophers, many suns, to rise and set. If only enough brains remain. Having been economical in my life (through my sister's care) I shall have saved enough to eke out the limited pension I shall get with the help of a few odd jobs which I may secure. For the present I think I shall stay on here in Manchester. But I dream of a long holiday after July, ending up with 3 months in Italy till the year begins. A brother philosopher there who owns vineyards and can keep a motor offered to motor me all over Umbria. . . . However these are dreams and may not come to fulfilment, for my brother's health seems not very good.'

He had the Italian holiday, and returned to a busy although not to a bustling retirement in Manchester. The ' odd jobs ' were examining for higher degrees, lecturing, reviewing, and the like. His house was a sort of Mecca for philosophers to visit from many lands; and he had many friends at home.

Honours came to him, almost as many as he deserved, and although I don't think he would like me to say much about his honours — none was so sweet as his election to the British Academy in 1913 — I shall give a list of his later academic honours. Birmingham gave him its LL.D. in 1924, Oxford its honorary D.Litt. in the same year, and Durham in 1923. He received the honorary Litt.D. of Liverpool in 1925, and of Cambridge in 1934. He was made an honorary Fellow of Lincoln College in 1918 and of Balliol College in 1925.

His attitude towards such matters is sufficiently indicated by the following letter *à propos* of Liverpool :

' Your V-C has told me Liverpool is going to give me a doctorate in June. I suppose it is you and —— who have wangled this, and I am greatly touched by it. I have given up asking myself if I deserve the honours which have been conferred on me. I just allow them to feed my vanity, which is marked. But what I like and have no inward reservations about is the personal side of these decorations ; and in particular I am warmly grateful to you people in Liverpool for thinking of me and cherish the friendliness which prompts the act.'

An honour that moved him very deeply was the presentation of his bust by Epstein in November 1925. It stands in the Hall of the Arts Buildings of the University of Manchester, and Alexander was very fond of taking his friends to see it. Its presentation was a great occasion, and I must quote the speech that Alexander prepared for it, omitting only his graceful references to the distinguished people who were present :

' I hardly recognise myself in all these kind and honorific words. But a man must accept with gratitude the opinion of his friends ; and it is sweet and heartening to me to know that they think these things of me.

'. . . I owe to the University the long 31 years that I was proud and happy to be a professor here, during which I tried to do my part, according to my lights, as a teacher, and otherwise as opportunity presented itself, and to contribute something to my subject, which also is a part of our duty. I have never satisfied myself in any of these capacities, however much the generosity of my colleagues and friends has overlooked my shortcomings. One thing I may claim some credit of fortune for, remembering in how large a measure the work of the University depends upon the quality of its younger teachers. I had the good fortune to bring to it a succession of gifted young colleagues in my subject (including Mr. A. E. Taylor now of Edinburgh), so gifted that, alas! they were always being taken away elsewhere after a very few years. Many of them, as was natural, came from Balliol; even Mr. Lindsay, who was one of the exceptions and did not come from Balliol here, went from here to Balliol. Only one of them up to the present has become head of a College; but two or three of them are still at an age at which anything may happen to them. I rejoice too and am grateful that my bonds with the University are still unbroken; and I hope, in closing one long chapter of my life and beginning another chapter, that it may be true of me what a member, real or imaginary, of my race said of himself, " The best is yet to be ".

' It is a great thing, I feel, to have secured the affection of my pupils and my colleagues and my other friends in Manchester and elsewhere; and I shall keep the list of names which I hold in my hands, along with the other list of my pupils and other members of the Philosophical Society who last year presented me with a holiday in Italy, among my most cherished possessions; and I shall add to those names in thought those others who for good reasons may not be represented in the lists. I cannot tell how I have won this affection; unless it be that I possess a fair stock of affection myself, which extends to all children and to dogs and cats and other animals. Apart from that, after careful self-examination, I can only conclude that there must be something in me which in the 18th century they used to call a *je ne sais quoi*. It is strange to me, reflecting how small a part of my teaching has played in the work of the Faculty of Arts, that my bust should occupy such a place of eminence in this Hall. But the very irony of this situation may be a happy reminder that we teachers of the several Faculties are all members of the one larger organic whole which is the University ; that the distinction and separation of Faculties is mainly one of convenience ; and that, at any rate, I have always regarded my subjects as the connecting link between the Arts and the Sciences.

' Yet I reflect that my position of eminence here is less a tribute to me than to the artist. A man may well be proud to be the subject of so great a work of art. In the future when I am forgotten this bust will be described among the University's possessions as the bust of a professor, not otherwise now remembered, except as an ingredient of the ferment which the earlier years of the 20th century cast into speculation,[1] but it will be added that it is an Epstein. I have heard the remark by some friends, who had seen the photograph of the bust which appeared some time ago, that it would have pleased them more if it had been less in repose, less serious. But, after all, during the greater part of my waking life I am in repose ; and though I shall be glad if it is said of me, " He was known for a certain gaiety of speech ", I prefer to have it said of me, " He contrived for some years to persuade people that he could think ". For, my Lord, in spite of appearances to the contrary, I am really and truly and fundamentally a very serious man ; it is only that I find it difficult to be dull. How accurately the artist has entered into my character is shown by his giving the portrait just a touch of mulish obstinacy, which is perhaps less known to my friends than it is to myself in the secret places of my heart. I must add gratefully what an experience it was to sit to Mr. Epstein. I do not think only of the kindness I received from him and Mrs. Epstein and from their little daughter. I am thinking of the opportunity it gave me of observing a great artist at his work ; how while he seemed to be, and was, absorbed in the faithful reproduction (which it is) to the minutest detail, of the form of my

[1] In 1930 Alexander wrote (to Professor Susan Stebbing) : ' The fact is I believe I am rather provocative than anything else ; and I've made up my mind that my business is to make people think, even if their reflections condemn me. I'm very deficient in soundness and thoroughness. And you know what W. James said, that any fool can be original '.

unworthy and in some respects eccentric head, his hand somehow (I do not understand how, but I suppose because he is a great artist) introduced into my features the imaginative increment which makes the bust something, as Miss Thorndike says of the bust of herself which was being done at the same time, which the subject himself would like to be.'

I have in my possession a newspaper photograph of the scene. My copy is blurred, and the bust is aggressively preponderant. It is a life-mask, too triumphant in its relative perpetuity. Beside it, but a little behind, stands Alexander, his elbow on the pedestal, a broad figure, simply dressed, shorter than some tall men beside him,[1] and stooping slightly, the fingers of the right hand grasping the back of the left, and the thumb, as it were, feeling for the pulse, the face grave, deprecating, wondering, and very wistful. That, as it seems to me, is the Alexander of later years — a man resigned to his many honours, but weary and modest and half-dismayed. His spirit, could it return, would be grateful, deep, and perplexed.

The greatest honour came in 1930, when the Order of Merit was conferred on him. Readers who have not yet received that decoration may be interested to learn that it will be announced to them in a missive from the King's Private Secretary typed in letters of an outsize. I do not know what Alexander wrote to his sovereign, but in a draft that he prepared he sent his humble duty, confessed that he would not have judged himself equal to the honour, knew that he could not judge in his own case, and continued : ' I remind myself of a famous conversation in which King George III had paid a very high compliment to Dr. Johnson,[2] and how, when asked by a friend afterwards whether he had made any reply, Johnson said, "No, sir. When the King has said it, it was to be." '

There was, of course, a chorus of congratulations—from colleagues, from the University, from the Mayor of Man-

---

[1] His precise height, in his maturity, was 5 feet $10\frac{1}{2}$ inches.
[2] See also my note on p. 133, *infra*.

chester, from Oxford pupils, from Manchester pupils, from the W.E.A., from the Chief Rabbi; a sheaf of telegrams (one from the Chief Constable of Manchester, another from Lord Rutherford, 'your meritorious brother'); tributes from all the world. According to a few the choice was a proof of the discernment of a Labour Government. According to most, it almost reconciled them to the existence of a Labour Government. Sir Frederick Pollock sent a postcard in Latin: 'Inter philosophiae studiosos minimo mihi haud paulum arridet principes nostros viris illustribus honores tribuentes philosophiae, praesertim tuae, non oblivisci. Vale.' The neatest thing that was done was done by a gentleman whom Alexander had presented for an honorary degree the month before. In presenting Professor Smithells for the honorary degree of Doctor of Science, Alexander began, ' I present to you a distinguished and too fortunate chemist upon whom at his birth the ungrudging gods, in bestowing upon him the gift of science, forgot that they had already bestowed the still greater gift of beauty'. Dr. Smithells sent Alexander his photograph with the inscription, 'From Beauty to Merit'.

In short, it was a joyful occasion. In doing honour to philosophy England honoured herself and honoured the best tradition of her culture. In doing honour to Alexander she honoured a philosopher in whom vigour of intellect and breadth of imagination mingled with a generous and gentle nobility of manhood in a degree unique in his generation.

Alexander replied to all these well-wishers, saying something a little different to each. To me he wrote on June 8: 'I've only just begun to answer my friends, quailing before a mountain of letters. . . . I think you know I entertain quite a modest opinion of myself. And ever since I got the letter from the King's Secretary (the most charming and gracious sort of formal letter) I have been feeling myself unequal to what *ought* to be the big tradition of the order. The pleasure it excites among my friends reconciles me to it. And to-day I got a telegram from Whitehead himself (unquestionably better fitted as a representative of philosophy) approving warmly. That only means that Whitehead is a dear, but it comforts me enormously. . . .

' I hope the vanity of my new honours won't damage my work and prevent me (through over-care for my reputation) from plunging as I have done hitherto.'

His vanity had to accommodate itself to knee-breeches, but Sir Philip Hartog, who, along with Dean Inge, was honoured at the same investiture, assures me that Alexander seemed more cheerful than most. A postcard to Sir Philip indicates some of Alexander's preparatory difficulties. ' If I hadn't had your remarks about the stockings I should have been puzzled by the arrival of 2 pairs, one cotton and one silk. But now I understand what to do (I am, as you know, proceeding on the most economical plan). I am glad to find I don't look such a fool as I had expected in knee-breeches, but a friend to whom I said this last night said, " Are you sure ? " '

But let me turn to the way in which Alexander honoured others.

The earlier system at Manchester had been to appoint a presenter *ad hoc* for each particular honorary graduand. In place of this system Alexander, comparatively early in his Manchester career, was appointed Public Orator, except in the name (which he declined).

He continued to present for honorary degrees at Manchester until 1930. ' It doesn't mean hard work,' he wrote me, ' but I enjoy so much hitting on happy phrases that it diverts me from my proper business.' In reality it meant very hard work; for Alexander took immense pains to get information (and especially what is called ' inside information ') about the men and women who were to be laureated. ' Tell me something about his doings and his character that will be interesting and picturesque ', he would write. ' You know the sort of thing. Not things out of *Who's Who*, but the character of his work and the man. This office of major-domo or butler is what I have come to in my senility.' But the major-domo had delightful wages. Many (indeed most) of the recipients wrote to him (and often wrote again, years after the event) recalling the pleasure that his delicate skill had given them. Here is a typical instance, from Bavaria : ' Having come home, I cannot abstain in thanking you for what you have said about me. It would give me an everlasting pleasure if I could have a copy of your speech. I would leave it to my daughter, who would be delighted in what you have said about me and my family.' Similarly Alexander received an astonishing number of letters from the unhonoured in the audience. It was he and his magic that made the ceremony for them, and they let him know about it.

He himself enjoyed these occasions very actively indeed. ' I manage ' he wrote me, ' (by stealing my friends' words from their letters) to make sketches of these people. For the rest my " good voice and pompous manner " of which I told you carry me through and help towards an excellent ceremony.' A variant of this statement was (to a lady) : ' You've discovered my secret, which is that my voice is the only good thing about me '.[1]

I shall not quote much from these admirable sketches. The flowers of ceremonial oratory are cut flowers that droop almost as soon as the platform party goes down the steps in all its would-be mediaeval array. I like the conclusion of Alexander's tribute to the present Archbishop of York : ' Nor amongst the claims which he has accumulated upon the admiration and affection of this place would I forget the good fortune which has been his (and ours) to have been aided in his work by a partner whose gifts and character, were it but the custom of the Church that the wives of

[1] He was fond of reading poetry aloud, to children and on holiday as well as on a public platform, and very proud of his skill in the art. In *Philosophy* of January 1939 Dr. Muirhead says : ' In his frequently solitary walks it was his habit to carry a book of poetry with him and to employ himself in committing favourite passages to memory. . . . One of my own liveliest reminiscences of him was once at Edgbaston in the twilight before the lamps were lit, when it was suggested that he should recite some poetry to us, and he unhesitatingly responded with long passages from Shelley in the rich tones of his beautiful voice.'

prelates should share the titles of their husbands, would singularly befit the title of Her Grace.' I like the reference to a former colleague ' whose departure diminished at once the gaiety and the volume of the spoken intercourse in our society '. I like the tribute to a generous man, ' With such pockets it hardly excites wonder that he has the reputation of being the worst-dressed man in Manchester '. Indeed I like too much to go on with these quotations, and, instead, will quote one of the speeches in full. It refers to Miss Eileen Power and I have chosen it almost, but not quite, at random :

' I present to you a scholar so various, and so excellent in each of her characters, that those who only know her books suspect the reputation of her social charm, and those who only know her personally suspect the reputation of her learning : both alike wrongly, for by some rare creation of natural history she unites the virtue of the bee with the glamour of the butterfly. Had she had her will, she would have followed in the traces of Marco Polo, and indeed, as the first woman holder of the Albert Kahn Travelling Fellowship, she visited China, and left so profound an impression on the learned of that country that barely to name her is to open every door of learning or of art. But her other gifts serve only to enhance her merits as a historical scholar. With capacities that might have won her fame as a traveller, or a connoisseur, or perhaps as an actress, she has chosen to spend laborious days in first-hand enquiry among the files of the Record Office. She has thrown light upon the life of English nunneries in the Middle Ages, and, by studies of the wool trade of the fifteenth century, upon the life of the class which later in Tudor times made England great, and has enriched our knowledge of economic history with commentaries on many a mediaeval and Tudor document. Professing to have no taste for abstract thought, as I must needs deplore, she read herself into her chair at the School of Economics with a masterly discourse on the philosophy of history. Need I add further praises to commend to you a scholar of the soundest achievement and a woman of infinite variety?'

Alexander also excelled as an after-dinner speaker. I shall quote part of a speech that he made at a dinner given to the present Master of Trinity College in Cambridge :

'If I am asked why you, Sir, and the Committee have conferred on me, more or less a literary man, the privilege of proposing the toast of the Master of Trinity, I cannot answer. Perhaps they remembered that this Society is literary as well as scientific, and they know that he is not only a great man of science but is also a considerable historian. For he is an authority on the history of the pirates, and has been heard to discourse learnedly on the performances of Gentleman Jones. Perhaps they remembered that physics and philosophy are returning to their old friendship; that the best sellers are inimitable compositions by eminent scientists of the latest discoveries with an appendix of suggestions in philosophy; that in the persons of Earl Russell and Mr. Whitehead we are returning to the great tradition of Descartes and Leibniz and Kant when physics and philosophy were combined in the same person; and they may know my own deep sympathy with that movement, however incompetent I am to help it on.

'Whatever the reason of their choice, I am proud to have been chosen and the task is an easy one, for we welcome to us the discoverer of the electron, who is the father therefore of modern physics, who has opened up to us a new field of knowledge, a new chapter in the history of human thought. He is the father of a long series of eminent investigators, some of them taught by himself, like his own successor Lord Rutherford (well known to us in this place where he counted the alpha-particles), others taught by his own pupils (and may I add that the line includes the name of his own distinguished son?). It was thirty years ago that he brought the electron to birth by a strange process of midwifery, unbending with an electric field a stream of cathode rays that he had previously bent with a magnetic field. Since then the electron has been the spoiled child of physics, learning new tricks in each decade; not many years ago it learned to spin, in the hands of those who have followed on in the Master's own footsteps, and now it has learned the trick of hiding itself in the disguise of a nebula of probability waves, trimmed with quanta in front and of diffraction patterns behind it.

'. . . I cannot forbear to praise his immense alertness of mind and to give an instance in illustration of it, that when he was in the chair at a scientific meeting on a very hot day and he was using, apparently, his legitimate privilege of sleep during a heavy paper, when the reader declared that two atoms could not be held together by a single electron, a voice from the region of the chair said suddenly, " Yes, they can. I've seen them. . . ."

' He is a Manchester man. He was not actually born in Manchester but in Cheadle. . . . I regret that he is not everywhere remembered in Manchester as he deserves. Only the other day, speaking to a scientific observer here, an old man declared " that he did not hold with education. These bright lads who do so well at school, they aren't no good afterwards." He added, " Why, I was at school with a fellow called Joey Thomson, and he got all the prizes, but I should like to know whoever's heard of Joey Thomson since ? " That is not the case in this Society here,' etc.

Alexander spoke on many platforms and for many causes — about the oppressed, about the University, about Miss Rathbone's candidature for Parliament. (She was a friend from Suffragist days.) He also took pleasure in lecturing, once the burden of day-to-day lecturing had rolled from his shoulders; and his Samuel Hall orations were great University events. For the most part he lectured about art, but also about theism, and the new science, and other such topics. His audience was sometimes laic, sometimes sophisticated. He gave public lectures in Manchester, lectures to Jewish societies in various cities, addresses to learned bodies including at least half of the universities in Great Britain. Often he would choose a hackneyed theme the better to exercise his remarkable talent for draining honey from a wilting flower. 'First I thought I wouldn't', he wrote to a young philosopher at Bangor, '(I always do) and then I thought I would, and now I think I will. . . . When must you know? It will have to be something about art, *e.g.* " Science and Art " or " Truth, Beauty and Goodness " or some such damned *cliché*.' The ' damned *cliché* ' always turned out to be supple. No one was more skilful than Alexander in reaching originality by what might seem to be mere logical permutation or in finding something new about the art in science or the science in art, or the morality in either.

His manner on these occasions was a perfect blend of unselfconscious dignity with the skill of a finished speaker, and he was at his best with questioners, usually contriving to catch their meaning despite his deafness, and using the deafness itself as the graceful cloak of a kindly gladiator. Sir Philip Hartog has supplied me with an admirable instance from a general audience (the date doesn't matter). Questions being invited, one of the audience (shall we say, Mr. Theophilus?) became thoroughly abusive about Alexander's theological views, and ended with the statement that the views were absurd. Alexander, gentle and altogether good-natured, slowly replied, ' Mr. Theophilus thinks that what I have said of the deity is absurd. Well, perhaps it is. But then ' (a pause and a dawning smile in eyes and voice) ' the *truth*, you know, is so often absurd.'

I have often heard him myself on the annual occasions [1] when our philosophers congregate in July to air their opinions in some hospitable university seat. In his later years Alexander had become the seraph in attendance at these congresses. If he were away the congress failed; but usually he was present.

He knew his power and described it very well in his habitual mixture of introspective acuteness with unselfconsciousness. ' The only reason they ask me to speak at these meetings ', he wrote, ' is because I am so good

[1] He could not resist contributing to a French International Congress when the letter of invitation addressed him as ' cher maître '.

tempered and because I generally like the young 'uns and so they are kind to me.' Another thing he sometimes said (although few believed the concluding part of it) was, ' My difficulty is not so much age as the deafness. Age enters in only so far as I find I can't keep up with what you young people think about, and so I tend " stare super altas vias ".' His success, however, delighted him. For instance, I remember the frankness of his pleasure about a speech he made at Oxford when Locke's tercentenary was being celebrated. ' I burbled ', he said, ' but they *liked* it. They *all* liked it.' And so they did.

Alexander didn't attend all the meetings at such congresses, but when he played truant he had usually a little private congress of his own. Here is an instance : ' I enjoyed most of all a long conversation I had with Eddington and Broad in the lovely garden of New College about Relativity. It was like a dialogue out of the *Alciphron*. I failed in my duty of attending ——, but was rewarded for my default.'

I have frequently referred to Alexander's deafness, partly because it made his beautiful good-temperedness all the more remarkable. How it arose I do not know. I have heard, but do not necessarily credit, the lay suggestion that the origin of the trouble was a severe attack of German measles in childhood, the only obvious illness that Alexander had.

When Alexander was over seventy there was a fibrous growth. ' Is there any remedy left but prayer ? ' he wrote. ' And is that likely to be useful ? '

Mrs. Ewing of the Department of Education for the Deaf in Manchester University has supplied me with some particulars. In 1919 when the Department was established Alexander said, ' It is not serious with me—yet. If I grow worse I shall ask you to teach me to lip-read.' He set about to learn that art in 1929. By that time he was too deaf to hear any of the consonants in speech, as audiometric tests showed. He could just hear the sound of a voice faintly. The effort of attention that his sociable nature required was, in short, prodigious.

MEMOIR

For long he had used an ear-trumpet; but it was asking rather too much to expect a friend to speak into the ear-trumpet and also to leave his lips visible. In 1932 Alexander began to use an electrical instrument, but showed, as he said, 'amateurish timidity' in shaking the microphone in a 'confident rough expert way'. He used it as little as he could help. By this time his deafness was almost complete for all the upper notes within the speech range. So he could hear only 'cracked voices' in conversation, although formerly nothing used to please him more than a musical speaking voice. He was interested in 'the percentage of mumblers among the English'.

From early days Alexander had been something of a journalist, but he was rather a reticent journalist until he ceased to be a practising professor. As an honorary professor he greatly extended these activities, especially in the writing of obituaries and reviews. The obituaries were written for various journals, and I cannot quote the best of them since their subjects, fortunately for the world, are still alive. The ones he published were chiefly about philosophers, but sometimes about other friends (including Mr. Tom Kilburn, inn-keeper of the Hill Inn at Chapel-le-Dale near Ingleton, who, with his wife, had perished in a motor accident). His reviews were nearly all for the *Manchester Guardian*. Of these I have seen 104, mostly written during the period we are now considering.

These reviews (for the most part either signed or initialled) ranged over all the philosophical and near-philosophical subjects, and one (signed 'A' instead of the usual 'S. A.') is about R. A. Knox's *The Body in the Silo*. It begins philosophically: 'A good mystery or detective story is a comedy of murder. Not pity and fear are the emotions excited but the thrill of successful iniquity in a crime too fantastically executed to horrify and whose unmasking, after long suspense, stimulates a gentle and unvindictive pleasure in the reader, who thinks less of the suffering of the victim despatched off the stage than of the skill of the perpetrator and the still greater skill of the detective.' For the rest, this notice reads like any other notice of an interesting detective story. (I may add that the backs of these cuttings give evidence that Alexander was fairly successful in solving crossword puzzles.)

Alexander, I think, was rather too kind to the unillustrious. They did not *all* deserve so much encouragement. With the illustrious he was firmer and, although never hostile, was often quite definitely unconvinced. Thus of A. E. Taylor's *The Faith of a Moralist* he wrote: ' Why should not the religious life be indeed precious, but reserved for the religious ? ' Of Dean Inge's *God and the Philosophers* he said : ' The whole philosophical doctrine, I should say, suffers from impatience. . . . With full recognition of the force of mind displayed in this work, I came away from it with the feeling that there are two kinds of minds which, in dealing with the all-important question of the connection of religion and philosophy, are apt to lose contact with one another. The one works ploddingly upwards from experience and finds religion and God at the end of it, never entertaining a doubt that a sound philosophy must find its place for a fact of experience so indefeasible as God, and the worship of him. The other takes the conceptions nearest to its religious wants, and I think distorts the conceptions in physical experience to suit them.'

Alexander's beautiful voice was twice heard on the air in National Broadcasts, once in 1930 when he took part in a series of talks on Science and Religion [1] (later published together), and once in 1934 when his subject was ' Philosophy and Beauty '. One of the results was a very large fan mail. Another result, Mrs. Naomi Mitchison tells me, was the repair of the roof of his house. Alexander was unaffectedly delighted that his voice had become a hundred-pound voice ; but he had a frugal mind. He said that the painting of the bath could wait.

[1] Alexander was disappointed with the plan of the series. He thought the too respectable B.B.C. hadn't given the honest-to-godlessness atheist a fair chance.

MEMOIR

The second of these broadcasts was in some sort a sequel to his book, *Beauty and Other Forms of Value*, which appeared in the autumn of 1933. The book may be described as a fresh discussion of the 80-page chapter on 'Value' in *Space, Time, and Deity*. It was a metaphysical discussion culminating in a theory of value. This time, however, Alexander began pretty near the top and worked downwards and across instead of 'plodding' from the bottom upwards as in the earlier work. He now tried the eagle's methods and not the mole's.

The book began with a chapter on 'valuation', thinking with the learned but talking with the vulgar, and it used beauty, its analysis, its genesis, and its forms as a long prologue to its metaphysical theme. Passing rapidly over natural beauty, Alexander developed his thesis that beauty is the satisfaction of a creative impulse that is also contemplative, mind being interfused with its material and, in fine art, bringing magic out of its craftsmanship. Such a union is artistic 'form' and the artist's impulse is always creative. But it does not create *ex nihilo*. It mixes mind with material, and, instead of imposing an 'image' upon the material, elicits the so-called image from the material. Here the distinction between poetry and prose, in the philosophical roots of it, is very apposite. 'It is that the poet places himself and places his hearer within the subject itself and works from within outwards, while the prosaist describes, relatively, from without.' Beauty has degrees of greatness. It is objective because it 'satisfies a standard mind' (this is Adam Smith) and because there really is a creative instinct that it really does satisfy.

The prologue occupied more than half the book; and that was deliberate. Alexander, because of his essays and lectures on art, had gained the reputation of being what is inelegantly called 'a great aesthetician', and the theme of aesthetics fascinated him. Therefore when he set to work to unite his 'scattered heresies' into 'one big clotted heresy' he lingered over his prologue on aesthetics.

It is permissible to suggest, nevertheless, that the earlier essays, although (or perhaps because) they ' plunged ' so provocatively, are severally more adequate than the later and smoother narrative.

There were, however, compensating advantages. The early essays were written very largely to invite criticism, and Alexander had hoped that artists of distinction might tell him how they worked. The response, on the whole, was meagre. Artists, perhaps, are not introspective. Or perhaps they are sometimes shy. There had, however, been a certain response from novelists, painters, architects, and musicians, for the most part, it is true, from persons who could not pretend to be very gifted, but also from some who were eminent and (what Alexander liked even better) from young authors of promise. His correspondents, to be sure, did not always agree with him. Some told him that ' the mind becomes the image ' — whatever that might mean. Others told him that ' appearances do not contain the explanation of themselves. They refer to the unapparent ' — a proposition that Alexander could accept in his own Alexandrian sense. He had, however, a great deal of encouragement from these first-hand sources,[1] to say nothing of the hearty support he had always had from such an one as C. E. Montague.[2] So he had useful material with which to supplement his earlier efforts and his very extensive reading in the biographies of painters and sculptors and musicians.

' He had an intense love of beauty ', a friend writes, ' in men and women, in pictures, in cathedrals and churches, in literature and music, in fabrics and furniture and household gear.' The last of these I have illustrated by the letter quoted that he wrote from Assisi. As for cathedrals, he could seldom talk enough about Salisbury, but he visited most of the finer English cathedrals on his bicycle in his

---

[1] Among others from Robert Bridges : ' There is one thing in your lecture that I especially wish to mention. You say " I believe it is through the Alexandrines ". . . . *That is absolutely true*. . . . I should like to tell you the story of the invention . . . a logical process ! '

[2] See quotations in my notes to p. 231 and p. 247, *infra*, in the present volume.

later years, and he may have loved the west front of Wells at sunset most of all. In literature his own admirable taste was his surest guide and he had an unusually accurate verbal memory for poetry. ' He told me ' Dr. Fiddes writes, ' that at one time he could repeat the whole of Palgrave's *Golden Treasury* by heart.' Regarding painting and sculpture he had learned much although he did not travel very often, and he seldom visited London without lingering over the greater exhibitions and sampling the smaller. Music caused him greater perplexity, and his deafness did not help, although he had not the same difficulty in hearing music as in hearing the spoken word. But he was tireless in collecting material about Mozart and Beethoven and others in that high company.

In particular he had a most lively and pertinacious interest in the process of artistic creation. He himself disclaimed such powers. ' Lord bless you ! ' he wrote, ' I don't know what artistic creation is unless making jests is artistic.' But he was sure he *must* be right about the process and, in that spirit, did a good deal of ' prosaic ' observing ' from the outside '. In this respect the experience of sitting for Mr. Epstein delighted him vastly, as may be seen from the speech quoted above at the presentation of the bust. He described the affair at greater length in an article on ' The Creative Process in the Artist's mind ' (1927) in the *British Journal of Psychology*. Admitting that he ' could not elicit a direct answer from Mr. Epstein ', he resolutely affirmed that that eminent man, intending a ' meticulous study of the sitter ' slowly and tentatively superinduced a work of genius that was ' rather a reading of the original than a transliteration of it '.

The short Part II of the book pursued the ' damned *clichés* ' of the true, the beautiful, and the good. Science was a special kind of art, the art of satisfying disinterested curiosity, but it was not simply a ' put-up job ' even if Eddington had said so. Truth (*i.e.* true knowledge) had value because it satisfied the scientific sentiment ; but its artistry was different, say, from the painter's. The painter personalises his material. The truth-seeker de-personalises himself, submitting to the control of the material. Morality, again, was an art of willing. Its material, in the main, was the wills of men, and that is what it attempted to control.

The still shorter Part III got on to the book's big business. There is a sense (Alexander said) in which everything matters to something else, and, indirectly, to everything else. In that sense ' value ' is pervasive, a category, and everything has a ' subjective pole '. Not everything, however, has a mind, and ' *our* precious values ', truth, goodness, and beauty, are *not* categorial. They are only ' empirical ' and not omni-pervasive. They are the objective relation of satisfactoriness to certain high-grade and unusual satisfactions. Hence the whole, the *omnitudo realitatis*, cannot be a ' value '; for it is not a relation and in any case could not be less than *categorially* valuable if it were a ' value '. Theological philosophers (Alexander was thinking of Taylor and Inge and Höffding among others, although he mentioned Höffding only) should take note. So should all idealists.

Alexander thought that the reception of the book was ' lukewarm and rather superior '. There I think he showed less than his usual equanimity; and without sufficient cause. I may, however, mention a tiny incident. ' I can't be mistaken in believing the excellent notice in the *Scotsman* to be yours ', he wrote to me. ' It would help the book if anything can, and it really says what is in the book. Thank you for it. But I can't think my prose is " beautiful and satisfying ". I call it just " good handicraft ".' That would have been very pleasant reading for me — if I had written the review. But I never wrote anything for the *Scotsman* in my life. The reference to mere ' good handicraft ' seemed to me to be an odd delusion. The description would have fitted Alexander's first book, and I am not suggesting that Alexander, in later life, was *not* a good craftsman. But I am confident that most of his readers would have agreed with an eminent critic who complained of his ' abominable eloquence '.

MEMOIR

Another tiny incident is this: Alexander used to relate with glee that a Spanish newspaper (*El Sol* of Madrid) embellished a review of the book on *Beauty* with a woodcut of Dr. Samuel *Johnson*. That really happened; but Alexander had quite enough Spanish (and, I think, quite enough curiosity) to know perfectly well that the purpose of the review was to proclaim the advent of a second great Samuel who was capable of refuting Berkeley.

The book on *Beauty* was not the last of Alexander's literary labours. He went on with writing that cost him very hard work, for example the paper on ' The Historicity of Things ' that he contributed to a volume in honour of Ernst Cassirer. (He called it ' minor stuff' and thought the name was the best thing about it. But if it is ' minor ' it is not in the least senile.) He complained, about this time, that a difficult book had to be *very* good if it sustained his attention; but others have had that experience before becoming advanced septuagenarians.

About the time of his retirement, Alexander ' in the physics of him ' was very strong. He went on a cycling tour and did his fifty to seventy miles a day for some days on end. At seventy he was still good for over thirty miles of this exercise in a day. ' I have been riding my bicycle about $32\frac{1}{2}$ miles a day', he wrote in 1930 to a friend who was a doctor, ' half of it hilly country with collar work. You as a physician can judge whether this indicates decrepitude on the part of an old fellow of 71, for it does me good, and I seem to have next to no heart.' He had colds and he had indigestion, but, in any ordinary sense, he had very good health. The leaf of his autumn seemed to be as the leaf of the ash.

All his life, it is true, he had been subject (as we saw) to periods of depression — *accidie* as he called it, or ' blue devils ' or ' inertia ' or ' brainlessness '. When he was younger, a few days in a bracing spot, Ingleton or Disley or even Blackpool, would exorcise the blue devils, and often they would vanish from slighter causes. They were rather more stubborn as he grew older ; but they were vincible.[1] He still maintained (and I think he believed) that he would live to be eighty-five ; and he clung to his bicycle despite all the dangers of his deafness in the Manchester streets. That particular habit disturbed the community, and when Alexander's old friend Miss Dodd died she left him a legacy of £200 to pay for taxis and rest the bicycle. Alexander used the legacy principally for the conveyance of his friends. He had no mind to discard the bicycle.

The following letter to Dr. Marie Stopes gives a good indication of Alexander's general attitude :

' After the luxury of your house and garden and the gorse of Hindhead these surroundings of mine are indefinitely banal. But the soul you know ! That perhaps rises superior to circumstances. Perhaps. The great thing is not to fall below them ; so I reckon the good things I have had, like my visit to you, as good ; and the jog-trot things are good too, and I thank the gods. This means that by contentment with my lot I make things easier for the future gods. Should they thank me rather ? The attribute of piety is the same, no matter in what language it is expressed.'

I remember the greater part of a day that I spent with Alexander about this time. I had agreed to become his literary executor and we spent the morning in discussing what the present volume should be. He had preferences and hesitancies and a very discerning modesty. But agreement was easy, and we were able to intersperse our business with the sort of discussion that philosophers are prone to, something about ideas, much about persons, a little about ourselves, and a lot about the world and its affairs. Alexander's study was pretty cheerless on a raw April morning. Its small fire of smokeless coal seemed reluctant even to glow. When lunch-time came he was too busy or too

---

[1] He liked to pay short visits. ' I am like the Wandering Jew ', he wrote, ' and restless.* I like to come away to my friends, but when I am there I want to get back : and then I am restless again.

* " will not look beyond the tomb
And cannot hope for rest before " (cp. *Childe Harold*).'

deaf to hear the loud buzzer that had been fixed in the room. His faithful maidservant, Mary Winifred Lloyd, had to come in and poke him on the shoulder as was her custom.

In the afternoon we walked towards Didsbury, although I think Alexander would have preferred to use his bicycle. He wore his second worst hat and an overcoat that was not new; but it was a triumphal procession. There were salutations (as it seemed to me) from nearly all the ladies and from all the nursemaids that we met—also from all the men who wore a municipal uniform (there were hardly any other men to be seen at that hour of the day). Alexander was the uncrowned king of Withington.

After tea, of which fluid, like another Dr. Johnson, he partook copiously (and he liked it very sweet), he turned to his proofs and I to some page-skimming in the dustier parts of his overflowing library. The proofs were the first of the book on *Beauty*, and Alexander, having authors' cold feet very badly, would frequently groan aloud. Once or twice he would complain of the thinness of his own ideas and marvel at the persistent thickness of Whitehead's.

In the evening, but only on my account, we took a taxi (from Miss Dodd's bounty) to let me deposit my bag at the station. We then repaired to an eating-house connected, I think, with some delicatessen establishment. Alexander had expatiated in advance upon the delights of *Leberwurst* and such-like things, but the actuality interested him less than the anticipation. (I never had a meal with him when the same thing didn't occur irrespective of the type of meal.) On this occasion there was a reason for his apparent disappointment. He had a cold which was visibly progressing, and as he was seventy-four I was much concerned. But I couldn't persuade him to go home. He must wait till eleven to see me off, and I had little doubt that he meant to ignore Miss Dodd's bounty in the matter of his own return. He said he was very tough, absurdly tough for a man of his years.

I think that, on the whole, Alexander's period of retirement was a happy period until near the end, when his heart was weakening. Certainly there was the *accidie*, and I have spoken of it. Certainly he was disappointed at the 'thinness' of some of his work. 'My late spring', he would say, 'no bud or blossom showeth' — or, again, 'I'm just not in my grave'. Certainly he thought that there were 'too many boys' among the Manchester professors, and he was rather too sensitive to his antiquity on his rare visits to their Common Room. But he had a wide correspondence, and troops of friends from all parts of the world, and a great company of young people to encourage, and matters of business that he found most interesting (such as the elections to the British Academy). If, like all who are ageing, he had to live too much with ghosts, he was too much of a man to forget the remedy, a vivid interest in the living and more especially in the young. A favourite institution, his open house on Wednesday evenings, continued. A friend has told me how, returning to Manchester after a dozen years or more and finding himself near 24 Brunswick Road of a Wednesday evening, he began to reflect about time's vicissitudes. But time had stood still. There was Alexander on his doorstep, saying good-bye to a pretty girl. Another quite recent account[1] says the same thing : 'Those parties of his were real occasions. They happened in his study. For the evening, piles of books were taken off the chairs (I don't think the chairs were actually dusted, though !) and put on the floor. There was coffee and cake and real conversation. One was ruthlessly moved on by the host when he thought the time had come, but friendships started there. He liked mixing people and always enjoyed a quarrel so long as it was an intellectual one.'

He would jest continually about his age. I cite a whimsical example in his more oblique manner from a letter to a lady who had youth to help her recovery :

'The *Manchester Guardian* says you have a broken ankle and influenza and cannot go to Rome. Alas for the

[1] From Mrs. Mitchison, an 'adopted God-daughter'.

bad news, which I have to suppose is true. The better people are the more highly organised and brittle they are (and I think you told me once you were brittle). So get well soon. Can't you live on lime and build up your bones? Influenza passes like the fashion of this world, but bones are bones. However, this comes of being worth while. Now I who am not worth while am not brittle.'

There was one great cause of sadness, the distraction of a mad and cruel world and the sufferings of the Jewish race in Europe. Although Alexander did not concern himself very closely with the Jewish community in Manchester, he was proud to be a Jew, and was proudly esteemed by all the Jews. He had a keen interest in Zionism and was a regular contributor to the Palestine Foundation Fund. He was an Honorary Vice-President of the Friends of the Hebrew University of Jerusalem, represented that University on several public occasions, sent its library all the books he could spare, and left it £1000 in his will. Alexander was Chairman of the Jerusalem University Library Committee of the Inter-University Jewish Federation.

Dr. Weizmann, the Zionist leader, writes me as follows : ' You ask me, What kind of a Jew was this man ? He was from early youth deeply attached to Jewish tradition. The first boiled egg I ate in his house was placed in front of me in a small silver egg-cup. He looked at it for a moment with his usual air of intent innocence, and then said, "I was given that cup when I was thirteen, at my barmitzvah." . . . He himself often told me too that in his youth he had known some famous German Jews, including Lazarus and Steinthal and others. When he became famous he lost no opportunity of appearing among his co-religionists. To the end of his life he was a member of the Kehillah [community]. . . . It was he who introduced me to Lord Balfour on one of the latter's visits to Manchester. He said of himself that he was "a total assimilationist who had ceased to believe in the possibility of assimilation " and he whole-heartedly supported Zionism long before it became fashionable.'

Therefore the sufferings of Jewish refugees deeply and permanently clouded his declining years. What he could do with purse and pen and voice, he did; but he knew, none better, that it was little. One of the last of his liberal acts was to dip into his capital in aid of Austrian refugees after the *Anschluss*. He said he wouldn't need it much longer; so the act was naught. 'My dear, I would like to make you a really handsome present', he told one of his 'god-children', 'but that damned Hitler takes all my money.'

The last time I saw him was in the spring of 1937. He had then a good deal of his old vivacity and some of his old vitality. A letter that he wrote to a contemporary in Australia, in September 1937, indicates his general attitude at the time: 'We grow insecure at our years, and we have to be prepared for what the gods may send us, with no great trepidation, I trust, of regret or of joy. But let us not anticipate, and I hope to have more letters from you and, if possible, to see you. But you may not find *me* in when you come. I jog along in the condition in which you saw me last, not of much use to myself or to others, not very contented, sometimes depressed — but I do not complain of the universe. There are books to read and friends to see. Only one may live too long, and I don't like to see much younger men depart before me.'

He had an active disbelief in human deathlessness, or *post mortem* survival of any kind, except, of course, the continuance of a dead man's influence among the living, and his imagination did not falter in the application to his own case. 'Should the extension of mind beyond the limits of the bodily life be verified,' he wrote in *Space, Time, and Deity* (II, 424), 'so that a mind can either act without a body or may shift its place to some other body and yet retain its memory, the larger part of the present speculation will have to be seriously modified or abandoned.' Here he made no reservations, as Spinoza did in Proposition xxiii of Book V of his *Ethics*, 'Mens humana non potest cum corpore absolute destrui, sed eius aliquid remanet quod aeternum est', although, in general, Alexander was willing to say 'if they inscribe on my cinerary urn *Erravit cum Spinoza*, I am well content'. Alexander also did not falter about this matter when he wrote letters of condolence, however deeply his feelings were stirred. 'I have always been content to think', he wrote on one such occasion in the last year of his life, 'that our minds are too closely identified with our bodies (being indeed another aspect of them as Spinoza held) for any personal survival. To live on in the thoughts and memory of our friends and descendants and whoever else we have affected or may affect is of course impersonal — George Eliot's verses are satisfying to me. And equally any way of absorption into the great good is impersonal. I can't help thinking that it is even more inspiring (I don't say consoling) that each of us has his chance and his responsibility for making good use of it while he can, that is, while he lives. That is certain, all the rest is insecure. . . . I am only trying to be candid. And so I'll add this. Many and perhaps most would say I entertain a bleak prospect. The thought of personal continuance does not appeal to me, and I am ready to think that a deficiency on my part. It is rather, I believe, resignation to the inevitable, but perhaps some want of human feeling. At any rate, it's what I mean when I repeat as I always do to my friends, let us be grateful for what we have had. And let us do our work as well as we can.'

Late in 1937, at Lord Rutherford's funeral, all Alexander's friends were shocked at the change in his looks. At the turn of the year, however, although 'grumpy' and 'dumpy' he was still undertaking to give lectures on Pascal and on the relations between science and history — old themes, no doubt, and old for him, but he meant to bring novelty into them. About Eastertime in 1938 he scoffed at his old persistent intention of living to be just precisely eighty-five, and told a friend who went to see him that they would never meet again.

In the summer, the candle of his life began to burn very

low. On August 21, 1938, he wrote to one of his oldest comrades:

' You have always been a faithful and dear friend to me, and getting your letter was a great blessing. My case is bad — I don't know how long it's going to last — it looks like a prolonged illness — a trouble which is inoperable and so cannot be cured. I hope my friends will just hope I may go as soon as possible. Only otherwise I am strong. So I must make the best of it, and not talk about it lest I should be too sorry for myself. My love to you all.

'. . . I am not up to writing now. I fear we shall not meet again. But if you see the report of my departure: don't grieve, for it's what I most want.

' There's no pain. Only discomfort in writing.'

He was sent a copy of the service used at Dr. Montefiore's funeral. He replied on a postcard on September 2: ' Thank you for letting me see this — a beautiful service '.

He died on September 13, 1938, and was cremated at the Manchester Crematorium on the 15th. On October 14 the ashes were buried in Manchester Southern Cemetery in the section reserved for the British Jewish Reform Congregation. He left directions that there should be a simple stone with his name on it and the dates of his birth and of his death. Having bequeathed the bulk of his estate, in due course, to the University of Manchester, he left directions that the bequest should not be commemorated by his name.

I have read many charming things that were written about him, and many charming things that were written to him. None could be charming enough; but a letter from Dr. Montefiore came nearer than most to saying what his friends would have liked to say had they known how to say it. Here is the whole of the letter:

' Many thanks: you are an old dear, and quite unique. You do walk humbly with your funny God, and are so beautifully unconscious that you are *really* a great swell.'

JOHN LAIRD

Oct.-Nov. 1938

I

THE MIND OF A DOG

(Reprinted from *The Cornhill Magazine*, July 1906)

I AM often asked if my dog is intelligent and good, and I cannot say yes without qualification. Again I am often told, or I find it assumed, that he is intelligent and good, and I will not say no without qualification. It is the kind and limits of intelligence and virtue that matter. The case is the same as with literary style. The style that suits an essay is not good for a novel. The style that suits a book is not good for conversation; and Sir Walter, who understood dogs, knew that his own big bow-wow style, as he calls it, was not adapted to the delicate homeliness of the subjects which were chosen by Miss Austen. My dog is intelligent and good, as becomes a dog, more so than some dogs, and less so than others; but his mind is a dog's and not a man's, and it is better to be a whole dog than half a man. He is of about the same age as the infant child of a friend, and I have compared their growth. When they were both about eighteen months old the dog could do much more than the boy, but when I renewed my comparison at the age of five the dog had remained a child but the child had ceased to be a dog.

At the same time, while to me it is his differences from human beings that are most interesting, there is much to be learned from the likeness, and more particularly from the likeness to children. There is much truth in a rhyme which I remember from my childhood. You were asked what little boys were made of, and the answer was — rats, and snails, and puppy-dogs' tails. Of rats I shall have something to say later. As regards snails, I have no evidence that concerns their affinity to children, except that children are said like those animals to creep unwillingly to school. But undoubtedly the puppy-dog (for I assume that the poet when he spoke of the part intended the whole animal, by the figure of speech known as metonymy) enters into their composition. Though my dog has not the makings of my human friends I can trace him in them, and the description of his mind and of his education may throw some light on the growth of theirs.

The intellectual education of my dog, I may say at once, has been almost entirely technical. Literary training I have found to be possible only in a very restricted form, although it is extremely significant. For the rest, he has been schooled in certain practical occupations, and has acquired a certain amount of what, on the analogy of manual training, I may call 'buccal' dexterity. If he could have used his paws in the way he has learnt to use his mouth he would have had hands, have watched them, and become reflective and human, and would perhaps have adopted permanently the upright attitude which he now adopts upon occasion. Neither in his linguistic nor in his technical education can I trace the growth of character which underlies such education amongst children and makes it liberal. Though in the course of these exercises he has acquired moral qualities, he has not acquired them through the exercises themselves, and accordingly his moral education may be considered apart from his intellectual education.

His education has been limited by the deficiency which makes the difference between him and a child. I may as well state at the beginning the general character of his mind. He has learned the golden virtue of self-control, or, in another form, obedience. But his actions are based on habit, and on a certain considerable inventiveness determined by desire. They are a kind of outgrowth of instinct, as, indeed, all well-based action must be, and it is of great interest to me to observe in his different actions just where they fall short of real instincts because they are artificial, and where they fall short of human action because they are

THE MIND OF A DOG

essentially instinctive. Roughly speaking, what distinguishes him from children is that though he learns to do things he does not learn their meaning. He can take means to ends, but he does not know why he must take them. He does not analyse situations but takes them in as a whole. He knows the hang of things but does not know why they hang together. The young Clerk Maxwell used to ask of any toy or machine or other object which interested him, ' What is the go of it ? ' Now my dog learns how certain things go, but he does not learn the go of them, and, therefore, though he has inventiveness he has never become an inventor. He may be, though I doubt it, a Clerk Maxwell amongst dogs, but he is certainly a dog amongst Clerk Maxwells. His virtues, even his obedience, are limited by the same defect. He has not learned the reason of them, and so he is never safe against the temptations which he has not forgotten.

His use of language is limited, but it is most instructive. He has acquired a reasonable vocabulary of some dozen or more words and phrases — bone, cat, boots, slipper, stick, dinner, postman, brush (his own brush), come out, bed, paw, good dog, and bad dog. They are signals to actions, and are unaffected by qualifications. ' Bone ' and ' no bone ' mean the same thing to him when the word bone is pronounced with identical intonation. When someone has said 'cat' in his hearing he is not reassured by being told that there is no cat until he has been to see for himself. Each word pulls a trigger in him and discharges an action. He has not arrived at the stage of considering the word and its meaning for its own sake. His condition of mind is much like that of an admiral who should fire when he hears the word torpedo-boat. To speak strictly, his words are not language at all, though they serve the same purpose. In some cases it is not the word he acts upon but a corresponding intonation or gesture. Thus, unlike a much-regretted dog of a friend of mine, I have never been able to teach him to discriminate the gift of a biscuit from a Manchester man as distinct from a man of some other city. I have to alter the tone of my voice when I name Manchester. Similarly, if he is to take the biscuit when I count three, he watches for the change of tone, and if three is said in the same tone as one and two he will not act. But I am more concerned to describe the different effects of different words. Some of them, like bone or cat, or good or bad, produce an emotion, an attitude of excitement, and to some he responds by a vocal difference — the cat-emotion produces a whining bark, the bone-emotion a bark of joyful excitement, to 'postman' he responds by the mixture of ferocity and kindly welcome with which he usually greets a stranger. Such actions are closely allied to instincts, because of the excitement of desire from which they proceed. Other words excite actions by the simple process of the association of the word with the action, and betray little emotional excitement. Now, when the word fails to excite an emotion the act is likely to become hesitating. He sometimes forgets what the word means, or, in stricter language, he has lost his signal code. He often, therefore, gives the impression of stupidity when, in reality, he is perhaps languid or disinclined, or has simply forgotten. Under these circumstances frequent repetition of the word may be necessary before the impression becomes vivid enough to discharge the action. When I tell him to bring my boots he may go to the door and then look round with enquiring eyes until the word has been repeated several times impressively, when he goes off with a look of satisfaction. A person unused to my dog might suppose he had failed to understand the order and was waiting until he understood. The truth is merely that the trigger that day has got a harder pull. On the other hand, when he is in good spirits and ready to play, the order 'boots' will send him off at once with quick elated step and wagging tail.

The meanings of words are one sort of habit and are acquired as those habits are acquired — by association. Of his other habits I give as an example his training to domestic service. He had been taught as a young puppy to fetch and carry sticks and balls. Much patience on my part, helped by moral persuasion, evoked in him a secondary instinct, a liking for carrying things in his mouth which, in later life, has become an absorbing passion. He learned to bring things, like boots, from the ground floor to my study. My housekeeper gave him the articles, and on her giving a signal to me I called him. In a few repetitions he learned to bring me not only my boots, but cards telling me that my meals were ready, and sometimes, though not so easily, he would take cards from me asking for coals or tea. In the early stages of this process he had been sent down with a card, but on the way, hearing the postman's knock, he dropped the card and rushed for the letter and brought it back to me. He soon learned when he was in my company, and was ordered by words to that effect, to go downstairs and find the boots and bring them up to me when they are ready, or bark for them if they are not; and when I tell him to see if dinner is ready he will generally go down, especially if he is hungry himself, and bring up the card. It is not the usefulness of these actions or their endearing character for the sake of which I describe them, but rather the fluctuations to which, like his intelligence of words, they are subject. In themselves they are mere associations (to use a loose term) in virtue of which the object suggests the action required. As such they are repeated with automatic monotony even when the circumstances are unsuitable. When I am in the house anything which the dog is given or seizes he is apt to bring up to me, and he is not so easily persuaded to take things from me and give them to another person. I frequently take him with me to College, when I am usually provided with a bag and sometimes ride on my bicycle. He does not like being taken to College because he is left alone, and the sight of the bag and the bicycle is often enough to drive him to bed. When I was in Wensleydale, in Yorkshire, amid surroundings as unlike those of Manchester as possible, and had occasion to carry some books in my bag to a friend three or four miles away, my dog, who was

THE MIND OF A DOG

accustomed to do this journey with me almost every day, as soon as he saw the bag, declined to go. Moreover, not only are his actions repeated monotonously even on unsuitable occasions, but they are repeated in an identical form. Like a child when a story is told with some variation, my dog is disconcerted if he does not find the boots in much the same place as usual, and sometimes not searching for them comes back unhappy. On the other hand, again like a child in its use of language, he will extend actions which he has learnt in one connection to circumstances which are similar. He first practised begging for food, but he soon began to beg for anything that he wanted and that he could take into his mouth. When I am throwing a stick for him in a field and give up the game from fatigue, he will sit up in the field and beg for the stick to be thrown. As I have already explained in respect of words, these habitual actions have something of the nature of artificial instincts, and share with instincts their mechanical character; but they are, in some respects, less than instincts, for an instinct depends upon some inherited preformation which is accompanied by desire, and because of this, as we shall presently see, the instinct may become inventive. Hence it is that these mere habits, unless they light up a passion in my dog's mind, are liable to failure. When he is in poor spirits, he will not, as the children say, play, and he is subject to intervals of what looks like stupidity, which, like children to the discomfiture of their parents, he will take occasion to display to my discomfiture in the presence of visitors. It is only in the case of actions like fetching sticks or playing cricket with a slipper, where he has an acquired passion, that he can always be counted on for response. With him, as perhaps with children, the things to be learnt have to proceed from their liking, or else fresh likings have to be created.

His acquired dexterities are the best illustration of the inventiveness of instinct, while at the same time they indicate where inventive instinct falls short of rational action. He is skilful in getting a walking-stick through a narrow opening in a wall, or a railing. An observer, seeing him push the stick along with his teeth till he gets it at the crook and then draw it through the hedge, might attribute the act to reflection, and say, what an observer of Principal Lloyd Morgan's dog said on a similar occasion, ' Clever dog that, sir ; he knows where the hitch do lie '. Now this is precisely what my dog (and Mr. Lloyd Morgan's dog also) does not know. When he feels the hitch he knows how to get rid of it, but he does not understand it. I put him, in imitation of Mr. Morgan's experiment, behind some railings. The dog ran at them holding the stick by the middle, and did this more than once. Then, in the excitement of his desire to get through and join me he began to seize the stick at random, and seizing it near the crook he was able to bring it through. When I repeated the experiment he was clever enough to seize the stick, after a very few trials, at the right place, and I imagine that it is the rate at which the lesson is learned that makes the difference between one dog and another. Even now, when he has become expert, he first runs at the narrow opening holding the stick by the middle, and then when he has failed, he skilfully, and without further waiting, shifts his teeth to the right place. He learnt thus how to do the action by trying repeatedly at random and failing, until success crowned his desire, and he remembered the method of success. Compare his action with the same action as done rationally by a man. In a strict sense the dog does not know how to do the action because he has not analysed it into its means. His means are not deliberate means to secure an end, but they are a lucky device struck out by the urgency of desire. He has learned how it goes, but not the go of it.

My dog confirms many experiments that have recently been made. Mr. Thorndike put famishing cats into crates in which a door could be opened by sundry means, uplifting a latch, pulling a bolt, pressing a lever, singly or in combination. Outside the crate was a tempting piece of fish. The cat, in its hunger, scratched and tore at the door, and in this process it touched the latch or pulled the bolt and the door opened. This process took a long time. When the experiment was repeated the successful movement had been imprinted on the cat's mind, and the time it took to perform the action had been reduced considerably, say from three minutes to thirty seconds. Rats (I promised to mention them) exhibited to another American observer, Mr. Small, the same results. A hole was made in the wooden floor of a cage with wire walls, and a piece of cheese put by the hole. The cage was set on a mound of sawdust. The rat, in its desire to get to the cheese, burrowed through the sawdust, and after much vain effort reached the cheese. The next time it went more directly to the hole, and the time was reduced from one hour and thirty minutes to a few minutes.

Like these rats and cats my dog invents to satisfy his instinct, but like them he does not apparently stop to form to himself an idea as to how he is to achieve his end, and so he stops short even of a child's invention. Watch a baby trying to grasp. At first it behaves like my dog. It tries to grasp and misses its foot or the glittering toy. Then, under the urgency of desire, it tries again. If the glittering toy is not the moon, it succeeds, and so far it is like my dog. But later it can go farther, for it may begin to compare its unsuccessful efforts with the desired result, not merely feel like my dog its failure ; and it may also imitate its elders. After a certain age it begins to compare its drawing with the model. I say after a certain age, because at first it draws without attention to the model, puts two eyes in a profile not because it sees them in the model, for it does not look, but because it knows that a face has two eyes. But when this age is past the child notes the departure of its drawing from the original and seeks to remedy the error ; or observing the actions of its elders watches the movement and tries to imitate the several parts of their movement. It has begun to learn not merely how things go, but the go of them. We begin with the method of my dog, but we go farther. Sometimes, indeed,

THE MIND OF A DOG

we return to it: an unskilled dancer may watch the movements of a new step, and for all his rationality may be unable to repeat them, and perhaps only succeeds when a self-sacrificing partner has carried him through the steps.

My dog's actions, when they proceed from passion like his love for my stick, are plastic and inventive, and varied to suit circumstances, but they do not proceed from reflective ideas. They are intelligent, to use one of Mr. Morgan's words, but not rational. Give him reflection and he would cease to be my dog. But also let a child have no basis of motive or liking on which to work: how much will his reflection do for him?

I am far from saying that my dog has no ideas and does not act upon them. On the contrary, I easily observe in him both memory and imagination. I do not indeed know that he sees pictures when he dreams. I do not happen to have found him growling at his visions, but he can certainly retain ideas in his mind. His brush is kept in a corner of my study, and when he is there he will get it when ordered. But sometimes he will fetch it from the ground floor. He has not been taught to do this, and it always takes a little time to impress the order upon his mind; but he will at times do it, and this suggests that he must keep the idea of the brush vividly before his mind. But I question whether his idea serves any purpose except to keep alive in his mind the signal which is given him. Again, he exhibits spontaneity of action. He brings the slipper to be played cricket with, and his chief demonstration of good will to a visitor is to bring him the slipper and deposit it on his knees and ask for it to be thrown. The game goes in his mind with the joyful excitement, and it is difficult to say how far he forms a regular idea of bringing the slipper. Other cases, however, are clearer in which he appears to be visited by happy thoughts. For a long time he had not seen my former housekeeper, to whom he is much attached. As I shall more than once refer to her I shall speak of her by name, but, with the respect due from a biographer towards a living person, by a fictitious name.

THE MIND OF A DOG

When she came to live five minutes away from my house he was taken several times to see her. Not long after, the happy thought occurred to him after breakfast to pay her a visit; and though it may merely have been induced by a vague feeling of discomfort, of wanting something, and even of wanting Jane (he may have felt the Jane-emotion), or possibly the road before him happened to suggest to him the road he had been taken, still, he may have remembered her, and that image may have acted as a signal to him to take the road. Like his other thoughts it tended to become automatic. The happy thought was repeated for a week, and he left my house after breakfast and returned in the evening, an action of much psychological significance, to dine and sleep.

But such passing images which take the place of sensory excitements are a long way from reflection upon means to ends. Experiments by Mr. Thorndike, which are not indeed entirely above criticism, have tended to show that hungry cats, when they see other cats in front of them get out of the cages which I have described, do not do the same actions any the better for the example. On the other hand, a number of ingenious experiments were made by Mr. L. T. Hobhouse which he thought proved that even dogs and cats could act upon a kind of forethought of means to ends when the way was shown them. My own observation of my dog was not favourable to this interpretation. Imitating one of Mr. Hobhouse's experiments I chained my dog to a table and, placing a biscuit before him on the floor in the crook of a stick, showed him how by pulling the stick in he could get the biscuit. The dog pulled the stick. The floor, however, was uneven, and turned the stick over so that the crook ceased to hold the biscuit, but the dog went on pulling at the stick. I do not, however, think this single experiment at all decisive. But one incident occurred which left upon me a lively impression of how a dog may possibly make a discovery in a way which seems to imply thought, but does not. My house stands in a row, and there are green plots in front with a

THE MIND OF A DOG

low wall to the street and a rail above it. Coming home one day I shut the gate, and the dog, who was then a puppy, could not jump the rail. He tried at the rail several times, and then, backing a little on the pavement, looked up and down the street as if he were thinking how to get in. Then he was aware of a gate open at the end of the row, and with a sudden look of intelligence ran to it and reached his home. Such action was a little farther advanced than mere scrabbling with a stick to get it through a hedge, but it was less than thinking. He was filled with desire, and he saw how he could accomplish it. The road through the gate was not a means by which he recognised that he could secure his end, but it was part of the total situation. This is what I meant when I said that he could take in a whole but could not analyse. His action was little more than noticing that one particular gate would admit him. And I think it possible that in Mr. Hobhouse's experiments the explanation may be something of the same kind, if indeed this is not the meaning of the author himself.

Other actions which would seem to imply a train of reflection are capable of simpler explanation. My dog, as I have said, dislikes going to the College because he is left alone there, and though he is not tied up he feels tied up. He particularly objects to following me there on a bicycle. This dislike has grown upon him with years, and on several occasions lately he has lingered behind and given me the slip, as if deliberately. But the fact is, he was unwilling and lagged behind. Now he has not very long sight, and when he missed me he may have gone home in the ordinary course, or, not noticing me, he may have yielded to the idea of going home, which had been suggested by his unwillingness to come with me. He may, as we inaccurately say, have thought it a good opportunity for getting home without having any intention to trick me. He often comes up from his own bed to sleep in my study, and chooses an arm-chair. There is a deep cane chair in the room with a soft cushion against the padded back.

Lately my sister has discovered that he makes a nest for himself in this chair by dragging down the cushion and sleeping between it and the back of the chair. This suggests much cunning, but I do not know the history of this invention, and as he does not come to spend the night in the study till I have gone to bed, I shall never know. He may one night have found the cushion partly down, and lying on it, may have turned it still farther over and discovered the luxury of a padded hole. Or the explanation may lie farther back. I used to spread a newspaper on the chair because he does not like to sleep on one. But sometimes he was found lying on the cushion which he had pulled over on to the paper. He may thus have first discovered the method of pulling down the cushion to avoid the paper, and then advanced from this discovery (even when there was no paper) to that of the still warmer and delicious bed.

His intellectual exercises, as I have said, do not seem to me to have left any marked trace upon his character. He succeeded in them from the force of his own desire and persistence. They did not teach him the perseverance or attention or industry which should lead him to learn fresh dexterities. His whole moral education consisted in the lesson of obedience or self-control, and his dexterities (for I hate to call them tricks) depended upon his having learned this lesson, and they fortified it. But his morality is limited like his intellect, and even more so. It is an affair of artificial habit built up on instinct. It was acquired soon, for he came to me at four months of age, and Jane, and in a less degree I myself, supplied for him the place of mother and family. Counting upon his attachment, I could guide him by insistence upon my will, and I used the method of reward more sparingly than that of punishment. He learned to beg without the reward of food, but he only learned to carry after several whippings, more perhaps than I should use with a second dog. In teaching him to give up undesirable habits like uncleanliness and stealing, I found that mere displeasure had little effect, and I was compelled to whip him soundly. And here I remark, parenthetically, a trait of *human* nature. Parents and teachers sometimes tell their children that it gives them more pain to whip the child than the child feels, but though I disliked having to whip my dog, when I had begun whipping him and my blood was up, I liked it. Do I betray a latent vein of cruelty in myself, or discover to my friends a trait in themselves which they have not suspected? I could not leave him to the discipline of consequences, as it is taught by Rousseau and Mr. Herbert Spencer. For he was generally clever enough to avoid dangers; he did not put his paw into the fire and discover that fire burns, but drew back at once from a live coal. And the consequences of his other actions were too pleasant for any little inconveniences attending them to count. When as a puppy he stole from the larder half a pound of steak and ate it, though he was gorged he would probably have been content to repeat the offence at the cost of such pleasing pain. Accordingly I could not leave him to be disciplined by such consequences, and for such serious offences I whipped him, and various educationalists have advised that in offences of equal seriousness a child may also advantageously be whipped. At any rate, by much correction my dog learned good habits, through the association of certain desires with punishment and, in a less degree, with reward. He does not steal food except from the ash-boxes. He has acquired patience, and will not take a biscuit till he has received permission, and as his patience varies with his hunger, I use the time he takes to bark for the biscuit as a scientific measure of his appetite. But I cannot call his virtues moral; they are mere habits, and he has not learned the reason for them. He knows that certain things bring rewards and others punishment. He does not fear my disapproval, but the whipping or the discomfort which black looks from me cause him. Moral education depends on exciting sympathy with the likes and dislikes of others, and punishment in the case of a child makes him feel that a parent does not like stealing or

THE MIND OF A DOG

dirtiness, and it is sometimes the only way of making him feel this. But just as my dog cannot understand why means should be taken to certain ends, neither can he understand my reasons for punishing him. He only knows that he will be punished. Hence his conscience is purely naïve and instinctive. When he obeys a rule he feels pleased, and when he violates one he feels uneasy. Both the pleasure and the uneasiness are acquired, and they bear the mark of their origin. His sense of virtue is the presentiment of a kindly pat. His sense of guilt is the presentiment of a whipping. And, unlike a man, who may deliberately conceal an offence or deliberately confess it, my dog neither conceals nor confesses, but betrays it. I should never know of his offence of going to the ash-boxes if he did not come home with a grin on one side of his face which usually means deprecation. Accordingly he fails to distinguish between guilt and any accident for which he is blameless, like a primitive savage who counts a misfortune a crime. When he has been sick he is ashamed. He even confuses mere discomfort with guilt. If he has been left alone at College he sometimes grins at me when I return as if he had offended. His penitence is not the recognition that he has done wrong, but the desire to be relieved of the discomfort of my reproof. When he is whipped he goes to bed, though this whipping is rarely inflicted now because he offends less often and it hurts his feelings more. But when he was younger he would retire to bed sometimes angry, sometimes sulky, always unhappy. After a varying period of two or three hours he would come to make friends. Either he came of himself or I would call him. Sometimes he could not bear the estrangement any longer, and sometimes I could not. For I was sometimes sorry for him, and he was always sorry for himself. And then, in a figure, we kissed again with tears. Neither of us repented, for I had no need to repent and he could not; but he was happy again, and the deterrent from evil had sunk deeper into his habits. His obedience then has become semi-instinctive, and it never has been rational. Like his other artificial

THE MIND OF A DOG

instincts it is subject to failure. There are some natural temptations, like the insupportable enchantment of the refuse-boxes, which he still cannot resist; and when he is disinclined and lazy he only obeys upon authority. When he does not want to come with me to College he offers a stubborn resistance and only yields to imperative orders. Then, when he recognises that my mind is made up, he comes of his own free will. I do not wish to introduce the problem of free-will into this biography or to balance the claims of determinism and indeterminism; but I am sure that when under these circumstances my dog comes of his own free will it is because he recognises that he must.

When I mentioned to the friend with whose child I have lightly compared my dog that I was going to state my view of my dog, he told me that I had much better state my dog's view of me. It is difficult to do so, but I will try. It is sometimes said that a man is a god to his dog. This may be true in the case of Jane, who deserves it, but I almost hope it is not so in my case, for if it were so he has so often brought me my boots that he must long ago have discovered that the feet which wear them are of clay. Yet there is some little foundation for this very metaphorical statement. He finds me mysterious and arbitrary, and while I provide him with food and the pleasure of exercise and company in games, I am, he must think, a creature of moods, and if I cause him pleasure I also cause him pain, and he has perforce to be content. In this respect he feels as any child may feel to a father, or as any man may feel to a person he does not understand. And the changes which psychologists like Mr. J. M. Baldwin describe in the growth of a child's consciousness of its personality have their analogue in my dog. A child learns to understand its father or nurse by doing the things which they do; and by imitating its equals, its brothers and sisters, it finds it can master some of them and must yield to others, and so it comes to be aware that it and other human beings are all alike persons, some to be obeyed and some to command.

THE MIND OF A DOG

Mysterious as I am, no doubt, to my dog, he learns that he can put his desires against mine, and that in certain respects he can master me, while in others he obeys. He finds me to yield to his imperative requests to go out or for the stick, and that I adapt the pace of my bicycle to his pace. I taught him instead of bringing the stick back and dropping it at my feet, in which case I had to stoop to pick it up, to put his paws up and give the stick into my hands, and now he will only give up the stick willingly when asked to do this. But even then the stick has to be taken from him in a certain way, and he has a rule about it which must be observed. I call it, after the trial scene in *Alice*, Rule No. 43, and I cannot discover what it is, and I am not sure that it does not change each time. He has so far, however, learned to measure me, and therefore also himself. But the process is far removed from that sympathetic insight into one another which is possible to human beings who can form ideas and reflect upon them. My dog learns by tact how far he can go with me; otherwise I am a mysterious force which he must obey. I am more to him than other dogs with whom he can fight. I am more perhaps even then a superior dog; perhaps if he could he would describe me as a human dog. But he does not treat me as a person, for he does not know himself as one. I am, I suppose, to him a feeling animal with strange unaccountable flashes of some unintelligible and compulsive energy to which he submits. His sympathy is equally limited. It is a community of feeling and not of imagination, and it arises from attachment, and is modified by habit and custom. Accordingly it varies from one person to another. To me his attitude is one of constant and reasonable affection varied only by occasional displays of transport. And as his memory is short he sometimes exhibits more joy when he sees me again after an absence of twenty-four hours than he does when I have been away for weeks. But to Jane his attitude is one of passionate devotion. In her society he enjoys that combination of rapture with short intervals of contentment (I borrow the

THE MIND OF A DOG

distinction from Goldsmith) which I take to be the meaning of bliss. When he was a puppy she fed him and nursed him when he was ill, and when he misbehaved she reported him to me and left me to whip him. I do not say this to depreciate her real and essential claims upon his affection, but rather to show in what way the natural basis of affection may be varied by circumstances and the qualities of his companion. But in a strict sense he does not sympathise with her or with me. To me, as I have said, he is undemonstrative, and he rarely licks me. When he used to bring up my letters to me in the morning he jumped upon my bed, dropped the letters in front of me, put his nose into my face to smell my identity, and then curled himself up at the end of my bed. I have never observed that he behaves any differently to me when I am well and when I fancy that I look ill. Perhaps the reason is that I only fancy that I look ill. But when he came home dripping blood from a hole in his neck which had been apparently torn by a spike, he came and licked my hand. His sympathy is not one of imagination, but of instinct refined by intercourse, and I should be very ungrateful if I did not here record the perpetual little manifestations of loving-kindness which arise on his part from this *rapport* between himself and me. I am, I suppose, a kind of support or background to him. I am a part of himself, or rather of the atmosphere in which he lives, and sometimes there is thunder and lightning in it. He has not quite so independent a character as some other dogs, and I verily believe that when he is away with me from Jane or my family, and I leave him alone, the sun of his day is for a time extinguished quite. We cannot remember our early babyhood, but I imagine he is in somewhat the same position as a baby to a mother, modified, however, by all those developed activities of companionship in games and exercise of which a baby has not yet had experience. Or perhaps a better analogy can be found in the attitude of a man living in a country governed by custom to whom the custom is his air with which he feels himself one; who obeys the chieftain as the interpreter of that custom, however arbitrary the interpretation, and for whom to have broken the tradition is a source of discomfort as acute as it is to one of ourselves to break through a convention of fashion.

I have written a biography, and I have omitted the first duty of a biographer. I have not mentioned the date of my dog's birth, I have not mentioned his breed, nor even his name. I have thought these things less important than his mind. His breed would be a more important matter if I had been able to describe the early growth of his instincts, as Mr. Wesley Mills has done in the case of certain dogs and cats, or to compare their growth with the growth of instincts which Miss Shinn has traced so faithfully in her little niece. But he did not become my dog until he was four months old. He is an Irish terrier and of distinguished origin, though he does not outwardly do credit to it. His good breeding may in part explain why in certain respects he is perhaps less clever than some other dogs. Mr. Mills found that a mongrel pup, when it was put with other dogs, developed very rapidly as compared with well-bred pups. There are other features of my dog, like his early delicacy, which if I had been giving a fuller life of him, might have been mentioned as accounting in part for a certain want of independence and for an extreme gentleness of disposition which he has. His gentleness and sweet temper are persistent, in spite of his readiness, like other dogs of his breed, to fight, and in spite of the fear which his affection for them inspires sometimes in the breasts of children; a characteristic which has been touched in the course of some Latin verses by my former colleague Mr. A. E. Taylor, addressed to Hobbes, from which I must give myself the pleasure of quoting:

> Floreat et Griffius (for that is the Latinised
>   version of his name),
> Acer ille canis,
> Omnibus philosophis
> Carus, at puellulis
>   Timor suburbanis

THE MIND OF A DOG

— dear to all lovers of wisdom, but to little girls in the suburbs, *timor*: how delicately the word is chosen to describe the character of my dog; not *terror*, a terror to little girls in the suburbs, but *timor*, a source of apprehension. But the more civilised traits of his character have arisen, doubtless, in much larger degree from his constant, perhaps too constant, association with human beings like Jane and myself.

I may have appeared to some readers to take a delight in minimising his qualities. I can only protest that I have tried to deliver the truth without exaggeration, and it is no easy task. For if it is difficult to tell the truth about one's own mind, it is also difficult to tell the truth about the mind of one's dog. But I repeat that the limitations of my dog, which make him less than a child, but leave him a dog, do not lessen my regard for him, but rather increase it. After all, if we did not know that our children act as they do because they know no better, should we, for all their endearing qualities, even tolerate them? We like them because they are children, and not because they will be men. When we learn that their apparent mendacity is imaginativeness, their apparent selfishness instinctive appetite, their apparent cruelty inexperience of pain, and their apparent stupidity adenoids, we find them adorable. So is my dog.

II

DR. JOHNSON AS A PHILOSOPHER

(Reprinted from *The Cornhill Magazine*, October-November, 1923)

SPEAKING of Bacon's *Essays*, Sir Joshua Reynolds, in an unfinished ' Discourse ' he has left us on Johnson's influence (M. ii. 229),[1] says that Dr. Johnson was of opinion that ' their excellence and their value consisted in being the observations of a strong mind operating upon life '. Johnson's judgment of Bacon may be applied to himself, and more aptly describes his claims to be considered a philosopher than any attempt to rank him as a philosopher in the strict sense of the term. His qualifications to that title are of the slightest ; he is rather the wise man or sage than the philosopher.

For philosophy has a strict and a vague sense. In the special and proper sense, it is a science more or less systematic dealing with certain ultimate questions about the nature of things, as has been illustrated from Plato down to Mr. Bradley in our own days by all the great philosophers. Johnson was very little of a philosopher in this stricter sense. Carlyle has at the end of his famous essay on Boswell compared Johnson and his contemporary Hume, calling them the two great half-men of their time, complementary to each other. Now Hume *was* a philosopher and in the first rank. Johnson on the other hand was not.

But in the vaguer sense of the word he was eminently a strong mind operating upon life and as full of wisdom as he was of essential goodness. He has sometimes been compared to Socrates and I shall return presently to the com-

[1] References are to the *Life* (L.) and the *Johnsonian Miscellanies* (M.) in the editions of Birkbeck Hill, to whose labours all my gratitude is owing.

DR. JOHNSON AS A PHILOSOPHER

parison. But Socrates, though he was all that Johnson was, a very wise and strong mind, was a strict philosopher — we should now say a professional philosopher — as well, or in the first place, and it is doing him less than justice to think of him only as a very able and stimulating thinker, as all readers of Messrs. Burnet and Taylor now are aware. Johnson was like one-half of Socrates. Perhaps in our own time the nearest parallel to him is Jowett, who was a devoted Johnsonian by some sense of affinity — Johnsonianissimus, Birkbeck Hill calls him quoting Boswell's word, in the dedication of his edition of Boswell. Jowett was hardly, I may even say in no way, a philosopher in the strict sense. In his introductions to the dialogues of Plato you will find in a high degree the operations of a strong mind upon life, acuteness, largeness of view, over and above the charm of a delicate but vague style ; but you will find no real feeling for metaphysics, nor any profound insight into the mind of Plato. He appears rather to think of Plato as a highly gifted man groping vaguely in the theory of ideas, or, in the later doctrines of the *Sophist*, vaguely and ingeniously and fantastically involved in the difficulties and entanglements of his problems, offering rather illuminating observations about them, than what Plato actually gives us — the intensest insight which speculation has ever possessed into the nature of things. It may indeed be doubted whether Jowett really believed in philosophy for its own sake, or except as a form of wisdom. He rather restrained the enthusiasm of his pupils than incited it. Once when on returning from a vacation I told him that I had been reading Hegel (I must have said all Hegel), he said : ' It's a great thing to have read the whole of Hegel ; but now that you have read him I advise you to forget him again '. No one who believed in philosophy could have said that, whatever view he took of the positive merits or demerits of Hegel. Unfortunately I believe I took his advice in large part and have regretted doing so ever since. On another occasion he said : ' It's extraordinary what an attraction metaphysics seems to possess for certain minds ; it's like falling in love ; but you get over it after a time '. There seems to be some doubt whether Jowett ever fell in love. I think he certainly did not fall into metaphysics. This is written with no thought of belittling him, which would ill become a pupil who fell under his influence and remembers with gratitude his genuine kindness. It is not for his philosophy that we remember him with gratitude, but for the qualities which he shared with Johnson, his humour, his clear and vigorous intellect, his power of direct vision of things, his love of truth and hatred of insincerity and sentiment, his largeness of mind, his love of goodness, his real piety, and his sound sense of the value of material things, perhaps also his prejudices whether we shared them or not — such as his dislike of Thackeray and Carlyle (how glad, he said at breakfast one morning when we told him from the newspapers that there was some apprehension that the comet then visible might collide with the earth and set us on fire, how glad Mr. Carlyle would have been if he could have been alive to know this) ; and more than all, notwithstanding his deprecation of enthusiasms, his steady encouragement of his pupils to pursue knowledge wherever their tastes led them. He would have agreed with Johnson's statement somewhere that all knowledge was of value. Asking one of his pupils one day after graduation what his age was, he said gravely and kindly : ' You have thirty or forty years before you of reading and writing '. The pupil remembers sadly how ill he has justified the prediction, to which he listened then and remembers still with so warm an emotion.

I

In the imaginary University which Boswell one day suggested should be set up by the Club at St. Andrews, Johnson, after first saying ' I'll trust theology to nobody but myself ', on second thoughts left practical divinity to Percy and chose for himself logic, metaphysics, and scholastic divinity (L. v. 109). It may be suspected that

DR. JOHNSON AS A PHILOSOPHER

there would have been more divinity than metaphysics. In 'Prayers and Meditations', No. 27 (M. i. 17), there is a prayer 'on the study of philosophy as an instrument of living' — a significant description of what philosophy meant for him — but even then he adds, 'This study was not pursued'. In the Preface to the *English Dictionary* he writes, referring to subtle distinctions of meaning, 'Many of the distinctions which to common readers appear useless and idle will be found real and important by men versed in the school philosophy, without which no dictionary can ever be accurately compiled or skilfully examined'. But this is probably not to be understood as a claim to be himself considered deeply versed in that subject.

To judge from his conversations and writings, his treatment of philosophical topics testifies rather to the strength of his general powers than to any special philosophical gift. The most famous incident of all suggests the absence of any such gift. Boswell had said of Berkeley's 'ingenious sophistry to prove the non-existence of matter and that everything in the universe is merely ideal' (both statements inaccurate) ' that the doctrine could not be refuted, though we are satisfied it is not true. Johnson answered, striking his foot with mighty force against a large stone till he rebounded from it, " I refute it *thus* ".' Johnson's *argumentum ad lapidem*, of course, only showed that the stone was different from and offered resistance to his body, and was irrelevant to the doctrine that both stone and body were ideas. If it proved anything it proved that Johnson had not understood and was probably too unspeculative to understand Berkeley's point. That the doctrine left the practical nature of things unaltered, Johnson might have learnt from a parallel incident in Molière. In the delightful foolery called 'The Compulsory Marriage' (*Le Mariage Forcé*) the old man Sganarelle, having doubts of his wisdom in proposing to marry his young ward, goes to consult two philosophers, one of whom is the sceptic philosopher Marphurius, whom he tells he has come to consult him in the matter. 'You must please amend', says

Marphurius, 'this way of speaking. Our philosophy orders us to pronounce no decisive proposition, to speak of everything with uncertainty, always to suspend one's judgment; and therefore you ought not to say I have come but it appears to me that I have come.' Sganarelle can, of course, get no satisfaction out of the sceptic, and at last is provoked into beating him. Marphurius cries out, ' Commit such an outrage on me, beat a philosopher like me!' and Sganarelle replies ' Please amend this way of speaking. Everything must be doubted; and you ought not to say that I beat you but that it seems to you that I beat you.' ' Ah,' says Marphurius, ' I shall go to the magistrate and complain of the blows you have given me.' Sganarelle washes his hands of the affair; but Marphurius is right. For though everything is apparent, the apparent judge will condemn Sganarelle to apparent confinement with a diet of apparent porridge and skilly.

Johnson's mind was much occupied with philosophical problems, and even where he shrank from certain questions like freewill or death, Boswell gave him no peace from them. It is doubtless true, as Boswell and others have observed, that his attitude was determined largely by his theological beliefs or his political prejudices, which he held with the sturdiest pertinacity and did not wish to be disturbed in them. They stood in the way of any deep probing of the questions, such as the metaphysician with his equally pertinacious freedom from prejudice requires. He had no eye for the significance of Rousseau's doctrine of society and the state. It offended his conviction of the necessity of subordination of ranks, and disgusted him as an upholder of customary virtue : ' Rousseau, Sir, is a very bad man. I would sooner sign a sentence for his transportation than that of any felon who has gone from the Old Bailey these many years ' (L. ii. 12). He laughed at his preference of the savage state; and he was blind to all that has made Rousseau an inspiration in his own time and in our own. He thought that Rousseau talked nonsense and knew that he did. ' Why, Sir, a man who talks nonsense so well must

DR. JOHNSON AS A PHILOSOPHER

know that he is talking nonsense' (L. ii. 74).[1] But he has in mind chiefly the earlier writings, and perhaps he exaggerated because of Boswell's infatuation for Rousseau.

He had no inkling of what Hume was to mean for subsequent philosophy, or if he did he only saw its disruptive character. A real philosopher was needed to appreciate that, and he was not found till the end of the century, and Johnson was content to acclaim Beattie. What he saw in Hume was, as he thought, the opponent of orthodox Christianity, and it must be remembered that even Adam Smith was afraid to publish the *Dialogues on Natural Religion* which Hume had bequeathed to his care. He declared that everything which Hume had advanced against Christianity had passed through his own mind before, and he urged (L. i. 444) that after a system is well settled upon positive evidence a few partial objections ought not to shake it. 'There are objections against a plenum and objections against a vacuum; yet one of them must certainly be true.' And against the essay on miracles all he could urge was that 'although God has made nature to operate by certain fixed laws, yet it is not unreasonable to think he may suspend those laws in order to establish a system highly advantageous to mankind', such as he profoundly believed Christianity to be. Accordingly for him 'Hume and other sceptical innovators are vain men and will gratify themselves at any expense. Truth will not afford sufficient food to their vanity; so they have betaken themselves to error. Truth, Sir, is a cow which will yield such people no more milk and so they are gone to milk the bull.' Vanity enough Hume had; but there was more in him than vanity.

But though Johnson did not possess the speculative mind, his strong intellect fills his discussion of such questions with sound and wise observations which may be generally accepted, and with pointed and acute criticism of the deficiencies of others. At the end of *Rasselas* there is

[1] He added: 'But I am *afraid*' (chuckling and laughing) 'Monboddo does *not* know that he is talking nonsense'.

talk of the immateriality of the soul, and the astronomer urges that the soul may be material, for matter may have qualities with which we are unacquainted. To which the prince's mentor Imlac, who may be taken to represent Johnson himself, returns, ' He who will determine against that which he knows, because there may be something which he knows not ; he that can set hypothetical possibility against acknowledged certainty, is not to be admitted among reasonable beings '. Your modern philosopher insists after Leibniz that bare possibilities are nothing. Johnson makes a distinction between satisfaction and happiness to show that not all who are happy are equally happy. ' A peasant and a philosopher may be equally *satisfied* but not equally *happy*. Happiness consists in the multiplicity of agreeable consciousness. A peasant has not capacity for equal happiness with a philosopher ' (L. ii. 9). Plato had said something of the same sort before him, and J. S. Mill draws a similar distinction, not quite the same, in a famous passage of the *Utilitarianism*, where he says it is better to be Socrates dissatisfied than a pig satisfied. Supposing the pig and Socrates were equally satisfied, Socrates would have the greater happiness. The trouble is that Johnson with all this insight leaves the matter there and goes no further.

One of the questions which Boswell was always agitating was that of freewill. Once Johnson said impatiently, ' Sir, we know that the will is free and there's an end on't '. On a more favourable occasion (L. iii. 291) he talked more freely, summing up by saying, ' All theory is against the freedom of the will ; all experience is for it ', a judgment repeated in our time by Henry Sidgwick. Boswell's difficulty was the familiar one, how to reconcile freewill with God's foreknowledge. Johnson urges that ' you are surer that you are free than you are of prescience. But let us consider a little the objection from prescience. . . . If I am well acquainted with a man, I can judge with great probability how he will act in any case, without his being restrained by my judging. God may have this probability increased to certainty.' All sound good sense; but it does not carry us very far. Boswell even congratulates himself on finding Johnson ' so mild in discussing a question of the most abstract nature, involved with theological tenets which he generally would not suffer to be in any degree opposed '. Johnson was on the way to the view of freewill which regards a man as willing freely whose will is determined from within himself. But he adopts neither the plenum nor the vacuum. He could not trace freewill like Spinoza to our ignorance that we were determined; nor like Hume treat willing as like all other causality; nor could he boldly assert man to be a centre of indetermination, as Mr. Bergson was to maintain at a later day. What was enough for practical life was enough for him. To go deeper was to probe mysteries which for him were closed.

The best known, and Boswell says the best, of Johnson's minor writings was a review of Soame Jenyns's *Free Enquiry into the Nature and Origin of Evil*. From Johnson's account Jenyns seems to have adopted more or less the easy optimism of Pope's *Essay on Man*, and he writes of the book much what he afterwards wrote on the Essay in the ' Life ' of Pope. He points out the vagueness and difficulties of the conception of a scale of being continued up to God in which man has his proper place. Jenyns had not the advantage of Pope's genius of expression to make up for the weakness of his argument. Like Pope's, his attempts to justify evil were in themselves insufficient at the best.

For my own part I do not think that Pope at any rate deserves all the charges of superficiality that are brought against his poem; it does not owe everything to its felicity of style. But when all is said, its optimism is too facile, and it had little chance with Johnson, and Jenyns's *Enquiry* still less. Johnson had the gloomy temperament which did not suffer him to endure solitude, and drove him to seek relief from his own thoughts in the society of his clubs. He was all his life oppressed by disease and melancholy; and more than all, he had known the misery of extreme poverty. He had spent nights walking about London streets, because neither he nor his companion Savage had money enough to buy a night's lodging in a cellar — though indeed Johnson affected at a later day that they had not been depressed; and when he was drudging for Cave he had signed one of his letters to his master *impransus* — dinnerless. The revolt against the spirit of optimism which had been provoked in Voltaire by the earthquake at Lisbon was provoked in Johnson by inherited temper and bitter experience. Johnson was, says Boswell (L. iv. 300), decidedly for the balance of misery in life upon the whole; although Tom Tyers seems to say he held the opposite (M. ii. 360). One of his poems ends with the words, ' And screen me from the ills of life '. In its earlier form it had been stronger and Boswell says more Johnsonian : ' Hide me from the sight of life '. In the passage which concludes *The Vanity of Human Wishes* on what a man may pray for, he writes :

> These goods for man the laws of Heaven ordain,
> These goods he grants who grants the power to gain.
> With these celestial wisdom calms the mind,
> And makes the happiness she does not find.

When he recited his own lines on the misery of the scholar's lot, he burst into tears. *Rasselas* and *Candide* are on the same theme. But the first is suffused with an atmosphere of gloom.

Johnson could not bear to think of evil, and arguments to explain evil away were likely to weigh little with him. Jenyns committed himself to an outrageous proposition that perhaps our misery makes sport or gives utility to beings higher in the scale of existence, as the death of animals serves our happiness. Johnson's melancholy did not dry up his inexhaustible humour, and he annihilates Jenyns in prosecuting this idea in a passage which is too long to quote, though it is an admirable example of Johnson's better style, but of which I cannot deny myself

DR. JOHNSON AS A PHILOSOPHER

the pleasure of citing one paragraph :

> One sport the merry malice of these beings has found means of enjoying to which we have nothing equal or similar. They now and then catch a mortal proud of his parts, and flattered either by the submission of those who court his kindness, or the notice of those who suffer him to court theirs. A head thus prepared for the reception of false opinions and the projection of vain designs they easily fill with idle notions, till they make their plaything an author : their first diversion commonly begins with an ode or an epistle, then rises perhaps to a political irony, and is at last brought to its height by a treatise on philosophy. Then begins the poor animal to entangle himself in sophisms, and flounder in absurdity, to talk confidently of the scale of being and to give solutions which he himself confesses impossible to be understood. Sometimes, however, it happens that their pleasure is without much mischief. The author feels no pain, but while they are wondering at the extravagance of his opinion, and pointing him out to one another as a new example of human folly, he is enjoying his own applause and that of his companions and perhaps is elevated with the hope of standing at the head of a new sect.

Vastly amusing all this is, and Johnson has an easy victory. But we learn little from his shrewd criticism of the weaknesses of Pope and his follower, except that optimism and pessimism alike, whether in a Pancrace or a Johnson, are the reflection in the main of different temperaments, and that if it is folly to deny the reality of evil, its positive reality, it is as hard to reconcile life with the excess of misery as to reconcile misery with the wise benevolence of God.

II

If Johnson had not the speculative gift, or his prepossessions debarred him from the exercise of it, he had in the largest measure the qualities which make the philosopher in the vaguer sense. Besides a wit and acuteness of mind which never failed, he had the large view ; and some portion of that quality of grace and symmetry of mind which Plato regards as one of the chief intellectual virtues of the true philosopher, a natural predisposition to and affinity with truth, always in Johnson's case within the limits set by his passions and his prejudices. His fertility and force of argument were amazing; he fastened on the central point of his subject or exposed the fallacies of others with unerring acuteness, though he sometimes argued fallaciously himself. The teacher of logic [1] is grateful to Boswell for an unlimited collection of illustrations of common forms of argument and fallacy. His readiness and concentration in an encounter of wits were the expression of his strong intellect. 'Depend upon it, Sir', he said once in answer to someone who said that an address which was supposed to have been written by the famous Dr. Dodd in Newgate (and was really written by Johnson himself) showed more than Dodd's usual force of mind, 'depend upon it, when a man knows he is to be hanged in a fortnight it concentrates his mind wonderfully.' Johnson's mind needed no such stimulus, it was always concentrated, and his weapons of attack were always bright or loaded. His wit is a trained one, forcible rather than charming; alert rather than rippling. There is his well-known retort to a proser who had told at great length a story about a flea: how long would he have taken if it had been a lion? Compare that humorously annihilating reply with Goldsmith's equally famous retort to Johnson himself. Johnson had praised Goldsmith because in a fable about little fishes he had made them talk like little fishes, and shook his sides with laughter over Goldsmith's simplicity. Goldsmith replied, 'If you were to make little fishes talk, they would talk like whales'. That is the more delightful wit, though no one but Goldsmith or Garrick would have dared to use it against the great dictator.

Alas! Johnson often talked for victory. His passions would not allow him to be beaten. And sometimes when he was beaten he resorted to rudeness. 'When his pistol missed fire', as was said, ' he knocked you down with the

---

[1] Alexander made very extensive use of Boswell for this purpose in his own teaching of logic, and had several excerpts printed for the testing and toughening of academic neophytes in the subject. [Editor's note.]

DR. JOHNSON AS A PHILOSOPHER

butt end of it.' In the report of his conversations allowance has always to be made in seeking to know Johnson's real opinions for this habit of taking the other side. He would, as many persons said, have been an excellent barrister. Yes, if only he could have been trusted not to bully the witnesses and the judge. And an excellent judge, if only he would not have bullied witnesses and counsel and his brother judges.

Perhaps he might have defended himself as he defended the practice of counsel, on the ground that it is of importance that we should know the best that can be said on both sides. Perhaps he might have said that conversation was a game of wits. At any rate he had a passion for veracity. He always talked, says Thomas Tyers, as if he was talking upon oath (M. ii. 365). 'Truth,' says Reynolds (M. ii. 223), 'whether in great or little matters, he always held sacred. . . . " It would have been a better story," said he, when Reynolds had suggested an addition to a story Johnson had told, " if it had been so, but it was not." Our friend Dr. Goldsmith was not so scrupulous, but he said he only indulged himself in white lies light as feathers, which he threw up in the air, and on whomever they fell nobody was hurt. " I wish ", said Dr. Johnson, " you would take the trouble of moulting your feathers." '

With his love of truth may be reckoned his downrightness. He was always either for the plenum or the vacuum. Of one of his friends whom he calls Poll, apparently one of those to whom he offered the hospitality of his queer household, he said at the Thrales' (*Diary*, i. 64):[1] 'Why, I took to Poll very well at first, but she won't do upon a nearer examination. . . . Poll is a stupid slut ; I had some hopes of her at first, but when I talked to her tightly and closely, I could make nothing of her ; she was wiggle-waggle and I could never persuade her to be categorical.' Johnson himself was nothing if not categorical.

He hated excessive flattery, and all kinds of exaggeration, especially of praise. They distorted the truth. He

[1] *Diary and Letters of Madame d'Arblay.*

said to Mrs. Thrale (*Diary*, i. 77), that he 'was always sorry whenever he made bitter speeches, and he never did it but when he was insufferably vexed'. Among the things which vexed him insufferably were the insincerities in which people indulged in society in their estimates of one another and the expression of their own feelings. Thus he deprecated the pretence of excessive distress for others, and upon a famous occasion rebuked Mrs. Thrale for it. ' Suppose now, Sir,' said Boswell, ' that one of your intimate friends were apprehended for an offence for which he might be hanged.' ' I should do ', said Johnson, ' what I could to bail him and give him any other assistance; but if he were once fairly hanged I should not suffer.' Yet no man loved his friends more than Johnson did. He knew hypochondria himself, but was impatient with Boswell's lamentations about his own gloom, believing them to be cultivated. He carried his impatience with the untruthful self-consciousness of people so far that in despite of all fact he declared that climate and the weather had no effect upon happiness (L. ii. 195).

Johnson had the strong mind which, with his experience, operated upon human life to seize the essence of a situation. But he had also the largeness which is not coloured by egotism. He had suffered much, but he did not complain of the world (L. iv. 116, 172). ' It is rather wonderful ', he said, ' that so much has been done for me. All the complaints which are made of the world are unjust. I never knew a man of merit neglected : it was generally by his own fault that he failed of success.' On another occasion, when Boswell said that the great, who Johnson said had seen enough of him, must certainly be highly pleased with his conversation, he answered, ' No, Sir ; great lords and great ladies don't love to have their mouths stopped '. He had the fair judgment which did not spare himself. For he considered himself for all that a polite man ; and I think he was really right. Once he said that the wife of a certain author 'had a bottom of good sense', and when his hearers tried to suppress their laughter said angrily, ' I say the

DR. JOHNSON AS A PHILOSOPHER

woman was *fundamentally* sensible '. I believe Johnson was fundamentally polite. But the great lords and ladies might not see it. His attentions were often, it must be confessed, like the hug of the bear. Another example of his fairness of mind was his feelings towards the booksellers. They paid him little ; even for the *Lives of the Poets* he had only £200 when he was at the height of his fame. But he did not complain and said the booksellers were generous men.

Like other wise men he did not think meanly of material advantages. There are few ways, he said, in which a man can be more innocently employed than in getting money (L. ii. 323), and of authors he said that no man but a blockhead ever wrote except for money (L. iii. 19). In this proper regard for the goods of life he was more in accordance with the sentiment of the great Greek philosophers than with his own orthodox Christianity. Aristotle thinks the absence of a sufficient quantity of these goods is an obstacle to happiness, and even that a man cannot be happy who is very ugly. Johnson is inclined to agree with him. He was indeed impatient of people who said they were happy, for he thought that, like himself, no one was happy, and he held such statements to be cant. But how Greek he was in his reasons may be judged from what he said of the sister-in-law of a dear friend of his who said of her in his presence that she was really happy. ' If your sister-in-law ', he said to his friend, ' is really the contented being she professes herself, her life gives the lie to every research of humanity ; for she is happy without health, without beauty, without money, and without understanding.' This story he told Mrs. Thrale herself and when she expressed something of the horror she felt, he said, ' I tell you the woman is ugly and sickly and foolish and poor ; and would it not make a man hang himself to hear such a creature say it was happy ? ' (M. i. 335).

He shared with the Greeks a feeling of contempt for the profession of acting, though it must be admitted he was not alone among Englishmen, and that even Molière had been refused a Christian burial. Even his friend Garrick he spoke of as 'a player — a showman — who exhibits himself for a shilling' (L. ii. 234). But woe to anyone else who had said so of Garrick; and after all Garrick was buried in the Abbey.

Johnson was like a great Greek philosopher in another respect. 'I always wonder at you, Socrates', said Phaedrus, 'for when you are in the country, you really are like a stranger who is being led about by a guide.' 'Very true, my good friend', said Socrates, 'and I hope you will excuse me when you hear the reason, which is that I am a lover of knowledge, and the men who dwell in the city are my teachers, and not trees or the country.' Johnson had the excuse which Socrates had not, that he was too short-sighted to see scenery; he thought 'prospects' were nonsense. 'Let us', he said, 'if we *do* talk, talk about something; men and women are my subjects of inquiry' (M. i. 215). London supplied him with all the material of life. 'Why, Sir, you find no man at all intellectual who is willing to leave London. No, Sir, when a man is tired of London he is tired of life; for there is in London all that life can afford' (L. iii. 178). And again, 'A great city is the school for studying life' (L. iii. 253). 'He that lives well in the world', says Imlac in *Rasselas*, when they are discussing monastic retreats (ch. 47), 'is better than he that lives well in a monastery. But perhaps everyone is not able to stem the temptations of public life; and if he cannot conquer he may properly retreat.'

To Johnson at any rate retirement and solitude meant misery, and temperament settled his choice. And he showed his largeness of mind in the interest which, like Socrates, he took in every kind of person. He thought the man Johnson should be encouraged who rode three horses at a time, 'for his performances show the extent of the human powers in one instance and thus tend to raise our opinion of the faculties of man, and so every man may hope by giving as much attention to be equally expert in whatever profession he has chosen to pursue' (L. i. 399). Partly his reason was genuine human geniality, which led him to pursue acquaintances of the most varied and at first sight not attractive kind. Johnson's own knowledge was of immense range. It was not merely that in talking to an educated person he might, as Smart the poet said he did (Tyers, M. ii. 365), begin with poetry and end with fluxions. It covered all kinds of occupations. He dabbled in chemistry and medicine, and at one time he entertained the idea of editing a *Bibliothèque*, and he trusted to himself for giving an account of Continental literature on all subjects; when it was suggested that he might use the assistance of the French scholar Dr. Maty, who had done something of the sort for England, he said, ' He, the little black dog; I'd throw him into the Thames '. However, literature was in the main the point of contact between him and his friends, and he could meet men and women in conversation easily. One of his queer acquaintances was Bet Flint. He said he had known all the wits from Mrs. Montagu down to Bet Flint. She was, he said, habitually a slut and a drunkard and occasionally a thief and a harlot. But she figures also in the literary world and brought him her verses to correct, but he gave her half a crown and she liked it as well. There were others of these queer persons whom he described at the Thrales' who are recorded in the same passage of Fanny Burney's *Diary* (i. p. 42).

Moreover Johnson, like the wise man that he was, took the world as he found it and did not expect from it too much. When Mrs. Thrale complained of a lady who had talked of her family and affairs till she was sick to death of hearing her, Johnson defended the lady:

Why do you blame the woman for the only sensible thing she could do — talking of her family and affairs? For how should a woman who is as empty as a drum talk upon any other subject? If you speak to her of the sun, she does not know it rises in the east; if you speak to her of the moon, she does not know it changes at the full; if you speak to her of the queen, she does not know she is the king's wife; how then can you blame her for talking of her family and affairs? (*Diary*, i. 90).

DR. JOHNSON AS A PHILOSOPHER

Johnson had genuine simplicity of character and mind without which no man oppressed like him with a gloomy temperament could have taken the fair and large view of things and himself which I have attempted to illustrate. But if it explains some of his merits it accounts also for his unwavering faith in what he thought good and never suffered to be questioned. Asked by Boswell if he would not, perhaps, have done more good in his conversations if he had been more gentle, he said, ' No, Sir, I have done more good as I am. Obscenity and impiety have always been repressed in my presence ' (L. iv. 295). Upon virtue and religion he was immovable. There was another prepossession which he held almost as firmly: his belief in the value of subordination of ranks in society. The topic is perpetually recurring in his conversations and in his writings. He allows no praise to Swift (*Works*, iv. 136) for the familiarity and frankness which he maintained in his dealings with the ministers. ' No man ', he says, ' can pay a more servile tribute to the great than by suffering his liberty in their presence to aggrandise him in his own esteem. Between different ranks of the community there is necessarily some distance ', and he thinks that as Swift preserved the kindness of the great when they wanted him no longer, his childlike freedom was overpowered by his better qualities. No passage illustrates better Johnson's sturdy and self-respecting recognition of rank and the justice of distinctions of rank. ' Sir ', he said, ' I am a friend to subordination, as most conducive to the happiness of society. There is a reciprocal pleasure in governing and being governed ' (L. i. 408). He showed his sense of this most delicately on the occasion of the famous interview with the King in the library. The King had asked if he was then writing anything, and Johnson replied that he thought he had done enough, whereupon the King said ' I should have thought so myself if you had not written so well '. (At least the honour of that gracious speech cannot be taken from George III.) When one of his friends asked him afterwards at Sir Joshua's whether he had made any

DR. JOHNSON AS A PHILOSOPHER

reply, he said, 'No, Sir. When the King had said so it was to be so.[1] It was not for me to bandy civilities with my Sovereign ' (L. ii. 35). I think most of us in the same situation would have been silent like Johnson out of a sense of what was proper. The difference is that he acted not merely from obedience to rules of good breeding but from simple faith in the natural fittingness of the relation in which he stood.

Failure to recognise the natural subordination roused his wrath. Whiggery was to him anathema. The first Whig was the Devil, and every Whig was at bottom a rascal. Burke he loved although the dog was a Whig. When radicalism combined with irregularity of life, as they did in the person of Wilkes, all his animosity was roused. Yet he had humour, and politics were not religion or virtue. He consented to meet Wilkes, or rather to attend a party where Wilkes was to be present, and everybody knows how the charm of Wilkes prevailed over the prejudices of the old Tory. Jowett called our attention to the art with which Boswell has told this famous episode of the dinner at Mr. Dilly the bookseller's, the prelude to it and the sequel, and how Boswell had turned it into an epic.

[1] I have given an illustration in my Memoir of the appeal this story made to Alexander. I think myself that Alexander had something of a Johnsonian attitude towards royalty, although not, in general, towards rank, and although it isn't evidence (because of the occasion) I should like to quote a speech that Alexander made when he planted a tree to celebrate George VI's Coronation. ' It is by your kindness my honour and happiness to plant this tree, and to dedicate it to our King and Queen who have been crowned to-day. I hope that many generations of students seeing it will go on to think of them with affection and devotion — for I do not doubt that our personal affection will gather round them as it gathered round the King's father and mother, King George and Queen Mary, and around his brother, King Edward VIII. But our duties contain something more important than affection. The King means for us our country, under which word " country " is included the whole nation and empire, and it is not from mere egotism that I remind you that both your warden and I come from one of the dominions. The King embodies for us our whole polity and the spirit of British life, and he is at once one of ourselves and above us. The thought of him may spur us to maintain that spirit and hand it on, stronger and better if we can make it so, to those that follow us, just as he has received and will transmit his crown. This modest tree may well be for us the emblem of something worthy of all our devotion. God bless King George and Queen Elizabeth." [Editor's note.]

DR. JOHNSON AS A PHILOSOPHER

I have referred above to the comparison which Carlyle makes between Johnson and Hume, and it is very interesting to think of the different fates of the two great men, which Carlyle speaks of. The easygoing, prosperous Hume was loved by all who knew him, even by the great French ladies at Paris who laughed at his corpulence and his incompetence in speaking French; and he was of European reputation in his lifetime, and since his death is one of the greatest figures in the history of philosophy. Johnson, poor and melancholy, afraid of his own company, shrinking from the thought of death, though loved was feared, and though he was a literary dictator, his influence in his lifetime and since never extended beyond his own country.

What, we may ask, are the reasons which have made him, apart from his real importance in our literature, so familiar a figure and so well loved? The consummate art of Boswell's biography accounts in part for this result. But all the other memoirs of him are also brimful of interest and delight, and Boswell after all was reporting the man himself, and Johnson himself knew well enough that he did more good by his conversations than by his writings. He appeals to us partly because he was a great independent character and partly that it took a form which we are accustomed to consider typically English, that of the sturdy conservative, with the prejudices of that type, and supremely gifted with intellect and good judgment and knowledge. He was the wisest person, said Tom Tyers, and had the most knowledge in ready cash that he had the honour to be acquainted with, and Tyers in his roving life had seen presumably many kinds of men. We may or may not sympathise with Johnson's opinions: many would love Goldsmith more, and more reverence Burke; but great character and great wisdom always command affection.

And in Johnson's case they were combined with an astounding wit and what appeals to us perhaps still more, an abundant and overbrimming humour. In a very interesting letter which Birkbeck Hill quotes (M. ii. 98),

DR. JOHNSON AS A PHILOSOPHER

Jowett thinks that Boswell has misrepresented him in one respect: by representing him more as a sage and philosopher in his conduct as well as his conversation than he really was, and less as a rollicking 'King of Society', and he cites a remark of Sir John Hawkins: 'He was the most humorous man I ever knew'.[1] In conversation Jowett once said that he thought Boswell's being a Scotchman was responsible in some degree for this. But I imagine he made this remark in the spirit of Johnson's own quips at the Scotch, which, though Boswell did not see it, were half sheer fun. When someone said ' Poor Old England is lost', Johnson said, ' Sir, it is not so much to be regretted that Old England is lost, as that the Scotch have found it' (L. iii. 78). Boswell does himself, as Dr. Hill says, mention Johnson's merriment and pleasantry. And no one can fail to feel the humour of Johnson's talk even in Boswell's narrative, if he reads between the lines. Sometimes Johnson laughs and shakes even in Boswell's pages; on one occasion he indulged in some pleasantry with Chambers the lawyer, and, unable to get over his merriment, on the way home with Boswell he laid hold of one of the posts at the side of the foot-pavement and sent forth peals so loud that in the silence of the night his voice seemed to resound from Templebar to Fleet-ditch (L. ii. 262). A gentleman was pleading for the future life of brutes, and said, ' But really, Sir, when we see a very sensible dog, we don't know what to think of him'. Johnson (rolling with joy) said, ' True, Sir, and when we see a very foolish *fellow*, we don't know what to think of *him*'. Still, it is true that Boswell approaches Johnson with such reverence that the fun of his hero is suppressed as not quite suitable to his dignity. Moreover, we must remember that Boswell's records are

---

[1] Apparently not quite correctly quoted. Hawkins says, ' In his talent of humour there hardly ever was his equal '. Jowett probably did not know Hawkins at first hand. One of the minor sorrows of my undergraduate days was this. He told me he had not seen Hawkins' *Life* and much wished to. Shortly afterwards I bought a copy in Great Portland Street for a shilling and promised myself the pleasure of giving it to him. But, going home, I left it behind me in the Underground.

DR. JOHNSON AS A PHILOSOPHER

mostly of conversations in societies of men, and those often men of the first distinction, when Johnson was on his mettle, and felt he must maintain his position. Once when he was ill and someone mentioned Burke, he said, ' That fellow calls forth all my powers. Were I to see Burke now, it would kill me.' So much was he accustomed to consider conversation as a contest (ii. 450). The result is that you have much more the impression of wit than of humour from Boswell's own words ; he took his hero a little too seriously. Fanny Burney, on the other hand, says, ' Dr. Johnson has more fun and comical humour and love of nonsense about him than almost anybody I ever saw ; I mean when with those he likes ; for otherwise he can be as severe and bitter as report relates him ' (*Diary*, i. 136). To know Johnson as it were in undress we must hear him at home at Streatham among the Thrales and go to the pages of Fanny Burney's *Diary*. I have not space to quote an inimitable instance of his prejudices and his fun in a passage between him and Sir Philip Jennings Clarke in Chapter V of the *Diary*.

But when all is said of his wit and his humour and good-humour (he said he looked upon himself as a good-humoured fellow), it is not these alone or so much which endear him to us as his wise humanity and the tenderness of his nature, and the materials of life which they supplied his strong mind to operate upon. He cared for all sorts of men, and while he was never sentimental, he never shut his heart to genuine distress or failed to appreciate genuine goodness. Everyone knows how he carried a sick unfortunate woman of the streets on his back to his house and kept her till she was restored. He spoke of Levett the doctor, one of his housemates, as a brutal fellow. Yet he made him the constant companion of his mornings, and when he died wrote upon him and his good works a beautiful and affecting poem. Of poor Christopher Smart, the mad poet, he said : ' I did not think he ought to be shut up. His infirmities were not noxious to society. He insisted on people praying with

DR. JOHNSON AS A PHILOSOPHER

him ; and I'd as lief pray with Kit Smart as anyone else. Another charge was that he did not love clean linen ; and I have no passion for it ' (L. i. 397). Which is strongest here, humour or wisdom or tenderness ?

Johnson was in the first place a man of letters ; and now that the superficial misjudgment of his style, which at its best is pure and nervous, though at its worst too much inclined to a ' Roman ' vocabulary and too fond of the then fashionable habit of personifying abstract qualities, has disappeared, his writings, or at least some of them, besides the classical *Lives*, are recovering their value. At any rate all their merit flows from the full and strong mind operating upon life, which made him a wise and just man. Other men of letters stand equal or superior to him in our literature ; few have been so tried by experience of men and life and emerged so noble from the assaying.

III

THE ART OF JANE AUSTEN [1]

(Reprinted, by permission, from the *Bulletin of the John Rylands Library*, July 1928)

EVERYONE likes to pay a debt of gratitude if he can; and that is why I have seized this opportunity to record a lifelong devotion to Miss Austen. When I was an undergraduate at Balliol, it was the custom (and it may be the custom still) for the College to set an essay every week to be done by everyone in his first year, and the first such essay I did for my tutor was on Jane Austen's novels, and I chose *Mansfield Park* to make her acquaintance by. Since that time I have read all the novels over and over again, still forgetting them according to my wont, and still renewing the old delight. When I am asked which of them I like the best, I am apt to answer, the one I have read last. Exception has to be made against *Sense and Sensibility*, but a recent reading only convinces me of the extraordinary merits even of that work. In my heart of hearts I know that I love *Persuasion* best, and I shall give my reasons later. But except for my devotion, I have no other claim to speak, and still less to be listened to, upon Miss Austen, being no practised critic of literature, but only dumbly attached to a few great writers, of whom she is one. And except that I have read Mr. Elton in his *Survey*, and the admirable paper of Mr. A. C. Bradley in the *Essays of the English Association for 1911* (from which with proper acknowledgments I shall borrow freely) and the introductions to the 'Everyman' edition, I know almost nothing of what has been written on Jane Austen as a writer, and have deliberately refrained from reading the most recent

[1] A lecture delivered in the John Rylands Library on March 14, 1928.

writings upon her, such as Mr. Brimley Johnson's book,[1] and Miss Spurgeon's paper, deliberately, lest I should find myself left with nothing of my own to say.

Yet for one who is concerned not so much with the direct appreciation of literature as with questions of aesthetics, Miss Austen offers a natural and obvious starting-point and subject. She is admittedly a consummate artist, and at the same time her range of subjects is the narrowest. ' Three or four families in a country village ', she writes to her niece Anna (*Letters*, ii. 351, No. 87),[2] ' is the very thing to work on ', and this is for the most part the substance of her own novels. She spoke herself (*Life*, p. 377)[3] ' of the little bit (two inches wide) of ivory, on which I work with so fine a brush as produces little effect after much labour '. But this comparison with miniature painting is a singular misdescription on her part. The miniaturist takes a large subject and paints it on a small surface, ' crowds all his spirit in little ', as Browning says. Miss Austen takes a considerable canvas — even the shortest of the six novels extends to two volumes — and paints a little subject. The only thing that is apposite in the comparison is the delicate and subtle workmanship both of herself and the miniaturist. She uses the methods of miniature over the canvas of the painter, and she succeeds because she is neither painter nor dramatist but is writing novels. Extreme minuteness in a picture distracts from the unity of the design, because a picture is not drawn out in time but is stationary, and even if it represents motion conveys only a significant moment. A drama *is* drawn out in time, but the characters of it are left to tell their own story, while the novelist, according to

---

[1] From a notice I have seen I expect I should find I owed much to his book if I had read it. I have of course used the *Memoir* and the valuable later version of it, the *Life and Letters* by W. and R. A. Austen Leigh (1913), which is naturally much fuller than the *Memoir*, though it lacks the charm of that direct testimony.

[2] References to the *Letters* are to the Winchester edition of the works (Edinburgh, 1912) but the number of the letters is added. References to the novels are to the paging of the ' Everyman ' editions.

[3] Letter to Edward Austen. Also *Memoir*, [1] p. 212 ; [2] p. 153. I owe those references to Mr. R. W. Chapman.

THE ART OF JANE AUSTEN

Plato's well-known description of epic poetry, blends narrative and drama, allowing the persons, like Homer, at intervals to speak for themselves. Miss Austen is so great an artist, because within her very limited range of subject, her work is so nicely adapted to her subject.

For what makes a work of art beautiful is just this adjustment of its material, *i.e.* its style, to its subject. The subject may be small or even trifling, or it may be grave and splendid. Beauty lies not in the choice of the subject but in the use of the material, whatever that material may be, whether words or pigments or stone, so as to render the truth and significance of the subject. That can never be done by successful imitation or mere faithful description of the subject. There enters into it always the magic by which the artist transforms his subject; he would otherwise be practising science and not fine art. But it needs close observation such as science also requires. When as is most often the case the subject is some piece of human nature it needs the minute observation and acquaintance with men, on account of which Molière used to be called *le contemplateur*; and above all, the sympathy and insight which supplements and anticipates and may even dispense with direct observation, which makes Shakespeare so great a master. The truth which the artist conveys is not altogether the truth which he discovers but which he makes. He may use many means of finding his truth; sometimes it is his depth of passion, sometimes his amplitude of thought; sometimes, as with Miss Austen, the transforming spirit is humour. Her subjects are rarely, perhaps only in one instance exalted; they are not mean, but they are mere ordinary human nature in persons with no great range of interest, for the most part the common intercourse of persons in middle-class society in the country, living the ordinary domestic life, making love, visiting, engaged mostly in the pleasures of life, with a little vice to chequer the ordinary course of virtuous commonplace existence, not too bright or good for human nature's daily food, not frivolous and not over-serious, but always alive; never a dull surface, but stirred by the ripple of alert if placid adventure. She is so great an artist because with an unfailing skill of words she can so weave her story that all these minutiae of conduct and incident and character fall into an intimate design, and her delicate portrayals of character, like Lady Bertram's, or the clear-cut delineation of reserved strength like Mr. Knightley's, or, rollicking braggartry like John Thorpe's, or the malicious portraits of Mrs. Norris, or the good-humoured absurdity of Miss Bates, or the vulgar angling of Ann Steele for her doctor whom we are glad to think she did not land (*Memoir*, ed. 1883, p. 148); all these in their variety and in their several places enhance one another and create in soft tints unified portions of her human comedy, which is also *the* human comedy on the level which she knew and depicts.

These outstanding features of Miss Austen, her exquisite art and the limited range within which she draws human nature with such variety and discrimination, stand in the way of a just estimate of her rank as a writer. She suffers from two different kinds of judges ; the indifferent, and the fanatical admirers. Some she leaves cold through her coolness and want of passion and her classical decorousness of air, the tameness of her incidents, her detachment from the larger interests of her own day ; their latter-day blood asks for the play of strong passion and romance, for vividness and heat ; they seek romance and cannot easily think themselves back into that quiet England when the eighteenth century was changing over to the nineteenth, when there were no trains in the country and few newspapers, when people made love much as they do to-day, but at once talked more about it, and were more circumspect and decorous in their general behaviour, when women still led the sheltered life, and having fewer general concerns were naturally absorbed in the most important of all private ones. Such judges may recognise her excellence but they turn to Charlotte Brontë or Meredith. They do no harm to Miss Austen ; they are only insensitive. *Non ragionam di lor.*

THE ART OF JANE AUSTEN

Her worst judges are those who exalt her above her proper place, and put her on a level just below Shakespeare. Macaulay began the habit, but temperately, and dwelling upon her skill in the discrimination even of characters of the same profession, such as the three clergymen, Edmund Bertram and Henry Tilney and Edward Ferrers. I have known lovers of Miss Austen outraged at the statement that she is not so great a writer as Scott. Now Sir Walter and Miss Austen themselves understood each other. She writes jestingly of him (L. ii. 356, No. 88): 'Walter Scott has no business to write novels, especially good ones. It is not fair. He has fame and profit enough as a poet and should not be taking the bread out of the mouths of other people. I do not like him and do not mean to like *Waverley* if I can help it, but fear I must.' And everyone knows how Sir Walter wrote of her: 'The big Bow-Wow strain I can do myself like any now going; but the exquisite touch which renders ordinary commonplace characters interesting from the truth of the description and the sentiment is denied to me. What a pity such a gifted creature died so early' (Lockhart's *Life*, vol. vi. ch. 7). Now I do not hesitate to say that Scott is inferior to Miss Austen as an artist, is indeed often careless, but is a greater writer. Shakespeare himself is full of passages that fall short of beauty, and Miss Austen rarely does. The dull episode in *Persuasion* of Mrs. Smith she did not live to revise, and it is natural to think she might have done so. And yet the four novels which remain when *Northanger Abbey* and *Sense and Sensibility* are excluded leave her still one of our greatest artists and yet hardly among our very greatest figures in literature.

For there is a distinction in art as there is in morals between two orders of attainment. In morals there is the order of goodness, in which every good act is equally good, and the order of perfection in which some acts, though not better than others, are more perfect or greater. The widow's mite is the classical example of the first order. It is as good as the disinterested endowment by a rich man of a hospital. But it is not so splendid. In like manner there is beauty in art and there is greatness, which I hesitate to call the order of perfection, because we commonly speak of excellent art as perfect. Miss Austen for instance is typical of the perfect art. Beauty is beauty wherever it is found, and no matter what the subject. But the subject makes a difference to the greatness of the art. ' Drink to me only with thine eyes ' is perhaps as beautiful in its kind as ' The baseless fabric of this vision ' and ' The glories of our blood and state ' are in their respective kinds. But it is less great or splendid. And so when we are estimating the greatness of a writer, we have assuredly to take into the account not merely the beauty but the intrinsic value of the subjects and our judgments are always mixed. Beauty being attained, there is room for further appraisement. It may be difficult to perform, it may be impossible to say in particular cases which subject counts most in importance ; a light subject may feed a human want as valid as one with high seriousness. Yet there is still some weight in the consideration which puts tragedy higher than comedy, and of two comedies there is more greatness in *Le Misanthrope* than in *Le Tartuffe*, and in *Much Ado* than in *Love's Labour's Lost*, over and above the more complete attainment of artistic beauty in the first of this second pair. Again, greatness in the topic may compensate for defect in the art, just as perfection in the art may compensate for poverty in the subject. But isolated works of art hardly abide comparison. It is when we take as a whole and compare them one with another that we are compelled to grade them according to their weight of subject, their depth of insight, their feeling for what is important in the world of man and nature.

I take this to be the element of truth in the plea that art cannot be separated from conduct. It is wholly false if it is understood to mean that beauty depends on conduct, that there may not be as exquisite beauty in a base or vulgar object as in a noble one. Still it remains true that literature, to confine myself to that art, is about something.

THE ART OF JANE AUSTEN

The poet is no mere artificer of melodious and unmeaning words. And the greatness of a poet in the rank of poets cannot ignore the subjects with which he occupies himself. He is not only an artist but a man. His work as a man is rightly judged by his total performance. It is because Miss Austen is so supreme an artist that she holds so high a place in our literature. But when we turn to Scott we find a range of incident, of passion, of human insight, in the splendour of which we forget his defective art where it has failed and reckon him, I must think, on a higher level than Miss Austen, as what William James called a folio edition of humanity. Perhaps in admiring her sanely we do her more justice than in making claims for her which in the end cannot be maintained. A great and adorable writer she remains, too great to be merely the idol of a sect or coterie.

The truth is that to bring Miss Austen into comparison with Shakespeare is far-fetched and almost inept. Mr. Bradley has observed that only her minor characters have any Shakespearean likeness, Miss Bates for instance. He has made, I think, one omission, the one character in which she remotely approaches romantic passion, Anne Elliot, one of the noblest women in our literature. Anne has the weakness of having yielded her judgment to that of her cautious and unimaginative and rather stupid friend Lady Russell, and to have played for safety in rejecting Frederick Wentworth while he was still a young naval officer who had not yet acquired a competence out of prize-money. Much may be forgiven to a heroine of that time, brought up in habits of deference to her elders and of careful prudence in the choice of a partner for life. Apart from that forgivable blemish in her character, she is a figure of heroic fidelity which is with some justice comparable with Imogen. She gives to *Persuasion* the air of seriousness in the comedy which makes that novel in my opinion the greatest (though not necessarily the most delightful) of Miss Austen's novels, and a glory of English literature. If we are really to compare the classical and unromantic Jane with any

THE ART OF JANE AUSTEN

other great writer, it should rather be with Molière, and I believe the comparison is really fruitful.

Mr. Bradley has reminded us of Jane Austen's fondness in her youth for making plays for the domestic circle, and her regular visits to the theatre whenever she was in London with her brother Henry, and has noted how like the novels are to comedies. Perhaps this is true of all novels that they are dramas, only that, as I said before, the novelist helps out his characters with narrative. Some are comedies, some tragedies, some are of a mixed order. The novel has so largely replaced the drama, partly for external reasons, that it reaches a larger audience than a play possibly can and satisfies better a general want; partly I suppose that a good play is a more difficult form of art, for the novelist can explain the minds of his persons in their workings, he is in the interests of art a psychologist, while the dramatist must make them reveal themselves in their undissected personalities. At any rate, if ever a novelist was a dramatist it is Miss Austen, and all her novels are comedies, except *Persuasion* and perhaps *Mansfield Park*, which are what can only be called by the generic name of plays or dramas. And I choose to think of her along with Molière because he is the great pattern of the classical comedy, though I do not suppose she knew him well. I have not the learning nor the skill to contrast her with the other English novelists. She is utterly unlike the sentimental Richardson whom she knew; nor is there much affinity between her and Fielding. She knew Fielding well, and when she chose to imagine playfully that Tom Lefroy was inclined to pay attentions to her, she complained to her sister Cassandra of his wearing a very light-coloured morning coat in imitation of Tom Jones, ' his one fault ', she says, ' which time will I trust entirely remove ' (L. i. 223, No. 1), and adds later that if he asks her, he will have to give up his white coat. She has obviously been affected by Fanny Burney, and praises a friend because ' she admires *Camilla*, and drinks no cream in her tea ' (L. i. 237, No. 6). She laughs at Mrs. Radcliffe and the other horrid tales, which

Isabella Thorpe recommends to Catherine Morland, assuring her that they are all horrid, like the entrancing *Udolpho*. It is Miss Burney, I suppose, who is her real predecessor with *Evelina*, which the best judges of that day, Johnson and Burke, so highly praised, and some of Miss Austen's vulgar characters have their predecessors in the Brangtons. All these things are matters for the critic and historian. Still less can I attempt to trace her connection with the novelists of the nineteenth century from whom she differs so greatly, even from Thackeray. I am concerned with her art, and it is worth while to think of her for a moment along with Molière.

Like Molière's, her comedy is the comedy of manners, in which common sense shatters the absurdities or pretensions of the comic personages. Sometimes good sense is embodied in one of the characters, like Mr. Knightley in *Emma* sardonically reserving his disapproval of Emma's passion for arranging matches between unsuitable persons; or in *Pride and Prejudice* Elizabeth Bennet smiling at her sister Jane's inveterate belief in the virtue of others, or the admirable Gardiners, or even Mr. Bennet, the sarcastic and mordant judge of his wife and of all his daughters but Elizabeth, and at the same time too indolent to reform them, and perhaps giving up as a bad job the attempt to make Mrs. Bennet understand the meaning of an entail; for she, like Mrs. Allen in *Northanger Abbey*, ' was one of that numerous class of females whose society can raise no other emotion than surprise at there being any men in the world who like them well enough to marry them ' (p. 6); or again, Elinor in *Sense and Sensibility*. Most often good sense is embodied in the author herself or in her readers, taking, either of them, the part of the commenting chorus in a Greek play. Miss Austen clearly loves Elinor and Elizabeth and says so in her letters. But even when there is no one there to represent her, you feel her presence, watching with her detached good humour, not untouched by malice, the antics of her folk. Often it is circumstance itself which as it develops turns the comic situation into a more serious issue ; as when with the highest art of construction, Emma's last absurd attempt to direct Harriet's affections to Frank Churchill, while Harriet imagines she is being encouraged to aspire to Mr. Knightley, reveals to her that she is in love with Mr. Knightley herself. Mrs. MacCunn has in a paper on Molière's ladies — Henriette, Léonor, Éliante, even the coquette Célimène of *Le Misanthrope*, and others — compared them aptly with Jane Austen's women where she finds one to represent herself (*Cornhill Magazine*, April 1925). In either author one can observe at its plainest the operation of the comic spirit, the general social standard of conduct asserting itself against deviations from it in ripples of wit and humour, dwelling in both cases rather on the foibles of men than on their vices. It is not often that Molière lashes his subjects as in *Le Tartuffe* ; and Miss Austen in the last chapter of *Mansfield Park* says : ' Let other pens dwell on guilt and misery. I quit such odious subjects as soon as I can, impatient to restore everybody, not greatly in fault themselves, to tolerable comfort, and to have done with all the rest.' (It must, however, be remembered that there had been a good deal before which made for dishonour among the Crawfords and the Bertram daughters, and some actual achievement of it.) Even Mrs. Norris in the end, as Mr. Bradley says, redeems herself by devotion to the unfortunate Maria, though it is added with acid humour ' that it may be supposed that their tempers became their mutual punishment '. Altogether a pretty adjustment of well-doing and ill-doing, as befits a high comedian.

There is another interesting feature in the reference to Molière, that the growth and development of his art throws light on the maturing of Miss Austen's. Molière's comedy, as is well known, had its origin in farce, and to the end he relieved his writing of serious comedy with exuberant and outrageous farce. From farce he passed through the comedy of intrigue and circumstance to that of character. And as he grew, character more and more ceased to be of the abstract type and became full-blooded personality tinged with some prevailing colour, like Harpagon in *L'Avare* or the great figure of Alceste. Now in Miss Austen in the smaller range within which she moves we can note these same tendencies.

The novels fall into two groups, the first written at Steventon up to 1797, containing *Pride and Prejudice*, *Sense and Sensibility*, and *Northanger Abbey* ; the other group, containing the other three, were written between 1811 and 1816. Between these two periods, while Miss Austen was living at Bath or Southampton, before she returned to the Hampshire country at Chawton, she wrote apparently nothing. But there is a marked difference in the art of the two periods. When she resumed writing in her comparative maturity, she had passed to high and concrete comedy from abstract comedy and farce. The first group includes *Pride and Prejudice*, which is the most popular of all the novels, and undoubtedly the most brilliant. It is obviously the finest of the first group and I must confess to some consciousness of recklessness when I plead that, considered as a work of art, it is inferior to *Persuasion* and in certain respects even to *Mansfield Park* and *Emma*. The order in which these earlier novels was written appears to be somewhat doubtful, for though *Pride and Prejudice* was written before the other two in their present form, they seem to have existed in earlier drafts under different names. But all three have certain characters in common. *Northanger Abbey* is little more than exuberant farce, and some at least of the persons are embodied abstractions. Even Catherine, lovable and charming as she is, is only a romantic schoolgirl, incarnating the taste for a particular sort of romantic literature. Isabella Thorpe and her uproarious brother are even more abstract. The serious Miss Tilney and the gay clergyman brother who are the relief of good sense to these comic personages are admirably done, but their father, again, the General, is a caricature. It all reads like a delicious squib done by a writer of genius in an overflow of spirits, like some of Molière's farces. *Sense and Sensibility* in its very title betrays the abstractness of conception which is its outstanding defect. Even Elinor, though on the side of good sense and therefore beloved by Miss Austen herself, suffers somewhat, but she is far more real and concrete than Marianne, the Lydia Languish of this comedy. It is not the tediousness of the impeccable Colonel Brandon that makes our interest fainter than in the other novels. For my part I delight in the book, and I am sure that if Miss Austen had written nothing else we should feel her to have been a very considerable writer. Who can forget, or if as I always do, he forgets, can fail to revel in the minor comedy of it, the sense of duty to his own immediate family which compels Mr. John Dashwood to listen to his wife and put a limit on his intended benefactions to his mother and sisters; the perfect picture of Mrs. Jennings; the humour reflected in the comments of the wise Elinor upon Mrs. Dashwood's plans for extending her cottage when she has saved money; the overflowing hospitality of Sir John Middleton or Marianne's shrinking from the idea of marrying an old man of thirty-five who wore a flannel waistcoat? The major comedy remains too much the contrast of abstract types.[1]

And how shall any one dare to find defects in *Pride and Prejudice*? In the face of a character like Elizabeth's, which is both real and enchantingly drawn, of Jane, whom Mr. Bradley praises so justly, of the sententious Mary Bennet, from whom I shall quote presently, of Mr. Bennet and his immortal wife, cavilling seems sheer insensibility. And yet, the famous proposal of Mr. Collins is really farcical, as anyone can see who contrasts it with the true comedy of his courtship of Charlotte Lucas. Mr. Collins is as much a caricature as Mr. Stiggins in *Pickwick*. Even the great scene between Elizabeth and Lady de Burgh is strained beyond probability. But the real fault lies in the picture of Darcy, a figure drawn to embody pride. He

[1] In the early *Lady Susan* the chief character, brilliantly as she is drawn, is a mere abstraction, too wicked (even if delightful) to be credible; and the author was well advised to leave it an unpublished effort to fledge her wings. Luckily she preserved it.

becomes a living man only when his passion breaks in upon his pride and he offers himself to Elizabeth. And yet the terms of his declaration, while they maintain his abstract type, are as impossible as his rudeness when he declines to dance with Elizabeth in her hearing. True enough his pride is explained away as the result of his upbringing and he turns out in the end to be an estimable person. But the blot remains. When Miss Austen had reached her artistic prime she ceased to name her books by the contrasts of virtues and vices, and she showed a correct instinct, for she has ceased to deal in abstractions and her comedy has become that of the real world. I do not say that we are wrong in preferring *Pride and Prejudice* to all the others, I am only pleading that as a work of art it falls below the later three, though more brilliant in details than any of them. It is no great crime where all is art of a high order sometimes to prefer the less consummate art because of its extraneous enchantment. But who would say that in themselves for all their brilliance *Romeo and Juliet* and *Midsummer-Night's Dream* are equal masterpieces with *Macbeth* and *Much Ado*; or would rank *L'École des Femmes* with *Les Femmes Savantes*?

In the three later novels we are, as I have said, in the real world of flesh and blood, concrete figures moving about in the life which Miss Austen knew. *Emma* is I suppose nearest, in point of manner though not of time, to *Pride and Prejudice*, and hardly inferior in the brilliance of its humour and wit. True that Jane Fairfax is shadowy, and Emma and the silly Harriet repeat themselves a little too much, but they are admirably portrayed, and the work is a unity of design, secured by the pervading presence of Mr. Knightley, and I need not recur to the great solution which is brought about by Emma's own absurdity. And there are, by the way, the delights of Mr. Woodhouse and Miss Bates (who again is not mere garrulousness but a person of real and deep feeling, a genuine character) and Mrs. Elton, who is a real advance upon Lucy Steele and still more upon Isabella Thorpe. One of the few good things which will be remembered of George IV is that he liked Miss Austen's novels and graciously permitted *Emma* to be dedicated to him.

Mansfield Park is much more of a story than any of the others, and I am one of those who would place it above *Emma*, though I admit there is some absurdity in placing the novels in this fashion in order of merit. Miss Austen if you read her at all you know so intimately that it is almost impossible to avoid having preferences; and I wish merely to justify mine. The usual question is whether one prefers *Mansfield Park* or *Pride and Prejudice*, but that question I have discussed. The humour of *Mansfield Park* is less ebullient than in *Emma*, but there is the exquisite contrast of Mrs. Norris and Lady Bertram, who is perhaps the most altogether successful piece of pure humour in the novels. I cannot help giving a single example. When Sir Thomas returns from his long absence in Antigua, Lady Bertram's feelings ' were so warmed by his sudden arrival, as to place her nearer agitation than she had been for the last twenty years. She had been almost fluttered for a few minutes, and still remained so sensibly animated as to put away her work, move Pug from her side, and give all her attention and all the rest of the sofa to her husband. . . . She began particularly to feel how dreadfully she must have missed him and how impossible it would have been for her to bear a lengthened absence' (p. 148). There is no falling-off of the wit but it takes a more subdued tone. The contrast of the Bertram household under the efficient supervision of Mrs. Norris with the helplessness of the other sister's ménage at Portsmouth is incomparable. But it is not so much the details, as the movement of the complicated tale of intrigue and character which is the merit of the novel. For my own part, while no one can pretend to be interested in her as much as in Emma or Elizabeth, I love Fanny and the long-drawn-out story of her timid and faithful soul. And even Edmund, who inclines at times to be a trifle priggish, is a vital person, and is to boot a first-rate picture of the better type of parson — such as Miss Austen was acquainted with in her own family — and the conflict in his mind between his love of the flippant Miss Crawford and his conception of his profession which she despises is beyond praise. There is, it must be admitted, a certain dullness as compared with the sparkling *Pride and Prejudice* or *Emma*, but the construction and the interplay of its characters, and the constant relief of the serious tone by the gaiety of some of the persons and the comic absurdity of the others make it a first-rate novel.

Persuasion, the last of the novels, seems to me to be on the whole the finest of them as a work of art, because of the deeper note introduced into it through the character of Anne Elliot and the consequent greater difficulty of the task it solves. Possibly the approach of her end, which was to follow in the next year, may have cast a shadow of gravity on Miss Austen's mind ; [1] the tone is more ' solemn and serene ', to use Shelley's words, than in the other novels. But it is more natural to say that maturity disclosed in her case more fully the seriousness which is always present in great writers of comedy, like Molière or Shakespeare or Meredith or Dickens. There is no failing of power ; the old humour is there, but gentler and more subtle. There is, as Mr. Bradley says (who, however, prefers *Pride and Prejudice*), a more delicate balance of the humorous element and the interest of the love story. The elder Musgroves and the Crofts are delightful creations,[2] and even Sir Walter Elliot overcomes, though he betrays, the early tendency to caricature. And there is the notable comedy of situation in the history of the heart-broken Captain Benwick, who first begins to fall in love with Anne and when she leaves Lyme to return to the Musgrove family at Uppercross falls in love with Louisa recovering from her accident, and thereby saves Frederick

---

[1] As Mr. Bradley thinks.
[2] Mr. Bradley quotes what the Admiral says of the two Miss Musgroves, ' And very nice young ladies they both are ; I hardly know one from the other ' (p. 77).

Wentworth to return to his old allegiance. Against this background of comedy stand out the heroic figure of Anne and the hardly less engaging portrait of Wentworth, indignant at Anne's prudent rejection of his earlier suit, bent on finding his happiness elsewhere, and lucky enough to find himself free in the end to follow his true attachment. I must quote the great passage which describes the feelings of the two lovers, which, it should be observed, does not occur in the first draft of the final courtship, and is therefore among the latest things that Miss Austen wrote. Charles Musgrove has invited Wentworth to join him[1] and Anne and see her back to her home in Bath :

> There could not be an objection. There could only be a most proper alacrity, a most obliging compliance for public view ; and smiles reined in and spirits dancing in private rapture. In half a minute Charles was at the bottom of Union Street again, and the other two proceeding together ; and soon words enough had passed between them to decide their direction towards the comparatively quiet and retired gravel walk, where the power of conversation would make the present hour a blessing indeed ; and prepare it for all the immortality which the happiest recollections of their own future lives could bestow. There they exchanged again those feelings and promises which had once before seemed to secure everything, but which had been followed by so many, many years of division and estrangement. There they returned again into the past, more exquisitely happy, perhaps, in their re-union, than when it had been first projected ; more tender, more tried, more fixed in a knowledge of each other's character, truth, and attachment ; more equal to act, more justified in acting. And there, as they slowly paced the gradual ascent, heedless of every group around them, seeing neither sauntering politicians, bustling house-keepers, flirting girls, nor nursery-maids and children, they could indulge in those retrospections and acknowledgments, and especially in those explanations of what had directly preceded the present moment, which were so poignant and so ceaseless in interest. All the little variations of the last week were gone through ; and of yesterday and to-day there could scarcely be an end. (P. 205.)

[1] As a learned Austenite points out to me, Charles Musgrove said he had to go and see ' a capital gun ' and so asked Wentworth ' to take his place and give Anne his arm to her father's door '. [Editor's note.]

Persuasion has blemishes in the story of Mrs. Smith and Mr. Elliot, which has already been noticed. But with all its faults it is an incomparable work.

Her characters are drawn so vividly that it is not surprising to hear that, like other artists with their personages, Miss Austen used to give further information about them than the novels contain. In a picture gallery in London she says she saw the picture of Jane Bennet, Mrs. Bingley, though Mrs. Darcy was not there (L. ii. 185, No. 61). It is delightful to hear of the fate of the sententious Mary Bennet, aged nineteen, who when her sister Lydia eloped, and omitted the ceremony of marriage, said (p. 246): ' " This is a most unfortunate affair and will probably be much talked of. But we must stem the tide of malice, and pour into the wounded bosoms of each other the balm of sisterly consolation." Then perceiving in Elizabeth no intention of replying, she added, " Unhappy as the event must be for Lydia, we may draw from it this useful lesson: that loss of virtue in a female is irretrievable — that one false step involves her in endless ruin — that her reputation is no less brittle than it is beautiful — and that she cannot be too much guarded in her behaviour towards the undeserving of the other sex." ' Mary, it is satisfying to learn from Miss Austen, married a clerk of her uncle Philips the lawyer, to whom, no doubt, precision would be welcome. When William, the sailor brother of Fanny, left Mansfield Park to join his ship, his Aunt Norris said she had given him ' something rather considerable at parting '. ' I am glad you gave him something considerable ', said Lady Bertram with unsuspicious calmness, ' for I gave him only £10.' Miss Austen used to say that the something rather considerable was £1 (*Memoir*, p. 148).

There could not have been in her mind much difference between her imaginary persons and real life; for her letters, save for their greater unrestraint, are just like her books. She was clearly always observing the people she met, and one of them, Miss Milles (L. ii. 239, No. 68), must have helped to suggest Miss Bates. ' She undertook in *three words* to give us the history of Mrs. Scudamore's reconciliation, and then talked about it for half an hour, using such odd expressions and so foolishly minute, that I could hardly keep my countenance.' Her niece Fanny, who became in the end Lady Knatchbull, was earlier asked in marriage by a suitor, and consults Aunt Jane. The letters (L. ii. 317 ff.), part fun, part wise consideration of her niece's feelings, and prudent advice, might come straight out of the novels. No wonder that her nieces and nephews loved Aunt Jane and that one of them wrote the charming *Memoir* of her. In her letters there is sometimes more malice in the humour than in her writing, though there is gentle malice there too ; as when she tells Cassandra that ' Mrs. Hall, of Sherborne, was brought to bed yesterday of a dead child, some weeks before she expected, owing to a fright. I suppose she happened unawares to look at her husband.' It would be easy to quote sentences from the letters, with all Miss Austen's humour and aptness of language. Here is one : ' Single women ', she says to Fanny (L. ii. 335, No. 83), ' have a dreadful propensity for being poor, which is one strong argument in favour of matrimony '. And another : ' Many a girl on early death has been praised into an angel, I believe, on slighter pretensions to beauty, sense, and merit ' (than a certain Miss Mapleton who has just died : L. i. 382, No. 32). She writes to Anna about her book : ' Devereux Forester's being ruined by his vanity is extremely good, but I wish you would not let him plunge into a " vortex of dissipation ". I do not object to the thing, but I cannot bear the expression ; it is such thorough novel slang, and so old that I daresay Adam met with it in the first novel he opened ' (L. ii. 355, No. 88).

The same belief in the reality of her creations extends to her readers. They want to know where is Molland's shop in Millsom Street in Bath where the Miss Elliots waited while it rained ; and if they are at Lyme they are like Tennyson careless of where the Duke of Monmouth landed, and want to be shown the steps beside which

THE ART OF JANE AUSTEN

Louisa Musgrove jumped from the Cobb, fell on the lower Cobb, and in the language of the time was taken up lifeless. She recovered enough life, it will be remembered, to heal the wounded heart of Captain Benwick.

It is difficult to realise that in her years of authorship Miss Austen was a contemporary of Wordsworth in his productive years, of Keats and Shelley. She loves Nature, but it is still an eighteenth-century love for its gentler and more orderly beauty. It has nothing of Wordsworth's mystic passion. She is untouched by romantic passion, and if the passage from *Persuasion* seems to contradict that statement, we have to remind ourselves that the eighteenth century, for all its decorum and outward calm and good sense, was a century of men and women like ourselves, and that if it produced men who were cool and serene, it produced also the fire of Burke and Chatham and Fox and Johnson. She seems in her classic and ironical humour to have felt no breath of the change wrought in men's minds by the new movement of freedom. It has often been observed how detached she is from the great events of her own time, and how no one would guess from the unruffled calm of the novels that England was at the date of the earlier novels in the throes of the Napoleonic war, and at the date of the later ones, only just emerged from it. It is true we hear that Wentworth was made commander in consequence of the action off St. Domingo (*Persuasion*, p. 20), and there are admirals coming into the stories and mishipmen like William Price, and there is the Price family at Portsmouth; and Anne gloried in being a sailor's wife. Nelson and Buonaparte are not mentioned. Miss Austen was devoted to her two sailor brothers, Frank and Charles, who both in time became admirals, but when Southey's *Life of Nelson* appeared, she says (L. ii. 219, No. 65), ' I am tired of lives of Nelson, being that I never read any. I will read this, however, if Frank is mentioned in it.'

Her style of writing is in keeping with her classic and ironic mood. I have left to the end her manner of writing, though it is the very soul of her art, as the style of all literary art must be the soul of every literary artist. There is an old saying often quoted, *Le style c'est l'homme même.* We are told that what Buffon really said was, *Le style c'est de l'homme même*; and I am too indolent to check the statement. And there is no real difference. Whether the style is the man or of him, as the style so is the art. It is not a mere dexterity added to thoughts or images, as it may be in writing which is not art; but the very form of the material the writer uses, which is words with meanings. So long as a Milton is mute we cannot tell that he is a Milton, and thoughts which may be too profound for words are not the thoughts of a literary artist. An author does not merely need words, and those artistically wrought, in order to communicate to others what he thinks; if he is an artist he must speak or die. It would hardly seem worth while to say this were it not for a widely spread belief that technique is only the instrument of art instead of being organic to it and indeed the whole.

At any rate Miss Austen's style is her characters, and plot, and the humorous unfolding of her comedy, over again. It is natural and unaffected, without fuss or affectation, and its equable flow sparkles as it flows. It fits the subject as a glove follows the hand, as William James says somewhere of Mr. Bergson's style, and that is because it is the very substance of her art. Her English differs little in its general character from the standard English of the present day, except for the greater expansiveness and equableness which it possesses as belonging to the eighteenth century, and the occasional use of antithesis and balance which the writer may have acquired from her dear Dr. Johnson. Needless to say it is wholly alien, whether in narrative or in conversation, from the jerkiness of some later nineteenth- and twentieth-century English.

Not that it is always impeccable. When I was re-reading in preparation for this paper, I began to note the instances in which 'everybody' or 'nobody' is followed by 'their': 'Nobody put themselves out of their way to secure her comfort ', ' Everybody should marry as soon as they can do it to advantage '. I noted twenty instances of this usage in *Mansfield Park*, and when I found it occurred in all the novels, I gave up counting. It is a very popular misuse, and I suppose a solecism repeated continually by a great writer must be considered as promoted to the brevet rank of an idiom. Occasionally, but not often, she does descend to the distressing trick, practised so often by Dickens, of conjoining with one verb two heterogeneous complements — ' almost ready to overpower them ' (it is Miss Bates) ' with care and kindness . . . anxious inquiries after Mr. Woodhouse's health, cheerful communications about her mother's and sweet-cake from the beaufet ' (p. 156). These are small matters, and I could wish that the people who nowadays use the silly expression ' that's right ' when they mean ' yes ' would read this passage from *Mansfield Park* (p. 245) :

' You will divide your year between London and Northamptonshire ? '
' Yes.'
' That's right.'

and they will learn the difference between the expression of mere affirmation and that of approval, or of the confirmation of a statement.[1]

In the remainder of my time I shall now indulge myself by reading illustrations from the novels of Miss Austen's style. They are chosen without any special care, almost at random (except for one passage), just because her workmanship is so uniformly excellent. I shall first cite some longer passages and then a few shorter ones which may serve as examples of her peculiar aptness and wit or humour.

The first is taken from *Mansfield Park*. It has no particular claim to be chosen ; it illustrates the simple manner habitual to the writer. Sir Thomas Bertram has

[1] When I first read this paper I expected to be met at the appointed place by a Mr. Smith whom I did not know by sight. I asked the man who met me if he was Mr. Smith and he said, ' That's right '.

returned home and has been told about the theatricals, the very risky play, as it would then be thought, which was certain to shock his grave propriety :

> There was one person, however, in the house, whom he could not leave to learn his sentiments merely by his conduct. He could not help giving Mrs. Norris a hint of his having hoped that her advice might have been interposed to prevent what her judgment must certainly have disapproved. The young people had been very inconsiderate in forming the plan ; they ought to have been capable of a better decision themselves ; but they were young, and, excepting Edmund, he believed of unsteady characters ; and with greater surprise, therefore, he must regard her acquiescence in their wrong measures, her countenance of their unsafe amusements, than that such measures and such amusements should have been suggested. Mrs. Norris was a little confounded and as nearly being silenced as ever she had been in her life ; for she was ashamed to confess having never seen any of the impropriety which was so glaring to Sir Thomas, and would not have admitted that her influence was insufficient — that she might have talked in vain. Her only resource was to get out of the subject as fast as possible, and turn the current of Sir Thomas's ideas into a happier channel. She had a great deal to insinuate in her own praise as to attention to the interest and comfort of his family, much exertion and many sacrifices to glance at in the form of hurried walks and sudden removals from her own fireside, and many excellent hints of distrust and economy to Lady Bertram and Edmund to detail, whereby a most considerable saving had always arisen, and more than one bad servant had been detected. (*Mansfield Park*, p. 55.)

The second illustrates the contrast of the angelic Jane Bennet who never sees evil and the shrewd and caustic Elizabeth :

> She then spoke of the letter, repeating the whole of its contents as far as they concerned George Wickham. What a stroke was this for poor Jane ! who would willingly have gone through the world without believing that so much wickedness existed in the whole race of mankind, as was here collected in one individual. Nor was Darcy's vindication, though grateful to her feelings, capable of consoling her for such discovery. Most earnestly did she labour to prove the probability of error, and seek to clear one without involving the other.

'This will not do', said Elizabeth, 'you will never be able to make both of them good for anything. Take your choice, but you must be satisfied with only one. There is but such a quantity of merit between them; just enough to make one good sort of man; and of late it has been shifting about pretty much. For my part, I am inclined to believe it all Mr. Darcy's; but you shall chuse.'

It was some time, however, before a smile could be extorted from Jane.

'I do not know when I have been more shocked', said she, 'Wickham so very bad! It is almost past belief. And poor Mr. Darcy! Dear Lizzy, only consider what he must have suffered. Such a disappointment! and with the knowledge of your ill opinion too! and having to relate such a thing of his sister! It is really too distressing. I am sure you must feel it so.'

'Oh! no, my regret and compassion are all done away by seeing you so full of both. I know you will do him such ample justice, that I am growing every moment more unconcerned and indifferent. Your profusion makes me saving; and if you lament over him much longer, my heart will be as light as a feather.'

'Poor Wickham! there is such an expression of goodness in his countenance, such an openness and gentleness in his manner!'

'There certainly was some great mismanagement in the education of those two young men. One has got all the goodness, and the other all the appearance of it.' (*Pride and Prejudice*, p. 192.)

The third is from *Emma*, just after Emma and Harriet had been visiting a poor and sick protégée of Emma's in the village of Highbury, which, by the by, is Cobham, for as Sir Francis Darwin pointed out, in one place the author has written Cobham and forgotten to substitute Highbury:

'These are the sights, Harriet, to do one good. How trifling they make everything else appear! I feel now as if I could think of nothing but these poor creatures all the rest of the day; and yet who can say how soon it may all vanish from my mind?'

'Very true', said Harriet. 'Poor creatures! one can think of nothing else.'

'And I really do not think the impression will soon be over', said Emma, as she crossed the low hedge, and tottering footstep, which ended the narrow, slippery path through the cottage garden, and brought them into the lane again. 'I do not think it will ', stopping to look once more at all the outward wretchedness of the place, and recall the still greater within.

' Oh dear, no ', said her companion.

They walked on. The lane made a slight bend ; and when that bend was passed, Mr. Elton was immediately in sight, and so near as to give Emma time only to say further :—

' Ah, Harriet, here comes a very sudden trial of our stability in good thoughts. Well ' (smiling), ' I hope it may be allowed that if compassion has produced exertion and relief to the sufferers, it has done all that is truly important. If we feel for the wretched enough to do all we can for them, the rest is empty sympathy, only distressing to ourselves.'

Harriet could just answer, ' Oh dear, yes ' before the gentleman joined them. (*Emma*, p. 89.)

To the selection of shorter passages there is no end. Here are a few ; they are, except the last, in no sense selected as gems, a hundred other passages might be selected with equal justice ; they all show the true artist's fusing of the matter and the form.

From *Sense and Sensibility* :

[Says the egregious Willoughby], ' Brandon is just the kind of man whom everybody speaks well of, and nobody cares about, whom all are delighted to see, and nobody remembers to talk to.' [And when Elinor defends him as highly esteemed by all the family at the Park, he goes on to ask], ' Who would submit to the indignity of being approved by such women as Lady Middleton and Mrs. Jennings, that could command the indifference of anybody else ? ' (P. 40.)

From *Emma* :

When she considered how peculiarly unlucky poor Mr. Elton was in being in the same room at once with the woman he had just married, the woman he had wanted to marry, and the woman he had been expected to marry, she must allow him to have the right to look as little wise, and to be as much affectedly, and as little really, easy as could be. (P. 277.)

And this of old Mr. Woodhouse, when the news came from Enscombe that Mrs. Churchill was ill and that the ball must be dropped, and Frank could not come, and everybody was wretched :

THE ART OF JANE AUSTEN

Her father's feelings were quite different. He thought principally of Mrs. Churchill's illness, and wanted to know how she was treated; and as for the ball, it was shocking to have dear Emma disappointed; but they would all be safer at home. (P. 266.)

From *Pride and Prejudice* : Elizabeth and her sensible aunt Mrs. Gardiner are speaking about the sudden interruption of Bingley's courtship of Jane, and Mrs. Gardiner asks, demurring to the description that he had been violently in love with Jane :

' Pray how *violent* was Mr. Bingley's love ? '
' I never saw a more promising inclination; he was growing quite inattentive to other people, and wholly engrossed by her. Every time they met it was more decided and remarkable. At his own ball he offended two or three young ladies by not asking them to dance; and I spoke to him twice myself, without receiving an answer. Could there be finer symptoms ? Is not general incivility the very essence of love ? ' (P. 121.)

From *Northanger Abbey* :

Man only can be aware of the insensibility of man towards a new gown. It would be mortifying to the feelings of many ladies could they be made to understand how little the heart of man is affected by what is costly or new in their attire ; how little it is biassed by the texture of their muslin and how unsusceptible of peculiar tenderness towards the spotted, the sprigged, the mull or the jackonet. Woman is fine for her own satisfaction alone. (P. 54.)

From *Mansfield Park*, of Mrs. Price :

Her days were spent in a kind of slow bustle ; always busy without getting on, always behindhand and lamenting it, without altering her ways ; wishing to be an economist without contrivance or regularity ; dissatisfied with her servants without skill to make them better, and whether helping, or reprimanding, or indulging them, without any power of engaging their respect. (P. 325.)

And from *Persuasion* this passage, gay and exquisite, about Anne when the proposal from Wentworth was in the offing :

Prettier musings of high wrought love and eternal constancy could never have passed along the streets of Bath than Anne was sporting with from Camden Place to Westgate Buildings. It was almost enough to spread purification and perfume all the way. (P. 163.)

There is no end to this. I only hope the shade of Jane Austen will forgive me if in the interest of candour I have not left her defects unmentioned in estimating her merits. I think she would, but I should be afraid to wait to hear the mocking approval she would bestow.

IV

MOLIÈRE AND LIFE [1]

(Reprinted, by permission, from the *Bulletin of the John Rylands Library*, July 1926)

I

AT the conclusion of Plato's *Symposium*, the reporter of the dialogue says that when he was awakened towards daybreak by the crowing of cocks he found the rest of the company asleep or departed, but Socrates and Agathon, the tragic poet, and Aristophanes were still awake and drinking, and Socrates was discoursing and was compelling the other two to acknowledge that the genius of comedy was the same as that of tragedy, and that the true artist in tragedy was an artist in comedy also. Socrates was not the man to shrink from a paradox, and the assent of the other two must not be pressed, for the reporter says they were drowsy and did not quite follow the argument. It is greatly to be regretted that Plato has not preserved Socrates' arguments in some other form. We may be sure they were delightful and full of good sense and subtlety. Socrates had before him the practice of the tragic poets in winding up the trilogy of tragedies with a satiric play; if he had been living in the seventeenth century he could have pointed to Shakespeare and Racine and Corneille, and to the last with peculiar relevance for our subject. For although *Le Menteur* hardly rises above the level of a comedy of incident and errors, Molière himself has said, that if it had not been for this comedy he himself might have written his lighter comedies but would not have risen to the height of the serious comedy of *Le Tartuffe* and

[1] A lecture delivered in the John Rylands Library, April 14, 1926.

Alceste. Possibly Socrates was influenced unconsciously by the presence both in the tragedy and the comedy of his time of the chorus which in some fashion represents the grave opinion of the public and of life. For there is reason to believe that the chorus or its equivalent enters implicitly or explicitly (that is, in the person of some character or characters) into the very structure of comedy. At any rate in the comedy of Molière this is always so. On the other hand, the chorus is accidental to tragedy in its structure. From being originally a participant it becomes a commentary on the real participants and then disappears.[1] Now Socrates, impressed by the habit of his time, may have thought that both forms of the drama, sharing in so important a feature, were in essentials the same or had the same genius. His arguments would have been subtler and in appearance more profound. Yet perhaps it is here that the real difference of tragedy and comedy may be found, that in the one the judgment on the persons is absent or falls to the spectator, in the other it is in the structure of the play.

Socrates, while he said that the true tragic writer was also an artist in comedy, did not lay down the converse proposition that the true comic writer is also an artist in tragedy. Molière, at least, if he sometimes seems to skirt the borders of tragedy, is never really tragic. We have to be on our guard against reading into him feelings different from his intention or inspired by situations which are more seriously regarded at times different from his. I know one sensitive person who cannot read *George Dandin* because of sympathy with the hero so cruelly deceived. Yet he is too undignified in himself to be a tragic character — ' vous l'avez voulu, George Dandin ' : the helpless resignation of a foolish man ; and we must confess that Molière and his audience were accustomed to regard conjugal infidelity with levity when it did not touch themselves, and that the heartless wife in the play is meant to, and does, emerge triumphant. Our sympathy with the nobler side of

---

[1] C. E. Vaughan in *Types of Tragic Drama* sees it represented in later tragedy in the lyric element of the speakers.

Alceste's character may incline us to weep with him rather than laugh at him; but there is no doubt of the intention of the play. Molière comes nearest to tragedy in *Le Festin de Pierre*. Yet the fate which overtakes Don Juan may give us a thrill of horror but is too melodramatic to be tragic. In a tragedy the vengeance of insulted right would not be left to the strange machinery of an animated block; the just heavens would have embodied their vital presence in the person of some character of the play; whereas Done Elvira, who warns Juan of his doom, finds no more tragic solution of the conflict than to retire repentant into a convent. True to his comic inspiration, Molière, on the contrary, leaves us with the great exclamation of the valet bewailing the loss of his wages. Once, indeed, Molière tried his hand not at tragedy but at an heroic play, *Don Garcie de Navarre*. But he had the good sense to recognise that he was forcing his natural vein, and made the best use possible of his failure by taking passages from the tediously jealous harangues of Don Garcie before his serious and constant mistress, and inserting them into the worthier setting of Alceste's manlier, if still unreasonable, protests against the levities of Célimène.

In order to test the paradox of Socrates by a concrete instance let us ask why *Le Misanthrope* is a comedy and *Timon of Athens* a tragedy. Of the justice of the designations there is no doubt. Alceste upon the stage is laughable and meant to be so. *Timon*, which as a tragedy is not for a moment comparable in artistic merit with *Le Misanthrope*, and is indeed a poor tragedy and only in part, it is said, the work of Shakespeare, is a tragedy. They are worth comparing because in both the subject matter is the same, the turning of what is essentially a noble nature into misanthropy. In both, the hero is ennobled by passion and disfigured by foolishness; in both the issue is the rejection of the world. Here the likeness ends. The differences arise with the comic or the tragic development respectively.

The passion of Alceste lies in his sincerity and dislike of shows. The man who prizes the rude lyric, ' Si le roi m'avait donné', in spite of its archaic style and its poor rhyme, because it portrays a heartfelt passion may or may not have been a good literary critic (he was surely a good one) ;[1] but at least he was a man of noble disposition. Timon is mere good nature, till ingratitude makes him flame up into hatred ; adversity brings out the man ; he ceases to be the genial fribble, under which his real force was disguised. 'The old Timon with his noble heart', says Tennyson, 'that strongly loathing greatly broke' — though the words are perhaps exaggerated. Alceste has his passion within control. Even when he is most agitated by hatred of conventional lies, he remains of the world which practises them. In the great scene with Oronte he is the perfect gentleman — 'Je ne dis pas cela'. Only when provoked beyond bearing does he tell Oronte flatly and coarsely that his sonnet is worthless. Timon becomes hatred personified, through revulsion from his own good nature. The difference of their fates flows from the difference in their faults. Alceste is foolish through the extravagance of his expectations. Being a large and not a mean character, he unreasonably asks of human nature more than human nature can bear, and the high pitch and tension of his sincerity pervades him so that comic as he is he is one of the really concrete and organic types of personality ; like Tartuffe in this respect and unlike Harpagon in *L'Avare* perhaps, and certainly Argan in *Le Malade Imaginaire*. That is why, or one reason why, *Le Misanthrope* is so great a comedy and Alceste a comic hero.

[1] Si le roi m'avait donné
　Paris, sa grand' ville,
Et qu'il me fallût quitter
　L'amour de ma mie,
Je dirais au roi Henri :
　Reprenez votre Paris ;
J'aime mieux ma mie, ô gué,
　J'aime mieux ma mie.

Le rime n'est pas riche, et le style en est vieux ;
Mais ne voyez-vous pas que cela vaut bien mieux
Que ces colifichets dont le bon sens murmure,
Et que la passion parle là toute pure ?

His fault is not tragic for it is the basis of his character. Timon's fault is not so much extravagance of judgment as foolish and innocent confidence in men. When the unthinking spendthrift discovers that he has placed his trust in summer friends he recognises the tragic fault (the ἁμαρτία) and his trust is converted into passionate hatred. Were he a more organic person, were he less a mere prey to the revulsion of feeling and the desire to give it vent, he would be more of a tragic figure than he is.

All the same we can, in the indifferent tragedy, trace all those elements which have been discovered to lie at the basis of tragedy by Aristotle and Hegel, and by Mr. Andrew Bradley in our day. There is the tragic fault into which he slips out of the blind simplicity of his inexperience of mankind. And the play may be said to exhibit within this noble and serious person, turned nobly serious by the issue of his defect, the conflict in which overweening trustfulness is shattered against the real self-seekingness of mankind, and he perishes in the conflict. And at the end Alcibiades enters to pronounce, like Fortinbras in *Hamlet*, the words which reconcile his death with overruling providence. These features do not stand out so clearly here as they do in *Lear*, or *Othello*, or *Hamlet*; but they can be discerned in spite of the imperfections of the play.

In *Le Misanthrope*, on the other hand, there is indeed a clash or conflict between the high-strung demands of Alceste and the unbending reasonableness of the social standard. But the clash is not so much a clash as a contrast; and it can be so reduced in scale, and become comic, because the conventional judgment which laughs at Alceste for his extravagance and is embodied in the persons of Philinte and Éliante and even, in her way, of the gay and bewitching and entirely reasonable coquette Célimène who is the author of all Alceste's woes — because this conventional standard is not an elemental force in things and human affairs, but rather a matter of sweet reasonableness and moderate expectation, in which all men can settle down as to a minimum. Thus Timon's trust in human

MOLIÈRE AND LIFE

nature comes into conflict not with what we may reasonably expect of men in society, but with self-regarding human nature and the end is the destruction of Timon in the struggle. Alceste's revolt against society is not the simple failing of a sincere and noble nature, but a crude misapprehension on his part of the conditions under which society can be carried on. There wants in such a situation the seriousness of issue which in tragedy is always raised. Of the tragic poet it is true what Mr. Yeats says of himself with a different application :

> The elemental beings go,
> About my table to and fro.

The public standard against which Alceste rebels has not the high solemnity of a great power like jealousy, or, to take again the Hegelian case of the *Antigone*, loyalty to the state, or as in *Hamlet*, devotion to a father's memory. We are not torn in our sympathies between the sincerity of Alceste's passion for unbridled truth and our acceptance of current opinion. Conventional standards do not seem to us to deserve all that pother, and the gravity of tragedy is consequently replaced by light-hearted observation of how the revolter goes under.

It will be urged that Alceste is passionately in love, and there is tragedy in the sacrifice of his love to his sincerity ; and it is true that the conflict betrays a noble nature and excites our sympathy, and, if Alceste were different, contains a tragic possibility. The conditions of real tragedy are however wanting, the contention between vital elements in human nature. For Alceste's sincerity is vitiated by its unreasonableness, which it is the very gist of the comedy to expose ; it has not the ' high seriousness ' of Othello's simple trust and honour, poisoned by a friend with suspicion (' it is the cause, it is the cause '). The sacrifice of his love has not the inevitableness of the tragic calamity, nor is the pity it excites a ' cleansing ' pity ; it does but make the comedy a greater and higher comedy.

In his recent work on Psychology Mr. M'Dougall has

suggested that laughter is a preservative against excess of sympathy which would be exhausting. In this play we take the side of Philinte and Éliante, and even Célimène, and laugh in order not to sympathise with the honest sufferings of Alceste. Those who, feeling so strongly his essential but misguided goodness, weep for him fail to take the point of view of the comic poet and to laugh at the somewhat trivial defiance of an accepted code or anything firmly enough based on common practice to claim reasonable recognition : much as we laugh at Beatrice and Benedict for their playful refusal to acknowledge the claims of their attraction for each other. Hence Alceste, for all his enthusiastic rebellion against the insincerities of polite society, is no grave champion of virtue but a light challenger of the claims of moderation and reason. Noble as he is, he is surrounded with an aroma of triviality. In the end his indignation hurries him into his rupture with the world :

> Trahi de toutes parts, accablé d'injustices,
> Je vais sortir d'un gouffre où triomphent les vices ;
> Et chercher sur la terre un endroit écarté
> Où d'être homme d'honneur on ait la liberté.

The issue is too intense for the occasion. Significantly enough it is suggested that his resolution may not be unshakeable. The comedy ends, not like a tragedy with the hero's overwhelming, but with the hope that after all he may acquiesce :

> Allons, madame, [says Philinte to Éliante] allons employer toute chose
> Pour rompre le dessein que son cœur se propose.

I do not say that comedy is in the right to ridicule these generous rebellions against good sense and moderation. Heaven forbid that indignation at the insincerities of our accommodated social intercourse should cease. Rather than that, let our Alcestes claim the liberty of saying no word but unvarnished truth, at whatever risk of hurting the feelings of others ; or, if they are unfortunate enough to love in their own despite a Célimène who being young and full of the wine of life declines to abandon all society in order to devote herself to her lover's whims and bury herself in hiding with him from the world whose injustice he cannot endure, let them endure their discomfiture. The spirit of revolt is so precious that these sacrifices may be worth while. Yet comedy may still have something to say in its defence. It ridicules in Alceste not his sincerity but his petulance. It raises no laugh at the revolt against serious evils by the valiant champions of new ideals whose aim is to reform: your Francis of Assisi who, bred in luxury and the life of pleasure, gives his cloak to the beggar and embraces poverty. Comedy laughs at Alceste for rejecting what it is not reasonable or worth while to decline for the sake of something which it is not reasonable or worth while to secure. The standard from which it measures its victims may be itself a low one, may express no more than a minimum of requirement, may take human nature too lightly. But it can at least urge for itself that these standards are a solid achievement of good sense and at least something which it is worth while to conserve till a better is found.

The rights of comedy are more palpable when the sin against public use and wont is not the generous unreasonableness of Alceste, but the exaggerations of valuable elements of life into hypocrisy. When it ridicules the pretences of the false *dévot* it is still more obviously establishing the claims of moderation and good sense. It includes in its subjects (besides the Alcestes), the Tartuffes, and even, as in the *Femmes Savantes*, the supposed pretenders to a cultivation believed to be beyond their sphere, even when they do not, as in this play, carry their pretensions to the absurdity of refining their language into a ridiculous precision.

I cannot speak of comedy in general or the comic spirit. For that I must send you to Meredith's great *Essay on Comedy and the Uses of the Comic Spirit*. But of Molière's comedy it is true that always the part of chorus is played by common sense, or sound sense, current in the cultivated opinion of the time. The comic motive lies in the contrast of certain characters which deviate from this standard with the others which represent it. Such good sense is not merely good taste but right and goodness as they are conceived at the time in the general current of healthy life. Accordingly Mr. Bergson, who founds himself in the main upon Molière, declares in his book upon Laughter (*Le Rire*) that the comic character is one-sided and presents the appearance of something mechanical, something which does not share in the full tide of life. The point is well taken, for the exaggeration, which takes the hero out of the region of full good sense, whether as in Alceste it is an offence against good judgment merely, or as in Tartuffe against the true and balanced spirit of religious devotion, destroys the equilibrium of life. The criticism is, however, not perfectly good, if it implies that the comic personage is not in himself a personality organised completely by his controlling impulse. Such a view would not hold of Alceste, who is a very living person; it may be true of Harpagon or Argan, but it is certainly not of Tartuffe, who is a thorough-paced and vital rascal, who by a kind of fine art can harmonise his pretended exaltation of sentiment with very human sentiments of sensuality and vindictive love of gain. The great comic characters are in fact comic in proportion as they are also whole men, with not so much a mechanised life as a twisted one. Was there ever a more living man than Falstaff himself, who was perhaps beyond the reach even of Molière; whose want of principle is idealised into a new irresponsible kind of life, that is never troubled by current opinion and does not so much defy it as rather is innocent of it; who in no sense is like Satan who says ' evil be thou my good ', but rather enjoys a merry and delighted obliteration of moral distinctions ? The shock with common sense culminates in his case with his repudiation by the prince turned king, in whom indeed common sense in its harder and more brutal form is represented.

MOLIERE AND LIFE

In a paper in the *Cornhill* for April 1925, on 'The Ladies of Molière', to which I owe much, my friend Mrs. MacCunn dwelt on the good sense of Molière's women, and wisely compared them, Léonor and Henriette and Éliante and the rest, with the heroines of Jane Austen, with Jane Bennet, Eleanor Dashwood and Fanny Price. It is not only the Philintes and Chrysales who play the foil to the comic personages, but the wise coquettes like Célimène, the modest and gracious and dutiful Henriette of the *Femmes Savantes*, the Léonor of the *École des Maris*, and the enchanting Dorines and Nicoles. Meredith has dwelt on the equality of the sexes in Molière's plays, not equality of privilege but equal opportunity as members of society in their respective spheres. He even regards such equality as the true soil for the growth of pure comedy. 'Where women are on the road to an equal footing with men, in attainments and in liberty — in what they have won for themselves, and what has been granted them by a fair civilisation — there, and only, waiting to be translated from life to the stage, or the novel, or the poem, pure Comedy flourishes, and is, as it would help them to be, the sweetest of diversions, the wisest of delightful companions.' Such an audience Molière found not so much in the society of the Court of Louis XIV as in the bourgeoisie of Paris, 'sufficiently quick-witted and enlightened by education to welcome great works like *Le Tartuffe*, *Les Femmes Savantes*, and *Le Misanthrope*, works that were perilous ventures on the popular intelligence, big vessels to launch on streams running to shallows'. And again: 'Cultivated men and women, who do not skim the cream of life, and are attached to the duties, yet escape the harsher blows, make acute and balanced observers. Molière is their poet.' Meredith is doubtless right in the part which he assigns to women in the world comedy. 'The man seeks freedom,' says the princess in Goethe's *Tasso*, 'the woman observance' — *Nach Freiheit strebt der Mann, das Weib nach Sitte*. Whatever may be thought of that antithesis, it is at least true that the equal participation of women with men secures the atmosphere of ordered custom, which supplies the standard of well-regulated judgment against which comedy in its Molièresque example sets out the laughable follies or extravagances of mankind.

II

When I speak in the title of this paper of Molière and life, I mean by Molière not the man himself in his recorded life but in his plays. What we know of his life outside the history of his plays is scanty : his few years of study as a young man at the Collège de Clermont ; and in particular the conversations he had with and the lessons he had from the Epicurean or materialist philosopher Gassendi (Molière once began a translation of Lucretius which unfortunately is lost) ; the years of Bohemian experience when he was touring the provinces before he came to Paris ; the somewhat libertine life he then led ; while all the while he was equipping himself in knowledge of the stage and of human nature for the extraordinary facility and the more precious wisdom of his later years ; his tenderness to his actors and the dependants of his theatre, which made him persist in spite of his physical weakness in holding his performance lest they should lose their profits or their wages ; his final word as an actor when as the bachelor in medicine in *Le Malade Imaginaire* he engages to observe the statutes of the faculty — *juro*, and his hugger-mugger burial at night because of the prejudices of the Archbishop of Paris against him as a reputed infidel. These things and the happy incidents of his friendships with Boileau and others are irrelevant to the great artist. Not even the most poignant incident of his life, his jealousy of and passionate love for his wife whom apparently there is no good ground to acquit of the infidelity with which he and the world credited her ; not even this, though it affects us so deeply in reading him, is relevant except as supplying part of his experience of life. There is hardly anything more touching than the report which Sainte-Beuve [1] quotes

---

[1] *Portraits Littéraires*, vol. ii. pp. 41 *sqq.* (Paris).

of Molière's confession to his friend Chapelle in the garden at Auteuil of how, knowing the unworthiness of his passion for the unfaithful Armande, he was incapable of resisting it. Yet it is precisely not the legitimacy of the passion of the jealous husband which he portrays in the comedies, from the *Cocu Imaginaire* onwards, but the folly of jealousy and the constant fear of a fate regarded as only too probable and the commonest subject of comedy, for which he had no need to go to his own life and which perhaps a wise man would accept with resignation. Consider the diatribe against jealousy of Done Elvire, the mistress of Don Garcie, in her conversation with Élise (Act I, Sc. 1):

> Partout la jalousie est un monstre odieux :
> Rien n'en peut adoucir les traits injurieux ;
> Et, plus l'amour est cher qui lui donne naissance,
> Plus on doit ressentir les coups de cette offense.

The voice of good sense. In *Les Fâcheux* Éraste is called upon as arbiter between Orante and Célimène who champion respectively the unsuspicious and the jealous lover — and wishing to please both parties and be released from their detention of him, decides :

Le jaloux aime plus, et l'autre bien mieux. (Act II, Sc. 4).

A poet's life may supply him with all manner of material for his art, but it is not necessary to suppose that his works are a transcript of himself. The real Molière writhed under conjugal infidelity ; the dramatist mocks it. There is truth in Browning's retort to Wordsworth's saying of the sonnet : ' with this same key Shakespeare unlocked his heart ' ; ' Did Shakespeare ? If so the less Shakespeare he.' What the artist puts of himself into his work is not always the emotions which he shares with his personages but at most the emotion of the dramatic situation which he describes ; and this goes almost without saying. With this proviso, it is safe to identify Molière with the standard which laughs at his comic personages. Nor was it a particularly high standard. It was no more than the average standard of his time. But it was both serious and reasonable, according to those lights. He had no passion for virtue but he approved virtue. He was certainly not deeply religious, was probably enough touched with free thinking; as the story goes of what he said returning on a boat on the Seine from the house at Auteuil. Chapelle was maintaining the doctrine of atoms; Molière denied it but added, ' Passe pour la morale !' [1] But he hated pretence and he defends seemliness and wisdom and the good conduct of life, with all liberty for gaiety in the process. False devotion and the pretentiousness of the doctors he exposed, the first without mercy, the other laughingly and good-humouredly, though apparently the doctors did not take it so.

Of one thing we may be certain about Molière the man because it is attested by the poems themselves. His superabundant gaiety and humour and wit were the overflow of a profound and passionate mind trained into wisdom by experience and observation. His nickname of the *Contemplateur* was given him from his habit of watching people in barbers' shops, and milliners' shops, and elsewhere; but his observation was the intuition of a great mind. Perhaps, whatever may be true of wit, which is more the effect of intellectual skill, there has been no great humour which has not its roots in insight; it has been the outcome, where it has not been the cloak, of gravity and wisdom. The fool in *King Lear* is not mere comic relief to the sorrows of his master; he is continuous with them, and understands what he mocks. Consider as the first examples that occur the fatuity of the famous *le pauvre homme !* with which Orgon greets the recitals of Tartuffe's austerities. How funny it is but how true and sincere. Or Vadius's prefatory condemnation of the itch of authors to read their own productions; followed by his introduction of his own verses on young lovers.

[1] *Portraits Littéraires*, vol. ii. p. 45.

MOLIÈRE AND LIFE

> Le défaut des auteurs, dans leurs productions,
> C'est d'en tyranniser les conversations,
> D'être au Palais, au Cours, aux ruelles, aux tables,
> De leurs vers fatigants lecteurs infatigables.
> Pour moi, je ne vois rien de plus sot, à mon sens,
> Q'un auteur qui partout va gueuser des encens ;
> Qui, des premiers venus saisissant les oreilles,
> En fait le plus souvent les martyrs de ses veilles.
> On ne m'a jamais vu ce fol entêtement ;
> Et d'un Grec là-dessus je suis le sentiment,
> Qui, par un dogme exprès, défend à tous ses sages
> L'indigne empressement de lire leurs ouvrages.
> Voici de petits vers pour de jeunes amants,
> Sur quoi je voudrais bien avoir vos sentiments.

In the *Femmes Savantes* a delightful instance occurs at the dénouement. Ariste, his brother, and his charming and reasonable daughter Henriette, have persuaded Chrysale to play the man in his house and resist his wife Philaminte's proposal to marry Henriette to the poetaster. Chrysale is the embodiment of good sense and reason, though he has limited ideas of the function of women in society, according to our recent views though not according to the views of the seventeenth century. Unfortunately, as Henriette says :

> Il a reçu du ciel certaine bonté d'âme
> Qui le soumet d'abord à ce que veut sa femme.

His resolution, however, has been stiffened and he insists that Clitandre and not Trissotin shall marry Henriette. Yet when the moment arrives for the formal decision, Philaminte terrorises him ; and sheepishly he proposes the compromise that Clitandre, who had given up the *précieuse* sister Armande because of her affected prudery, and devoted himself to her younger and unaffected sister, should still take Armande and Trissotin have Henriette. ' Hé ! mon père ! ' says Henriette. ' Hé ! monsieur ! ' says Clitandre. And Ariste cuts the knot by his fictitious news of Chrysale's ruin, at which Trissotin retires from his suit.

Once more let me cite one of the confidential maids — Lisette, in *L'École des Maris*, who joins Léonor in protesting to Sganarelle against his treatment of Isabelle by locking her up from the approach of other men to keep her for himself:

> En effet, tous ces soins sont des choses infâmes.
> Sommes-nous chez les Turcs, pour renfermer les femmes?
> Car on dit qu'on les tient esclaves en ce lieu,
> Et que c'est pour cela qu'ils sont maudits de Dieu.

Perhaps the stately measure of the Alexandrines would hardly have permitted to Molière the conceits in which Shakespeare abounded in his younger days, and Meredith to the end of his days. In any case there is no effort after effect. As Meredith himself observes, the wit itself and the humour flow naturally, without emphasis, without any appearance of dexterity. And the reason is the artist's immersion in his subject and his conception of his characters as invested with life. Molière's sympathy with life is the insight of a very wise man. And the very effortless flow of his speech makes it difficult to select instances of particularly glaring wit or humour. The speech is pointed but it is the bubbling over of a personality and the comedy lies in the situations. Just so in real life, humour is so elusive because its expression is found in implications unexpressed, in lights and shades which shift as the speaker proceeds and partly conceal and partly reveal the mind engaged.

In the *Critique de l'École des Femmes*, itself an excellent comedy where Dorante plays the part of good sense and moderation, we have at once one of the best pieces of literary criticism ever written and the best exposition of Molière's attitude. The original play which it defends was a delightful exhibition of the triumph of human nature in the persons of Agnès and her lover over the silly old man (or comparatively old man) her guardian who had brought her up in complete ignorance to be the better wife for himself. Out of the very situation arose incidents which offended the purists in morals or language. Dorante, who is as it were a Philinte turned into a literary critic, urges in the first place that the object of a comedy is to please: 'Je voudrais bien savoir si la grande règle de toutes les règles n'est pas de plaire, et si une pièce de théâtre qui a attrapé son but n'a pas suivi un bon chemin'; and of the rules of art themselves he has just said what no aesthetic doctrine can improve upon: 'Il semble, à vous ouïr parler, que ces règles de l'art soient les plus grands mystères du monde; et cependant ce ne sont que quelques observations aisées, que le bon sens a faites sur ce qui peut ôter le plaisir que l'on prend à ces sortes de poèmes; et le même bon sens qui a fait autrefois ces observations les fait aisément tous les jours, sans le secours d'Horace ou d'Aristote'. Elsewhere he lays down this golden judgment on the right way of judging a play: 'la bonne façon de juger, qui est de se laisser prendre aux choses, et de n'avoir ni prévention aveugle, ni complaisance affectée, ni délicatesse ridicule'. 'Se laisser prendre aux choses' — there is the secret of your Shakespeares and your Molières and all great writers and artists, but particularly great dramatists. Comedy has its special difficulties as compared with serious pieces. 'En un mot, dans les pièces sérieuses il suffit pour n'être point blâmé, de dire des choses qui soient de bon sens et bien écrites; mais ce n'est pas assez dans les autres, il y faut plaisanter; et c'est une étrange entreprise que celle de faire rire les honnêtes gens.' Always good sense and the appeal is to decent men, 'les honnêtes gens'. And for the description of the measure by which they judge I will cite from the speech of Philinte at the beginning of *Le Misanthrope*:

> Mon Dieu! des mœurs du temps mettons nous moins en peine,
> Et faisons un peu grâce à la nature humaine;
> Ne l'examinons point dans la grande rigueur,
> Et voyons ses défauts avec quelque douceur,
> Il faut parmi le monde, une vertu traitable;
> A force de sagesse, on peut être blâmable;
> La parfaite raison fuit toute extrémité,
> Et veut que l'on soit sage avec sobriété.
> Cette grande roideur des vertus des vieux âges
> Heurte trop notre siècle et les communs usages:

MOLIÈRE AND LIFE

Elle veut aux mortels trop de perfection :
Il faut fléchir aux temps sans obstination ;
Et c'est une folie à nulle autre seconde,
De vouloir se mêler de corriger le monde.
J'observe, comme vous, cent choses tous les jours,
Qui pourraient mieux aller, prenant un autre cours ;
Mais, quoi qu'à chaque pas je puisse voir paraître,
En courroux, comme vous, on ne me voit pas être :
Je prends tout doucement les hommes comme ils sont ;
J'accoutume mon âme à souffrir ce qu'ils font,
Et je crois qu'à la cour, de même qu'à la ville,
Mon flegme est philosophe autant que votre bile.[1]

Not a great ideal, as we observe, but sound and sweet. Comedy does not deal with great ideals, not with grand passions. But it rests on the sound basis of usage established by serious men for the daily food of mankind. Perhaps in the passage quoted above from Dorante, Molière in drawing so marked a distinction between plays written to make the audience laugh (which was undoubtedly his purpose in the honest exercise of his craft, as much as Shakespeare thought mainly or only of pleasing in legitimate ways) is hardly conscious of the serious foundation of comedy and certainly does not do justice to it. On which subject enough for my purpose has been said above. It is in the long run only the serious nature which can amuse by legitimate means, and amuse eternally like Molière.

Two things follow from the standard which Molière works to. The first I half fear to mention lest it should be thought that I fancy art is under prudish obligations to morals. It is that Molière's comedy is always clean. Coarse enough he can be in the plain-spoken fashion of his time, calling a spade a spade. But he is never gross or inflammatory. (Our own time, just because it is less plain-spoken, conceals a greater peril or rather has a harder artistic problem to solve.) The reticence of the 'honnêtes gens' follows the author who writes for them; and it is only prudes who could blush at the so-called

[1] Compare Ariste in Sc. 1 of *L'École des Maris*.

indelicacies of the *École des Femmes*. On the stage, even the rollicking licence of speech of *Le Médecin malgré lui* disappears under the cloud of honest laughter. The other feature is that he is never venomous. Not even Tartuffe is drawn venomously, though indignation mixes with the laughter he provokes. Molière is a good fighter and strikes manfully, but though he mocks, and as a comedian therefore falls short of the ideal of his scientific contemporary Spinoza, like Spinoza he does not despise. Only, being a comic writer and not a philosopher, the honest emotions of the ' honnêtes gens ' are reflected in his comedy. He never wearies of exposing the doctors ; but it is their formalism and pretentiousness and traditionalism or professionalism at which he laughs. They seem not to have been altogether blameless. Locke in his diary describes a graduation scene in the medical faculty at Montpellier, where he was staying, in words of which the famous induction of the bachelor of medicine in *Le Malade Imaginaire* is hardly a caricature, and Molière may in his early days in the South have witnessed such a ceremony. But there is no trace in Molière of the venom which animates Mr. Shaw in our own days. Molière is content to laugh. Physiology was only beginning in his day, which saw the researches of Harvey, and medicine has now become a science. Yet possibly even now there would be honest physicians who would admit that their profession is in some degree open to the laughter of Molière. After all the doctors enter only into his farces, even the *Malade* is hardly more than half comedy, half farce. Molière did not believe that doctors were of much use. But whether the pitiful story is true that they refused to attend him in his last illness and revenged themselves, I do not know.

III

The doctors take us into the world of Molière's farces, which no lover of Molière dare pass by without some brief mention. In his excellent work *Molière* (2 vols., Paris, 1908) Mr. Eugène Rigal has shown how the true comedy of

MOLIÈRE AND LIFE

Molière grew out of his farce. His early comedies, *L'Étourdi* and *Le Dépit Amoureux*, were imitations of the current Italian or Spanish types of comedy of intrigue, and incident, though the second of the two is relieved by the charming scene of lovers' misunderstanding to which he was to revert in *Le Tartuffe* and the *Bourgeois*. He found himself and prepared for his mission of serious comedy by 'leaving clever and complicated intrigue and adopting the modest framework of farce, but filling it so well with studies of manners and character that the frame cracked'. He did this with the two farces which stormed Paris, the *Précieuses Ridicules* and *Sganarelle ou Le Cocu Imaginaire*, in which last the name Sganarelle replaces that of Mascarille borne hitherto by the farcical heroes of his plays. For it is still the Marquis Mascarille who in the *Précieuses* enters the drawing-room of Madelon and Cathos in the dress described by the diarists which sent the audience into vociferous laughter. After Sganarelle the name of Mascarille disappears for ever from Molière's plays, and the change marks the step from incident to character. Mr. Rigal reckons the *École des Maris* amongst the farce-like comedies, which lead on to the *École des Femmes*, and in the end to the great comedies which are the last stage of Molière's art. But all the while down to his death he was writing farces, and earning for himself the *fou rire* of his audience. Largely they were made to divert the Court, and often written with great rapidity. Mr. Rigal observes how unjust accordingly is Boileau's insinuation against Molière, when the ties of friendship between them had been loosened, that he wrote farces to please the populace:

> Molière, illustrant ses écrits,
> Peut-être de son art eût remporté le prix,
> Si, moins ami du peuple, en ses doctes peintures
> Il n'eût point fait souvent grimacer ses figures,
> Quitté, pour le bouffon, l'agréable et le fin
> Et sans honte à Térence allié Tabarin.

In the first place, it was the Court that ordered most of his farces; it was the bourgeoisie that made the success of the great plays; and next, Molière required no inducement to write farces and showed no repugnance in doing so. They reek, in fact, positively with their author's delight. Poor Molière had sorrows enough; but his spirits were irrepressible and the edge of his gaiety never dulled. When the writing of *Le Bourgeois Gentilhomme* became too difficult for the time at his disposal, he lapsed into farce after the third act. Some commentators please themselves in shrugging their shoulders over this lapse and over other cases in which more restrained farce turns into rollicking fun. For example, in *Le Mariage Forcé*, after the half-grave interview with the sceptical philosopher whom the old man Sganarelle consults as to the wisdom of his marrying his very young ward — the succeeding visit to the Peripatetic Pancrace is a scene of the wildest and most outrageous fun, repeating more exuberantly the scene of *Le Dépit Amoureux* in which Albert consults the philosophical tutor Métaphraste on the future of his pupil, Albert's son.

We may shake grave heads of disapproval over these frequent lapses of Molière from the highest levels of his art. But perhaps it is better to be thankful for what we have. Could the gaiety and wit of the comedies proper have been maintained had Molière had no outlet for his sheer love of fun? And does anyone seriously regret the conferring upon M. Jourdain of the dignity of Mamamouchi? or feel ungratefully unmoved when the Grand Turk and his attendants rise and pronounce the words, ' Ha la ba, ba la chou, ba la ba, ba la da?' A good critic has declared *Le Médecin malgré lui* to be the greatest farce ever written, and it is certainly the most famous one. I do not envy the feelings or the judgment of those who do not thank God for the Molière of the farces.

Moreover, even they are suffused with that air of good sense and reasonableness which is the very life blood of the comedies. The nurse, Jacqueline, in *Le Médecin malgré lui*, observes when they are going to bring in the new doctor to cure Lucile's dumbness, ' la meilleure médeçaine que l'an pourrait bailler à votre fille, ce serait, selon moi, un biau et bon mari, pour qui alle eût de l'amiquié '. M. de Pourçeaugnac, who thinks himself the incarnation of common sense, is mocked in the name of good sense for his foolish and impudent aspiration, being as he is a citizen of Limoges, to marry a Parisian girl; and, being charged in the teeth of all evidence with having already a wife, is gravely assured by two lawyers that polygamy is a hanging matter, on the authority of great lawyers and the customs of civilised peoples, whose names are strung together in a way which makes Molière the forerunner of our own W. S. Gilbert.[1] In the semi-farce, *Le Malade Imaginaire*,

[1] *Premier Avocat.*
La polygamie est un cas,
   Est un cas pendable.
    Second Avocat.
     Votre fait
Est clair et net ;
Et tout de droit,
Sur cet endroit,
Conclut tout droit.
Si vous consultez nos auteurs,
Législateurs et glossateurs,
Justinian, Papinian,
Ulpian et Tribonian,
Fernand, Rebuffe, Jean Imole,
Paul, Castie, Julian, Barthole,
Jason, Alciat, et Cujas,
   Ce grand homme si capable ;
La polygamie est un cas,
   Est un cas pendable.

Tous les peuples policés,
   Et bien sensés ;
Les Français, Anglais, Hollandais,
Danois, Suédois, Polonais,
Portugais, Espagnols, Flamands,
   Italiens, Allemands,
Sur ce fait tiennent loi semblable ;
Et l'affaire est sans embarras ;
La polygamie est un cas,
   Est un cas pendable.
    Premier Avocat.
La polygamie est un cas,
   Est un cas pendable.
      — (Act II, Sc. 3)

MOLIÈRE AND LIFE

Toinette the maid is the last of those adorable young women, half servants and half confidantes, from Lisette, and Dorine in *Le Tartuffe*, onwards, who embody just judgment in racy speech and are perhaps the great glory of Molière's women, unless we rather incline to the Henriettes and the Célimènes.

In fine, the story is always the same. Whether Molière is writing farce and leaving the judgment of his extravagance not so much to the characters who take the side of good sense and reason as to the audience itself; or is writing in the grave mood which befits the highest comedy, he is always the humane and wise, who makes faulty human nature in all its forms show itself up for its folly or its wisdom or in some cases for its harmfulness. It is only that in the great comedies he rises to the highest point of that insight into our strength and our weaknesses from which his whole humour issues. He is so great an artist because he has this command of subject and because with him ' se laisser prendre aux choses ' overflows into clear and graceful and witty speech.

I have said and intend to say little or nothing of Molière's artistry of words. For two good reasons, the first that I am concerned with his outlook upon life as we find it in the plays. The second because I have not the competence to judge him as a stylist. Boileau himself in earlier days lost himself in admiration of Molière's facility and elegance. He is accused by those who know of carelessness of style, and on many occasions he was writing against time. You are struck by the ease and unrestraint of the verse. You desiderate the lyric gift which makes Shakespeare's lighter fancies so enchanting, or turns some of his heroes like Macbeth into poets. Molière is no romantic but the dramatist of good sense and moderation. Yet in all this equable speech there is the greatest variety. He was not, as everyone knows, scrupulous about where he found his goods, and stole where he found. Sometimes he hardly varies a word, though the variation is critical, and his victim is forgotten and

MOLIÈRE AND LIFE

Molière is immortalised by his thievings.

>Le véritable Amphitryon
>C'est l'Amphitryon où l'on dîne,

is taken almost verbally from a poet Rotrou. He took Cyrano's ' que diable aller faire dans la galère d'un Turc ', and making the old father ask the question in a very slightly different form and with equally insane desperation he made it glorious. Perhaps the late E. Rostand did justice to poor Cyrano's generosity when he makes him say sadly of the rival (unhandicapped by a portentous nose) who displaced him in the affections of Roxane, and of the man who stole his wit :

>Molière a du génie, et Christian était beau.

I could not trust myself for want of knowledge to compare his style with that of other great writers of French. It seems to me both limpid and sparkling. I should not equal it with that of his great contemporary, Pascal, but what prose writer but Plato is worthy of such a comparison ? and what poets but some who are greater than Molière have such mastery of direct and passionate speech ? He is rather to be appraised in comparison with Corneille and Racine and Boileau, with La Fontaine and Voltaire ; and I have not the necessary competence. One quality of Molière's writing deserves a special mention. It is his amazing virtuosity ; his power derived, no doubt, from his habit of close observation, of making things and persons live by their details. The best example that I know is the speech of the hunting bore in *Les Fâcheux* (The Bores) : the play he wrote rapidly for Fouquet's entertainment of the king at Vaux (described by Dumas in the *Vicomte de Bragelonne*) from which the host went to his arrest and disgrace. The speech bristles with technicalities and detains the lover from his engagement with his mistress with the arresting copiousness which only a bore can inflict. This was ' se laisser prendre aux choses ' with a vengeance.

MOLIÈRE AND LIFE

Noscitur a sociis : a man is known by the company he keeps. I hope it may not weigh greatly against my character if I confess that two of my greatest intimates through life, perhaps the two greatest intimates, outside the circle of philosophers, have been Dr. Johnson and Molière ; with whom as the old scholar says in Southey's poem, ' I take delight in weal and seek relief in woe '. Others, perhaps, for hours of rapture ; for habit and solid felicity, these two. No one would for a moment put Johnson (even at his best in conversation as he appears in Boswell's book), with Molière as an artist or a literary figure. Johnson belongs indeed to the English-speaking people, but Molière to the world. They have, however, one trait in common, their knowledge of life and their wise humanity. With what amateurish inadequacy I have appraised Molière in this paper I know well. But at least I have tried to express in some measure the gratitude that I feel to a great man, a great artist, an inexhaustible spring of wisdom and gaiety, and a most dear friend.

V

PASCAL THE WRITER [1]

(Reprinted, by permission, from the *Bulletin of the John Rylands Library*, July 1931)

PASCAL, who was the inventor of the modern omnibus, anticipated also the extremely common modern habit of wearing a watch on the left wrist. He compares 'those who judge a work by feeling rather than by some rule to those who do not possess watches in their estimate of the time. One says it has been two hours, the other says, only three quarters of an hour. I look at my watch and say to the first, you are bored, and to the other, you hardly notice the time; for it has been an hour and a half, and I laugh at those who say that time is my time and that I judge its duration by fancy: they do not know that I judge time by my watch' (5, 137).[2] All the same, as Mr. Brunschvicg points out in his note on this passage, Pascal himself would insist that while precision in estimating time can be secured only by the watch, which is an invention of reason, time itself, the idea of time, is not given to us by reason but by intuition, like all the fundamental principles — categories people are nowadays apt to say — such as space or time or number or movement. All such parts of our experience we receive through what Pascal calls the heart, as in the famous saying, 'the heart has its reasons which reason does not know'. Reason pursues with precision and order the ideas which are supplied from elsewhere. Pascal himself is a model of the union

[1] Address given at the John Rylands Library on April 15, 1931.
[2] References are to the smaller edition of the *Pensées* by Mr. Brunschvicg. At the same time the marginal numbers of the passage in the original edition as given by Mr. Brunschvicg are noted after his number.

in a writer of precision, and order, the *esprit de géométrie*, and the delicate adjustment of words and thought to the subject, which he calls *justesse*.

It is a commonplace that he belongs to the great masters of literature ; and perhaps few would quarrel with the proposition, which I venture in my ignorance of general literature, that he is the greatest master of prose since Plato. Perhaps I should say the greatest master known to me since Plato. The comparison with Plato is obvious. The earlier *Provincial Letters* in which the writer records his visits to the several representatives of learned doctrine, Molinist, Thomist, Jansenist, and ironically sets their answers about the question of grace in relation to the Jansenist doctrine which he represents himself, recall the delightful comedy and irony of some of Plato's earlier dialogues, especially the *Euthydemus*. And then as the argument deepens and irony and playfulness are succeeded by the deadly tearing off the mask from the Jesuit books of casuistry, until at last he breaks out into direct and passionate invective, you are reminded of Plato's passionate attacks upon democracy in the *Republic*, and on the Sophists there and in the more famous pictures of the Sophist in the *Gorgias* and the *Theaetetus*. Plato's passion is indeed always under control and cloaked by an even urbaner irony than Pascal possessed. And the great passages in Plato upon philosophy and love, or rather upon philosophy as the highest form of love, are not unfitting exemplars in their beauty and elevation of thought of the more impassioned passages of the *Pensées*, such as those which show how the wretchedness of man's condition and his greatness in knowing his own weakness culminate in the knowledge of God as set forth in Christianity, or the sublime description of the two infinites, which I shall presently quote. Both writers illustrate how hard it may be to define the limits in such exalted passages between prose and poetry, harder when we think of Plato than, as I shall try to show, when we think of Pascal.

Pascal is a great master of the natural style, and even of

what is called the plain style, simple and unadorned, of which our own best example is Swift. He does not appear to have been a student of literature, except of Montaigne and except that he knew Descartes, who was one of the influences in making classical French prose, of which Pascal himself is generally acknowledged to be the consummate master. In clearness and precision he must have been helped by his studies in mathematics and physics; and he possessed by natural gift the unselfconsciousness which is the prerequisite of the highest art. Whether by nature or habit, he had acquired the power of saying things in the simplest possible manner, with exact accommodation to the needs of the subject, which is characteristic of the 'universal' manner, so that his greatness as a writer is as manifest to the stranger as to his own countrymen, and no intimacy with French literature is required of me to accept the judgment upon him of an expert historian of French literature like Mr. G. Lanson. His perfection of style, though it would seem to have been spontaneous with him, was by no means without labour, witness his own famous saying about one of the 'provincials' which had been very long, that he could have made it shorter if he had had more time. And the manuscript of the *Pensées* is scored with corrections. These great artists who talk ordinary language exquisitely are not the less artists because they seem to write at ease. Yet in thinking of Pascal we can never forget that his limpid style was the work of a mind, subtle indeed and complex, but utterly sincere, and so much a creature of natural beauty as makes it difficult to speak of him in measured terms of admiration. I feel myself unequal to the task of describing him as a thinker or as a religious teacher,[1] and am limiting myself to speaking of him as a creator of great literature, which anyone who fails to appreciate, because repelled perhaps by his austerity and melancholy or by the now hopeless anachronism of his theological learning, is self-condemned.

[1] I may refer to the excellent book of Mr. Clement Webb, *Pascal's Philosophy of Religion*, Oxford, 1929.

PASCAL THE WRITER

Pascal has himself in the first section of the *Pensées* given his ideas of the natural style. It partakes both of the *esprit de géométrie* and the *esprit de finesse*. The distinction is well known, but I must quote it (1, 405). 'In the one the principles are palpable, but remote from common usage; so that it is hard to turn one's head to that side, from want of habit; but however little one does so, one sees the principles in full; and one would need to have a quite perverse mind (*l'esprit faux*) to reason ill upon principles so gross that they can hardly possibly escape one. But in the *esprit de finesse* the principles are in common use and before the eyes of everyone. One has not to turn one's head or do oneself violence; the only need is to have good sight, but one must have it good; for the principles are so minute (*déliés*) and so numerous, that some of them can hardly avoid escaping one. Now the omission of a principle leads to error; thus one must have very clear sight to see all the principles involved, and, next, one must have insight (*l'esprit juste*) not to reason wrongly upon known principles. Geometers who are nothing but geometers have correct minds, provided only that everything is explained to them by definitions and principles; otherwise they are perverse and unbearable, for they only keep straight and correct upon well-explained principles. And fine minds which are nothing else have not the patience to descend into the first principles of things of speculation and imagination, which they have not seen in the world and which are outside of common use.' Pascal himself, so far as we are concerned with him here, is, as said above, a geometer in respect of his order and precision, but he is more particularly an *esprit fin*. 'True eloquence', he says (15, 130), 'consists in establishing a correspondence between the mind and heart of the persons to whom one is speaking on one side, and on the other the thoughts and expressions which one uses; which supposes a previous study of man's heart in order to know the springs of its action, and to discover next the proper proportions of the discourse to be adjusted to them. We must put ourselves in the place of those who are to hear us and make a trial on our own heart of the turn we give to our discourse, to see if the one is made for the other and if we can feel sure that the hearer will be as it were compelled to surrender. We must constrain ourselves as much as possible within what is simply natural ; not make big what is small, nor small what is big. It is not enough that a thing should be beautiful, it must be suitable to the subject, with nothing too much and nothing wanting.' Or again, ' There is a certain model of beauty and agreeableness which consists in a certain ratio between our nature, weak or strong as it may be, and the thing which pleases us ' (32, *129). He laughs at so-called ' poetic beauty ' which decks out its object with superfluous ornaments. ' Imagine a woman on this pattern, which consists in saying small things with big words : you will see a pretty girl covered with chains and glasses (*miroirs*), and will laugh at her, because you know better in what consists the agreeableness of a woman than the agreeableness of verses. But the inexpert would admire her in this array ; and there are villages which would take her for the Queen ' (33, *129). Hence (29, 427) ' when we see the natural style we are astonished and delighted ; for we expected to see an author and we find a man '. Those who speak or write thus are universal persons, the *honnêtes gens* : they carry no badge of poet or mathematician ; these talk the language of cultivated men. And the natural style in writing is the same. It is ' the manner of Epictetus, of Montaigne, and of Salomon de Tultie ' [that is the supposed author of the *Provincial Letters*] (18, *443).

The inimitable ease and force and urbanity of the *Provincials* I cannot find short passages to illustrate by. With the *Pensées* the difficulty is the opposite. I read a few passages almost at random :

On *Diversion* (139, 133). How is it that this man who lost a few months ago his only son and who, overwhelmed with lawsuits and quarrels, was this morning so disturbed, thinks of it no more now ? Be not astonished ; he is entirely occupied in watching where the boar will pass, which the dogs have been pursuing with such ardour these six hours. Nothing more is needed. However full a man be of sorrow, if you can prevail upon him to enter into some amusement, he is happy for that time ; and a man, however happy he may be, if he is not distracted and occupied by some passion or diversion which prevents ennui from extending, will soon be sore and unhappy. Without distraction there is no joy, with it there is no sorrow (217). And it is this which constitutes the happiness of persons of great condition, that they have a number of persons to amuse them, and that they can maintain themselves in this state.

Or this, which calls up to mind a celebrated passage of Newman's *Apologia* :

(693, 1). Seeing the blindness and wretchedness of man, beholding all the universe dumb, and man without light, left to himself, and as it were astray in this corner of the universe, without knowing who has set him there, what he is come there to do, and what will become of him when he dies without the capacity of any knowledge, I fall into terror as a man who should have been carried asleep into a desert and terrible island and should wake up without knowing where he is and without means of going away. And thereupon I wonder how one does not fall into despair at so wretched an estate. I see others near me of like nature ; I ask them if they are better furnished with knowledge than I ; they say no ; and thereupon these wretched strays look around them and seeing some amusing objects give themselves up and attach themselves to these. For myself, I can make no such attachment, and considering how much more probable it is that there is something else than what I see, I have enquired whether this God would not have left some sign of himself.

I see many religions contrary to each other and consequently all false except one. Each claims its own authority for belief and threatens unbelievers. I do not believe them in this. Anyone may say so, anyone may call himself prophet. But I see the Christian religion in which there are actual prophecies, and this is not a thing that anyone can do.

(550, 194) I love poverty, because He loved it. I love money because it gives the means of helping the wretched. I keep faith with everyone, I do not return evil to those who do me evil ; but I desire for them a condition like my own, receiving from men neither good nor evil. I endeavour to be just, true, sincere, and faithful to all ; and I have an affection for those to whom

God has united me more nearly ; and whether I am alone or in sight of men I have before me in all my actions the sight of God, who will judge them, and to whom I have consecrated them all.

Such are my feelings, and all the days of my life I bless my Redeemer who has implanted them in me, and who out of a man full of weakness and wretchedness, of concupiscence, pride and ambition, has made a man exempt from all these evils by the power of his grace, to which all the praise of it is owing, for I have from myself nothing but wretchedness and error.

The general rhythm of Pascal's style is long and continuous, but it is diversified by pithy sentences of wit or passion. Sometimes they light up the sombre atmosphere of the *Pensées* with blinding flashes. ' The eternal silence of these infinite spaces terrifies me ' (206, Copie 101) ; '*gloire et rebut de l'univers*' (pride and refuse of the universe) which should be read in its context ; ' Judge of all things, imbecile earthworm ; depositary of truth, sewer of uncertainty and error ; pride and refuse of the universe '. These sayings have a lyric cry, and we may add to them the famous ' Be comforted, you would not seek me if you had not already found me ' (553, 89). There is the terrible ' naturally that will bring you faith and stupefy you (*cela vous fera croire et vous abêtira*) ' about following the practices of religion — masses and holy water, after accepting the argument of the wager (233, 3). There are others less charged with emotion but heavy with thought. Such are ' Man is but a reed, the weakest in nature ; but a thinking reed ', where again the whole context is needed for the effect. It goes on : ' It needs not that the whole universe be in arms to crush him ; a vapour, a drop of water suffices to kill him. But though the universe should crush him, man would be still more noble than his slayer, for he knows that he dies, and as for the advantage which the universe has over him, the universe knows nothing of it ' (347, 63). Other passages have by their felicity or profundity become so familiar that we forget their origin : ' if Cleopatra's nose had been shorter, the whole face of the earth would have been different ' (162, 487) ; ' Truth this side of the Pyrenees, error on the other side' (294, 23) — on the relativity of human justice.

Some of these passages illustrate the two salient features of Pascal's mind as it is expressed in the *Pensées*; his scepticism or Pyrrhonism as a thinker, and his religious fervour which resolves the perplexity and doubt into which he is thrown by his contemplation of the misery and the greatness of man. But I am not concerned with the substance of Pascal but with his style. It is the plain or natural style, but full of imagination and vivid in its presentation of things. If anyone fancies that the plain style does not admit imagination, he need only remember the charm of Berkeley (whom, by the way, Mr. Saintsbury takes to be the chief of our prose writers in English), or that Swift on occasion is both pictorial and eloquent. I will read two passages of Swift to point this statement. The first is a famous piece in *Gulliver* (p. 1571),[1] the second one from the *Tale of a Tub* (p. 61).[1]

For I remember very well, in a discourse one day with the king, when I happened to say there were several thousand books among us written upon the art of self-government, it gave him (directly contrary to my intention) a very mean opinion of our understandings. He professed both to abominate and despise all mystery, refinement, and intrigue whether in a prince or a minister. He could not tell what I meant by secrets of state, where an enemy, or some rival nation, were not in the case. He confined the knowledge of governing within very narrow bounds, to common sense and reason, to justice and lenity, to the speedy determination of civil and criminal causes; with some other obvious topics, which are not worth considering. And he gave it for his opinion, that whoever could make two ears of corn, or blades of grass, to grow upon a spot of ground where only one grew before, would deserve better of mankind, and do more essential service to his country, than the whole race of politicians put together.

The worshippers of this deity had also a system of their belief, which seemed to turn upon the following fundamentals. They held the universe to be a large suit of clothes, which invests

---

[1] These page-numbers are given, in the original, without explanation. [Editor's note.]

everything : that the earth is invested by the air ; the air is invested by the stars ; and the stars are invested by the *primum mobile*. Look on this globe of earth, you will find it to be a very complete and fashionable dress. What is that which some call land, but a fine coat faced with green ?, or the sea, but a waistcoat of water tabby ? Proceed to the particular works of the creation, you will find how curious journeyman Nature has been to trim up the vegetable beaux ; observe how sparkish a periwig adorns the head of a beech, and what a fine doublet of white satin is worn by the birch. To conclude from all, what is man himself but a micro-coat, or rather a complete suit of clothes with all its trimmings ? as to his body there can be no dispute ; but examine even the acquirements of his mind, you will find them all contribute in their order towards furnishing out an exact dress : to instance no more ; is not religion a cloak, honesty a pair of shoes worn out in the dirt, self-love a surtout, vanity a shirt, and conscience a pair of breeches, which though a cover for lewdness as well as for nastiness, is easily slipt down for the service of both ?

They are both full of satire in their several ways, but they serve to show how the plain style can vary even in a man like Swift who does not rank especially among the poets. But Pascal's writing is of a higher order, if only because he had the exaltation which Swift lacked. I will quote part of the passage on the two infinites :

This is where natural knowledge leads us. If it is not true, there is no truth in man ; if it is true, he has in it a great ground of humiliation, compelled as he is in one or other manner to feel his abasement. And he cannot live without believing it. I wish before he enters into larger inquiries into nature that he should for once consider nature seriously and at leisure, that he should also see himself and knowing what proportion he bears. . . . Let him then contemplate all nature in her full and exalted majesty, removing his eyes from the mean objects which surround him. Let him regard this brilliant light, set like an eternal lamp to illumine the universe ; let him see the earth as a point in comparison of the vast orbit which this star describes, and think with astonishment that this orbit is but a very delicate point compared with that which the stars that roll in the firmament comprehend. But if our sight stop there, let imagination go out beyond ; it will rather weary in conceiving than nature in supplying. All this visible world is but an imperceptible spot in the ample bosom of nature.

No idea approaches it. In vain we make big our conceptions till they reach beyond imaginable spaces, we do but produce atoms in comparison of the reality of things. It is a sphere whose centre is everywhere, whose circumference nowhere. And it is the greatest sensible mark of the omnipotence of God that our imagination is lost in this thought.

Let man return to himself and consider what he is in proportion of existence ; regard himself as strayed into this remote corner of nature ; and from this little hiding-place where he lurks (I think of the universe) let him learn to judge the earth, the kingdoms, the towns and himself at their just measure.

What is a man in the infinite ?

But, that he may be aware of another prodigy as astounding, let him inquire into the most delicate things in what he knows. A mite will offer him in its small body parts infinitely smaller, limbs with joints, veins in its limbs, blood in its veins, humours in this blood, drops in these humours, vapours in these drops ; let him divide up these last things again and exhaust his powers in such conceptions until the last object he can reach becomes the object we are speaking of ; he will think perhaps that he has reached the extremest minuteness in nature. I will make him see therein a new abyss ; I will paint for him within the circuit of this tiny atom not only the visible universe, but the immensity of what we can conceive in nature. He shall see therein an infinity of universes, each of which has its firmament, its planets, its earth, in the same proportion as the visible world : in that earth animals and mites in which he shall find once more what the first mites offered ; and finding again in the others the same thing without end and without rest, he shall be lost in these wonders as astounding in their smallness as the former ones by their largeness ; for who would not wonder if our body which before was almost not perceptible in the universe, imperceptible indeed in the bosom of the whole, should be now a colossus, a world or rather a whole, in comparison of the nothing which he fails to reach.

He who shall consider himself in this fashion will be terrified at himself, and, considering himself poised, in the mass nature has given him, between these two abysses of infinity and nothing, he will quail in view of these wonders ; and I think that his curiosity changing into astonishment, he will be rather disposed to contemplate them in silence than search them out with presumption.

For indeed what is man in nature ? A nothing in respect of

the infinite, a whole in regard of the nothing, a mean between nothing and the whole. Infinitely far from comprehending the extremes, the purpose and the principle of things are shrouded for him in an impenetrable secrecy, incapable as he is of seeing either the nothing from which he proceeds or the infinite in which he is engulfed.

What will he do then except apprehend some appearance and mean of things, in an eternal despair of knowing either their principle or their end ? All things come from the nothing and are borne on to the infinite. Who shall follow these astounding steps ? The author of these wonders comprehends them. None other can. (72, 347.)

Many would be inclined to say that this wonderful writing is, in spite of its prose form, poetry and the prose writing of a poet. And to two at least of the famous sentences I quoted before, ' Le silence, etc.' and ' Console-toi, etc.', it is difficult to deny the character of poetry. A French friend of my own, and a distinguished writer, declared to me that Pascal was not only the greatest French writer of prose, but the greatest French poet ; and I imagined at first that he might be using poetry as the name of all literary art, I mean writing which is not mere craft as most prose and much verse is, but in the strict sense art, and not merely skilful but beautiful.

But I understand that this is not ordinary French usage, as the word ' Ditcher ' is used in German for any imaginative writer ; and the proposition is staggering to one who thinks of Shakespeare as a supreme poet and Swift as a supreme prose writer. At any rate it is worth while, I think, to raise in respect of Pascal the old question of the difference between prose and poetry, for I shall plead that Pascal is not a poet, nor the great piece I have quoted the prose writing of a really poetic nature. I do not mean merely that he does not write the hybrid thing called poetic prose or prose-poetry. Pascal himself would have scorned such an imputation — that it could be said of him what he quotes from Petronius (29, 427) *plus poetice quam humane locutus es* (' you have spoken rather as a poet than a man'). What I mean is that for all the glory which imagination and vividness may throw over his words, he remains what he claims to be. The passage does indeed come very near to poetry. But Plato, who is a far more imaginative writer, comes even nearer to poetry than Pascal and yet he writes prose. In reading the *Symposium* and the *Phaedrus*, one asks if these speeches about love and philosophy are not really poetry written without metre and in the form of prose ; and one has to recall that sometimes Plato is parodying Agathon and Aristophanes, who were poets. But Plato, as it happens, did write poems, and to be convinced that we are reading prose and not poetry in these two dialogues we need only compare them with the two famous epigrams which have come down to us as being from him (at any rate they are worthy of so great a man) :

Once you shone among the living as the star of dawn, now that you are gone you shine among the dead as the evening star.

You gaze at the stars, my star ; I would that I might become the heaven, to look at you with many eyes.

Could anyone doubt that this imperfect English is not prose but a translation of a poem, itself of Wordsworthian simplicity of diction, into the mere form of prose and not into the diction of prose ; any more than he can feel the same doubt about passages in the Bible like ' By the rivers of Babylon ', etc. ?

Contrast, before I pass on, the Pascal passage with Hamlet's famous lyrical outburst whose topic is almost precisely the same as that of the first paragraph quoted above :

I have of late — but wherefore I know not — lost all my mirth, forgone all custom of exercises ; and indeed it goes so heavily with my disposition that this goodly frame, the earth, seems to me a sterile promontory; this most excellent canopy, the air, look you, this brave overhanging firmament, this majestical roof fretted with golden fire, why, it appears no other thing to me but a foul and pestilent congregation of vapours. What a piece of work is man ! How noble in reason ! how infinite in faculty ! in form, in moving, how express and admirable ! in action how like an angel ! in apprehension how like a god ! the beauty of the world ! the paragon of animals ! And yet to me what is this quintessence of dust ? man delights not me ; no, nor woman neither, though by your smiling you seem to say so (*Hamlet*, Act II, Sc. 2).

That is the work of a man who is a poet, and it is, I suppose, poetry, and if we ask why it is written in prose, the answer is (I borrow the observation) that Hamlet is playing a part to deceive his interlocutors. The speech is lyrical, but it is in prose form to suit the rest of the conversation. On the other hand, there would be no doubt that Pascal's lovely confession in the passage 550 quoted on page 193[1] is lovely prose but not lyrical, rather a statement of his feelings made for instruction of his reader.

I know that the difference of prose and poetry is almost insoluble in its difficulty. It might seem easiest to follow the Maître de Philosophie in the *Bourgeois Gentilhomme* and say that ' What is not prose is verse and what is not verse is prose ' — a mere difference in the form, metrical or unmetrical. But the answer is too easy. For in the first place there is the difference of diction, and Coleridge showed conclusively that even Wordsworth's diction, which Wordsworth took to be the diction of ordinary life and prose, is not really so, though it is true that sometimes in ordinary life men talk poetry because, as will be suggested later, they are not describing or expounding but are themselves, and talk as the bird sings out of the fullness of their life and passion, are in a word dramatic or lyrical. And in the second place the question still remains, what is it that makes one man adopt the form of prose and another that of poetry ? Some have said, like Mr. H. Read, that the difference is one of quality, and I believe that this is true. But it does not follow that, as he thinks, it is indescribable, or that it cannot at least be brought home to the mind by attempts, however imperfect, at analysis, or at the worst, setting it in its due relation with other things.

[1] Of these *Pieces*, *i.e.* the passage beginning ' I love poetry, because He loved it '. [Editor's note.]

PASCAL THE WRITER

It may be described, as some have thought, as a difference of purpose. The first virtue of prose, Sir A. Quiller-Couch says in the preface of his *Oxford Book of English Prose*, is persuasion ; whether his description of the first virtue of poetry, as a high-compelling emotion, which he substitutes for Clutton-Brock's word love, is right or not is open to question, as indeed the whole place of the element of emotion in the arts is obscure. We may say, perhaps, that the prose writer explains, and the poet sings, as it were, to relieve his soul. Perhaps these statements are true, and they are certainly helpful. But we should prefer to know what prose and poetry are rather than the differing motives of them, or what follows from their different natures. Now it is useful, I believe, to start from the vividness or imaginativeness which makes many think that highly imaginative prose is poetry, and to distinguish between the two in this very respect of vividness and imaginativeness. The prose writer may use all his arts to bring his subject before the reader's mind ; but it is one thing to exhibit a topic vividly to the mind so that the mind cannot help seeing it and believing it ; it is another thing to put the reader's mind actually into the reality he is describing, and that is what the poet does. The subject is not merely brought before the mind, but the mind is made to live in it, because the subject, whether a human being or daffodils or a flock of sheep that leisurely pass by one after one, or a battle, or Melrose Abbey, are depicted in their reality, as they live their own lives or live in themselves. The poet shares the life of what he describes and he communicates to us the life which he himself has shared.

In other words, for the statement is but a technical repetition, prose is analytical and gives a picture of what is described. Poetry is synthetical or if you prefer intuitive ; or better still it is concrete : it sees into the life of things, to borrow a famous phrase of Wordsworth. The objects of poetry are things as they exist, whether they are living things and live, or inanimate things which fulfil their destiny. You are not merely looking on at them, and seeing them clearly in consequence of the writer's skill; they are dramatic and you live in their lives. Poetry creates a world and prose describes it. The differing purposes of the two follow from these essential characters. Prose persuades and instructs; poetry is its own end and aim, it creates its object and has no thought of anything else. The varying choice of subjects and method of handling them are one alike with the purpose of the two and the motives from which they arise. Poetry has no aim beyond its own satisfaction, prose aims to enlighten.

Perhaps, however, we should rather say that the difference is relative and that in proportion as literature (for it is only literary art of which I speak) attains concreteness and the self-contained unity of concrete things it is poetic, and in proportion as it is content to analyse it is prose. The concreteness of poetry explains too why the poet needs for his expression (and he is not a poet without expression in words) greater resources of technique in comparison with prose: for metre and rhyme are, as Coleridge showed, means whereby the unity is secured in the object to which the poet gives life or depicts in its actual life; and poetic diction, in so far as it is genuine and not artificial, has the property of other magic that it helps to make real the world of things which the poet fashions to his own desires and makes us in turn desire.

The most satisfactory way to test these or any other suggestions of the kind is to set side by side with each other passages of acknowledged poetry and acknowledged prose whose subject matter is roughly identical, and note the difference of treatment of diction and how even the subject is altered in the two cases. I cannot do so here, but I propose to confirm my judgment of Pascal by contrasting with the *Pensées*, which so often approaches to poetry but remains prose, Robert Bridges' *Testament of Beauty*, which so often approaches prose and sometimes actually falls into versified prose and yet is throughout poetry. I do not ask whether it belongs to great poetry, it is too near ourselves to judge its place as yet. I should not dare myself to value it so highly as some have done; nor should I think it for a moment as great in poetry as Pascal's work in prose, for I remark that though poetry is a higher literature than prose, much poetry is inferior in greatness to much prose. But it is beautiful beyond question, and what is most to my purpose, though its subject is explicitly a philosophy, like the poem of Lucretius to which it is most easily comparable, and at the first blush recalcitrant to poetic treatment, it is beyond question poetry; and my object is to ask why; or rather to ask whether it conforms to the test which I have suggested.

Bridges' poem is long and it is didactic, and both these characters make the judgment of it difficult. A long poem cannot sustain itself always on the higher level. Inevitably it drops into mere verse. If this is true of the *Prelude* it is much more true of the *Testament of Beauty*, and it would be quite easy to quote passages of mere prose, passages, I mean, which except for the metre are indistinguishable from prose, especially in the Fourth Book, where the poetic inspiration flags in comparison with the other three parts. I will quote one such passage merely for verification (III, 151):

> Yet our distinction is proper and holdeth fast. Now BREED
> is to the race as SELFHOOD to the individual;
> and these two prime instincts as they differ in purpose
> are independent each from other, and separate
> as are the organic tracts in the animal body
> whereby they function; and tho' Breed is needful alike
> to plants as to animals, yet its apparatus
> is found in animals of a more special kind,
> and since race-propagation might have been assured
> without differentiation of sex, we are left to guess
> nature's intention from its full effects in man:
> And such matter is the first that will follow hereon.
> — (III, 151-162)

I cite this merely, as I said, for verification of my statement, not for reproach. A long poem must be taken as a whole if we ask whether it is truly poetical: we judge by the unity and spirit of the whole. For a different reason we dare not judge by thinking only of the special passages of lyrical beauty, which abound in this poem as they abound in Lucretius. Even Bridges himself, somewhat unfairly I must think, seems to suggest that he cared for Lucretius not as the poet of the atomic theory of Epicurus but as the author of the glorious invocation to Venus and we might add of those other passages in which he rises to the height of the greatest poetry, like the picture of the cow whose calf has been taken from her for the sacrifice or that in which he deprecates the fear of death. It is neither by more obvious poetical triumph of selected parts, nor the obvious poetical falling short of other selected parts that the poem produces its effect.

So much for its length. As to the drawbacks which are supposed to arise from its philosophic character, fortunately I need not speak for myself. I have only to borrow the words of Mr. Santayana's study of Lucretius and of Dante in his *Three Philosophical Poets* (Harvard, 1910). Of Lucretius he writes (p. 34):

There remains the genius of the poet himself. The greatest thing about this genius is its power of losing itself in its object, its impersonality. We seem to be reading not the poetry of a poet about things, but the poetry of things themselves. That things have their poetry, not because of what we make them symbols of, but because of their own movement and life, is what Lucretius proves once for all to mankind.

In urging that the poet brings things before us in their own movement and life I have been saying for myself what Mr. Santayana has said so much better years ago.

Of the fitness of a philosophical or a scientific theory to be poetry he writes in a passage not every word of which I should accept (p. 124):

The life of theory is not less human or less emotional than the life of sense; it is more typically human and more keenly emotional. Philosophy is a more intense sort of experience than common life is, just as pure and subtle music, heard in retirement, is something keener and more intense than the howling of storms or the rumble of cities. For this reason philosophy, when a poet is not mindless, enters inevitably into his poetry, since it has entered into his life ; or rather, the detail of things and the detail of ideas pass equally into his verse, when both alike lie in the path that has led him to his ideal. To object to theory in poetry would be like objecting to words there ; for words, too, are symbols without the sensuous character of the things they stand for ; and yet it is only by the net of new connections which words throw over things in recalling them, that poetry arises at all. Poetry is an attenuation, a rehandling, an echo of crude experience ; it is itself a theoretic vision of things at arm's length.

And again on p. 123, speaking of Dante's learning, he writes :

Such a constant dragging in of astronomical lore may seem to us puerile or pedantic ; but for Dante the astronomical situation had the charm of a landscape, literally full of the most wonderful lights and shadows ; and it also had the charm of a hard-won discovery that unveiled the secrets of nature. To think straight, to see things as they are, or as they might naturally be, interested him more than to fancy things impossible ; and in this he shows, not want of imagination, but true imaginative power and imaginative maturity. It is those of us who are too feeble to conceive and master the real world, too cowardly to face it, that run away from it to those cheap fictions that alone seem to us fine enough for poetry or for religion.

Now that I have, as I hope, removed these *prima facie* difficulties which arise from prejudice, all that remains for me to do is to read a few passages from the poem itself. Two things there are to note about them. The first is the singular power of the metre, these ' loose Alexandrines ', in securing unification of the picture. Lucretian hexameters read to me, who am no Latinist, rapider than Virgilian and carry you on on the tide of this movement and life of the atoms. These Alexandrines of Bridges are more effective still, and sweep you on through his moralities and reflections and scientific expositions until you cannot help feeling the life and movement of these things, to less reflective minds so arid. This is why I commented on Bridges' apparent ingratitude in speaking of Lucretius.[1] For Lucretius' atoms seem to me more interesting and alive than Bridges' own severe expositions of nature and man. And merely to gratify myself I recall how Lucretius in one place fancies the atoms listening to a certain theory and says they would bedew their cheeks with laughter over it (I, vv. 19, 20).[2] Could anyone have said so in prose? But for the poet the atoms are concrete and he shares their movement and life.

With this almost wilful parenthetical remark I have been leaving the matter of Bridges' workmanship, all important as it is for the artist, and have encroached upon the subject which concerns me most, which I am the most anxious that you should verify, the feature which distinguishes him as a poet and for all the closeness of his subject to a prose treatment, his concreteness by which his subject is not presented merely to our eyes but is enacted in itself; by which 'selfhood' and 'breed' and morals become for us a new world of living history. Doubtless such concrete vision is a reflection of the poet himself; the secret of a poem, he says (IV, 992), 'lieth in this intimat echo of the poet's life'. The question to be answered is whether this concreteness is there and whether it is not this which makes the poetic vision.

I will quote two passages which occur at the very beginning, I, 8-36 and 72-85, and two others from Book II:

'Twas late in my long journey, when I had clomb to where
the path was narrowing and the company few,
a glow of childlike wonder enthral'd me, as if my sense
had come to a new birth purified, my mind enrapt
reawakening to a fresh initiation of life;
with like surprise of joy as any man may know

---

[1] For Bridges on the Alexandrines, see p. 86 n. of this book. In the same letter Bridges said about Lucretius: 'I am very sorry that I seem to be hard on Lucretius. I didn't mean it, but had to kick at the coarseness of his materialism. I remember how (it is 70 years ago) when I first read him in one of my school vacations, how uninteresting and tedious his physical demonstrations were to me.' The letter also discusses Santayana. [Editor's note.]

[2]   Fiet uti risu tremulo concussa cachinnent
   et lacrimis salsis umectent ora genasque.

PASCAL THE WRITER

who rambling wide hath turned, resting on some hill-top
to view the plain he has left, and seeth it now out-spread
mapp'd at his feet, a landscape so by beauty estranged
he scarce will ken familiar haunts, nor his own home,
maybe, where far it lieth, small as a faded thought.
  Or as I well remember one highday in June
bright on the seaward South-downs, where I had come afar
on a wild garden planted years agone, and fenced
thickly within live-beechen walls; the season it was
of prodigal gay blossom, and man's skill had made
a fair-order'd husbandry of that nativ pleasaunce:
But had there been no more than earth's wild loveliness,
the blue sky and soft air and the unmown flowersprent lawns,
I would have lain me down and longed, as I then did,
to lie there ever indolently undisturb'd and watch
the common flowers that starr'd the fine grass of the wold,
waving in gay display their gold-heads to the sun,
each telling of its own inconscient happiness,
each type a faultless essence of God's will, such gems
as magic master-minds in painting or music
threw aside once for man's regard or disregard,
things supreme in themselves, eternal, unnumber'd
in the unexplored necessities of Life and Love.

Hast thou then thought that all this ravishing music,
that stirreth so thy heart, making thee dream of things
illimitable, unsearchable and of heavenly import,
is but a light disturbance of the atoms of air,
whose jostling ripples, gather'd within the ear, are tuned
to resonant scale, and thence by the enthron'd mind received
on the spiral stairway of her audience chamber
as heralds of high spiritual significance?
and that without thine ear, sound would hav no report,
Nature hav no music; nor would ther be for thee
any better melody in the April woods at dawn
than what an old stone-deaf labourer, lying awake
o'night in his comfortless attic, might perchance
be aware of, when the rats run amok in his thatch?

But heav'nward tho' the chariot be already mounted,
'tis Faith alone can keep the charioteer in heart —
Nay, be he but irresolute the steeds will rebel,
and if he looketh earthward they will follow his gaze;

and ever as to earth he neareth, and vision cleareth
of all that he feareth, and the enemy appeareth
waving triumphant banners on the strongholds of ill,
his mirroring mind will tarnish, and mortal despair
possess his soul : then surely Nature hath no night
dark as that black darkness that can be felt : no storm
blind as the fury of Man's self-destructiv passions,
no pestilence so poisonous as his hideous sins.   (II, 509-520)

For I think not of Reason as men thought of Adam,
created fullgrown, perfect in the image of God ;
But as a helpless nursling of animal mind,
as a boy with his mother, unto whom he oweth
more than he ever kenneth or stayeth to think, language,
knowledge, grace, love and those ideal aims whereby
his manly intelligence cometh to walk alone.   (II, 725-731)

    The fuller verification I must leave to the reader. But for my own selfish delight I must quote one of the greater and more lyrical passages. They are not necessarily more poetical, for when the poet is describing like Lucretius the inner life of the atoms or like Bridges the inner life of man, he is mastering material of greater difficulty than when he can surrender himself to sensible or let us say sensual pleasures (Keats speaks of the sensual ear, without reproach). I quote it because in such a passage the poet's characteristic virtue is more palpable and such passages might stand alone. The passage I choose is the one about the scents of flowers, towards the end :

The repudiation of pleasure is a reason'd folly
of imperfection. Ther is no motiv can rebate
or decompose the intrinsic joy of activ life,
whereon all function whatsoever in man is based.
Consider how this mortal sensibility
hath a wide jurisdiction of range in all degrees,
from mountainous gravity to imperceptible
faintest tenuities :—The imponderable fragrance
of my window-jasmin, that from her starry cup
of redstemm'd ivory invadeth my being,
as she floateth it forth, and wantoning unabashed
asserteth her idea in the omnipotent blaze

ของ the tormented sun-ball, checquering the gray wall
with shadow-tracery of her shapely fronds ; this frail
unique spice of perfumery, in which she holdeth
monopoly by royal licence of Nature,
is but one of a thousand angelic species,
original beauties that win conscience in man :
a like marvel hangeth o'er the rose-bed, and where
the honeysuckle escapeth in serpentine sprays
from its dark-cloistered chamber thru' the old holly-bush,
spreading its joybunches to finger at the sky
in revel above rivalry. Legion is their name ;
Lily-of-the-vale, Violet, Verbena, Mignonette,
Hyacinth, Heliotrope, Sweet-briar, Pinks and Pear,
Lilac and Wallflower, or such white and purple blooms
that sleep i' the sun, and their heavy perfumes withhold
to mingle their heart's incense with the wonder-dreams,
love-laden prayers and reveries that steal forth from earth,
under the dome of night : and tho' these blossomy breaths,
that hav presumed the title of their gay genitors,
enter but singly into our neighboring sense, that hath
no panorama, yet the mind's eye is not blind
unto their multitudinous presences : I know
that if odour were visible as color is, I'd see
the summer garden aureoled in rainbow clouds,
with such warfare of hues as a painter might choose
to show his sunset sky or a forest aflame ;
while o'er the country-side the wide clover-pastures
and the beanfields of June would wear a mantle, thick
as when in late October, at the drooping of day
the dark grey mist arising blotteth out the land
with ghostly shroud. Now these and such-like influences
of tender specialty must not — so fine they be —
fall in neglect and all their loveliness be lost,
being to the soul deep springs of happiness, and full
of lovingkindness to the natural man, who is apt
kindly to judge of good by comfortable effect. (IV, 459-506)

I have said nothing about special features of the workmanship of the poem such as the Miltonic revelling in proper names. These are matters which concern the literary critic ; my concern is not with them, even if I had the competence ; I am concerned with the one point. Admitting that a poem and its workmanship are one thing and one thing only, and that a poet without words, and melodious words, is nothing, we may still ask whether there is not such a difference in treatment and subject and its concomitant diction, which makes one artist in words choose the form of prose and another the form of poetry. This difference I have tried to suggest by setting the transcendently beautiful prose of Pascal in contrast with the beautiful poetry of the *Testament of Beauty*.

A further question is at once suggested, whether it is not likely that this same difference verified here in Pascal and Bridges has not its counterpart in the other arts as well. But I have already wandered far enough away from the ostensible subject of my discourse which was Pascal, and have made him the excuse for a more general discussion. Still it is a character of the greatest men (and Pascal belongs to the very greatest) that they raise questions which they themselves do not answer.

VI

ART AND THE MATERIAL

The Adamson Lecture, 1925. Separately published by the Manchester University Press, here reprinted by permission

BY the material of art I mean the physical embodiment of the artistic experience, whether that embodiment be words, musical sounds, pigments, or stone, the so-called expression of the experience in one of the many senses of that word.[1] My object is to show that without this actual physical embodiment, even if actual embodiment be only imagined, the artistic experience does not exist.

A view which is commonly entertained, perhaps it is the view most widely entertained, contradicts this assertion. It is believed that the external work of art is a kind of translation into material form of something purely mental. The artist's mind, it is said, is filled with an imaginative experience, which he transfers to the canvas or utters in words — though doubtless it would be admitted that his image is modified as he works. Even reflective writers imply this conception and regard the outward expression as in the main a means of publicity, of communicating to others the individual experience of the artist. Thus in his *Theory of Poetry* (p. 58) Mr. Lascelles Abercrombie (himself a poet and therefore particularly valuable to hear) writes: 'The moment of imaginative experience which possesses our minds the instant the poem is finished possessed the poet's mind the instant the poem began. For as soon as there flashed into complete existence in his mind this many-coloured experience with all its complex passion, the poem which we know was *conceived*

---

[1] See Mr. L. A. Reid's paper in *Psyche* (vol. vi. No. 1) on 'Some Aspects of Expression', with which I am in general agreement.

ART AND THE MATERIAL

as an inspiration. . . . So that it is also possible to consider the inspiration of a poem as distinguishable from the verbal art of it : namely as that which the verbal art exists to convey, and which can be distinctly known as such, however impossible it may be to describe it or express it at all in any other words than those of the poet.' Even Mr. Croce, who identifies the image or intuition of the artist (or anyone else) with expression, and laughs at those who fancy they could themselves be Raphaels or Shakespeares if they had but the skill to express their beautiful imaginations, still urges that the artistic experience, though it is essentially expression, is purely mental, and that the actual physical embodiment of the experience is a technical matter and merely serves the purpose of communication. I do not desire to press the words of these writers, and in what I shall say I shall sometimes say what they would take for granted. But I believe there is at least much obscurity in their doctrines and even in the end error.

To some extent indeed the view that the outward physical embodiment is a practical or technical concern depends on accidents. In the first place, in certain arts like poetry or music there are purely technical or conventional expressions which are irrelevant, the printed or written word or the musical notation. A poem is not marks on paper, but words spoken or heard. Secondly, in certain arts at least there may be a real disparity between the artist's expressive experience (*i.e.* between the thought of what he wants to do) and his technical skill (*i.e.* what he can in fact do). A sculptor may imagine his marble of a shape which he fails to execute, and is conscious of his failure, or a painter imagine nuances on his canvas which his brush misses. Even so, it is actual physical marble which he imagines, or actual physical pigments on the canvas, though he cannot produce the result he desires. Contrariwise, a pupil may be technically more perfect than his master, and in executing the master's design (as is said sometimes of Michelangelo's pupils) rob the conception of its vitality. In other arts, however, this disparity may be hard to find. If the poet's experience is essentially expression, as Mr. Croce rightly thinks, a failure in language is also a failure in the experience; unless it may be he happens to be suffering for the moment from some nervous defect, like aphasia.

Apart from these accidental matters, however, the common view raises really fundamental questions, one of which concerns the practice of the artist — the condition of mind in which he works; the other a more directly philosophical one, to be described later.

I

The first question is, what is the artistic expression the expression of ? Is it, as the common view holds, and as Mr. Abercrombie seems to imply, the embodiment of imagery or thought in the artist's mind ? What the poem means, we are told, is what the words say; does the poet write it because he has in his mind images or thoughts which the words express ? Has he in his mind what he means to say, and does he write or speak because his mind is possessed of these ideas ? And, if we include the expression in the image or intuition, does he speak because he has in his mind thoughts which are already words ? When Shakespeare makes Othello say ' Wash me in steep-down gulfs of liquid fire ', had he that very image in his mind when he wrote; or because he was passionately excited by Othello's remorse for his murder of Desdemona did his excitement overflow into these words in the same way as the excitement of anger overflows into a blow ?

The second alternative is what I wish to suggest as the truth. I suggest that the artist's work proceeds not from a finished imaginative experience to which the work of art corresponds, but from passionate excitement about the subject matter; that the poet sings as the bird sings, because he must; that his poem is wrung from him by the subject which excites him, and that he possesses the imaginative experience embodied in his words just in so far as he has spoken them. In no sense is the poem the translation of his state of mind, for he does not know till he has said it, either what he wants to say or how he shall say it — two things which are admittedly one. The imaginative experience supposed to be in his mind does not exist there. What does exist is the subject matter which detains him and fixes his thoughts and feeds his interest, giving a colour to his excitement which would be different with a different subject matter. Excitement caused and detained by this subject, and at once enlarged, enlightened, and inflamed by insights into it bubbles over into words or the movements of the brush or burin or chisel.

Strictly to decide between these two alternatives would need an inductive enquiry into the experience of artists themselves, to be gathered from such records as they may have left or by direct enquiry from living artists. This I have not been able to perform. Certain more or less familiar reports like those of Mozart and of Goethe's comparison of his own condition in writing some of his poems to somnambulism [1] favour the second alternative; Mr. Abercrombie's version may be regarded as against it. Two young writers of imaginative literature whom I have consulted tell me that in their best work they do not know beforehand what they meant to say, but one of them admits that sometimes the work is thought out consciously beforehand with much labour and never with so satisfactory a result.

Pending any such enquiry we may find approximations to an answer in readily accessible quarters. For each of us is called upon to do modest artistic work, as in the ordinary exercise or essay of a student in so far as he tries to make a finished composition. He does not, if I may trust my own experience, try to think out his work in an artistic form, but steeps himself in the subject, 'moons' over it, as we say, and when his interest is sufficiently strong lets himself go and the words come of themselves. Anyone who happens to be blessed or cursed with the gift of humour — I mean, of course, spontaneous humour as

[1] Eckermann, under date March 14, 1830.

distinct from the odious habit of premeditated jocosity —
and practises it to some degree as a fine art may test his
own procedure. A person or topic releases within him a
hidden spring of gaiety, flavoured perhaps with a slight
submalicious ingredient, and the spring issues forth into
jest. It is his gaiety which produces the words, and no
image of what he means to say. Hence it is that the
jester so rarely laughs at his own jest. His laughter has
preceded the jest and has been done with; for him it is
part of the cause of the jest, and not, as for the hearers,
the effect. A third illustration may be gathered from portrait painting. From observing the different results I
imagine that what the artist, if he is successful, does is to
stare literally and metaphorically at his sitter so as to
fathom form and personality, and that the portrait proceeds not from imaginative anticipation of the portrait
that is to be executed but from a lively and intelligent
excitement, using the skilled brush-hand as its instinctive
organ; much in the same way as the vaulter keeps his
attention fixed upon the bar he has to leap and does not
think of the leap itself. Without this more or less passionate interest in the sitter, the portrait, however perfect
technically, fails as a work of art, and is flat or insipid and,
as we commonly say, ' uninterested '.

How this passion, or, as I have called it generally,
excitement, feels, from which the artistic work proceeds
and which it satisfies, can best be understood by reversing
the experiment and contemplating the work of art itself.
The hearer or spectator is thrown by the work into what
may be conjectured to have been the condition of the
artist in which it was produced. I have used the word
excitement in order not to imply necessarily that it requires
emotional storms of sympathy with the persons represented.
It is, I suppose, the nervous excitement set going by an
object seen or thought of, but it is felt in secondary excitements of the organic system, and may extend all over the
body and be felt around the heart and down the spine and
in the secretory and excretory parts. It is, at any rate, a

mass of feeling with a dominant feature of pleasurable tension.

Any work of art will serve as a test. For instance, the scene in Meredith's *Vittoria*, where the prima donna sings the song of Italian freedom in the opera-house of La Scala at Milan. In the agitation which such a passage throws us into (so violent that some readers can hardly proceed beyond this point in the book) it is perfectly possible to distinguish (however much they are interwoven) the passionate sympathy with the actors in the situation from the proper aesthetic excitement, felt in the fitness of the words both of the narrative and the song to express the situation. It is not necessary to suppose that Meredith or Shakespeare actually felt the emotions of his characters, but only that he understood them. Doubtless such emotional sympathy may and probably often is present as well, but, if it is, it is present to add fuel to the excitement of the proper creative tendency, the tendency I mean to expression not in the ways of anger or remorse or love, but in the ways of speech or movements of the hand directing brush or chisel. Herein is the answer to the old controversy raised by Diderot (upon which Molière before him had expressed an opinion in the same sense as Diderot [1]) whether the actor should feel himself or not into the emotions of his personages. With different actors the conditions of success will vary. Some may be content with the semi-intellectual excitement of understanding their parts, another may be able more readily to imitate his part by feeling its emotions or at least may have his imitative procedure heightened by the simulation of the passions themselves.

The alternative which I have endeavoured to recommend has been deliberately overstated to point the issue. It is true only in general and as an ultimate statement, but is subject to qualification. Probably in an inductive enquiry into the actual practice of artists the qualifications

[1] *Impromptu de Versailles*, Sc. 1 : ' You show what an excellent comedian you are by expressing so well a character contrary to your own humour '.

will be more interesting and more difficult to state than the proposition itself. Probably all artists employ both procedures. In proportion to the expertness and long acquaintance which the artist has with his business, that is, to his skill and learning, will he be anticipating in imagination the work of art itself; and there will always be periods when excitement runs dry and he depends upon his skill. Yet this is only an apparent exception to the general rule, for though imagination of the actual material is sufficient it has been acquired by the more original process of finding images by work upon the actual material. Thus it is told of Leonardo that being employed to paint the Last Supper he spent three days staring at the convent wall, and being told by the prior that he was engaged to paint and not to stare at a wall, replied that he was doing his work. The great artist can dispense with the actual laying of colours on the wall because of his trained imagination. But it is actual colours he imagines there. And it is clear that Leonardo's answer is wholly irrelevant to prove what Mr. Croce takes it to prove — that actual colours are a matter of indifference, and that the painter's experience is wholly mental. It could bear that use only on a particular philosophical theory.

More important is it to remember in the next place that the excitement in question is a *directed* one, and in two senses. It is detained and fixed by the subject matter, and again, because of the specific character of the excitement, it is always on the point of expressing itself in the medium. Thus the artist will always be having ideas of the subject matter flitting before his mind, and the greater his absorption in the subject the more freely will his imagination play about it. These images, however, are not anticipations of the expression contained in the work of art. But, secondly, his mind is always being traversed with inchoate tendencies to such outward expression: traversed in the sense in which the poet says that he 'felt through all this fleshly dress bright shoots of everlastingness'. Such inchoate tendencies *are* anticipatory of the ideas embodied hereafter when the labour is complete in the work of art, but are for the most part vague directions or aspirations of the mind which receive definition in the finished work. Some of them may even take the form, say, in a poet's mind of verbal images, or painted shapes in a painter's mind. The tension of passion will not only reinforce these two kinds of images or imaginative efforts, but will lead the one group to stimulate the other into greater activity. It is these more or less vague efforts of imagination which mislead us into supposing that all the artist does is to translate his images into material form. They are, however, not the artistic experience itself, but preliminary stages of it before the experience is consummated.

Another source of error is to be found in the perpetual process of correction of the work of art before the artist rests in it contented. How, it may be thought, can he be sure he has failed unless he compares what he has done with some idea or image in his mind of what is more perfect? The question betrays a psychological misreading. If the perfect image were in the mind he would, except for weakness of technique, have no need to compare his result with it — he would have already translated his image into fact. What really happens is that the work fails to give complete satisfaction to the passion which drives him into outward expression, and he alters his work until satisfaction is reached — much as the cook alters his dish till it satisfies his palate, remedying the pinch of salt too little, the soupçon of onion too much. It may even be that when the artist has done his best he is still unsatisfied, not because of the better images in his mind, but because his passionate desire is unstilled by his product. Here perhaps we may verify the existence of those ' breathings for incommunicable powers ' of which Wordsworth speaks in a difficult passage of the *Prelude* (Bk. III, l. 187).

II

So far I have been dealing with what is ultimately an issue of fact, and have urged that the work of art is the expression of the artistic passion or excitement, and not of any imaginative artistic experience. That experience is generated in and through the expression itself. The philosophical question arises when we ask what is the relation between the expression and the experience which it embodies in physical form. Verbally our result agrees with Mr. Croce's doctrine, that the artistic or any other intuition is itself expression but in reality is different from that doctrine. For the expression is for him as much mental as the intuition. Consequently the existence of the expression in external physical form is a merely practical matter and indifferent to the artistic experience. I do not propose to examine the philosophy on which such a statement could be justified — if it could be. My trouble with it is that it leaves in complete obscurity the sense in which the expression can be called expression at all. In the ordinary usage of words, in which expression means either the movements which issue from some mental condition or the product of those movements, no purely mental event is expression.[1] On the other hand, to plead as Bosanquet so forcibly does [2] that the physical constituent

[1] In the *Problemi di Estetica* (which is later than the *Aesthetic*) the intuition appears to be the expression of the artist, and hence art is said to be essentially lyrical. Besides the authoritative paper *L'intuizone pura e il carattere lirico dell'arte*, there is a highly interesting one further on in the volume, *Una theoria della ' macchia '*, in which the pure intuition is identified with the 'macchia' — the blurred motive which forms the basis of the finished work. I still find that these papers leave three distinctions unclear: (1) the difference between the ideas of the subject matter and those of the work of art, *e.g.* in poetry, between the images the poet has in his mind of what he writes about and the images of the words he uses; (2) the difference between passion as the source of the work of art and passion as entering into the work of art — I cannot help feeling that the work of art is not lyrical unless it is a lyric; (3) the difference indicated above between the passion which leads to expressive practical action and the passion which leads to artistic expression. I am quite willing to believe that I am doing less than justice to Mr. Croce's doctrine from not having appreciated him completely, and that, as friendly hearers of this lecture have said, there is nothing in it to which Mr. Croce would not assent. But I leave the text unaltered in the hope of getting things clearer. (The essay of 1917, *Il carattere di totalità della espressione artistica*, published in *Nuovi Saggi di Estetica*, 1920, which I did not know when I wrote the paper or this note, modifies the doctrine of the *liricità* of art.)

[2] *Three Lectures on Aesthetic*, pp. 67 ff.

is as necessary as the mental one is to say what is true without assigning a reason. I propose, therefore, without entering into criticism of rival philosophies, to trace the connection of the experience of beauty with the experience of external things in general. We shall find that, while art introduces a creative act, the specific artistic experience, like the cognitive one, is a discovery or revelation. And in the old phrase I must take the matter pretty deep, or rather I must fetch a wide compass and say something very comprehensive.

All error in understanding what knowing is arises from holding the principle that our actions are determined by knowledge, that we first know and then act. All truth in these matters depends on recognising the opposite principle that we know in and through acting. Not only in religion is reality revealed to our apprehensions; all knowledge from bare sensation up to the highest truth is revealed to our apprehensions and revealed through action. The most obvious illustrations come from sensible things, percepts, which appeal to our instincts or appetites. The apple is not first apprehended as food and therefore eaten; but in so far as the physical apple excites us physically through the disposition, which is also bodily, to grasp and eat it we are aware of it as eatable. We do not recognise the earwig as repulsive and shrink from it; the earwig compels us to shrink from it because of our instinct which it excites, and shrinking from it we recognise it as repulsive. The little boy who, standing too near the edge of the railway platform, rushes in terror from the approaching train to his father's knees (the story is from William James) does not apprehend the train as dangerous and run away from it, but, forced by the monster to run away, apprehends it thereby as dangerous.

Pass from such manifest instances where an instinct is involved to simple sensation or perception. The red-cheeked apple excites the retinae and thereupon the eyes move towards it and the hand to grasp it. In those actions the apple is revealed as visible and tangible. I insist on

ART AND THE MATERIAL

the simplicity of this matter, because the notion of revelation to the subject is apt to seem mysterious. The light from the apple excites the brain through the retina by a purely physical or physiological process, the nervous response to the excitement issues in or is expressed by certain movements directed upon the object, which movements are thus literally squeezed out of the subject (in the literal sense of 'expression') by the external object. That is the situation we describe as having the sensation of colour or visibility. Whether the whole situation has been described in these physical terms, or whether we are to say that the brain excitement carries with it a quality of consciousness, is for our present purpose of less importance. The point is that an external quality extorts from us through our susceptibility to it an expressive response, and in that response reveals itself.

I am describing roughly and on broad lines. The mere coarse outward behaviour of turning the eyes towards an object to see it is not finely enough graduated to distinguish a red apple from a yellow one. It is but the so-called common path into which more finely graduated complexities of outgoing nervous response embouch. That such differentiations exist is sufficiently in evidence from the experiments which indicate preference in the young for certain colours and an order in the growth of these preferences. Here, in the differences of minute nervous outgoings, terminating perhaps in common paths and common gestures, the beginning stage is to be found of the discriminating reactions through which differences of sense qualities are revealed to us. The older writers used to say that afferent nerves conveyed sensations to the brain and mind, awakening there pictures which represent external things, upon which pictures we then behave appropriately. These pictures are mythology, and exist only in the fancy of theorists who are not content with facts. What the afferent nerves convey to the brain is nervous (or mental) excitements. It is the efferent or motor reactions (always in their continuity with the

ART AND THE MATERIAL

afferent processes) in which these excitements discharge in virtue of which we apprehend the qualities of external things. Through those responses the objects are revealed to us, not in their fullness but only in such features as can stir the senses to react, and, it may be added, only correctly if the organ be appropriate and the response undistorted.

It remains to add that images or ideas are equally revelations of objects, only that in their case the neural or mental response is not wrung from us by the object itself but is initiated from within. They are best understood by reference to preparatory or anticipatory movements in a complex experience. I see a loose stone upon the edge of a wall and I prepare to duck my head. I have, then, the idea or image of the stone as about to fall, though the stone is not actually falling. The movement of ducking the head is discharged from within by the responses which enable me to apprehend the looseness of the stone, being connected with that first step either through past experience or as the next stage in the serial development of an instinctive process. Images may in this sense be described as expectations. That is, we do not expect because we have ideas of what is to come, but in expecting we have ideas. Memory, which differs from expectation only in its orientation to the past instead of the future, may be understood on similar lines ; but I fear to complicate the exposition by difficult details. Enough to say that when mind or body from any internal cause — it may be a physical stimulation from the blood, it may be some other mental condition acting through association — adopts the behaviour appropriate to a really present object, that is, the behaviour which is normally elicited by that object, the object is presented or revealed in idea.

The greater part of our knowledge is present in our minds from past experience in its ideal form, so that through appropriate neural or mental behaviour we know real things without having them really acting upon us. So Leonardo in the story quoted above. But even in presence of actual things, part of our experience of them

ART AND THE MATERIAL

is always anticipation by way of ideas — the man is perceived as a thing with a solid structure though I see only his surface: I behave to him as a body. Such ideal elements which enter into the constitution of all our experience of things may be said to be 'imputed' by us to the things. The statement has a direct bearing upon the work of art, for the object there is always coloured by our imputations, so that the Hermes in the marble block is for the aesthetic appreciation alive and divine. The difference, in fact, between an aesthetic object and a natural one is that our imputations, if they are well chosen, belong to the natural object, but belong to the work of art only in the aesthetic appreciation and do not belong to it as a physical object.

Fundamentally then, and originally, things are known to us as they reveal themselves through practice; and at first the responses through which we know them are practical in the narrow sense, and are directed upon the object so as to alter or use or avoid it. But upon this original stage of knowing there supervenes a second stage of cognition, knowledge for its own sake, or theoretical, or speculative, knowledge. This comes about through a special kind of responses, equally instinctive though of a different order, whereby the subject of knowing is emancipated from purely practical interests, though they too are doubtless used in the first instance in the service of practical interests. The commonest form of such responses is speech, but any gesture may equally occur, like 'gestures' proper or movements which imitate the object by the hand. Why these responses occur we cannot say; we are made so that we have them. And they spring from and express dispositions, such as curiosity or mere imitativeness, which are, like the ordinary practical instincts, stirred into excitement by the external object. Now, these responses do not, like the practical ones, alter the object or the subject's relation to it. The result of practical acts is to affect the object. These others, however, leave the object unaffected, but they bring into existence as

ART AND THE MATERIAL

their product fresh physical objects, or arrangements of them, words or sounds or drawings or pictures or even sculptured stones, external things independent when once created of the creative art. It is these physical creations which become in the end the material of art.

Even now we have not arrived, however, at the distinctive feature of the work of art. The products of what I will call expressive excitement may, and in the beginning do, serve merely as signs for the objects which have excited the expressive disposition. That is the general function of words, and may be of drawings (like the drawings of thieves on walls for information of other thieves), or even sculptured blocks.

Words or other expressive products become the material of art when they are used not for the sake of the things which they mean but in themselves and for their own sake. It is therefore mistaken to hold all spoken words to be aesthetic ; they are in general purely semantic. Language becomes aesthetic only when it in turn becomes an object, and as such is revealed to the speaker charged with its meaning. It now not merely means its meaning and serves as a guide to the thing it means, and as in general happens, passes out of the mind when the mind is directed upon the thing through it ; but is held there and becomes itself the thing which occupies the mind, and no longer merely has a meaning but is charged with meaning or fused with it

I must dwell a little longer upon this ; for a word charged with meaning becomes a different thing from a word *with* a meaning. There is no mystery about meaning. A thing (*e.g.* a word) *means* the real things or qualities or patterns of things for which it stands. But in art the word or marble or drawing has welded into its being the things which it means. Its meaning is part of it in the same way as in the perception of an orange the round yellow form does not merely stand for the juiciness of the orange but is actually qualified by it and fused with it into one. In the marble block the Hermes does not

ART AND THE MATERIAL

merely mean life and divinity but is divine and alive, in so far as we appreciate it as a work of art. Its imputations, which come to it from the appreciating mind, and, unlike those of perceived objects, do not belong to it as a physical thing, are, for the appreciating mind, part of its nature. The artist or the spectator do not ask if the Hermes is really alive; they raise no question of true and false;[1] they see it so. This which is so clear with the statue is true also of language in art. The words are no longer mere sounds, but are alive with the qualities they mean. Paradoxical as it may strike us that a word has taken on in art qualities which it does not possess as mere sounds, that is the fact; and when considered it is not stranger than that the dead marble is alive. It may not be single words; it may only be whole phrases, or it may only be the poem as a whole. Certain it is that in a poem the words are new things altered from their common use; enchanting they may be, but they are always enchanted; magical in both senses of that word. Any illustrations from great poetry will serve:

> St. Agnes Eve, ah, bitter chill it was:
> The owl, for all his feathers, was a-cold —

the enchanted version of the scientific or historical fact that it was a cold night, so cold that the birds felt it through their feathers. Or Hamlet's dying words to Horatio:

> If thou didst ever hold me in thy heart,
> Absent thee from felicity awhile,
> And in this harsh world draw thy breath in pain
> To tell my story.

The words are bewitching music, as Mr. A. C. Bradley says; my point is that they are bewitched. Or this of the flowers in *Winter's Tale*:

> Daffodils that come before the swallow dares,
> And take the winds of March with beauty.

---

[1] Well brought out by Mr. R. G. Collingwood in *Speculum Mentis* and in his *Outlines of a Philosophy of Art*.

These are examples of easy or facile beauty, as the critics call it. Here is difficult beauty, again from *Winter's Tale* (Leontes to Camillo) :

> Dost think I am so muddy, so unsettled,
> To appoint myself in this vexation ; sully
> The purity and whiteness of my sheets,
> Which to preserve is sleep, which being spotted
> Is goads, thorns, nettles, tails of wasps ?

Or an example of artistic humour, Lamb's comparison of the silence of a Quakers' meeting with ' the uncommunicating muteness of fishes '.

There may be, as in some of the above passages, some strangeness in a word which makes the passage magical. But consider, in its context, a familiar line in which Wordsworth seems to approach most near, not to prose, but, according to his own distinction, to scientific description :

> And never lifted up a single stone.[1]

The line does not merely describe the old man's grief : the grief is, for the aesthetic appreciation, actually in the words. Paraphrasing reduces words to useful and significant description, turns them into bare words again.

I am not concerned to exhaust the conditions of the existence of the work of art. But one further feature I will mention in passing, since it concerns the expressive character of the material. A poem does not consist of single words, however much fused as has been explained with their meaning and not merely indicative of it, but is a complex unity, and every work of art exhibits unification into an expressive whole. This unity, which inspires so many valuable pages of Mr. Abercrombie's book, corresponds to and expresses the unity of thought or purpose in the artist's mind, which distinguishes the creative imagination, the creative passion as we have learned to

---

[1] One or two of these instances are taken from Matthew Arnold's introduction to Wordsworth. The example of difficult beauty is cited by Mr. Abercrombie as an illustration of Shakespeare's later style.

consider it, from the idle play of fancy or reverie, and arises from the dominant interest of the subject matter which detains and guides creation. That dominant purpose is reflected in the organisation of the product, and as the artist works he alters or amplifies his expression until his passion is satisfied by the external expression. I need not dwell further upon this topic here, except to point out that the unity of interest in the inspiration is helped and augmented by all the means of rhythm or metre in poetry, or generally of balance and recurrence in all the arts. Such devices are not mere conventions or mechanical resources of technique, but are the spontaneous overflow of unified feeling into expressive gestures. The bodily life is rhythmical in its nature, and such features of recurrence sustain as in the joy of the dance, give order and stability to the product, and fit it at once to express and knit together the dominant passion inspired and excited by the subject matter.

I return to the more immediate topic. Hitherto I have been concerned with the creativeness of the artist's act, by which he brings into existence a fresh physical object. But it is important to limit the exact measure of his creativeness. Words and musical sounds are produced by the speaker or singer or player. But when we turn to the sculptor's stone we see that what is created is not the raw material itself but its form. Words, too, are not the property of the individual, but the common possession of his fellows, and in this sense exist before him in the language he uses. His creativeness lies rather in his choice of words, though since language, unlike marble, is a growing thing he may actually bring new words into existence as well. This is comparatively accidental. What he does is so to select and to combine as to endow his language with what it does not possess in its ordinary or scientific use, with his magic. The poet, like the sculptor, creates a form which owes its aesthetic character to his imputations, and hence can never be dissociated from his or the spectator's appreciation, so that beauty, whether

ART AND THE MATERIAL

in nature or art, involves a coalescence of the material and the mind.

Creativeness once thus understood, we can now advance to a more important and final result already hinted at more than once. All cognition is discovery in which the object is revealed to the mind. The work of art, being the expression contemplated for its own sake and not merely as a sign, however much it owes its form to the artist, reveals to him his own meaning, and the artistic experience is not so much invention as discovery. In sculpture, where the block already exists, it is easier to recognise the truth of this. In Michelangelo's unfinished statues of slaves in the Academy at Florence we can feel the artist not so much making the figure as chipping off flakes of the marble from the figure which is concealed in it, and which he is laying bare (vivos *ducunt* de marmore voltus). Has he not said himself that there is no thought which the sculptor expresses in marble that does not exist there already? R. L. Nettleship [1] applies to the sculptor the words of Browning:

> The thousand sights and sounds that broke
> In on him at the chisel's stroke;

and the words describe how the sculptor's discovery, elicited by his own creative art, surprises him with the definition of his own mood of mind; in the same way as with no foreknowledge of the truth but with the passion to find it and to use the methods calculated to attain it, the scientific thinker is surprised by the discovery in nature of the law or fact which he is seeking. What is true of sculpture is true also of poetry. Shakespeare discovered *Hamlet* in the English language as the sculptor discovers his figure in the block. Full as that language is of the knowledge of nature and man for which it stands, of history and thought and emotion, Shakespeare, with his artistic excitement over the subject of Hamlet's story and with his profound insight into Hamlet's imagined

[1] In his essay on Plato's Education in *Hellenica*.

nature, could discover there in the language of English folk the selection and combination of words which were fitted to be the expression of his excitement, and in their turn surprised him as they surprise us with the imaginations they embody. Great artists know or believe that they are inspired from something outside themselves. Why should we suppose them to be deceived ? It is true that to make the discovery the gifts of Shakespeare were needed ; that is why great artists are rare. But equally the gifts and skill of Newton were needed to discover the law of gravitation in its first form, and other gifts and skill have been needed to discover that law in its later and preciser form. You cannot discover Hamlet unless you have Shakespeare's mind. But equally unless you have eyes you cannot discover the green trees. 'Ripeness is all.' Except for the features which make the artist's act creative, there is no difference in kind between the discovery of the tree by perception and the discovery of the Slave in the block or of Hamlet in the English language. The artist's creativeness conceals from us his real passivity. Every artist is in his degree like Shakespeare, who was a reed through which every wind from nature or human affairs blew music.

I have thus returned to the position sketched in the earlier part of this lecture : that the actual physical expression is the *sine qua non* of all artistic experience, and that that experience is the discovery which comes to the artist himself as well as to the spectator as a revelation vouchsafed to him. The difference is that we now can understand that artistic experience is unmysteriously in line with the simplest revelation of physical objects in nature to the mind. It will thus be clear how far they are from the truth who think that the actual physical work of art merely subserves publicity, is needed to convey to others and make public the private experience of the artist. For it is only through the public object of art, which all the world can see and hear, that the artist acquires that very private experience which is embodied in the work.

ART AND THE MATERIAL

There are certain corollaries from this conclusion, probably very many, of which I will mention two. The first is comparatively obvious, that in virtue of the material one art may be more suitable than another to express a given subject, and a particular art even wholly unsuitable. The same distinction may arise within any one art, which employs various material. Who would put the Apollo of the Belvedere into the form of a Tanagra statuette, or those delightful terra-cottas into marble statues? In architecture, great unwindowed spaces which may be stately and impressive or sublime in stone may look mean in brick or terra-cotta. And not only does the subject choose its material, but the material (as repeatedly said) chooses and modifies the images and the artist finds himself compelled by his material to fresh or altered imagination. Thus a word chosen by the poet may suggest and demand other words and the corresponding image grows under his eyes or hearing. The need of rhyme or metre may work to the same result; and all this with no violence to the artistic effect, but rather to enhance it. When, on the other hand, ideas are altered or enlarged in order to suit these exigencies and for no other reason, the result is disturbing and unaesthetic, as in the tags which Molière so often introduces (the French call them *chevilles*) to eke out his metre, or the grotesque rhymes introduced by Browning in wilfulness to save his lines and not with the legitimate object of grotesques, so often achieved by himself elsewhere, and by Byron often.

I may add, as an illustration of the reciprocal moulding of material and images upon each other, the familiar difficulty of translating poetry from one language to another. It is difficult because the corresponding words of the new tongue alter the images, or because certain shades of meaning which suit the genius of one language (comparable in this respect to the difference of stone and wax) cannot adapt themselves to that of another without loss of flavour. Nor is it altogether an accident that some writers cannot write without a pen in their hand, that Oliver Goldsmith[1] could write like an angel and talked like poor Poll. It is asking us too much to believe that the pen merely serves to recall words; the reason is that without the intention to use words for an artistic purpose the images will not flow. Similarly, to take another illustration which is not far-fetched, a dull man may sit down to write French and find himself pointed in thought because the expression compels him to be so.

A less obvious and far more important corollary is the answer to the question, what makes the difference between natural beauty and the beauty of art? The answer is that there is no difference of kind, but only one of circumstance and proportion. In natural beauty the material already exists, in art it, or rather its form, is the artist's work. In both alike there is creativeness and there is discovery, but in nature discovery, in art creation, bulks more largely in the proportion between the two. The real difference is in the circumstances of initiation; the impulsion in natural beauty comes from the beautiful thing itself; in art from the artist's mind. In the appreciation by the spectator of the work of art the difference vanishes, except so far as he throws himself back voluntarily into the artist's position. Even for the artist the raw material already exists in the unhewn block, and the language in which the poet works is not so much created by him as recreated after a standing pattern preserved in the minds of men and forcing him to observe its ways of going on. In appreciation of natural beauty the object is before the eye; at most the observer omits the features or things which jar. But his creative-

[1] C. E. Montague, writing to Alexander about this Lecture, 'on the way the artists magnoperate', said, 'It fairly delighted me to see the thing put just right at last. Of course Goldsmith is a specially good case, but everybody ought to understand it who has had the common experience of meeting a famous author or artist (when he is not excited above himself by functioning in his art) and feeling let down by his relative dulness in talk. Was it Johnson who called some great actress an "inspired idiot" for the same reason? I fancy every writer when he reads something that he wrote with the proper excitement on him, thinks " How the devil did I ever do anything as good as that?" Didn't Thackeray say something of the sort, afterwards, when he read his scene between Lord Steyne, Becky and Rawdon?' [Editor's note.]

ness is not limited to omission, for he endows the natural object with his own interpretations. There are the familiar words of Wordsworth in *Tintern Abbey*, which he says resemble closely a line of Young's:

> all the mighty world
> Of eye and ear, both what they half create
> And what perceive;

(the words have to be read in their context), and the equally familiar words of Coleridge:

> O lady, we receive but what we give,
> And in our life alone does nature live.

Even natural beauty is a fusion of the object with the observing mind, and a beautiful face or sunset possesses not bare physical reality but aesthetic reality; in the same sense as, to use the old example, the Hermes is alive and divine, though physically a piece of dead marble. But it would be long to develop this theme, and I have written upon it elsewhere.[1] There is no tertiary quality of beauty written on the face of nature, as there are primary and secondary ones. Its tertiary quality requires the supplement of our imputations and penetration by them. But in the proportion of discovery and creation the emphasis is upon discovery.

In the work of art creativeness is palpable. It needs reflection to recognise that the artistic creation is discovery. It has been one main purpose of this paper to make this clear. Therewith vanishes any ultimate disparity between natural and artificial beauty. Only the seeing and intelligent eye discovers natural beauty. Only the work of art reveals or, in the old usage of that word, 'discovers' to the eye its intelligence.

[1] *Hibbert Journal*, October 1924.

VII

ART AND INSTINCT

(The Herbert Spencer Lecture, delivered at Oxford, May 23, 1927.
Separately published by the Clarendon Press, reprinted here by permission.)

I FEEL deeply the honour done me in entrusting me with this lectureship, the more that it commemorates the work of Herbert Spencer, to whom I owe a debt of gratitude.

I begin by referring to a book much studied in this place, the *Ethics* of Aristotle. Contrasting true courage with animal courage which proceeds from anger or pain, Aristotle says that true courage is inspired by desire for the noble or beautiful or good ; and it is in keeping with his whole doctrine of virtue to say that virtue arises out of the natural passions, and exists when they are so qualified as to be directed upon the noble or, as he sometimes puts it, upon their proper objects for their own sake. The passions are thus the material which is fashioned and refined to virtue. But over and above these materials there is the noble, of which so far as I know he gives no further account. Any contemporary treatment of the subject may be expected to supply this account if possible.

Now in respect of art a similar question is raised acutely at the present time. It is the contrast between the ideas contained in the famous saying, ' poetry is a criticism of life ', and the phrase ' art for art's sake ' or ' poetry for poetry's sake ', which last was the subject of a well-known lecture by Mr. A. C. Bradley. Is there or is there not a specific aesthetic emotion, or is the aesthetic attitude or feeling nothing but ordinary feelings or attitudes towards the subjects of art, in a certain condition of refinement and complication? Mr. Clive Bell [1] and Mr. Roger Fry [2] are upon the one side; Mr. Richards in his excellent *Principles of Literary Criticism* [3] upon the other. And because it is well to have a balanced statement which avoids extremes, I will quote here the familiar passage of Mr. Bradley, which really avoids the difficulties of either extreme. 'What then', he asks, ' does the formula Poetry for Poetry's sake tell us about this experience? It says, as I understand it, these things. First, this experience is an end in itself, is worth having on its own account, has an intrinsic value. Next, its *poetic* value is this intrinsic worth alone. Poetry may have also an ulterior value as a means to culture or religion. . . . But its ulterior worth neither is nor can directly determine its poetic worth as a satisfying imaginative experience; and this is to be judged entirely from within. . . . For its nature [poetry's] is to be not a part, nor yet a copy of the real world (as we commonly understand that phrase), but to be a world by itself, independent, complete, autonomous.'

Now I humbly think Mr. Bradley and Mr. Bell and Mr. Fry to be right; though I think Mr. Bell in particular goes too far. I believe with him that art both proceeds from a specific aesthetic excitement in the artist and produces an aesthetic excitement or emotion in the spectator or hearer. I understand his claim that true visual art, that is the painting of what he calls significant form, excites in the true appreciator the ecstasy he describes, although I have it not myself, for, like most of us, great poetry does arouse in me an ecstasy. But I question if this ecstasy transports us into an altogether different world from that in which natural objects and we ourselves live. Witness the whole of natural beauty, which, though I believe it owes its beauty to our unconsciously artistic vision of it,[4] is easily accessible to us all. In any case there is always a prejudice felt against

[1] *Art*, London, 1914.
[2] *Vision and Design*, London, 1920; *Transformations*, London, 1926.
[3] London, 1925, p. 16, chapter on ' The Phantom Aesthetic State '.
[4] See on this subject ' Art and Nature ' in *Bulletin of the John Rylands Library*, Manchester, vol. 11, No. 2, July 1927.

those who seem to claim that they are hierophants of a peculiar mystery. If the claim for a peculiar aesthetic emotion is to be maintained, it must be traced to some impulse in human nature, and even if no further account can be given of it, we must at least trace its affiliation with some recognised impulse or instinct. We must be able to put our finger on the particular side of us to which art makes appeal. In the same way, it is not enough to say that in conduct we aim at the noble and leave that impulse to be accepted, as Aristotle apparently did, without further account; nor to refer science to the passion for truth. There is an underlying instinct which in each case is the root of these human products, and we have to try to identify it in each case. I believe it can be done, easily in respect of truth and morality, much less easily in respect of art. That more difficult problem is what I shall endeavour to solve in this lecture.

In this endeavour to affiliate the artistic impulse with certain instinctive tendencies I can appeal for authority not only to Spencer himself, who derived art from the play-impulse, but to the example of Burke. That great man showed his originality in his earliest work by tracing back the sublime and the beautiful to the instincts first of self-preservation, and secondly of society including in particular the instinct of sex. Sublimity was aroused by dangerous and terrifying objects, which threatened existence; beauty by objects which appealed to our tenderness. So far as beauty is concerned he thus anticipated Darwin's attempt to establish a relation between the decorative appendages and colouring of animals and the purposes of mating. Burke knew well enough that the sense of the sublime is not the same thing as terror, nor the sense of beauty mere animal tenderness. He was not misled into that blind alley. Unfortunately he does not tell us wherein the difference lies. Herein lies his failure. His merit lies in the appeal to the instincts, though he missed identifying the really relevant instinct. The reason of his failure is that he began with beauty or sublimity in natural objects,

ART AND INSTINCT

and fell into one of the two errors which beset the enquirer into art. From beauty in nature he could not pass, and no one can, to beauty in art. We have to enquire first into the beauty of art in order to understand the beauty of nature.

In this appeal to instinct he contrasts with Hume, it is worth while to observe, in much the same way as in ethics Adam Smith contrasted with Hume. For Hume the moral sense (for he insisted that virtue is such because it pleases after a certain fashion) sought the foundation of virtue in the pleasant consequences of good action; Adam Smith found the criterion of virtue in whether an action was in tune with the desires of persons in a society. He looked to the reasons why men act rather than to the effects of what they do. About beauty Hume has comparatively little to say; but he regards beauty as founded either in the usefulness of a thing, *e.g.* of a house to its possessor, or as in a beautiful animal or plant, in the proportion and adaptation of its parts so as to serve the purposes of the thing in question. He fell into the second of the errors I have mentioned, of looking for the nature of beauty in the characters of beautiful things rather than in the human impulses which beauty satisfies. And I do not say that Burke was free from this error likewise. Hume was a far greater philosopher than either Adam Smith or Burke; but in spite of his enormous influence on subsequent thought, both Burke in aesthetics and Adam Smith in ethics are closer to the thought of our own time. Kant, who was greatly influenced by Burke and immensely excelled him in the analysis of the psychological conditions of beauty, who indeed made by this analysis the first real step in aesthetical science, failed to recognise what Burke had seen, the ultimate instinctive basis of the aesthetic sense.

The thesis which I submit to you is that the aesthetic impulse and the aesthetic emotion which goes with that impulse and is part and parcel of it are an outgrowth from the instinct of constructiveness, and are that impulse or instinct when it has become first human, and next, contemplative. Accordingly I should describe or define the beautiful as that which satisfies the constructive instinct when it has reached the stage of contemplation. I know that the word instinct is used loosely and that there is dispute as to what impulses are instinctive. I am content to follow Mr. McDougall in treating constructiveness as an instinct. Illustrations of it are the dam-building of the beaver, the hive-making of the bee, the song of the nightingale, or the nest-building of the rook. These are animal chains of action which are really instinctive, though doubtless employed in the service of simpler and more fundamental instincts like that of preservation of life and the sex and family instincts. When they appear in man, they are so qualified and complicated by human prerogative as scarcely to deserve any longer to be called instinctive. They are but human manifestations of what is rooted in an animal instinct. By saying that we have the aesthetic impulse and the aesthetic emotion or excitement when constructiveness becomes contemplative, I mean that we have it when the artificer uses the materials of his construction not for a practical purpose but for their own sakes. If the beaver, instead of building his dam from the urgency of his practical desire, could observe his materials so as to watch their effect in their mere form as materials, he would be an architect. If the male nightingale sang for the love of singing, for the sake of the mere sounds he was producing and the delight he takes in their combination, he would be a musician. In fact he is merely a lover, or when he is not actually wooing he sings love songs from force of habit ; or in play, delighting not so much in the song which he produces as in the exercise. I know that the wise thrush is said to sing the selfsame song twice over, for reasons which suggest that he is really an artist and wishes to make sure of his musical effect. But it is a poet who speaks, and he playfully. The cold truth is that the thrush is in earnest with his wooing, but being less modest than the famous Bellman he thinks it enough to say what he says twice over for it to be accepted as true.

ART AND INSTINCT

Between animal constructiveness and artistic production there is an intermediate stage of handicraft or, in general, technology, in which constructiveness remains practical but is humanised for a purpose. No reason exists to suppose that the nest-building bird or hive-building bee has any idea in its mind of the work it means to produce; its actions follow in train by an instinctive ordinance which it brings with it. The instinct is plastic and the details of the train of action may be varied to suit special circumstances. Not finding shards to form a house in which to conceal itself, a crab may pick up bits of glass through which it can be seen. And recent enquiries seem to show that there are actions amongst the higher mammals which, still falling short of purpose, still dictated by blind desire for food or other object, exhibit a kind of flash of insight into the construction of means by which the object will be secured. Such devices we humans practise ourselves, but they are still removed from proper handicraft. In general, in animal construction each act performed is a signal to the performance of the next, but that next action is prepared for by the organisation of the instinct.

In distinctively human construction there is purpose of the end to be secured, and purpose arises only in a creature which possesses ideas and has memory and expectation, a creature which looks before and after. We can reflect on the next step to be taken, and how to weave acts together so as to attain our end; we are guided by our past experience of the behaviour of things. We can use our knowledge of levers and wheels to plan the construction of our engine. Even when we do not actually reflect about our procedure we can bring our acquired experience to bear upon the attainment of our purposed end as animals apparently cannot. Human construction becomes through memory and prevision a connected method, and we make plans of construction, putting our experiences together, so as, under the pressure of our purpose, to create novelties.

This human feature of construction is of particular interest because it is often called in a looser and more general usage constructiveness. When I speak of the constructive instinct and its human transformation, I am using the word in the sense of combining material objects, as the bird does in building a nest, or producing a physical object like a note, as the nightingale does when he sings. Constructiveness in the more general sense in which it might better be called synthesis or described by the adjective constructional is not confined to construction in the specific sense. The animals have construction in the specific sense, but in general have it not in the vaguer one.

Synthesis with its accompanying analysis or selection, the habit of systematising our experiences, is the most obvious feature of science of all kinds. Now scientific impulse, the impulse to true knowledge, is the outgrowth of an animal instinct and is its humanisation through ideas and memory and imagination. That animal impulse is curiosity, and truth may properly be viewed as the satisfaction of humanised curiosity. The animals too are curious to examine things, but their curiosity is guided by sense and is limited to practical issues. A dog is inquisitive about certain classes of smells, but only because they are the forerunners or at least the indications of practical delights. Our curiosity when it becomes scientific ceases to be practical, though it may of course be connected with practice, and there is also technological curiosity intermediate between animal curiosity and scientific. Now scientific curiosity depends for its working out on a high degree of constructional synthesis ; but it is not itself constructive in the specific sense. It views nature as something to be understood, not as a field for the creation of fresh objects ; though such fresh creations may be its incidental result and often its most impressive result, like wireless telegraphy.

I have dwelt on this point because it suggests that science may profitably be treated in its kinship with art. If we wish further to see how close the analogy of science and art is we may compare truth not with artistic but with natural beauty. For natural beauty is presented to us ready made for inspection or rather for discovery, and our hands or voices have had no part in fashioning it. If I am right in saying that nature is beautiful only if we see her with the artistic eye, the delight in natural beauty lies very near to the delight in truth, where also nature is taken as she is and analysed and reconstructed as it were, so as to produce the highly artificial product we call science, which is not nature herself but our vision of her, though that vision follows her as faithfully as our powers allow, and our truth, if it is not nature herself, is founded upon her. The difference between truth and natural beauty is that in science we divest ourselves of any personal interference; in beauty, even in natural beauty, our imaginations not only select and combine but add, seeing nature differently as we are grave or gay, neglecting what does not suit our particular point of view or interest, eking her out, as when we delight in a pure colour by added suggestions of contrast with impure ones, sometimes even adding our thoughts or fancies so as to be a part of what is there, as we say, in nature. Witness the poet's gloss upon the wise thrush, which I have quoted. The lover of natural beauty adds his personality to nature, however unconsciously; the man of science sets himself, by a supreme exercise of personality, to keep his personality out of, I was about to say, the picture.

Finally, to conclude my remarks on the intermediate stage of practical or technological construction or handicraft, it is because architecture is the most elementary and necessary art (I do not say the lowest art, for I decline the question of grades of art) that it unites most closely artistic and practical construction. A house which cannot be lived in is not beautiful, and a house may be built which is neither beautiful nor ugly but is merely useful and arouses no aesthetic emotion. The architect as craftsman is concerned with utility and can never forget it as artist.[1] But he is an artist not from his practical success but in so far

[1] See an address by Mr. J. H. Worthington, *R.I.B.A. Journal*, vol. xxxiv. No. 7.

ART AND INSTINCT

as he constructs his house for its own sake, and satisfies himself as contemplative. All the crafts like pottery, weaving, engineering, become arts so far as they follow the same motive.

Constructiveness then becomes art when it ceases to be merely practical; and it is much less easy to describe the step which is then taken to contemplation than it is to distinguish human practical constructiveness from animal constructiveness. But we have an analogy or a precedent for it in the passage from our ordinary experience of things, by which we become aware of them through the senses or otherwise, into knowledge of them in the proper sense which is theoretical. In describing this transition I am inevitably repeating what I have said on other occasions. I can but plead the importance of the subject, and the more personal plea that as I have not secured attention to the matter, I have to go on until I do. Our acquaintance with things begins then with practice and is an incident of practice. For simplicity, I confine myself to physical things. They secure for themselves our consciousness of them because they act physically on our sense organs and elicit from us and our brains a physical response. A red patch acts upon our retina and we turn our eyes to it and perform other specialised responses. In responding we become aware of the red patch. We do not first see it and then respond; it compels us in consequence of the sense organism to which it appeals to respond or react, and so far as we react appropriately the object is before us or is revealed. The same account applies everywhere. I repeat an illustration I have used recently. A motor-car with blazing head-lights bears down upon me. I do not say, ' This is dangerous; I must get out of the way '. It acts upon my instinct of flight; I get out of the way, and then I say I have escaped that danger. I do not first see that a fruit is good to eat, but if I am hungry it induces me to eat, and in eating it I discover it to be edible, just as in running away from a dangerous object I discover it to be dangerous. The statement is of course over-simplified and

ART AND INSTINCT

takes no note of the effect of past experience in determining a particular response. Broadly it remains true that knowledge comes in the first instance through action upon objects which themselves by a physical and not a mental compulsion elicit from us that response. We do not first perceive and then act; we perceive in so far as we act. We do not first know and then do; we know in doing, and the knowledge is the revelation which comes from practice.

From this elementary practical experience of things we advance to theoretical experience of them, to speculation in the most general sense of that word. We reach this condition when the normal response is diverted into another path. Instead of acting upon the thing, we speak; this is the commonest method of the diversion of our response. An enemy presents himself to me; instead of striking him, I say, 'I hate you'. That is speculative or theoretical knowledge; still an affair of practice (for of course everything we do is practical in the widest sense), but not practice in the ordinary sense of practice, which means doing something to an object itself. Had Eve instead of eating the apple spoken merely and said it was an apple, she would have arrived at theory and we should not be bearing the burden of original sin. The diversion of the practical response may take other forms than speech. The object may suggest to me ideas and divert my mind to them; or I may merely note in it other qualities and divert my response to those. When I am on the point of striking my enemy, I may remember that he is good, or note that he is big. Always the normal response to the object apprehended is diverted into other channels, and then the apprehension ceases to be practical and becomes theoretical.

This account of theory may help us to understand how constructiveness becomes contemplative, for there are at once likenesses and unlikenesses, both of which I must indicate. Speech may form the starting-point, for speech is itself an act of construction. Construction differs from practice in this, that practice is a response directed upon the object towards which we respond, while construction is productive and is not directed upon the object which provokes the construction but upon something else. When I strike a person, I affect or alter him ; when I curse him I do not alter *him*, the original object, I make a new object, the words of the curse. Speech is creative of fresh objects though they follow accepted patterns ; but construction need not be creative of its actual material : the architect does not make his stones ; what he makes, and this is production, is the arrangement and form of them. Constructiveness thus is always productive either of the materials themselves or of their transformation or of both. And in every case what it produces is something different from the thing which evokes the construction. The nightingale's mind is fixed upon his mate ; his response is not mating but his song. Even the beaver or the bee makes something and does not merely respond. The bee's end is to store his honey, and the beaver's to secure his winter home. The bird's nest-building is incidental to its care for its young, and so far as its mind can be said to be fixed upon anything, it is the premonition of its young which makes it construct.

Now in so far as construction produces a new object, other than that which fired it, it brings to the creature's apprehension a new revelation. Having been constructed the work is there to be observed. The animal, however, is no further interested than in taking note of what it has produced ; in the same way, though perhaps with warmer feeling, that it notes the other things that surround it. Even the craftsman, with all his reflectiveness and purpose, though he may watch the work in its progress, is guided still by his practical purpose ; he observes in order to see if the machine is doing its work. His constructiveness is indeed human and has the prerogatives of his possession of ideas, but does not otherwise differ from the animal's. He observes his work, even observes his work theoretically, but with an eye bent on the purpose for which his construction is undertaken. How may he come, as an artist, to detach himself from this practical preoccupation, and follow lovingly the lines of his own invention, and possessed by that passionate contemplation perhaps even alter his machine here and there so as to achieve beauty?

Let us take the case then of speech and ask how speech becomes artistic, whether poetry or prose. Speech is creative, and that fact offers such foundation as there is for a doctrine that has acquired authority in our own time, that linguistics and aesthetics are the same subject. It misses the difference of aesthetic from ordinary speech. For speech of itself is a construction for practical purpose. Either it is the means of creating theory or speculative consideration of things, and then it has the practical purpose of description, as in science. Or else it is manifestly practical, because it is the indication of our needs. To say ' I am cold ' means in general ' help me to get warm '. It is a winter's night and friends are gathered together, and one says it would be comfortable to have more fire. That is constructive practical speech, and it may require not only for scientific description, but even for practical needs, much skill and niceness in the construction. Compare those words with familiar ones :

> Dissolve frigus, ligna super foco
> Large reponens.

' Thaw away the cold, piling generous logs upon the fire.' The subject is indeed practical, but the words are not practical speech ; they are used lovingly as words, though they express the same practical thought as before. They are not indeed striking as art ; but for a striking difference take an accurate description of spring and the appearance of the fields at that time, which would be speech practical, and compare it with

> When daisies pied and violets blue,
> And lady-smocks all silver white,
> And cuckoo-buds of yellow hue,
> Do paint the meadows with delight.

ART AND INSTINCT

There, at least in the last line, is enchantment, not from the thought alone but from the words.

But I have only illustrated and not explained. How do words get diverted from their practical use, and become enchanted? How does the magic get in? When physical objects, instead of being apprehended through practice, as originally they are, are apprehended theoretically, it was, we saw, because the normal response was diverted into another response and primarily into speech. But when speech itself, instead of being used as a practical means, becomes the end, there is no other response into which the speech response can be diverted. If there were, we should be contemplating the words theoretically, as indeed we do in the science of them. Now the very thing which the poet does not do is to contemplate his words theoretically. He makes an artistic and not a scientific use of them. Since then there is no other action to detach words from practice, except the action of poetic construction itself, what is it which effects the detachment?

It is, I suggest, the constructive excitement itself which attaches the words to the artist and detaches them from their practical issues. The constructed object (the word), instead of leading the mind on to its practical effect, stimulates or serves as a signal for the continuance of the constructive activity itself, and leads on to the next constructed object (word) in the connected work. Just as to pass from one thing to another in a train of ideas loosens the first thing from its practical urgency and makes it an object of theory, so the first element in a constructional whole may lead on, through the constructive process, to the next element, without regard for the practical outcome. Then we have art. In the constructive process the objects then are held or possessed by the constructor. The poet makes himself one with his words and so holds them to himself, and detaches them from the subject matter which excited his constructive impulse. In practical speech or the use of speech for the practical means of description, there may be constructive passion, as anyone may attest who recalls the effort of bare accurate description. But it is the subject described which interests him : his use of speech, his constructiveness, is a means to describing the subject, which remains outside him and he a looker on. It is the subject which excites his constructive passion and he has to use his constructions in order to satisfy the subject matter. The poetic excitement of constructiveness seeks to satisfy the poet himself, at least to satisfy himself as well as be adequate to the subject matter. And in this passionate constructive effort he blends himself with his materials, which are words, holds them to himself, and thus constructiveness in speech becomes contemplative.

It has been said by others, by Mr. Middleton Murry for instance, that poetry differs from prose in its greater passion ; and it may be added that artistic prose, that is good prose, differs from ordinary speech in its being felt more deeply — anybody who tries to write as well as he can will note the rising tide of constructive excitement as he chooses his speech. But there is more in the artist's excitement than a greater intensity of passion. There is a difference in kind. The poet's specific passion is about words and finds expression in them. Two persons may be excited in equal intensity about the same subject matter, but the specific excitement from which they work may be entirely different and have different results. Spinoza thought with as much passion as Wordsworth upon the spirit which pervades nature, probably with more, and with greater insight. But in the one the constructive excitement issued in poetic words, in the other it issued in science or philosophy.

The constructive instinct then becomes artistic when it ceases to be practical ; and it ceases to be practical when it is pursued for its own sake, and the constructed object, in our case the words, is used as the satisfaction of the constructive passion itself. The passion takes possession of its object and lifts it out of practical consideration. It is not play, for play is still the shadow of practice, and continues practice when the urgency of practice is removed. Spencer was mistaken, therefore, when he affiliated art with play.

ART AND INSTINCT

If one thing is more true of art than another it is that art is serious, not play but work, not mere exuberance but a vocation; and if it were not so there would be no room for art in serious life. It is the constructiveness of play from which art is descended and not the playfulness of it.

In order to mark the absorption of art in its product, of poetry, say, in words, I have overstressed the poet's preoccupation with words, as if his attention was primarily directed to them. On the contrary the poet's attention is fixed upon his subject matter, the person he loves, the flowers he describes, and this passion sets him constructing language, by the natural or instinctive action of his constructive habit. He sings spontaneously as the bird sings, and he is not occupied with words in the sense that he thinks out the words to express his ideas.[1] The greatest

[1] See on this point further *Art and the Material*, Manchester, 1925; and 'The Creative Process in the Artist's Mind', *British Journal of Psychology*, vol. xvii. pt. 4, April 1927.

[The second of these papers began with a quotation from C. E. Montague's then recent novel, *Rough Justice*, in which the hero made some very Alexandrian remarks about 'how the feeling itself was changed just by being expressed'. In a letter M. wrote: 'I'm the most honoured of cheap deal pegs for the very best of hats. It's cheek of me to say it, but you seem to me enormously right all through. On p. 315 of your paper, in particular, every sentence is supported by what I have noticed when watching artists at work. Muirhead Bone and Francis Dodd are the two I have seen most. In both the rising excitement was obvious and I was pretty certain that this excitement and delight varied in direct proportion to the quality the man was putting into his work at the time — and he was exhausted afterwards in the same proportion.

'Some sort of analogy between this creative excitement in art and the mental exaltation attending the begettal of children can't help suggesting itself, and I have sometimes thought the sexual exaltation may be the nearest the common man ever comes to the sort of ecstasy in which a line like

" And visited all night by troops of stars "

is written. But there's such a plague of sloppy talk about everything's relation to sex that one rather wants to think there may be nothing in it.

'It's splendid that you write about these things. I've always been simply bewildered and numbed by Hegel's treatment of fine art and by Bosanquet's treatment of Hegel's. They seem to know everything except the one extraordinary thing that befalls the first-rate artist when he is functioning well. It's strange, for, as you say, we all experience it in our degree, and might suspect that the tip-top artist is differentiated from others by his supernormal powers of being excited into something far above his ordinary form, and this very quickly, in response to the stimulus of physical contact with his paints or clay.'—Editor's note.]

poems have their spontaneity written upon their faces. The poet's words are selected by his constructive passion, and reveal to himself or to his hearers the more intimate details of that passion as fixed upon the subject which inspires it. The words are used for their own sakes, not as external objects to be examined but as the means by which the constructive passion is assuaged. The words are part and parcel of the process of construction ; though of course they may also need to be handled technically as well. So complex and subtle is the difference which removes art on the one hand from practice, on the other from theory.

The aesthetic emotion is the emotion proper to the aesthetic impulse and contains many elements blended into one corresponding to the various elements in the impulse itself. There is the predominating element of sheer constructiveness, the delight in making ; there is the element of synthesis or the constructional element, that of composition ; and there is the sensuous pleasure of the material, in poetry the mere pleasure, improperly called beauty, of the words as sounds, and of the images they convey, as well as the added pleasures of metre and rhythm and rhyme which partly trench upon the pleasure of the composition. The constructional element or composition is shared by art with science and morals, and is thus not distinctive of art. The experience of aesthetic form is the experience not merely of relations but of relations within stone or pigments or words ; that is to say, relations among constructed objects. Undoubtedly the form of the work of art (in the sense of its internal relations, not in the mere sense in which artistic objects are distinguished from practical objects which may be consumed) provides a large ingredient in the total of the aesthetic condition of mind. The predominating ingredient is still that of delight in construction itself. But without the other ingredients it would not be different from the constructive pleasure directed to practical ends of the nightingale or the bee. This has helped probably to confirm some in mistaking art for play.

To avoid misconception there are certain things I must

ART AND INSTINCT

make clear, even if it delays me. I have assumed that the poet is occupied about words, that is spoken sounds, with the meanings and the pictures they convey. They are his material as pigments are to the painter — spoken words, not marks upon paper which are no more poetry than a musical score is music. It is believed by some that what a poet deals with is pictures or thoughts, and words are merely his technical means of expression. I plead that a poem is made of words in the sense described. Without the meanings they convey, the words of a poem would be mere sounds, and, though they may be so handled as to approach music, they are not, as bare sounds, poems. Words are sounds which carry meanings with them and the two cannot be parted. But the meanings belong in poetry to the essence of the word and the words are not mere symbols to indicate meanings as they are in practical or scientific speech. So understood, I trust the plea may be accepted as that of plain fact. If the business of a poem is merely to excite ideas, give me Spinoza rather than Wordsworth. When I want poetry I go to Wordsworth, as I go to Shakespeare, because the enchantment is in his significant words. Alas! Wordsworth himself has taken a different view.

In the next place, when I say that constructiveness in words becomes art, whether poetry or prose, because the speaker in his aesthetic passion detaches his words from practice by blending himself with the material in which he works, I mean no mysterious union of spirit and matter; I am only describing imperfectly a real occurrence. I mean two things. First, that words in a poem, say (to confine myself to poetry, and bearing in mind that, as Wordsworth said, the difference is not between poetry and prose, but between art and science), are art only for one who says them, whether it be the artist who makes them or the hearer of them when they are made. When we hear, we are thrown back into the aesthetic or constructive passion from which the artist wrote, and at second hand reproduce the conditions of the poem's origin.

ART AND INSTINCT

Secondly, there is no strange amalgam of material and passion, as if there were mind or passion in the words. The artist's passion enters into the poem by finding there material expression. It is a means to his creation, and that creation in turn serves us to recover the passion which is our means to apprehending the poem. The constructiveness issues in the poem itself, the choice and fashioning of the words, with all their qualities of sound and meaning in thought or picture. The structure of the material is the counterpart of the constructive passion of the poet. Only in this way does his passion form part of the poem.

There is another aspect, however, in which the poet's construction of his material affects the product. It is a construction from his whole personality, which includes what is vaguely called imagination. The excitement in which the subject matter of his poem throws him — the fields in spring, the beauty of a woman, his own material feelings of love (to be distinguished carefully from the passion of constructiveness by which he speaks his love) — this excitement spreads and evokes from his mind, from his experience of the past or his forecast of the future, ideas and impulses which feed his constructive impulse and are embodied in the poem. Hence it is that the poem is never the mere language of ordinary speech, whatever Wordsworth has said to the contrary; but there is always a strangeness in it, whether by the employment of unusual words, or something unusual in the combination of them, or some suggestion of human or other interest which they do not bear in their common usage. Who ever spoke outside a poem of painting the meadows with flowers, and even if he did, who ever outside a poem spoke of painting them with delight? I content myself with quoting two passages from Wordsworth himself, used often by others in aesthetic discussion. The first is the line which Matthew Arnold so deservedly praised:

> And never lifted up a single stone;

which might indeed, taken in isolation from the context,

be prose but is certainly art, for it introduces despair as practical speech could not. The second I borrow from Mr. Abercrombie :

> Rolled round in earth's diurnal course
> With rocks and stones and trees :

and leave it without comment. Even in such passages we can see how the poet does not merely take words as he finds them, but gives the material by his art an import which it does not of itself possess. Poetry shares in this respect with other arts the illusory treatment of its material, which is so much more easily recognised in sculpture, where the stone lives and the bronze breathes. But I add this for completeness' sake, and to indicate that the constructive impulse in artistic man does not merely use the physical properties of its materials, but introduces elements of meaning which their physical properties alone do not contain. He enters himself into the product because his materials are used, by artistic illusion, to mean more than they do in practical usage. Further remarks would take me far afield, and I fall back upon the song which paints the meadows with delight.

Poetry has been chosen, because it is only there that I can have the least pretension to form a judgment. I have the faith that what has been said of poetry will be found true of other arts, with the necessary changes and qualifications, which will be without doubt considerable. The object has been to identify and describe the artistic—or, better, the aesthetic—impulse, to indicate its instinctive basis, and how it exists when the constructive instinct becomes contemplative. To identify it does not affect in one iota the actual passion which is the form it takes in emotion. The ecstasy which may be felt in seeing a perfect picture or in reading or hearing a perfect poem remains ecstasy, no matter how cold reflection may describe it. And perhaps there is an advantage in recognising that these precious feeling are after all human, and do not separate us from the common life. For though there are few poets or painters or musicians and few architects who are also artists, the rest of us may have our constructive impulses excited to enjoyment and we thus share in the artist's life. The gift is 'in widest commonalty spread', awaiting education. And it is something for the artist, too, to recognise that his gift has an instinctive root, and that artistic action, that is, contemplative construction of the materials he uses, is really one of the series of human instincts. In its artistic shape it is derived and secondary, but remains instinctive in its nature. The artistic construction is compelled in him by the excitement which certain subjects provoke, and he is at a certain remove, and not so great a one, allied to his brother the nightingale and his humbler and dowdier brother the beaver. He sings and builds because he must.

So much in order to bate the pride of art, if thinking of its peculiar ecstasy it should exalt itself too high above nature. At the same time, if contemplative construction only exists through the blending of the artist or the spectator with the material, so that the material means what he makes it mean, it remains true that, as Mr. Bradley said of poetry, art transports us into a word of its own, 'independent, complete, autonomous'. It adds to the world a fresh reality, and that reality is not a part of the real world as commonly understood; for though the poem is a physical thing, and the picture still more plainly so, these are not artistic realities, except to the appreciating mind (we may now subjoin the constructive mind), which blends with them. And yet it remains a part of the world. It is our privilege to make new realities of our own construction, based on ordinary reality, but different, as we do when we make science or morals as well as when we make art. The very element of illusion which art employs when it gives its materials characters which as physical they do not possess, secures for the work artistic reality, and adds it to the real things of the world, which are called values.

Another conclusion follows which also is implied in Mr Bradley's statement. When, turning from the aesthetic impulse and its emotion, we ask ourselves what corresponds in the work of art to the constructive act, we find materials and relation amongst the materials which is I suppose what is meant by form. Now in poetry at least the materials which are words have meanings, and the meanings are the thoughts and images of the subject matter which enters into the poem — its subject matter as the subject matter is 'transformed' in the poem. And since the aesthetic impulse and emotion is conversant with the construction, it follows that the subject matter before it enters into the poem does not determine the aesthetic value. To use the happy word of Mr. Fry, it is the transformation of the subject into a character suitable to the constructive form which makes it an ingredient of the poem. As such it is, as the meaning of the words, part of the so-called 'content' of the poetic form. And while there can be no poem unless the words have meaning, the choice of subject matter does not affect the aesthetic appreciation. The art of a poem whose substance is nothing, like Peele's exquisite dialogue between Paris and Oenone ('Fair and fair and twice so fair', etc.), light as air, may be as great as the art of *Lycidas* or 'Like the baseless fabric of this vision'. No doubt the greater the subject, the more splendid the poem, but the subject as such is indifferent to the art. These are distinctions not of beauty but of what may be called perfection. It is the construction or form of the poem which makes its beauty, not its subject, except in so far as that subject is transformed into the content of the words.

Equally it follows, to turn back to the artist, that the aesthetic emotion is the constructive emotion. That the poet must have or he would be no artist. But he need not have in his mind the emotions which he portrays, unless indeed he is writing a lyric and his feelings are his subject matter. The passions of the dramatic personages of a play the poet may or may not have in his own person; it is his insight into them which makes Shakespeare a great dramatist, not that he must have felt their feelings. Thus the aesthetic emotion is distinct from the emotions which enter into the artist's subject.

We are here returned to that statement of Aristotle to which I referred at the opening. The gist of Aristotle's view of virtue may be put in words which are not his: that the passions are the subject matter which is transformed into virtue, and that in the end they are transformed by direction to the noble. Now the difference of virtue and the arts is that the material of virtue is the passions of the actors; the material of the artist is a physical medium, which the art fashions into a form, which, as held to the artist's or the spectator's mind, becomes an aesthetic experience. But the doctrine may be transferred from the one problem to the other. The problem of good conduct is to establish nobleness amongst the passions; the problem of the artist is to establish beauty in the form assumed by his materials. So far as he does so, his work is beautiful and he has the aesthetic emotion. Merely to influence the passions of the spectator about the subject, and to work from the passions congenial to the subject matter and not from the passion of construction, is to produce not art but illustration. In painting, the distinction is easy enough to draw. In poetry, which is a so-called representative art, it is harder to draw, but there, too, if sympathy with the subject as such, even if it be pity and fear in a tragedy, prevails over the delight in words and their construction and destroys the equipoise of sounds and their meanings, the result is not poetry but illustration or sentiment.

To extend these considerations from poetry to the other arts is beyond my scope. Painting in the past has been representative, though it has not been great art when it has descended, as it often has, to illustration. Now it is familiar knowledge that contemporary painting is passing through an experimental stage of new ideals; and a claim has even been preferred for abstract painting, which is said to be concerned with relations of space, as music with relations of time. No room, if this were true, would be left for

ART AND INSTINCT

subject matter in any picture. I cannot raise this question at the end of a lecture, even if I were competent. It may be that there is painting which has for its object merely 'significant form', reducible to nothing but spatial relations and colour. But significant form is significant of something. And even music, the most abstract of the arts to which these innovators attempt to assimilate painting, according to the classic statement of Hanslick, has for its subject ideas of movement ; and if this be true, it is hard to see how painting can avoid the question — form of what, or significant of what ?

But these topics are beyond my time and my powers. My purpose has been the limited one of defending the existence of a true aesthetic emotion, and to draw a lesson from nightingales and beavers and bees.

VIII

ARTISTIC CREATION AND COSMIC CREATION [1]

(Reprinted, by permission, from the *Proceedings of the British Academy*, vol. xiii.)

PICTORIAL imagination is a wondrous blessing not only for the lunatic, the lover, and the poet, but for the philosopher as well. Perhaps few philosophers have been devoid of it altogether, and nearly all persons who, without being philosophers by nature, attempt to think philosophically (and these are, I suppose, the majority of men, just as most men have the sense of beauty but only a privileged few are artists) possess it and are dependent on it. But here is the provokingness of it. Just when we reach ultimate problems or ultimate conceptions it deserts us. Either it is replaced by intellectual imagination or thought construction; and this is what happens to the philosopher proper; or it leaves us a prey to error or helplessness, which is often the case of the generality. For pictures are of the finite and the developed and of that which is distinct in its limited outlines. But they fail us when we touch the infinite or undeveloped and that which has no outlines but is the source of everything which has. And so a great imaginative writer like Plato, before he attained his full and abstruse and rigorous maturity, has recourse, when he comes within sight of his ultimate questions, to myth and symbol, glorious prefigurements of abstract conceptions like categories and numbers.

These rather trite reflections are suggested by the

[1] Read November 23, 1927. Annual Philosophical Lecture of the Academy.

problem of creation, that is, of cosmic creation. For the creations we know are finite products of nature or manufacture or art. But when we ask ourselves about the creation of the world we stumble, because we carry these pictures about with us and we try to intrepret by their help what is beyond the reach of pictures. Thus because for us a statue or a picture or a scientific theory or a steam engine is brought into being by a mind or spirit operating upon matter, or a great and beautiful fancy comes or seems to come out of our minds, we imagine a spirit which is an indefinite enlargement of ours, which educes the world from we know not where by the fiat of his will. Or we may even in our naïver moments imagine some man-like creator hewing the world out of some rough quarry, as drawn in a picture which used to delight me as a boy in Pouchet's *Universe* which I got for a prize. Strictly speaking, we cannot ask of the whole how it came into being, for all these conceptions, coming into being, production, causation, willing, decrees, belong to the parts of the world and not to the world as a whole. The philosopher Lotze is never tired of saying that to ask the reason why the world was created is a question *mal posée*. Yet the philosopher may expose the unfitness of the question as he will; the unregenerate man, and the philosopher himself, when he relaxes from his tension of thought, persists in it. He is not content to accept the world; it is so mysterious a thing that the world should be, not merely the sort of thing that it is in its details and its laws, but that it should be at all, that he finds himself unable to dispense with the imagination of a creating agency. And, as if by some instinctive feeling, he does not go on as he rightly should to enquire into the origin of this spirit — if God made the world, what made God? The obscure and correct sentiment that no further question can be asked leaves him content with the ultimate Spirit which is, and from which all existence flows. But using as he does imaginative ideas derived from finites, he is content, because happily for him he does not think, and he can explain neither how this immense finite which he calls infinite got there nor how it can produce the world.

I too shall join the philosophers and shall try to show that our question is not how the world came into being, but what sort of a thing the world is in its ultimate and simplest nature, within which we may legitimately say that creation takes place and things are produced and events come to be and are caused. I am sure that if I say Spirit is there that I cannot rest content with using this picture of the most developed thing we know, without asking how it came to be. But I know also how hard it is to avoid asking the question even if the elementary world is correctly conceived, and I too am beset with the pictorial habit of going outside the world, as it were, and asking for its author. It seems to me, therefore, useful for myself and perhaps for others to enquire first what creation is where we are familiar with it, and to use the answer to that problem to interpret what creation must mean when we speak of a creative principle in the whole world. It may be that to find the source of the world in a spirit is to make a mistaken use of the analogy of artistic or other finite creation. At any rate the first enquiry is feasible.

I

For the ways of the Universe may be past finding out, but the ways of art need not be, and it is a good rule that we should go to what experience presents us to, before we indulge in conjecture or hypothesis. I am not proposing to examine fully the nature of beauty, either what it is in itself or what the feeling of beauty is. And I am not going to raise the question whether nature or natural objects may not be beautiful of themselves without the need of an appreciative mind; whether, that is to say, beauty is not in beautiful natural objects themselves, a property of them independent of our human eyes and ears. I think myself it is not, and the mind is always there as a party to the beautiful situation. I limit myself to the beautiful in art, and there at least one thing seems to me clear, that in such objects spirit and matter are blended and at one. The object embodies the artist's thought or fancy, while the moulded object is aesthetically significant only to his appreciation, or of course in minor degree to that of the spectator whom in a manner he teaches to see with the aesthetic eye. More than once I have pointed out how in the beautiful object the significance is supplied in part from the artist's mind; how it is he who makes the flat Madonna seem, as Mr. Berenson puts it, a tangible three-dimensional being, or who gives divine playfulness to the Hermes, or motion and dance to the motionless maidens in the picture of the Spring, or who finds the perfect, the only fitting word, to express a meaning that springs from him, in what manner we shall presently see. And I have contrasted the object of art with the mere percept where also half comes from the perceiver's mind and half from what he directly sees: the coloured moving shape is perceived to be a man, though sight alone without memory does not say so. The contrast, if I may repeat myself, is this: the characters we impute to the object perceived, if we perceive correctly, really do belong to the object and may be sensed there on proper occasion; the coloured shape is the visible surface of a man; but in the work of art there is always illusion: the Hermes is not divine only but seems so, and the girls in the Spring are not in motion. At the same time, I have added, the artistic illusion is unlike ordinary perceptual illusion, for that illusion disappears to better acquaintance, is recognised to be an illusion. Whereas the illusion is of the essence of the work of art — ceases, therefore, to be illusion and makes the object significant. Hence the Hermes which you see in the gallery or which the Greeks saw at Olympia is not a mere marble block, not even a mere block so shaped. Only to the aesthetic eye is it really divine or even really alive, and when you see it so you are in the aesthetic attitude. Hence as mere marble, so shaped, it belongs to the natural world; but as Hermes, the playful god, it has a new reality, compounded of the marble and the spectator's mind. This does not mean any mysterious blending of stone and mind, but merely that the stone has qualities which it only has so long as it is contemplated by the mind. This inner compenetration of the two is effected by the marble's being so shaped, so textured, so played upon with light and shade, or it may be so draped or even coloured. *There* was the artist's creation; he found by his hand this body to be the bearer of his thought. I pass deliberately over many points of interest or difficulty, in particular the sense in which the statue or picture is expressive. I add another illustration to drive in the main lesson that I learn. Take a beautiful portrait of an ugly person. The picture is beautiful, the real person represented is, let us say, repellent. The artist has seized the essence of the person's character and embodied it in the form of his ordered pigments, has made the form significant of, say, a noble character or at any rate a character that counts for something, even if bad or weak. He makes this subject significant and he has lent significance to his pigments out of himself and therefore signified himself as well; he has, in expressing himself, made his subject characteristic. Presently you meet the person and you recognise him to be the noble or characteristic man he is. He does not therefore become beautiful; he is still a man with a repellent face and an attractive character. If, after seeing his picture or for other reasons of your own, you see him beautiful, you are imposing upon nature the aesthetic interpretation. That is why I said a moment ago, that in my belief natural objects were not beautiful or ugly in themselves; there's nothing beautiful or ugly, if I may parody Hamlet, but aesthetic imagination makes it so.[1]

So intimately in the work of art are form and significance blended into one; and hence it is that different

[1] The above statement, that the work of art implies, besides the material, imputation from the artist may seem less easy to justify in those works where, as for instance in certain paintings, the representative element is in abeyance in comparison with the formal one, or in music in which at first sight there is no human addition or subtraction. Yet I believe the statement is true even here.

writers can say that form is the essence of art, or meaning (characteristic) is the essence of it.

But at this point I find myself confronted with a doctrine which appears under different forms, that the embodiment of the work of art in external physical form, in stone or pigments or musical sounds or words (I mean of course spoken words, for mere writing or print is notation and nothing more), is unessential, a matter of technique. Even Wordsworth has given currency to this idea:

> Oh! many are the poets [he says in a famous passage of *The Excursion*] that are sown
> By nature; men endowed with highest gifts,
> The vision and the faculty divine,
> Yet wanting the accomplishment of verse.

As if poetry lay in the poet's vision and the words were nothing but an added and not an intrinsic element. Nowadays it is often said that the work of art exists in the artist's mind as an image or intuition, and that since the image is his private possession it needs embodiment in physical form to give it publicity, to communicate it to others, and give permanence to the transitory mental existence, and that this is the sole purpose of technical embodiment in material. If this were true, there would not be the fusion of external material and the artist's mind which I am suggesting is vital to art in all its forms, and the analogy of the arts would lead to a different result when used to illustrate cosmic creation.

Elsewhere [1] I have given reasons for believing that this conception is mistaken and that the physical material work is organic to artistic creation. Artistic production is on a line with the other organic actions by which we become aware of the physical things in perception. When I see a colour, I am not first aware of the colour and then turn my eyes to it. On the contrary the coloured object, by its

---

[1] *Art and the Material* (Adamson Lecture), Manchester University Press, 1925; and *Art and Instinct* (Herbert Spencer Lecture), Oxford, 1927.

action on my retina and my brain, compels me to fix my eyes upon it, and in doing so I become aware of the colour. I do not first know and then act, I know through acting; the object is revealed to me because it wrings from me an appropriate action. Artistic production is of the same sort, but more complicated. For the practical actions we perform on physical objects are directed towards those objects: we alter them or, in cognition, attend to them. While in our artistic actions, in production, we create a new thing, the work of art. But the general character of the process remains the same. The subject matter of the artist, the face he is painting, or the feeling, say of love, or the dramatic situation he is thinking of or is possessed by, throws him into a state of artistic excitement which issues in the act of speaking verse or painting the face or sculpturing the head in stone. The action is wrung from him by the subject matter, through the excitement it produces, in the same way as turning his eyes to a colour or sniffing an odour by his nostrils is wrung from him through the nervous excitement the colour or odour produces in his brain. And, just as the object known is revealed through the ordinary reaction to it, so the work of art is revealed to the artist himself through the productive act wrung from him in his excitement over the subject matter. Accordingly, he does not in general first form an image (if he is a poet, say) of what he wants to express, but finds out what he wanted to express by expressing it; he has, in general, no precedent image of his work and does not know what he will say till he has said it, and it comes as a revelation to himself.

The only way to test this statement is by appeal to artists themselves. But in part I can refer you to such experience as anyone may have of artistic production when he tries to write an essay or even a letter as well as possible. I will take two illustrations and put the question to you. The first is very familiar to you. I may say in practical prose, 'I love you and always shall'. That is a practical proposition. It is a long way from that to Burns:

ARTISTIC CREATION AND COSMIC CREATION

> As fair art thou, my bonnie lass,
>   So deep in luve am I;
> And I will luve thee still, my dear,
>   Till a' the seas gang dry.

Do you think the poet had first in his mind some vision of an eternity of love which would last till the seas dried up, or that in the aesthetic excitement of his feeling or thought about his feeling the thrilling words were out of him before he knew?

My second example is even more familiar and it is far graver:

And Ruth said, Intreat me not to leave thee, or to return from following after thee; for whither thou goest, I will go, and where thou lodgest, I will lodge; thy people shall be my people, and thy God my God. Where thou diest will I die, and there will I be buried; the Lord do so to me, and more also if aught but death part thee and me.

The writer's mind is occupied with thoughts and images of the devotion of the alien daughter to her husband's mother. Does he, playing with the pictures suggested by that devotion, merely translate the pictures into this perfection of words? Or does he in his artistic understanding of the passion of Ruth allow his artistic excitement to overflow at white heat into words which reveal to himself as well as to us the situations of life appropriate to her devotion?

Thus it is not true, as you might suppose from Wordsworth's words, that poetry lies in the vision and that putting into words is an added accomplishment. A man may have vision, even the most imaginative vision, of his subject matter, but it is only when that vision excites him into the more or less unreflective[1] issue in words that he is a poet,

---

[1] I say more or less unreflective. For I do not mean that his action is absolutely blind. On the contrary there may be at the back of his mind all manner of literary or other artistic experiences and learning, and the habitual correction by poets or painters of their work in subsequent versions is enough to show the part which reflection may play. Yet even when a poet corrects he is prompted by dissatisfaction with the existing word as an expression of his aesthetic emotion in its spontaneous action.

ARTISTIC CREATION AND COSMIC CREATION

and that depends upon far more than education in speech. Poetry exists in the spoken words, rhythmical and passionate and enchanted. It is they which contain and reveal the exact working of his mind; though words are no more poetry in themselves without their meanings than the vision of the poet about the subject is poetry without issuing in ordered speech.

There are, however, various reasons which may deceive us into supposing that the physical material is indifferent, a mere means of publicity, and that the work of art is finished in the imagination of the artist. In the first place, all artists in respect of certain parts of the work, and some artists in respect of the whole of it, anticipate the finished product in idea or imagination. There is no doubt of the fact, but the fact is misinterpreted if it is taken to imply that the physical execution is unessential. For the image of the product is to be distinguished from the image of the subject matter however much thought and insight and vision gather around that subject matter. The image of the finished product, of the picture or the poem or the statue, is the image of the product; it implies words or pigments or stone, and perhaps it involves also images of the very movements which the artist makes with his brush or chisel or his voice. The difference between artists who work in this way and those who do not is merely the difference between doing a sum in your head and on paper. The work of art is done in the head, but whether it is real pigments we deal with or imaged pigments is a matter of no importance. It is through experience of the actual pigments and words and stone that the artist can dispense with their actual presence. The real problem is how from his vision of the subject matter the artist proceeds to his product; but whether that product is left in his head or he is aware of it only by seeing or hearing the actual (as distinct from the imagined) material is insignificant. In the first case, he does but transfer into physical reality what is imaged as physical reality. The image which he forms in the first instance of the picture or the statue or the verse is wrung from him by his artistic excitement about the subject matter.

Another kind of misinterpretation arises in this way. An artist, without imagining the product, the painting, etc., may form a vivid and detailed image of the subject matter, and he may fancy that he is merely transcribing this image in much the same way as a man of science transcribes exactly the facts he is engaged upon. It is not so easy to fall into this deception with painting or sculpture, for the more suitable the vision is for mere imitation the more it approximates to an image of the finished product, that is, the case we have just dealt with. But in poetry, the artist sometimes does appear merely to imitate in words, or describe, as it were in a transcript, the image in his mind; and so it might be supposed that it is really this vision of his of the subject, the moaning of the doves and the like, that is the poet's model which he faithfully describes. Now, in the first place, such imitative or purely descriptive passages are never the highest poetry, nor is descriptive music the highest music. And, in the next place, the words never are purely a transcription of an imagined scene, but in the intoxication of the picture the poet as his words flow alters the picture from which he works under the influence of the words, as in the enchanting picture of Eden in *Paradise Lost*. Out of the wealth of images which arise in his mind he has to select and amplify and modify to suit the condition of his mind, and the history of his imagination is never distinct from the history of his speech, but the two are moulded together one upon the other, and the images are half-spoken words, and moreover are subjected to the needs of language, at the behest of rhythm or rhyme.[1]

We may safely, then, conclude that the material of the work of art is no mere technical ingredient but vital: that poetry is words of a certain sort and a painting pigments,

---

[1] Some further discussion of these topics will be found in a paper on 'The Creative Process in the Artist's Mind', *British Journal of Psychology*, vol. xvii. pt. 4, April 1927.

and a statue physical stone, idealised to contain the artist's meaning or his passion, and chosen to be such and such, this word and not that, this shade and not that, this outline and not that, because thus and thus only can the subject matter receive the significance he imparts to it.

I have spoken of the artistic excitement without attempting to describe it, and it will be as well to do so shortly,[1] because recent theories about the motive which produces art lend colour to the notion that art is the translation of images into material form. The aesthetic excitement is not to be identified with the practical passions which the subject matter may arouse in the artist's mind, which overflow into words, as anger for instance into expression of hate. The artist may or may not feel such emotions; in lyrics he does, in drama he need not. It is almost a commonplace that poetry or painting which does no more than excite in the hearer's or the spectator's mind such emotions is, in itself, no more than story-telling or illustration, which by itself has not artistic but only practical value and may easily degenerate into sentiment. The passion proper to the artist and communicated to others in minor degree, the aesthetic impulse with its aesthetic emotion is of a specific sort. It is, I believe, the formal impulse of constructiveness, which is an outgrowth from or a modification of the instinct of constructiveness which we share with such animals as the bee, the beaver, or the bird which sings for courtship or builds a nest for its young. It is so overlaid with human characters, so refined, as to seem remote from its instinctive origin. In particular it has become diverted from practice and contemplative. When the instinct of constructiveness seeks not practical gratification but is satisfied for its own sake; when the maker beholds his work and sees that it is good, the constructive instinct has become aesthetic and the work which satisfies it is beautiful.

The artist then works upon his clay or words or pigments under the compulsion of this impulse, but with his

[1] Cf. *Art and Instinct* for fuller treatment.

ARTISTIC CREATION AND COSMIC CREATION

eye directed upon his subject matter, which partly is present to his mind in all manner of conscious perceptions, images, and thought, and partly affects him unconsciously. Of these unconscious elements, some are the familiar subconscious motives which enter into ordinary waking experience; but some may well belong to that deeper unconscious which, according to a well-known discovery, is revealed in the imagery of dreams. Indeed, it has been suggested that art is nothing more than a dream expressed in external form through the strange gift of translation which the artist possesses; that, for instance, the moving force of Dante's art is his love for the real Beatrice Portinari. I submit that his love would account for the thoughts of Beatrice which are woven into his poem but not for the art of it. Such motives belong to the subject matter. They may appear as images in dreams, but dreams are not in themselves art but only reveal the stirrings in the mind of the dreamer which are connected with the topic of his art. Impulses which might appear in his dreams as imagery are in his waking life only part of the background of his topic, exercising doubtless an important, even perhaps the chief, influence over the materials which go to constitute his subject matter. They do not in him take the form of imagery, but are unconscious movements in his brain which have no conscious object while he is not dreaming. There is, I suspect, a confusion in this doctrine between the artist's mind when he is at work upon his art and his mind as it might be if he were dreaming. In either case the unconscious elements belong to the subject matter and not to the art. The artist must have something upon which to work, but his artistic impulse lies in the choice of his materials, to which there corresponds in the work of art its design which gives it form.[1]

[1] The problem is discussed in Mr. J. M. Thorburn's suggestive work *Art and the Unconscious*, London, 1925. He has a felicitous if paradoxical way of connecting art and dream; he says the artist's external material, clay or stone, hypnotises the artist into sleep.

ARTISTIC CREATION AND COSMIC CREATION

II

This digression has been long, but it has removed from the work of creative imagination the last trace of accidental elements ; that product is a material thing of speech or instrumental sounds or solider pigments or stone, dyed through and through with meanings, and these meanings sustained and supplied by the appreciating mind. With this conclusion we can proceed by the help of analogy to the cosmic problem. But what might seem to the hasty glance the natural application of the analogy, to suppose a creator, spiritual and more than man, fashioning a material which he finds or even creates from himself, is in reality to misuse the analogy by exploiting its accidental features and neglecting the essence. The essence of the work of art is that in it creative mind and the material are indissolubly fused. That this fusion is the meeting of two separate beings, the man who creates and the material which receives from him its form, is indeed vital to the artistic situation, but arises from the finitude both of the creator and his material.

Now the use of an analogy lies in its relevance ; it misleads if it is not adapted to the new situation in which it is employed. It was from such neglect that, to take an illustration from psychology or biology, instinct was so long misunderstood as proceeding from explicit purpose. Closer inspection, freed from the anthropomorphic or pathetic fallacy, showed that below the level of strict purpose there was something which simulates purpose, or of which purpose is an explicit form, which is nothing more than the prearrangement by which one step in a complex of movements prepares, and flows continuously into, the next. We may call such purposiveness if we choose unconscious purpose, but we only substitute a phrase. But when we have learnt that actions may conduce to an end which is not foreseen, we cease to gape at the exceeding skill of animals lower than ourselves and still more to suppose them endowed with these powers by an all-

ARTISTIC CREATION AND COSMIC CREATION

foreseeing Creator; we adopt the modester and not less reverent method of seeking to understand them and their place in nature. The hardest thing is to understand that which is simple. We may and must approach it from the complex. But if we identify the simple with the complex we miss the sense of both. We use our knowledge of the complex rightly in interpreting the simple when we discount the circumstances which make it complex. And this is difficult and requires some pains.

In applying the analogy of the arts to the world we must then discount the finitude of the partners in the transaction, and when we do this the application of the analogy is exactly counter to the notion of a mind or spirit which precedes the world and creates it. For in the first place the infinite, being infinite, can have nothing outside itself upon which to work as an artist works on his material. On the other hand what is vital to art is not, in this connection, the separateness of the artist and his work before the work is done, but their fusion when the artistic product is achieved. Strip off, then, the finitude involved in art; we must look, then, to the world in its simplest expression, and there we find something which corresponds to the essence of art, the complete fusion in it of something that corresponds to mind and something that corresponds to material. To be stricter, we find rather something in which there is no fusion at all except metaphorically and by legitimate analogy; something which is anterior in thought to fusion, but in which thought can detect these different aspects. It is itself uncreated but is merely there. In it, as in a matrix, are formed the finite things which are said to be created and to have a beginning, which acquire a semi-independent existence, like crystals in the mother liquid in which they are deposited. It is, in the old phrase, cause of itself, *causa sui*, self-created. But though uncreated, it is creative, in the sense that these crystals or embryos grow within its womb; and it must contain in itself some principle or character which is manifested in this growth. It has no purpose, but its creativeness comes to fruition in certain finites which possess true purpose, and we should expect to find, as we do, gradations between what appears as mechanical action at one end and true purpose at the other. There is no creator of it except itself; but it is the creator of all finites that come into being within it. But to say that the world has no Creator is not to say that it has no God. On the contrary the whole hierarchy of things cries out for a form of created existence beyond what is hitherto created, and the whole universe regarded as engaged in producing this higher form of existence is God. God's deity, then, is created; but the whole world is divine as being big with this created quality, and God, therefore, though not the Creator of the Universe, is, so far as he is identical with the Universe, creator of all the beings within it.

Such is the true application of creation in the arts by analogy to cosmic creation, and it is just the opposite of what might seem at first blush the natural application of it. There is no room for any spirit which precedes the world, not even to say as Goethe does, in that metaphysical poem about the birth of colour in the Zuleikah book of the *Westöstlicher Divan*, that it lay in the eternal bosom of God; there is but the universe itself, whose name in one aspect of it is God. But such a simplification removes also, or at least helps us better to withstand, the temptation to ask for the origin of the world from something other than itself, a temptation against which, as I said, the philosopher is no more proof than the unphilosopher. For we who ask the question are products of the process of creation, and we dare not speak of the universe in terms of its parts. But if we think of the world as primordially a spirit, and not less of a spirit than ourselves but more of one, as we necessarily do if we indulge in such descriptions as I have named, we are not securing simplicity, but only interpreting the simple by the complex. We merely substitute for the complex human spirit which we know another complex spirit which we do not know. It is as if we were to seek simplicity in our lives and habits, not by

ARTISTIC CREATION AND COSMIC CREATION

dispensing with unnecessaries but by returning to staining our skins with woad or living on roots and cooking our game in a cave. We only vary our accidentals, choosing a more inconvenient form of them, which we imagine simpler. But the Universe in its basal character is fundamental to every form of product which grows up within it, and if we try to get down to fundamental simplicity it must not be in terms of the mind we know. The simple world may still contain its analogue to mind, but that mind will be more and not less elementary than ours. If we thus bear in our thoughts that we are units in the outgrowth of the fundamental stuff of the world, we shall accept that world as above our questioning, like Shakespeare in Matthew Arnold's sonnet : ' Others abide our question, thou art free '. We may question of ourselves and all other created things, but the world itself is subject to none of our ideas but is the source of them.

The only question, then, that is left for the metaphysician is of what nature is this primordial world which literally underlies the universe we know ; which is no fancied Absolute that, bare itself of all natural qualities, blossoms out into them as its appearances ; which is being itself, and neither cause nor substance nor one nor many nor things, but contains numbers and causes and things within itself, as real features or parts of itself and not merely as emitted from itself into precarious appearance. The answer to this question is open to much doubt. It has been suggested that the stuff of the world is space-time itself, which physicists hold to be no mere receptacle of things, no mere form of mind but something quasi-physical. And I have dared to think that the matter which the physicists postulate in addition is not fundamental but itself a growth within space-time. Such a stuff may also be described as motion ; happily or not I must not judge, for at least this primordial motion is not the motion of material particles, which is derivative. Motion, understood as the primordial stuff, is what change becomes if you strip from change the notion of some quality which is

ARTISTIC CREATION AND COSMIC CREATION

replaced by some other quality. Rather the name is used to indicate that passage of nature of which Mr. Whitehead speaks, and to insist that the stuff of things is events and groups of events, not something fixed and resting but something which contains in itself a principle of unrest.

As the work of art is the fusion of spirit and matter in finite ingredients, so within this space-time, which is below fusion, there is an element which corresponds to spirit and one which corresponds to matter, and these are respectively time and space. Time is, as it were, the mind to the body which is space. Or since we are helping ourselves out to describe the simple by the complex (though without the fallacies which pictorial imagination introduces) let us rather say that in spirit and body as we know them, whether in an organism or in the new creation by man which art supplies, spirit is the time, and body or material the space element in these highly developed creations of the world process. Our life is the time of our body, which is the space of our life; only for brevity's sake I have to omit the qualifications which are needed to make this proposition true.

Space and time are, however, indissoluble ingredients of the one reality which is space-time, and neither has an existence independent of the other. Each involves the other. Though I cannot make good this statement here, it is in keeping with the recent physical conceptions; and it serves me in passing on to two points of the first importance. One of them I have already indicated. Since space cannot be without time, it follows that all stable things, which we are apt to regard as fixed things which may undergo changes, are but groups of motions or changes; that as a river preserves its form while in reality it is a stream of changing matter, so the material and other things which crystallise within the matrix of space-time are but groups of motions which preserve their form. So far as regards the living organism this would be readily accepted, and certainly by those who have felt the force of Mr. J. S. Haldane's account, based on the processes of respiration which he describes summarily in his work *Organism and Environment* (Yale Press, 1917), of how the structure and constitution of one part of the system depends upon the needs of the other parts. ' The structure ', he says, ' is only the appearance given by what seems at first to be a constant flow of specific material beginning and ending in the environment ' (p. 99). The stress lies here on the word ' flow '. Extend this notion downwards from organic to material things (which Mr. Haldane would perhaps not be willing himself to do) and you have the conception of things, whether living or not, as stable configurations, as a whole of movements or, if you care to use organic terms, of functions.

The second point is less obvious and more contentious, but it is to my mind not less clear. The primordial world which is without parts breaks up into parts held together within the stuff of the world which I must not call the *one* stuff, for fear of describing the creator in the language of the creature. It germinates into the infinite variety of things in all their grades of development. This impulse of creativeness I call the nisus of the universe, borrowing an idea from Spinoza and agreeing, as I think, with the spirit though not all the details of Mr. Bergson's *élan vital*. This nisus not only leads to the formation of things and to the sustainment of them, but impels the world forward towards new creations, bringing forth the new out of the bosom of the old. It creates chemical bodies and keeps up their form by the stability of their functions; but also, and this is perhaps more striking, drives on ' the chemic lump ', in Emerson's words, to ' ascend to man '. Now this nisus is the element of time in the primordial world, its principle of mobility and restlessness. Yet lest it should be thought that space is something upon which time works and that time is the creator, we remind ourselves that time could do nothing, could not even be, except for space ; which is thus also creative for it is not without the element of transition, and space by itself is but the totality of *events* considered without their movement.

ARTISTIC CREATION AND COSMIC CREATION

This nisus is no effort on the world's part to extend its bounds ; such a notion is unthinkable, for the universe is boundless ; but a ceaseless impulse to produce parts and alter the grouping of events into things. Things, we have seen, are clusters of events ; and the world's nisus sustains some of these clusters and produces others new by fresh combinations which it strikes out in the heat of its desire.

III

The discussion of this topic would lead me too far. But I may endeavour here to remove a possible misconception. This primordial world of space-time is not the dance of atoms imagined by Epicurus or Lucretius. Atoms are a late and complex product of history, manufactured articles in a sense different from that of Clerk Maxwell in his famous phrase. They have long since been displaced in physics by something more elementary, and shown to be comparable to stellar systems, which may even in their internal coherence seem to adumbrate organic life. They suggest affinity with higher creations, and that affinity would, if what I have conjectured is true, stretch downward to more primitive creations and even to space-time itself and its spatio-temporal component events, which have in them all, in time some forecast of mind and in space of matter. I mention this because it bears upon a prejudice entertained by so many, to which in particular Lord Balfour has given so distinguished an expression, that only ordinary theism can account for the values of beauty, goodness, and truth. The prejudice against our descent from apes which was provoked by the Darwinian theory no longer exists ; we are even proud that we are so much better than our fathers. But it is replaced by this new prejudice or is revived in it under a different form. Half the repugnance that is felt to the affiliation of values with a world which did not already imply them is removed by removing the fancied antithesis of the mechanical or material and the spiritual. The mechanical is penetrated with time which is the predecessor of mind, and the mechanical is not opposed to life so much as that it is simpler, more uniform, and of more routine a character; so that the functions of life when they harden into custom recede into the material order, as the mental in turn hardens with custom into the physiological and unconscious. As elements of the world which are not included in the mere material order arise and introduce the beginning of freedom, the automatic life of matter is replaced by the less simple life, or living beings, and new elements of freedom enter further with the life of spirit.

For my own part I believe that, in the end, a theistic conception of God's deity is demanded by the facts of nature. But to hold that value demands a theistic creator appears to me to rest upon leaving the notions both of a theistic creator, with design and reason, and of value as well, in the obscurity of neglected analysis. The connection of God with his created world is left vague admittedly, and that of value at least is surrounded with the nimbus of emotional fervour which treats examination of it as a depreciation of its real worth. We forget that value is a human invention, not in the sense of an artificial product, but of an effluence of man's nature, and if the body is descended from the apes so may value be rooted in organic analogies. A successful genealogy of value would no more alter its preciousness or sacredness than material objects were altered, as Berkeley pointed out, by his proposal to treat them as ideas. If value were not an expression of man's whole nature, in its relation to its environment both natural and social, something might be said for an appeal to some divine forethought and wisdom. But the impulse to do, to learn, and to create, are parts of the human equipment; the values are but the discovered scale of the embodiment of these impulses in judgments of act, in knowledge, and in creative art.

Moreover when they are considered in relation to the history of the animal man, they are seen not to be unique things in the world, but foreshadowed. Natural selection is particularly made the stone of stumbling in the attempts

ARTISTIC CREATION AND COSMIC CREATION

to regard value as, like other things, historical and evolved. The exact share of natural selection in natural history has now become controversial. But so far is natural selection from being incompatible with value that value is rather one way of describing an essential feature of natural selection. For value always rejects unvalue and is established by that process. And it is precisely by that rejection that, so far as natural selection holds in nature, organic forms are stabilised under their conditions of value. Natural selection is in fact the history of value in the organic world. How much farther down it extends, what analogues it has in the mere material world, it would perhaps be presumptuous to attempt to say. But in the organic world, every time that a variety excels its rivals in the struggle it so far establishes an infra-human value. This does not mean that beauty and truth and still less right are made by force. Might is not right; that half-truth has brought down a great nation; pray God it may not bring down another. But right is might; only, because that proposition is so easily misapprehended, it were better replaced by the less pointed one, that right is what is suited to prevail in the judgments of men. And if we have faith that the world works out its salvation and not its destruction, we shall be apt to believe that what so prevails is rooted in the nature of things, including men. At least if it is not so, we act as if it were so; and if the pursuit of this faith leads to our extinction, value will perish with us.

The marks of providence and design in nature and in man which are thought to demand a provident and all-purposing creator of the world do not weaken but rather enhance the conclusions which follow ultimately from considering the analogy of the arts. Providence is, in the main, the name for the fact that the result of man's purposes is something which he never purposed. 'Nothing', says Victor Hugo, 'needs so much to be foreseen as the unforeseen.' But we do not foresee it; we hardly foresee what can be foreseen, else how could the statesmen of Versailles have forgotten the Nemesis that dogged the career of Napoleon, and forgotten the treatment of the Southern States after the Civil War by the Northern States of America ? And since the unforeseen is not foreseen but happens, we attribute it to Providence. But the procedure of the artist, if rightly interpreted above, may teach us that there the work is not foreseen, but the artist is driven on from behind by his excitement and reveals to himself in the end the consummation of his desire. So far as he does not forecast exactly the product itself, his action is blind. If revelation depends on a purpose partly blind where there is real purpose, why should we shrink from the idea that the so-called blind action of matter or of living creatures below man's level may produce a form of existence, as they do, higher than or at least other than themselves ? The adjective blind is in fact a misnomer. Matter is blind to what succeeds matter ; but so are we to what shall succeed us. Yet each grade of existence has the vision which is relative to its estate : the animal which does not foresee its end is not blind to the means by which the end will inevitably come. From the relative vision of matter, treading its accustomed round, may arise the relative prevision of man.

Neither does the appearance in the world of design, by which creatures do not so much secure their ends as subserve the ends of other living things, require an all-foreseeing purpose in a prevenient God. Hardly any can have escaped the reflection that since the higher organisms can live only by making use of the lower ones, only those higher beings maintain stability for which the lower are apparently created. Here once more we dare not gape at the wonders of purpose, but ask its lineage. When we do so we discover that it arises out of failure and is removed by success. It means not preordainment but the want of it. When the animal misses his 'end' he tries, in his excess of uneasiness, random or undirected movements, impelled thereto by the compulsion of his nature not to rest till the end is secured. The dog learning to carry his stick through railings is the familiar example, improved so often by American psychologists by delicate problems set to other and less appealing creatures, rats and mice and cats. Within the limits of their plasticity animals can vary their habitual instinctive acts. Suppose, now, the advent of genuine ideas as in man. The devices which the animal strikes out in the urgency of his desire become purposes, and, when crowned with success, subside and lay the foundation for other purposes. Thus purpose is one and the highest form of the consequence of failing adaptation, and it is the method under such circumstances of successful adaptation. It remains, therefore, as true as when it was said by Spinoza that to attribute an all-foreseeing purpose to God is to attach to him not perfection but defect. To accept purpose as the attendant in a conscious being capable of ideas of maladjustment is to place it in its descent from animal purposiveness and to suggest that, if aggregations of material atoms do not exhibit purpose that may be because their complexity is insufficient to admit plasticity, and they require for sustainment no degree of freedom.

If these considerations are sound, artistic creation, so far from being the prototype of cosmic creation, is itself a late product in the growth within the universe of the various levels of existence in which the nisus of space-time takes effect; is an incident in the life of the highest existence known to us. The questions which are raised by the stratification of the world of finites into levels, which, in Mr. Lloyd Morgan's phrase 'emerge', I must not discuss here, having, indeed, done so elsewhere. I add only the remark that the conception of the nisus, which cannot be supposed to cease with the attainment of man, points to a higher form of existence and suggests an alternative theism. Instead of the vague notion which misinterprets the analogy of artistic creation of a theistic creator which works from behind with intelligence and purpose, it substitutes the notion of a higher being or phase of being, itself a cosmic product, the idea of which impels the possessors of that idea forwards, and in that sense draws them on from in front.

IX

NATURALISM AND VALUE

(Reprinted, by permission, from *The Personalist*, Los Angeles, California, October 1928)

IF there was ever a philosophy which can be described as naturalism, it was that of Spinoza. Everything in the world, human minds included, was for him a particular mode of extension, and could be expressed in terms of motion and rest, or in the current phrase, in mechanical terms. Judgments of good and evil or beauty and ugliness or perfection and imperfection were subjective: things or actions were not in themselves good or beautiful or perfect; those adjectives indicated merely our human comparisons with human ideals of good or beauty, and the standards were, in a sense, human inventions. Yet Spinoza's naturalism not only left room for the divine, but in the end there was nothing real but God, and everything else was but a fragment of God, had its being in God, and only the weakness of our imagination allowed us to think of things as possessing an existence and reality apart from God. Though everything was a combination of motion and rest, it was not merely such; for though on one side it was a mode of extension, it was equally upon another side a mode of thinking. Though our judgments of value were products of our imagination and mere comparisons with our human standards, those standards were not arbitrary; on the contrary, there were degrees of reality, and in that scale of degrees good possessed more reality than evil. Vice was a real thing as much as virtue and equally with it proceeded inevitably from the character of the agent. But in the eye of God virtue contained more reality, was nearer to the fullness of God and, so considered, vice and error were indeed only absence or privation of goodness or truth.

In spite of the glaring instance from Spinoza's philosophy that naturalism could leave religion and values not only unimpaired but exalted, the method of naturalism has been regarded with suspicion as if it were incompatible with belief in the things that are most precious to us. It is supposed to destroy because it explains. It presents human affairs in their place in a whole system of things, and treats human beings as one set of things to study amongst others, and is thought therefore to do away with the distinctive pre-eminence of man. No one, or at least few persons, now believe that to demonstrate man's descent from the ape demonstrates him to be nothing but an ape. Most persons, even if they dislike their grandfathers, do not think that their origin affects their present value, and may even believe that it enhances their value. They have learned to keep their dislikes out of their science. Now it is precisely this which is meant or ought to be meant by naturalism. Spinoza's saying is often cited, that he sought not to praise or blame but to understand. We have prepossessions in favour of virtue and beauty and religion and some of us wish to be immortal. The method of naturalism is to study our prepossessions without prepossession. It is in fact to preserve, in dealing with human affairs, the same neutrality as natural science preserves in dealing with its subject matter. It treats virtue and beauty and truth as facts of human nature which are to be described and set into relation with facts of other nature. It does not imply that human beliefs are unreal or lose one jot of their essential character because they can be analysed and even explained. Religion is a fact of human nature. Naturalism seeks to understand that fact; and it may incidentally deepen the significance of religion by analysing its nature and tracing its antecedents. In no way is naturalism, any more than any other philosophy, committed to an attempt to show that the belief of religion is illusory.

Part of the prejudice against naturalism is due to con-

NATURALISM AND VALUE

fusing it with two different things, materialism and the mechanical view of things. Each of these may be represented as being a form of naturalism. But in fact materialism is a perversion of naturalism, and mechanism, if that convenient word may be used to describe a habit of mind, is only a particular and imperfect and mistaken form which naturalism may assume.

As for materialism, that is a word of abuse, and perhaps no reputable philosophy has ever been pure materialism, except in the days of the great thinkers before Socrates, and they were not strictly materialists because the contrast of materialism and immaterialism had not then dawned upon Western Europe : they had not yet discovered mind. If materialism means, as it is taken to mean, that there is nothing but matter and its forms, and that mind as something with a distinctive character of its own does not count in the system of things, which would be the same as it is without mind, it is neither naturalism nor a possible philosophy. For at least minds are not stones, and the world of physical matter has at any rate ended by producing minds. Materialism can only become reasonable by allowing an element to exist in matter which has affinity with the latest outgrowth from matter which is mind. But then matter ceases to be sheer matter and acquires life.

The mechanical conception of things stands upon a different footing, and it has for a long time dominated thought. Its error is not that it is inadmissible but that it omits a vital factor in things, namely the emergence of novelties in the course of development. There may well be, as Spinoza held, a mechanical substructure of things, but special constellations of mechanical actions may be the basis of new modes of existence like life and mind. Minds are mechanical but not merely such. When once this is perceived the antithesis of the mechanical and the vital or the mental is seen to be unreal. The mechanical comes to carry with it an element which corresponds to mind but is not yet mind. To follow out this thought would take us too far. The revolt against mechanism (with which naturalism is confounded) is founded on a dim feeling that in reality nothing is merely mechanical, not even matter. The mechanical is but the simpler and less complicated form of existence; it too, like life or mind, is structural, only its structure is simple. It has life without being alive. There is at least in it an element which makes it possible for life to be a later stage in a continuous development of which mere matter is an earlier stage. Pure mechanism if it existed would cut us off from the existing distinctive features of life and mind as a part in a continuous and integrated system of things. Spinoza avoided that dilemma. The truth is that pure mechanism does not exist at all. 'Mechanism' is thus only one particular form which naturalism has assumed, and its deficiencies are not inherent in naturalism itself.

These (it must be admitted rather general) reflections are suggested by the use which is being made of the conception of value by many philosophers at the present day, who almost conjure with it, as if it supplied the ultimate solution of the problem of reality. Goodness and truth and beauty are for human practical existence so precious (what else is the precious but what has value?) that it is straightway asserted that they are the most fundamental things in the world. No analysis is made of these ideas; being values, they are incommensurate with everything else and superior to it; and any attempt to show their affinity with other features, say of the world of nature, must, it is implied, necessarily be a failure. Just so, instincts before Darwin's time, being the wonderful things that they really are, could only be regarded as a special endowment of certain creatures like bees or beavers by a beneficent Creator. When they were watched in their evolution they ceased to be unintelligible and incommensurate with other actions of animals or plants, and did not cease to be wonderful. Without asking the meaning of value, to treat it as sacrosanct and containing therefore the secret of things, is an instance of that habit of taking what is practically dear and lovely for what is theoretically beyond explanation, the habit against which naturalism sets its face, as being the intrusion of our wishes into our science, and producing what Bacon[1] might have called an *ad quod vult* philosophy.

When we ask what values are, we cannot help recognising that some account *can* be given of them. Without accepting necessarily the particular teaching of Spinoza on the point, the two propositions which he maintains are in principle true : first that values are essentially relative to men and are in this sense human inventions ; goodness and beauty do not belong to things apart from their relation to men ; secondly, that while relative to men they are founded in the nature of things and are not arbitrary. What is valuable is in the last resort what is satisfactory to us. Even exchange value of commodities depends on the satisfaction of human wants, and the precise value in exchange is that value which satisfies the maximum number of wants on the part of buyers and sellers combined. It was not an accident that a great economist, Adam Smith, laid down as a principle of moral value that those actions are morally good which spring from sentiments that an impartial spectator can approve, or, what comes to the same thing, with which the sentiments of others can be in sympathy. If I disapprove thieving in you it is because I want to keep my own property and sympathise with the objection of the person whom you rob. A similar account might be given of the other values of truth and beauty. They satisfy persons, but in such fashion as never to be the satisfaction of a whim of an individual, but as to produce the maximum satisfaction of a whole group. Truth brings into harmony the scattered experiences of many ; and beauty brings a pleasure which is not personal to the possessor but disinterested, in which all can share, whereas the satisfaction of a mere appetite devours its object and is interested.

Thus values are always satisfactions but not capricious

---

[1] *Novum Organum*, 1, 49. ' Intellectus humanus luminis sicci non est ; sed recipit infusionem a voluntate et affectibus, id quod generat *ad quod vult scientias* : quod enim mavult homo verum esse, id potius credit.' [Editor's note.]

ones : they are satisfactions of human nature as that nature is discovered by men in their intercourse with one another. Consequently their standards are independent of any one individual as a language which is spoken by individuals enforces its habits and its genius upon each individual who speaks it. They are in fact languages by which men communicate with each other and in accordance with which they settle down into mutual understanding. They are therefore primarily facts of human nature or human institutions, and again to quote Spinoza, or to gloss upon him, there is no goodness or beauty in things apart from men.

Yet these values though they are human institutions are in intimate relation to non-human nature which by itself has not these values. Truth is truth about facts ; goodness is the doings of men in reaction upon their physical surroundings and in turn issues in physical results which are part of the physical world. Beauty belongs to natural objects or to works of art which in turn are physical objects, pictures or sculptures or the spoken words of a poem. Why not then say that the values really reside in the facts or actions or beautiful things ? Because without the minds or persons which possess these facts or acts or things there is no truth nor goodness nor beauty. That this is so is most easily seen from art or from beautiful nature. For the work of art is only beautiful to the appreciating mind which reads character into the dead stone and charges the spoken words of the poem with meaning which they do not possess as mere signs of things ; and of natural beauty Wordsworth himself has written the words, ' all this mighty world of eye and ear, both what they half create and what perceive ' — beautiful nature and beautiful works of art possess qualities which they have not as physical things but have when the appreciating mind is blended with them. And in a certain sense, and with qualifications, truth and goodness are works of art, only not of fine art. Truth is not fact, but a system of facts held in the minds of men and woven into a consistent and objective whole, but fitted to facts as a glove fits the hand. Goodness is the satisfactory life of men under the external conditions of their existence and secures the permanence of human nature under those conditions, but it does not consist in external actions but in the system of approvals which are embodied in institutions like property or the family. It is not wrong to drink to excess because to do so will kill me ; that is mere imprudence. It is wrong because it is disapproved and it is disapproved because it destroys my relations to my society, which dislikes such conduct.

The values, when we treat them apart from prepossessions, appear then to be human creations founded on things but, as compared with nature, humanly artificial. How can we erect these precious artifices which are founded in reality because they express the best of human nature in its connection with reality — how are we justified in adoring them as if they were the keys to the understanding of things in general ? By such brief solutions do we do more than shorten the labour of thinking our problems out ? For naturalism, which is supposed to be fatal to value, has more to say than merely to indicate what value is. It also indicates that value, far from being something unique, has parallels in the world below the human level, and helps to make our human values more intelligible by finding their correspondents elsewhere. Herein lies for philosophy the significance of Darwinism. In human affairs the values prevail and establish themselves by ostracising the unvalues. Virtue (the kind of moderate virtue which is all that is permitted to the condition of man) imprisons vice or otherwise makes its life difficult. The moderately good enforce their own tastes on the moderately bad, and compel the bad to at least apparent conformity. Truth in the end, after long years, drives out error (though not ignorance). Beauty drives out ugliness ; in the end it is the beautiful imaginations which remain. The separation of value and unvalue is always a matter of experiment or trial, and it is a struggle of opinions or sentiments which uses the forces of persuasion or tradition. It may even use violence in extreme circumstances; though this statement is by no means convertible with the pitiable error that, because an ideal may sometimes need force to prevail, force is part of the ideal.

Now, what Darwinism means is that successful and permanent types of life in the plant and animal world are those which can prevail under the conditions of existence over real or possible rivals. From this point of view the question now debated whether variations are of all possible infinitesimal degrees, or nature proceeds on limited lines, is relatively indifferent. So far as natural selection operates it secures the success (of course not because of natural selection but because of intrinsic endowment) of certain types to the exclusion of other types. There is therefore in the natural world not indeed value but something correspondent thereto, namely, the process of preference whereby one type establishes its superior permanence. Darwinism is often thought to be antagonistic to the claims of human value; and so it is if those conceptions are used without analysis of their meaning, and treated (again to use a phrase of Bacon) as statues to be adored. For the habit embodied in naturalism, Darwinism is in fact the natural history of value. In the infra-human world it exhibits under appropriate conditions the operation of the same process whereby our human values establish their supremacy over unvalues in the growth of valuable institutions. So far from disparaging human values it traces their antecedents, much as, to revert to an earlier statement in this paper, matter presents the antecedents of life in the form appropriate to life at that earlier stage of existence.

The hands of alarm need not therefore to be raised against naturalism in defence of value. Naturalism at once sustains the practical significance of value and makes it intelligible. If it fails as a philosophy, its failure must be demonstrated on other grounds.

X

VALUE [1]

(Reprinted, by permission, from the *Bulletin of the John Rylands Library*, July 1933)

THE idea of value has become the subject of so much loose usage and loose thinking, which does almost more harm than false thinking, that the very name has an ill odour in philosophy. At a recent conference of philosophers at Reading a remark made incidentally that the word was detestable was received with applause. The reason is that the name is used to suggest something admirably mysterious, to be received with reverent acceptance, and no questions asked of its authority. The highest values, the old triad of truth and goodness and beauty, stand for something precious in our lives, and the word value has acquired an aroma rare and exquisite. But in science and knowledge we dare not allow our practical prepossessions to colour the ethical neutrality (I borrow a phrase of Bertrand Russell's) we have to observe in theoretical enquiry. We need to ask what value is without prepossession.

There is a general feeling in the air that value is an essential feature in the constitution of the universe. But till we know what value is, and what the word means, we may be fancying that the highest values themselves may be the most important features of the universe. Whereas it may turn out merely that there is something in the universe which at a higher stage is familiar to us under the form of the highest values, but is in itself something very simple and divested of emotional trappings. Mr. Laird [2]

[1] A lecture delivered in the John Rylands Library on March 8, 1933.
[2] In *The Idea of Value*, Cambridge, 1929.

VALUE

has offered to find this simple and pervasive feature in what he calls ' natural election ', the fact that everything in the universe has something else which matters to it or to which it matters, like the magnet and the iron filings. Before him Mr. Perry of Harvard [1] had extended the meaning of value to cover any kind of interest. Whatever is interesting to a conscious being is a value or valuable for that being. That would be making value something purely psychological, and the highest values would be (though we have yet to hear Mr. Perry on the subject in a new volume) particular cases of such interest. Mr. Laird goes further and extends the meaning beyond conscious beings to all beings, and I see no reason why we should stop at conscious beings. Now if Mr. Laird is right, and I think he is,[2] value would be a very important feature in the universe, and would be another way of expressing the fact that everything directly or indirectly, closely or remotely, is connected with the whole of things, that, as Mr. Whitehead puts it, everything in the world has all the rest of the world for its field.[3] But at least we know here just how much and how little value means, and we are not tempted to loose talk about beauty and goodness. For in a simple and comprehensive notion like this we have got very far away from our own highest values. They may be instances of natural election or of interest. But there is nothing exciting or emotional about natural election, and that is its great merit. It is an attempt to show what value ultimately means. And I am persuaded that we must give up talking at large about value till we have found out what makes a thing valuable.

[1] In *General Theory of Value*, London, 1926.
[2] Alexander himself had anticipated such views, for example in the VIIIth Essay in the present volume, especially at p. 276, and in the IXth Essay at p. 286. The Stoics and Spinoza had been equally foreseeing. It was always Alexander's habit to be a spendthrift in his acknowledgments to contemporary philosophers. In this instance he made the same acknowledgment in all his writings about ' value ' after 1929 : so I could not conceal it. [Editor's note.]
[3] Compare Locke's saying : ' Things, however absolute and entire they seem in themselves, are but retainers to other parts of nature for that which they are most taken notice of by us ' (Essay, Bk. IV. ch. vi. sect. 11).

VALUE

I propose to confine myself to the familiar highest values and to ask what it is in them which makes their value. Now there are two things which strike us at once about these values of beauty and goodness and truth. The first is that they are relative to us humans and satisfy us in certain respects ; and the second is that when we value anything as true or good or beautiful the objects we value under these terms are regarded for their own sakes. When we answer the question how such objects come to be regarded for their own sakes, we shall be answering also the question in what respects they satisfy or are satisfactory to us. I will deal with the first question, I mean how objects come to be regarded for their own sakes, first, because the need of answering it is often overlooked. It is so easy to say that a good act or a good character is regarded for its own sake, or contemplatively ; or that a beautiful face or statue or picture is regarded for its own sake, that this contemplation of objects for their own sakes seems hardly to require accounting for. Yet when we have accounted for it we have in fact solved the question how such objects have value.

Take morals first. It is a commonplace of the unsophisticated mind that we tell the truth and pay our debts not for the sake of the consequences or to avoid the pains and penalties of the law or public opinion, but because the two objects in view are respectively telling the truth and paying debts. Then sophistication comes in with ethical theory. One kind of theory says we approve these actions because they bring with them happiness, and some even go so far as to hold that we desire not the paying of debts but the happiness that comes of it. Now it may very well be that good actions do bring happiness, and yet it need not be true that they are approved for that reason. This theory hardly concerns us, for it holds that it is only by force of habit that we desire good ends for their own sake. Moreover, all the time there may be a different answer : that we are temperate and pay our debts not because it pays us better (though on the whole it does pay us better), but because we prefer temperance and honesty.

There is a different form of sophistication possible. Because when we do good actions we do them for their own sakes, this may be taken to mean that we do right because it is right, and that there is a right or a good which is a fundamental character of goodness, quite distinct from all consideration of consequences or motives. Kant followed this line when he tried to show that the goodness of good action lay in its categorical character, its universality, and set up a barren criterion of goodness. Our latter-day moralists follow a different line, and declare that right action is something which only intuition of its rightness can settle. Here again possibly there is an alternative which has been overlooked. Utilitarian theories hardly account at all for why actions are desired for their own sakes. These other theories offer a theory but it goes beyond the necessities of the situation. For actions may be desired for their own sakes not because of some mysterious property of rightness they possess, which we learn by intuition or by rationality, but because they satisfy some desire different from the desire which leads to the action. I desire drink, but I desire temperance in drinking because I carry my fellows with me when I stop, and do not when I exceed. Or I respect your right to life because I and other people dislike murder, as the Bible illustrates when Cain, after killing Abel, is met by the wrath of God. Now this suggests that I come to regard actions for their own sake, not because of some mysterious standard, but because of another passion which makes me sympathetic with the wishes of other persons in society.

Consequently we desire ends for their own sakes, as ordinary moral experience tells us we do, because there is a controlling passion which does not allow us to satisfy any particular passion, thirst or jealousy or what not, as it arises, but subjects that particular passion to the control of another passion, that of sociality or regard for the wishes of others. The social feeling, or the tribal self, confronts

VALUE

and limits the mere particular self. In this way any object when subjected to this control is lifted out of the mere class of objects which satisfy my individual or material passions, and becomes an object desired for its own sake. As I said before, by discovering how objects come to be desired for their own sake, we at the same time learn that such objects satisfy the social self or the social impulse. Goodness thus derives its value from its satisfying the social impulse in a man. The two questions have been answered together. We may add that the value of the good act or character is thus the relation between the act in question and the impulse it satisfies and that value is experienced by us as the pleasure of having our social passion gratified.

Consider, next, truth which may be described as acquaintance with the world of things, in so far as that acquaintance is pursued for its own sake. Our acquaintance with things is in the first instance practical: we know things in their uses for us. Indeed it might be maintained, were this the proper place to do so, that knowledge comes to us essentially through practice. We do not first know things and then act; we know things through acting upon them. The things which surround us excite us physically to response or, as we commonly say, to reaction. In that reaction upon them we become aware of them or know them. Light provokes us to turn our eyes to it and we then see it as light. All our knowledge is thus a revelation to us of things which first provoke us to respond to them. Differences in things provoke different responses, and difference in the response brings us face to face with the things as we know them. This relation begins with the data of sense, it is completed through the other responses of our so-called cognitive processes, and in the end the world as we know it is a vast system revealed to us through all the ways of sense, imagination, thought. But things which begin by being instruments of practice become emancipated from their practical uses and are observed and thought about for their own sakes. The

VALUE

connection with practice is never severed ; just as right and goodness are never severed from their roots in passion and desire. But as in morals a new passion enters to emancipate us from the pressure of personal passions, so in knowing we leave the calls of utility and study things for themselves and create science. Science begins with practical uses, leaves them and enters the pure empyrean of theory and returns to practical uses again.

Now what makes acquaintance with things into truth and gives it the value of truth ? It is that we seek to systematise our acquaintance with things, which gives us varying and often contradictory information about them. The data of the senses conflict with one another and with the other data supplied through memory. For man is a creature of ideas, and while the animal is content with the data of the moment, or is so for the most part, man brings, through his gift of imagination and memory and reflection, all the scattered fragments of his experience together and weaves them into an integral whole, makes theories and systems, invents hypotheses to unite his separate data, and, always under guidance from the world he is subject to, may construct systems which at first seem remote entirely from the sensible world, but in the end are verified by that sensible world, under pain of modification or rejection.

It is this passion for systematic enquiry which, with all the helps of his cognitive powers, turns his acquaintance with things from practical knowledge into truth acquired for its own sake. The impulse which leads him on is curiosity, not in the mere animal form which makes a dog sniff about in the interests of food or sex, but in the form of humanised and systematic curiosity. It is animal curiosity sublimated as it were through the presence of ideas. Such curiosity is of its own nature systematic.

As before with goodness so with truth. Truth is truth because it satisfies curiosity in this refined and human form, and its value lies in the satisfaction it brings to us thus. Truth has no doubt many other characters which there is not space to describe, all flowing from this original character. But truth is a value or has value because it satisfies this human curiosity, always under guidance or control from things themselves. The passion of enlightened curiosity which we call enquiry makes knowledge desired for its own sake and at the same time makes that knowledge a value as the satisfaction of a human need.

When we come to beauty, the third of these highest values, the situation is still plainer, and I am myself more interested in beauty just because the study of it affords a readier approach to the essential nature of value. Here too the beautiful object is not merely seen or heard but contemplated for its own sake. The beautiful object, whether in nature or art, is a material thing; in art, where the fact is sometimes overlooked, it consists of tones or pigments or bronze or marble or, as in literature, of words. Now these objects, whether in nature or in art, convey practical pleasures or, as they may usefully be called, material pleasures. Partly the actual material pleases, as with tones or the texture of marble; partly the subject (when, as in representative art, there is a subject distinct from the materials themselves) pleases. These pleasures enter into the total effect of beauty but they are not themselves the pleasure of beauty and may even divert the mind from beauty itself. An erotic lovesong or an unskilful or inartistic painting of the nude may excite and please material passions, and when such pleasure is predominant the experience is not aesthetic. Even in a portrait the mere pleasure of recognition which accompanies a successful likeness to the subject is subsidiary to the aesthetic success which is different from mere likeness. In a beautiful lovesong, say, ' My love is like a red, red rose '; or the charming conceit of Carew quoted by Edward Fitzgerald in one of the first in the collection of his letters,

> Ask me no more where Jove bestows,
> When June is past, the fading rose, etc.,

the material passion is indeed excited or suggested but in such subordination to the unity of the whole poem that it does not excite practically. The green field may give pleasure to a cow, but it is not appreciated by her, we may presume, as beautiful just because though seen it is not contemplated for itself.

How do sights and sounds as in a work of art or as in nature seen with an aesthetic eye come, then, to be thus contemplated? I have tried to give the answer in a paper of some years ago [1] by pointing to the fact that a beautiful object is never seen as it actually is but the mind introduces into the object its own interpretations and imputes to the object characters which it does not really possess. I have to repeat myself. The marble which is dead looks alive or full of character; the words of a poem not only have their meanings in the sense that they stand for objects, but the meaning and the word are blended, the words as I have put it are charged with meaning. Even such simple beauty as that of a pure colour or a pure tone pleases aesthetically or is beautiful because the mind is aware of its purity, its freedom from admixture of other tones or colours; such purity has its basis in the material fact, but needs the presence of the mind to apprehend through contrast or comparison. There is the added interpretation by the mind itself. So much truth at least there is in the famous notion of 'empathy', which has played so large a part in recent aesthetical theory. I need not stay to ask how we thus alter the actual material things so as to give them a meaning they do not themselves possess. The sculptor portrays a Hermes and he shapes the marble so that it means for the appreciative onlooker godhead and playfulness. The marble has this meaning in the same way as we see the ice cold. The marble takes a significant shape because the artist's choice of line and plane and volume embodies the ideas or images or thoughts the artist himself brings to the work.

Thus the work of art is according to the old phrase which C. E. Montague quotes *homo additus naturae*.[2]

---

[1] *I.e. Art and the Material.* [Editor's note.]
[2] In a letter in his memoir by O. Elton, London, 1929, p. 272.

VALUE

Now it is this addition to the physical material of a 'foreign' meaning from the side of the creative or appreciative mind which lifts the object out of its practical character and allows it to be contemplated for its own sake. Observe that this applies not only to art but to nature as well. For nature when it is seen beautiful and not merely pleasing to the sense is altered by our interference: we select those elements in the natural object which suit our mood. Nature when she is seen beautifully is subjected to our interference, according to the well-known lines of Coleridge,

> O Lady we receive but what we give
> And in our life alone does nature live;

which, however, does not allow for nature's existence apart from our finding her beautiful. The addition from our mind of interfering elements which we attribute to the material, not only brings those elements themselves before our minds but it divests the actual material elements present of their purely material character. By being interfered with they are diverted from their normal practical function and become the subject of contemplation. I have quoted elsewhere Shakespeare's line,

> Do paint the meadows with delight.

Delight and painting are introduced plainly by the poet, but the meadows themselves are transfigured in the process.

It is not always so easy to see that this statement holds in a non-representative art like music or in architecture, which comes nearest to music. Nor am I able to deal with the difficulties as they deserve. I must refer you here, if you care to pursue the theme, to what I am about to say in a more systematic treatment of the whole subject of this lecture which I hope may shortly appear.[1] Everywhere it will be found, I think, that where there is beauty, even in the most formal art, significance belongs to the work through the interference of the artist or the spectator.

[1] Under the title of *Beauty and Other Forms of Value*. (Messrs. Macmillan.)

And the study of non-representative art forces upon us the conviction that the beauty of the beautiful does not belong as such to the material effects of the beautiful but to its formal character, which it owes to the active constructive operation of the mind, which, out of elements, some of them given in the material, some of them supplied by the mind and expressed in the material, gives unity and harmony to the whole according to the old Greek account of beauty as unity in variety.

In discovering how the beautiful object is contemplated for itself, we have discovered what beauty is and what makes it a value. Beauty is that which satisfies the impulse of constructiveness, that is, constructiveness of materials, not the mere construction which the man of science uses in thinking — when that constructiveness has become human and contemplative. For constructiveness is found also among certain animals, but their constructions, like the hive of the bee, or the beaver's dam, or the nightingale's song, are part of practical arrangements, storage of food, or care for the young, or courtship. Human constructiveness is pursued for itself. Beauty or the beautiful is what satisfies this impulse, and beauty is a value because of the particular pleasure it brings to this impulse. They are therefore right who say there is an aesthetic sentiment, and I add that it is the human representative of animal constructiveness.

The value of beauty is thus eminently a relation, as between the beautiful object and the mind which creates, or appreciates; for appreciation is but creation at the bidding of the creator, it is going over again the work of creation when that work has been already performed. How essentially beauty is relative is seen from the constitution of the beautiful object itself, part given, part added by the mind; so that the relation of beauty to the mind is implied in the very nature of beauty.

The situation then is a complex one. An object is created or discovered which satisfies the impulse of constructiveness, and is a value because it so satisfies. Beauty

VALUE

is referred to the object as belonging to it, but it is not a quality of the object like yellow or sweet, but is the relation which the object has to the constructive person. He experiences the pleasure of beauty in the satisfaction of the constructive or, let us say now, of the aesthetic sentiment. The pleasure belongs to the person who feels it, the beauty is referred as a quality to the object which so pleases. Strictly it is not a quality at all, but a value, that is, a relation of the object to the person of satisfying the aesthetic sentiment.

One feature has been, however, omitted in each of these three cases, namely, the objectivity of value. None of these values is such for the individual alone but for many individuals. Virtue satisfies the social sentiment, truth the sentiment of disinterested curiosity; beauty satisfies the sentiment of constructiveness when that sentiment is emancipated from practice and thereby becomes impersonal. Thus all three values have their value in relation not to a particular individual but in relation to what may be called a standard individual, in morals the wise or good man, in truth the knowing man, in art or beauty the aesthetic judge. The mere disinterestedness of these values is enough to indicate their being satisfactions, not of one but of many and in general of a society of people. It is this impersonal character which gives a meaning to the 'absoluteness' of the highest values. Relative to individuals at any one time, they are at that time not relative to a particular but to a standard individual. And if you ask me how the standard is set up or discovered I answer, by trial, by finding out who are in agreement with it. The good and the knowing and the tasteful discover themselves and they exclude from those titles those who do not come up to the standard. The judges are discovered at the same time as the rule by which they judge. From one point of view the standard is set up by a piece of tyranny, but the tyranny is established in the effort to secure goodness and truth and beauty.

Now if, bearing in mind the standard or objective

character of the highest values, we go down the scale and consider what corresponds to these values among the animals (including man as an animal) and lower down amongst plants, we see that what is valuable to them is what satisfies generic wants. Food is valuable to the animal because it maintains the life of the species. Merely as pleasant to him, it has not value but is pleasant; in so far as it is nutritious it secures life in the animal's kind. Thus even lower than beauty and goodness and truth, the feature of objectivity of value is retained. Only what is established amongst ourselves by trial or experiment is already fixed in the animal in the needs of his species.

Descending still lower than life, we find that there is value amongst material things in so far as one thing can satisfy another, as the chemists used to say long ago about the satisfaction of one atom by another within the molecule. Here, too, value remains objective. Only the distinction between the individual and the species has not yet emerged in the scale of existence, and all interest of one thing in another is objective : there is no room for that difference of individuals from one another which makes one man's interests differ from those of another, and may, if he cannot submit himself to the standardisation of value, make him the subject of purely personal values, called so merely because they satisfy him as true value satisfies the standard man. Such so-called values are miscalled value, omitting as they do the reference to the generic or standard which, as we have seen, lies at the basis of real value. In other words, it is only when the notion of value, that is, standard satisfaction, is familiar, that it becomes possible for the individual to claim that his satisfactions are 'values' for himself. Thus standard or real value is not as it were a compromise between a multitude of personal values, but rather personal likings arrogate to themselves the title of value to which they have no claim. Personal value is a defect from real value, and not value a growth from personal values.

XI

NATURAL PIETY [1]

(Reprinted from *The Hibbert Journal*, July 1922)

I DO not mean by natural piety exactly what Wordsworth [2] meant by it — the reverent joy in nature, by which he wished that his days might be bound to each other — though there is enough connection with his interpretation to justify me in using his phrase. The natural piety I am going to speak of is that of the scientific investigator, by which he accepts with loyalty the mysteries which he cannot explain in nature and has no right to try to explain. I may describe it as the habit of knowing when to stop in asking questions of nature. The limits to the right of asking questions are drawn differently for different purposes. They are not the same in science as in ordinary intercourse between men in conversation. I may recall an incident in the life of Dr. Johnson. ' I was once present,' says Boswell, ' when a gentleman [perhaps it was Boswell himself] asked so many [questions], as " What did you do, sir ? " " What did you say, sir ? " that at last he grew

---

[1] Sir Samuel Hall Oration (University of Manchester), March 1922.
[2] In the fragment beginning ' My heart leaps up ' and ending
' The Child is Father of the man :
And I could wish my days to be
Bound each to each by natural piety.'
Wordsworth also used the phrase in *The Excursion*, Bk. III, line 266 :
' Such acquiescence neither doth imply
In me, a meekly-bending spirit soothed
By natural piety ; nor a lofty mind
By philosophic discipline prepared
For calm subjection to acknowledged law.'
A. C. Bradley, on a post card, said that the sense was ' plainly ' the same in the two passages, but several correspondents wrote to Alexander complaining that he had mistaken Wordsworth's plain sense. [Editor's note.]

enraged, and said, " I will not be put to the *question*. Don't you consider, sir, that these are not the manners of a gentleman ? I will not be baited with *what* and *why*. What is this ? What is that ? Why is a cow's tail long ? Why is a fox's tail bushy ? " ' Boswell adds that the gentleman, who was a good deal out of countenance, said, ' Why, sir, you are so good, that I venture to trouble you '. JOHNSON. — ' Sir, my being so *good* is no reason why you should be so *ill*.' The questions which Johnson regarded as typically offensive in conversation about the cow's and the fox's tail might quite legitimately be asked in science, and, I fancy, answered by a naturalist without any particular difficulty. There is a mental disease known as the questioning or metaphysical mania, which cannot accept anything, even the most trivial, without demanding explanation. Why do I stand here where I stand ? Why is a glass a glass, a chair a chair ? How is it that men are only of the size they are ? Why not as big as houses ? etc. (I quote from William James). Now the very life of knowledge depends on asking questions. Is it not called enquiry ? And its limits are not drawn by considerations of politeness or by shrinking from insanity. But it does recognise that, however far it may push its explanations, the world presents characters which must be accepted reverently as beyond explanation, though they do not pass understanding. And I call this habit of acceptance of nature by the name of natural piety, because simple-minded religion is accustomed to speak of events for which it can find no reason as the will of God.

I will illustrate my meaning from human matters, before passing on to the proper subject of nature. Familiar with the style of Shakespeare, we might with sufficient knowledge of his antecedents, his physiological inheritance, the influences upon him of the company in which he lived, the common speech of the time, and its literature, persuade ourselves that we can understand how he came to write as he did. But the distinctive flavour of it we could not with any amount of knowledge predict, as possibly we might predict with a style such as that of R. L. Stevenson, which carries with it the traces of its origin ; we can but acknowledge it as a new creation and confine ourselves to enquiring into its conditions. The same thing may perhaps be said of the style of Plato, or of Pascal. The French Revolution introduced into political and social life a conception which, however hard to define, was new and gave a new direction to the political thought of Europe, inspiring even those who in the end overthrew the revolutionary régime. That a change was about to occur could have been foreseen by those who considered the evils of the aristocratic polity of France and the direction of the thinking of political writers. But that the change would be the new idea of democracy could not have been foretold. A new feeling had arisen in men's minds of the claims of the common man. Even at the present moment, when the sanguine hopes which were entertained of a regenerated world which was to arise from the war seem to be swept away by the recrudescence of evil passions of domination, or terror, or selfishness, it can hardly be doubted that the world has suffered a political change, which we are too near the event to describe, which owes something to the ideals of the conquered as well as of the conquerors, a new flavour of political life, of which we can understand the conditions but can only feel the presence. We can tell how it has come about, but we do not explain why it should be what it is, and we hardly as yet realise what it is. Compare the teaching of Jesus with what we know of the Judaism of the first century of our era. If our authorities are to be trusted the difference appears to be far smaller than accounts for the immense consequences of the new teaching. That there was novelty, a new conception introduced into morality and the relations between man and God, it would be impossible to deny, and it provided the material when the organisation of Christianity by Paul came about. A religion had come into existence, not put forward by its founder as more than a reform of Judaism, and yet possessing a flavour of its own which was the mark of its originality. What may seem a mere difference of emphasis, a brighter flame of passion (I believe I am taking these phrases from Mr. Montefiore) — all these things, for which the historian can note the antecedents, were fused and welded into a new and distinctive idea. All great historical transformations might be used to supply further examples — the marvel which was born when men of Dorian birth adopted the civilisation and the arts of Egypt and Phoenicia; the limited idea of constitutional liberty for which the Great Rebellion in our own country was fought; the Reformation itself; and a hundred such great changes, of which once more we can understand with sufficient knowledge how they came to be, but not how they should have taken the particular colouring or flavour which actually they possessed.

In these critical changes, further, there is a constant feature. The new creation inherits the ancient ways out of which it grows, but it simplifies the old complexity. There was a chaos of conflicting forces; men's minds were groping confusedly in a tangle of divergent and intercrossing interests; there was a vast unrest; the old habits were lingering on though they had lost their convincingness and bred dissatisfaction; experiment after experiment upon the traditional lines had failed; yet the newer thoughts that were abroad had reached as yet no more than the condition of subterranean and indistinct rebellion. Suddenly, at the bidding of some great single mind, or oftener perhaps of some conspiration of many minds, stirred to their depths with obscure foreboding of the future birth of time, and finely if still vaguely touched to the fine issues, a light has arisen; the discordant elements fall into their places, and the complexity gives way to simplicity. The synthesis is no mere reconciliation; it is creative. So the historians have traced for us the birth of democratic freedom out of the turmoil of the eighteenth century, when once its complacence had broken down; or the preparation of the world to receive the Gentile gospel, when the dull universalising régime of the Roman Empire was fired with the deeper thinking of the Palestinian prophet. So, too, we may feel to-day that our minds are moving this way and that in a sheer confusion of old with new; the complexity and disorganisation of the world are more patent than its unification; and yet we doubt not, or at least we hope, that we have not passed through the ordeal in vain, and that some time and somehow the tangled skein of our present condition will be unravelled, and our conflicting ways may be found convergent towards a simpler and clearer ideal of national and international life. Hence it is, because the creative simplicity is conditioned by so immense a confusion and welter of interests, that it is sometimes more plainly revealed away from the place of its more immediate origin; that the smaller peoples may exhibit more definitely the principle for which larger and better organised nations have striven.

Nor is it only in political and industrial affairs that the creative simplicity emerges from the chaos of complexity. The same feature is even more palpable in science and all pursuit of knowledge. Simple and illuminating discoveries presuppose an immense labour, conducted upon older lines, of material which remains, till the new creation, incoordinated and blind. The new thought or theory reduces the old material to order, while it emancipates us from its confusion. The physical science of to-day uses a language singularly unlike that of the nineteenth century, which it half seems to forget; considered more closely, it is at once the continuance of that work and the discovery of a new and simpler world. Other sciences may not have reached this fulfilment so soon. In history I am told the vast accumulation of detailed investigations awaits as yet the constructive thought which is to give it coherence and simplicity. Philosophy exhibits at the moment all the signs of approaching creation, but is for the time a chaos of discordant doctrines, all of them containing their measure of truth, testifying the awakening of philosophy from its complacent dream, but none as yet completely binding experience into its desired unity. The extreme forms of idealism and realism, the traditional idealism and the antagonist ideas inspired by the revolt against intellect taken alone, or rather by the passion for seeing in the world the fulfilment of man's practical or aesthetic or religious ends; Bradley and Bergson, Croce and William James with his later followers, James Ward and Bertrand Russell; the 'discovery' of Time and the invasion of our ideas by the march of relativity, with its meaning and issues as yet half understood and certainly undecided; the breaking down of the older literary conception of philosophy and its return to its ancient unity and kinship with science, physical and biological; here is a picture of a world distraught by its own complex and abundant vitality. Yet the philosophic believer in philosophy never doubts the imminent birth of a more satisfying thought for which these labours have supplied the favouring marriage of unlikes feeling out towards their blending, and which once attained will set the mind free, as the older idealism has done for a century, to explore with a new guiding thread the vast provinces of special philosophical enquiry.

These features which have been traced in human affairs; new creations which lend an unexplained and strange flavour to existing institutions and remodel them; external habits and ways of life retained but their inward meaning transformed; immense complexities of elements, hitherto chaotic, now gathering themselves together and as it were flowering into some undreamed simplicity; these features are found in the nature of which man is but the latest stage. Nature is 'stratified', and if we apply to it our customary conceptions of growth and development, we can regard it as a geological formation with a history. But the comparison is still inadequate; for new geological strata are but fresh deposits laid down upon the subjacent ones, not drawing from them their new life. Nature is rather a history of organic growth of species, in which the new type of organism is the outgrowth of the older type, and continues the earlier life into a form at once more complex and more highly simplified. As there is in the

NATURAL PIETY

animal world or the plant world a hierarchy of forms, so in nature there is a hierarchy of qualities which are characteristics of various levels of development. There are, if I may borrow a metaphor used by Mr. Sellars of Michigan in his recent book,[1] ' critical points ' in the unfolding of nature when she gathers up her old resources for a new experiment and breeds a new quality of existence. The earliest of these qualities of being which is familiar to us is that of physical matter, whatever we are to suppose it is that materiality consists in. Other well-marked levels are those of chemical structure and behaviour, and life, which is the quality of things which behave physiologically.

I am not concerned to offer a complete enumeration of these levels of existence with their distinguishing qualities. The three qualities mentioned are but a selection. Every attempt at completeness raises questions of difficulty. Certain, however, it is now that mere physical materiality is a highly developed stage, late in the history of the world : that there are forms of submaterial being, and the line between the submaterial and the material is not for me to draw. Neither is it for me to say whether electrons are the lowest existence in the scale. Again, beyond life, some have maintained that mind is itself a new quality which arises out of life, while others treat consciousness merely as a function of all life, and for them consciousness and life are one, and accordingly all the knowing on which we pride ourselves so much is in the end only a special form of vital behaviour. There is another debatable question. To me, colours and sounds and tastes and all the sensible characters of material things appear to be resident in things themselves ; and coloured existence to be a critical point in nature. When a physical body is such that the light which it sends out to our eyes has a determinate wavelength, that body is red. To others, and they are the majority, the colour depends upon the possession by the percipient of eyes. These questions I need not raise in this place because they take us away from the central

[1] *Evolutionary Naturalism*, R. W. Sellars, Open Court, Chicago, 1922.

theme into historic problems which have occupied physics and philosophy from the days of Galileo and before. There is still another matter I leave open. Life is without doubt such a critical point in nature. Are the various gradations of life, first of all the difference of plants and animals as a whole, and next the marked differences of kinds among animals and plants themselves, to be regarded likewise? The differences which part a humble amoeba or hydra from the monkey, or even from the lizard or crab, are vast. Are they critical differences? All I need answer is that if they are not, at least the outgrowth of the higher from the lower forms of life helps us mightily to understand the outgrowth at the critical point of the higher level of quality from the lower. Further, if it is right to treat colours as real qualities, not dependent for existence on the physiological organs; which are but instruments in that case for apprehending, not for creating them; if this is so, the different kinds of colours — red, green, and the rest — are comparable to the species of animals or plants, and if they do not mark a change of level they mark differences upon that level. All these matters of debate I leave aside, in order to insist on the vital feature of nature that she does exhibit critical changes of quality, which mark new syntheses, that we can but note. We may and must observe with care out of what previous conditions these new creations arise. We cannot tell why they should assume these qualities. We can but accept them as we find them, and this acceptance is natural piety.

These bodies with new qualities, these 'creative syntheses', which arise at critical points from a lower level of existence, are therefore no mere mechanical resultants of their lower conditions. If they were they would have merely the quality of their antecedents or components, as the component pulls upon a body along the sides of a parallelogram are equivalent to a resultant pull along the diagonal. Even the chemical combination of sodium and sulphuric acid, though it leads to something new and its process is not purely mechanical, does but issue in a new chemical body, just as the pairing of two living beings may lead to a new variety, but still a variety of living being. They are, therefore, after the usage of the late George Henry Lewes, described as emergents by Mr. Lloyd Morgan, with whom I have for many years shared this conception of things, which he has expounded with a simplicity and lucidity beyond my powers in a chapter of his book, *Instinct and Experience*, and with particular force in the address with which he inaugurated the independent section of Psychology at the recent meeting of the British Association at Edinburgh (1921).

Without attempting to take in the whole field of nature, I will confine myself here to life, considered as an emergent from the realm of physico-chemical bodies. A living body is, according to this conception, a physico-chemical body of a certain degree and kind of complexity, whose actions may severally be viewed as physical or chemical, but taken in their integration, or entirety (to borrow a word of Lord Haldane's), have the quality of life. Life is therefore resoluble without remainder into physico-chemical processes; but it cannot be treated as *merely* physico-chemical. Certain of its functions may be referred to physical or chemical laws, but it is not these separable processes which constitute life. Life exists only when we have that particular collocation of such physico-chemical actions which we know as living. It is the special co-ordination which conditions the appearance or creation of the new quality of life. We might therefore be disposed to describe the living body indifferently as being a physico-chemical body which is *also* vital, or as being vital and *also* physico-chemical. In reality only the second designation is satisfactory. The first would imply that a certain grouping of such processes remains no more than physical and chemical, that life is not something new but a name for this integration, whereas it is a new quality conditioned by and equivalent to the particular complexity of integration. Given life, we can hope to resolve it into its physico-chemical equivalent. We can even hope to reproduce partially or wholly by artificial means the existence of life. It is well known, for instance, that certain foams or emulsions of oil have exhibited streaming movements like those of living protoplasm. But life has been already attained, and it is our clue to the invention of the necessary machinery. Given merely physical and chemical processes, we can only generate life when we have hit upon the requisite form of integration. Thus life is *also* physico-chemical, because in its separable activities it is comparable with other physico-chemical processes. But it is not *merely* physico-chemical, because merely physico-chemical processes are not alive, and they do not give us life until the requisite complexity of integration is attained. So important is it to remember that besides elements there is the form of their combination, and that the form is as much a reality as the elements and gives them their significance ; that it is not the patches of colour alone which make the picture, but their selection and arrangement which make the separate patches contribute to the expressiveness of the picture ; that a melody is not merely the notes by which it is conveyed, but the choice and order which the musician has introduced into them ; that in the choice and combination of the parts the whole receives a meaning which does not belong to the several components ; and that while a combination of sounds is still a sound, and the blending of male and female elements in a human being is still human, there is still room at critical points for the combination to carry us into a new quality of being. Even where there is no such new quality of being, the change that is due to form may shadow forth these greater and more creative changes ; as when, to revert to former illustrations, the choice of words generates the indescribable flavour of style, or, in music, to quote the often quoted words :

> Consider it well : each tone in our scale in itself is nought ;
>   It is everywhere in the world — loud, soft, and all is said :
> Give it to me to use ! I mix it with two in my thought
>   And, there ! ye have heard and seen : consider and bow
>   the head !

That attitude is an illustration of what I am calling natural piety.

It is here that we are brought face to face with the long-drawn-out dispute between the so-called mechanistic explanation of life and vitalism. The latest contribution to the controversy is to be found in the highly interesting work on 'the mechanism of life',[1] by Mr. Johnstone, the professor of Oceanography at Liverpool. I do not mention his work in order to discuss his own explanation of life. He distinguishes the vital and the material mechanism in this way. All material mechanisms expend a part of the energy supplied to them not in doing work but in the form of heat which is no longer available for work; in the technical phrase they increase the sum of entropy or unavailing energy, and they represent a progression towards the condition of general dissipation of available energy. Living machines, on the contrary, delay or reverse the accumulation of entropy. It is beyond my competence to inquire into the correctness of this view. Rather I wish to direct your attention to the point that there is upon this doctrine such a 'mechanism' of life; because it suggests that the sharp distinction of the mechanical from the vital is unfounded, and that life may be a mechanism and yet have, as I have said, a new quality (though this view I am not attributing to Mr. Johnstone himself), and that while there is no new entity life, there is a new quality life, with which certain combinations of matter may be endowed. Vitalism supposed that there was an actual vital force, non-physical, which interfered with and directed the physical behaviour of the organism, and it has been reintroduced in our day by Mr. Hans Driesch under the guise of a presiding psychoid or entelechy, as he names it, a distinguishable principle, not resoluble into chemical or physical action. In this controversy a middle position is occupied by Mr. J. S. Haldane, who has called attention to a number of delicate adjustments performed by the

[1] *The Mechanism of Life*, London (Arnold), 1921. Cp. W. M'Dougall, *Body and Mind*, p. 245.

organism which cannot be accounted for, he thinks, by the separate chemical processes of the body. Thus the respiratory actions under the guidance of the nervous centre are so delicate that they preserve the pressure of carbonic acid in the air in the lungs and therefore in the blood-vessels, and restore it to the normal when the amount of it has been disturbed even in the slightest degree, as by taking deeper breath and so diluting the carbonic acid. The arterial blood has, as he otherwise puts it, a normal faint alkalinity, and if this is disturbed, however slightly, by defect of carbonic acid, the pressure is restored. In the same way the blood has a normal salinity, which is kept constant in the face of the slightest changes by delicate reactions on the part of the kidneys. Mr. Haldane takes this delicacy of adjustment to mean that physiological action can only be understood by including in any function the organisation of the whole creature. Here we might seem to have a matter upon which only a physiologist has the right to speak. Still, a mere philosopher may be allowed to consider the wider issue raised. If this concept of organisation means only that vital action implies, and is not rightly described without, it, a philosopher must declare Mr. Haldane right. If he means that vital action precludes the resolution of life without remainder into chemical and physical action, he is open to the charge that, in his zeal for this new fact of life, he is forgetting that the whole make-up of the organism is itself, as Mr. Lloyd Morgan has pointed out, a factor in the chemical and physical processes in question. The moral which I draw from his work is not his own, but precisely the statement made at the beginning, that that organisation which is alive is not merely physico-chemical, though completely resoluble into such terms, but has the new quality of life. No appeal is needed, so far as I can see, to a vital force or even an *élan vital*. It is enough to note the emergence of the quality, and try to describe what is involved in its conditions. That task will be, I imagine, difficult enough, and Mr. Johnstone's own

NATURAL PIETY

account [1] may be valued as an attempt towards performing it.

The emergence of life with this new collocation of conditions implies that life is continuous with chemical, physical and mechanical action. To be more explicit, the living body is also physical and chemical. It surrenders no claim to be considered a part of the physical world. But the new quality of life which it possesses is neither chemical nor mechanical, but something new. Thus the parts of the living body have colour but life is not coloured, and they are material but life itself is not material, but only the body which is alive is material. The lower conditions out of whose collocations life emerges supply a body as it were to a new soul. The specific characters which they possess are not continued into the new soul. The continuity which exists between life and the material does not mean that the material is carried over into life. There would not in that case be continuity between the living body as a new emergent and its predecessors; the living body would be nothing more than an elaborate material mechanism, which would illustrate material action, but could not claim a position of privilege. The characters which *are* continued from the lower level into life are not the specific qualities of the lower level; they are rather those characters which all existence shares in common, such as existence in time and space, intensity, capacity of affecting other existences, all which belong to life as much as to matter.

From this it will be clear that when we draw a sharp contrast between life and mechanism, as too often we do, we are guilty of exaggeration if not of confusion.[2] It is more to the purpose to indicate their differences after we have assured ourselves of a fundamental continuity or resemblance. What is salient in mechanical bodies is their general uniformity of response, the routine character

---
[1] *The Mechanism of Life*, chapter xi.
[2] Compare on this subject chapters vi., vii. of Mr. R. F. A. Hoernlé's *Studies in Contemporary Metaphysics*, New York and London, 1920.

of their behaviour. What is salient in life is its capacity of fine adjustment to varying conditions, a capacity such as no merely material body possesses, not even any machine made as yet by human design. This capacity of variation in its response may seem even to amount in certain cases to an originality which has led some to credit life with genuine freedom from determination by previous conditions, with indetermination, such as is supposed to appear in human beings as freewill — not in the ordinary sense in which we are undoubtedly free, as directing ourselves consciously to foreseen ends, but in the sense of making new departures without determining reasons. How, then, we may ask, if life is resoluble without remainder into mechanical, physical and chemical elements, can a living body be other than the automaton which Descartes declared it to be? (Descartes, observe in passing, would, if I am right, have been justified, if he had only realised that an automaton of sufficient complexity would cease to be a mere automaton.) Now these questions are put because of confusing the determinate with the purely mechanical. All behaviour, it is safe to assert, is determinate, and its fine capacity of variation and spontaneity are determined by its delicately complex organisation. But not all determinate action is therefore mechanical. The mechanical is simple and its responses broadly constant; the vital is highly complex and its responses, though definite, may vary according to circumstances; and that is all. If one thing is appearing more clearly than another from recent science, it is that material action is not so much that from which vital action diverges, as a first approximation towards vital action. The idea of life tends in our day to be extended downwards towards more primitive kinds of existence. Not that material existence is to be regarded as a form of life, but that it exhibits features which correspond to life; so that the transition from matter to life is no longer the passage to something absolutely heterogeneous but the manifestation of a single principle operating under conditions of various complexity, and generating

NATURAL PIETY

emergents with distinctive qualities, and yet retaining them all in one linked progression of affinity.

We are to combine in our thoughts this fundamental unity with the recognition of emergent qualities which can only be accepted but cannot be accounted for. One difficulty in the way of effecting this combination in our thought is the idea that if the world is a determinate growth, each new creation determined by its predecessors on a lower level, the history of the world must be capable of prediction, according to the famous assertion of Laplace. But this conclusion does not follow. Laplace's calculator might foresee that at a certain point a certain complexity might arise, whose actions were capable of measurement and would be those of living things. He could never affirm that this form of action would have the quality of life, unless he lived to see. He might predict ethereal waves but could not predict them to be light; still less that a material body would be material or when touched by light would be red, or even merely look red to a living body with eyes. All known forms of action could be predicted in their measurable characters, but never in their emergent ones. Not even God, if we suppose a God presiding over the birth of the world, in accordance with the conception of the crudest theism, could predict what these emergent qualities would be; he could only accept them like ourselves when the world he made had originated them.

I have chosen as illustrating the attitude of natural piety our acceptance of the emergence of these qualities. They remain for ever a mysterious fact. But they are after all only a part of the mystery which encompasses us and which we have no right to ask to penetrate. They are themselves related to simpler conditions, which it is the object of science to discover. Some persons have even supposed, following the precedent of the early Greek philosophers, and in particular of the chief Pythagorean speaker in Plato's great dialogue, the *Timaeus*, that all these features in the world are but specifications of some ultimate stuff of which the world is made. If this were true, it might be repugnant to the feelings of some, but natural piety would accept it, as it accepts the law of gravitation, or the law of the progression in the forms of life according to evolution, whatever the law of evolution may turn out to be ; or as it would accept, if we are compelled to think so, that the four-dimensional space-time in which we live is bent in the neighbourhood of matter. All science attempts to connect the variegated phenomena of the world by expressing them in terms of measurable motions. It seems to take the colour and richness from the world of secondary sensible qualities and expresses them in terms of primary qualities which in the end are terms of space and time. It does not, nor does it pretend to, remove the mystery of the secondary qualities, and in all its explanations it does but bring us in face of other mysteries which we must needs accept.

We are thus for ever in presence of miracles ; and as old Nathan said, the greatest of all miracles is that the genuine miracles should be so familiar. And here I interpolate a remark, not altogether irrelevant to my subject, upon the uses of great men. The emergence of qualities is the familiar miracle, but great men, and in particular great men of science, are for ever enlarging our mysteries, simplifying them and extending their scope, as when they record the law of attraction, or the idea which lies at the basis of the notion of relativity. And thus with their fresher insight they keep for us our sense of piety to nature alive. Compared with other men they are like the springs of a river. Perhaps some of you may have shared with me the exquisite experience of seeing the springs of the Aberdeenshire Dee below the top of Brae Riach in the Grampians. There the clear water bubbles to the surface through mosses pink and yellow and green with all the varying shades of green ; and as it gathers to the edge it falls in tiny trickles which unite with one another into rills, and these with like rills from other portions of the plateau, until in the end they combine to form the river which you see at the foot, already a considerable stream. The stream

NATURAL PIETY

is discoloured in its course by the soil through which it flows or the products of human labour, and is put to the service of man before it reaches the sea. And as its springs are fed by the sea into which it falls, whose vapours are drawn up and fall in rain so that a continuous life is maintained between the ocean and the fresh waters on the heights, so it is that the thoughts of great men keep up for general mankind our communion with the circumambient mystery.

The mystery of facts, whether these facts are the individual facts of experience or the larger universal facts which are scientific laws, or such facts, more comprehensive still, as may be discovered by a prudent and scientific philosophy, is the last word of knowledge. The reverent temper which accepts them is the mood of natural piety.[1]

---

[1] Commenting further on the title of this essay, I may be excused, perhaps, if I remind the reader of the opening lines of Shelley's *Alastor*:

> 'Earth, ocean, air, belovèd brotherhood !
> If our great Mother has imbued my soul
> With aught of natural piety to feel
> Your love, and recompense the boon with mine.'

The lines that follow in this invocation are in Shelley's most majestical vein and must have stirred the reverent temper which Alexander felt all his life for that supreme poet. [Editor's note.]

XII

THEISM AND PANTHEISM

(Reprinted, by permission, from *The Hibbert Journal*, January 1927)

THEOLOGY is a science which, like any other science, sets out from a certain department of experience, of which it attempts to give an orderly and rational account. That experience is the experience of the divine, the sense of the divine element in the world, of an object towards which man adopts the attitude of worship and feels the sentiment of religious devotion. In this feeling and through this feeling an object is made known or revealed to the person who has the feeling, and he calls it God. There may be persons who are rarely or never visited by such feelings, just as there may be persons who are unmoved by the beauty of a sunset. And the object itself may be revealed to the worshipper in all manner of ways : it may be an overpowering presence which compels him to his knees or terrifies him into submission ; or it may be a being evoked through his desire for support in anguish, and answers his desire ; or more vaguely something to lean on in his sense of dependence ; or a gracious presence which responds to him mysteriously with love and excites his love. He may find it in the awful or the kindly face of nature, or in the inner promptings of his own spirit (like that strange daemon of Socrates) or of his conscience. Always, under whatever shape of sensible experience or fancy or reflection, there is the awareness of a mysterious something which enforces or pleads for recognition. And in that experience itself there is no question raised of whether the object experienced exists or not ; it is for the worshipper as much a fact as a green leaf or the sun is for a dispassionate observer. The religious feeling and its object are given in one and the same experience.

Now, theology attempts to give a more explicit account of this object of the religious sentiment, describing it as it presents itself immediately to the mind, and then further the characters which it possesses when it is considered reflectively, both in itself and its relation to the worshipper. God is a god for men, and is credited with moral, social, and natural qualities which link the religious with all the other experiences of men. These characters of the godhead are embodied in the legends or the sacred books or prophetic writings of the believers; and besides this, as soon as any level of reflection is attained the current ideas of reflective thought are employed about the object of religion, and are used to describe it more accurately. Thus theology as a science has first of all to provide an accurate statement of the meaning of religious documents, and to sift their value as evidence, and then in its more abstract parts has to present a coherent and rational account of the divine. For to have the religious experience is one thing, to describe it and make it a matter of discourse is another and different thing, which can only be achieved, as all orderly description is achieved, by the use of appropriate rational and unmysterious means of bringing home to other men the mysterious. Since the religious experience varies from people to people and from age to age, there will be special Jewish or Christian or Buddhist theologies within the general ambit of theology as a whole; or, rather, it is these particular theologies from which theology in general might be gathered. It follows from this limited scope of theology and still more of special theologies that, attempting as it does to give a rational and orderly account of a certain set of data, theology like any other science is a kind of art, though not a kind of fine art. It takes a part of human experience and makes it as far as possible self-consistent, using ideas congenial to the subject matter, so as to make a rounded-off body of knowledge. Every other science is an art in this same sense, and mathematics, which is perhaps the ideal of the sciences, is more palpably than all the rest a human construction.

Philosophy approaches theology, in the character of the philosophy of religion, in the same spirit as it approaches the other sciences, the spirit of criticism and comprehension. Necessarily, in Bacon's fine phrase, philosophy takes all knowledge for its province; not in the sense of arrogating an impossible erudition, but in the sense that it asks whether the ideas used in any science are compatible with those used in other sciences or in the ordinary unscientific possessions of the mind. No topic raised in the sciences, so far as it does not fall strictly within that art which is the special province of the science — and is therefore subject to the rules of the scientific artist (what philosopher in his senses would question the demonstration of the binomial theorem? He leaves such doubts to the skilled craftsman, the mathematician) — is exempt from his enquiry. His dearest privilege indeed is to organise knowledge, to find a comprehensive view of the whole. But comprehension means scrutiny. Of theology it asks, granted that the object of religion is such and such, what place is there in the rest of the universe for such a being? Is the being so described consistent with other well-attested facts? Hence, as in regard to the ordinary things of sense, it asks whether these are indeed real, apart from our awareness of them, or exist only in so far as there is a knower of them; so it asks of theology, may not the object of religion be a fancy projected into reality by the wishes of man?

Philosophy is critical of theology in another fashion, which is more to my immediate purpose. Theology is exposed to a peculiar danger. The more it penetrates by reflection into the notions of religion the more it tends to employ conceptions on the borderland of philosophy. Some theologies do more or less without philosophy; it is always said that the Jews are not a philosophical people on the whole, and are content with moral notions. But Christian theology has been, in its more abstract parts, very philosophical, and has attracted to itself some of the greatest speculative intellects. Now the danger arises thus: the demands of the religious consciousness — I mean, of course, the clarified religious consciousness — are insistent and must be met, and they lead to ideas which are mysterious indeed, but whose mystery passes more or less unnoticed by the ordinary mind; which are indeed pictorial embodiments of these insistent claims. Thus the intimate harmonising of God and man, their communion in the relation of child to father, is embodied in the idea of a God-made man, which is found in other religions, but in none with such grace and winningness as in Christianity. But the purely religious data of the Incarnation, the Atonement, the Resurrection, data which are the starting points of Christian theology, lead on to the subtlest metaphysical conceptions, such as that of the Trinity, which are introduced to satisfy rationally the data contained in the religious consciousness, which is not of itself rational at all in its inception. It is in the employment of philosophical conceptions that theology has to tread most warily and to beware of taking them over except after scrutiny. Much of the theology which I have read of to-day (and it is very little) seems to me not to avoid this danger; one instance is the indiscriminate appeal made to the idea of value or the valuable, as something which must be accepted as admitting no further analysis, although psychologists and writers on morals have offered such analyses more than once.

It is one such question of the legitimate use of conceptions taken from philosophy to which I am about to call your attention now — the question whether the notions of transcendence and immanence can be combined, as it is commonly thought they can be and are combined in the dominant Western conception of the Godhead. The same question may be put thus: Can theism and pantheism be combined in one conception? 'For pantheism', says Ward (*Realm of Ends*),[1] ' God is the immanent ground of

[1] P. 234.

the world, for deism he is the transcendent ground, for theism he is both.' I put aside for the moment the correctness of the statement, which would exclude Judaism from theism, and I ask merely, is the proposed conciliation possible, and in what sense ? Perhaps after all the question is not inappropriate to raise in a Jewish society. For while Judaism would, I think, be admitted to be undoubtedly theistic, Jewish philosophy has produced in the heretical Spinoza the greatest example of pantheism known to the Western world. Even Mr. Roth, who in his work on *Spinoza, Descartes and Maimonides* maintains the debt of Spinoza to Maimonides and his affinity with Maimonides, admits that God could not be equated with the world by Maimonides as he is by Spinoza, God being for Maimonides an immaterial intelligence beyond ' the order demanded by the universal claims of the thinking mind '. Maimonides, I suppose, represents the theology of the Old Testament. Spinoza's pantheism, whatever its antecedents, is unorthodox. Both, however, arise within the womb of Judaism.

To speak strictly, a transcendent being is one which exists outside the material world — which includes our own material life as embodied spirit, and if there should be creatures higher than ourselves in the scale of existence, transcendence would mean existence beyond even such. The Jewish God is clearly transcendent, and in the Old Testament, at any rate, the writers are so much absorbed in moral considerations and so little occupied with metaphysics that questions like that of the possible existence within nature of higher creatures than ourselves, or even that of an after-life of human beings, in which they exist as immaterial intelligences, scarcely trouble their minds. The God of Aristotle is eminently transcendent. Perhaps the distinctive note of theism which marks it off from deism is that the transcendent God of theism is conceived predominantly as possessing moral attributes and as entering into personal relations with his human creatures. Deism is no longer a living doctrine, though it played so large a part in England in the eighteenth century. It is often hard to distinguish it from theism, though not from Christian theism. Mr. Sorley quotes [1] from Samuel Clarke a passage enumerating four classes of deists. One class maintained the existence of a supreme intelligence which made the world, but having made it, concerns himself no further in its government; others allowed divine providence, or the moral perfection of God, or the duties of man towards God, with the accompanying notion of future rewards and punishments. But doubtless it is the externality of the Creator to his created world which predominates, and deism shades off into theism according to the extent to which God is believed to enter into relations with man or nature. Deism, in fact, is opposed not so much to theism as to revelation. Its God and his attributes and goings-on are discoverable by the light of nature only.

Thus theism in the strict sense of that term believes in a transcendent God, who is also the creator of the world, who enters into intimate relations with man and natural events. He is always conceived personally, though his infinity, eternity, and perfection make him so distinct from human persons that the notion of personality of God dare not be pressed. The theistic God is at least a person, but he is more.

Immanence, on the other hand, in the strict sense means something more than God's entry into intercourse with any part of nature, or in particular with ourselves. It means that God is a principle which pervades the whole of nature and has no existence outside. Whether God is identified with nature as with Spinoza (*Deus sive Natura*), or is simply a breath which inspires the world, is indifferent. To be immanent, God lives, and lives only in his world. This notion is the essence of pantheism, and pantheism assumes a less or a more exalted and satisfying form according as God is conceived merely as the indwelling presence which animates things, as in the familiar passage of Pope, or the world is conceived rather as consisting in

[1] *Moral Values and the Idea of God* (Cambridge, 1918), p. 458.

THEISM AND PANTHEISM

its parts of existences which owe their being to him, are in a manner shadows of him, possess only a relative individuality compared with his, are fragments of his total existence, and owe their being to their roots in him. Such is Spinoza's conception of immanent God, and various passages of Wordsworth approximate to it, though they do not reach it wholly. Goethe's thought was directly influenced by Spinoza; how far Wordsworth's was I do not know, though he must have learned of Spinoza in his intercourse with Coleridge. Hegel expressed the difference between these two varieties of pantheism in the phrase that in true pantheism God is not merely in everything, but everything is in God. Whatever form pantheism assumes, there is no room for God outside the world, and immanence in the philosophical sense does not mean residence in this, that, or other part of the world, but throughout, so that the immanent being is coextensive with the world which he indwells.

Now we may if we choose dilute the meaning of the word immanence and declare God to be immanent wherever he may be said to be present, to be immanent in us when he speaks to us in our conscience, or in the thunder when he provokes it. But to be present *at* a thing is not to exist *in* it. Immanence is not the same conception as omnipresence. If a being is immanent where its effects may be traced, if the cannon is immanent in the fractured arm, everything in the world is immanent in all the rest, and God has no prerogative place. The God of theism sustains the life of all his creatures, but he is not in them, any more than the man Shakespeare who is dead and gone is as the living man Shakespeare existent in *Hamlet* which he created. To act as in the sight of God is to be aware of God, but what is in the agent, what is indwelling in him, is not God but this awareness of God. A man would not be what he is but for his parents; but they are not in him. At most, according to a well-known doctrine, only a portion of their actual germ-plasm is continued into him. Handel is immortal, Samuel Butler says, in his music, and I for one believe that this posthumous continuance in our effects and our creations is the only immortality which experience can verify. But it is just because such immortality is not the personal continuance of the man, soul and body, that it seems to most persons cold and repugnant. For theism each part of the world implies God, but God is a being apart from them, and though each thing testifies to him (so that theism continually drops or rises into the language of pantheism) he does not live as God in them.

We may even conceive a special being, a God-man, in whom God is historically revealed, in whom divinity has taken human shape ; and in such a person God would really be immanent. But if we pretend that in this way theism and pantheism are combined, we expose ourselves to that besetting danger of theology to which I have alluded above ; we divert our conceptions from their proper use. For it is vital to immanence, in the proper sense, that God is as much immanent, in the looser sense, in a stone as in a man, and that God as an integral individual cannot be wholly present in either. At most he can be *implied* in either and then implied equally in both. And we cannot hope to clear up a religious mystery by a philosophical obscurity. Supposing that the highest religious consciousness demands a historical personage, who is a man but really God (and I am not calling that demand in question as a matter of religious experience), so that, in some recent words of Mr. Rabindranath Tagore (*Manchester Guardian*, August 5), ' God remains essentially what he is while manifesting himself in the Son's being ', that experience is not to be described in rational terms as a synthesis of immanence and transcendence or of pantheism and theism; but if it can be rationalised at all, demands different conceptions.

The thesis which I desire to commend, then, is that transcendence and immanence are not reconcilable, that God cannot be, as Ward suggests he can be, at once the immanent and the transcendent ground of the world. If

God is coextensive with the world, he does not transcend it. If he transcends it, he is not immanent in it. Alike for pantheism and for any theism which is likely to satisfy our minds, God enters into relations with every part of the universe, and is in that sense coextensive with the whole. But if transcendent he is necessarily not identical with it. It would seem to follow, and this is what I am about to suggest, that the transcendent God of theism is, in truth, a part and a part only of that very world of which he is said to be the ground or the creator, a distinguishable divine individual within the world itself, not the whole world, and yet related to every part of it. In what sense such a God could be said to be immanent remains to be seen. At any rate, it will be plain that his transcendence of everything below his own rank within the world (for that will be the only possible way in which he can transcend) will not be true of him in the same respect as his immanence.

The problem is one of supreme importance for the philosophy of religion, for neither pure transcendence nor pure immanence satisfies the mature religious sentiment, which requires in its object of worship elements which are characteristic of both. It is natural enough therefore that theology should help itself out with maintaining a synthesis of them. All that I am concerned for is that we should not conjure with these ideas, because God is felt to be in some sense immanent, and in some sense transcendent, without enquiring in what precise sense either is true. The need of reconciliation is palpable, even apart from the entrancing prepossession drawn from historical sources in favour of a God who becomes man.

For pantheism and theism have each of them defects for the religious feeling which the other supplies, and merits which the other lacks. The God of pantheism, being a pervading presence, is already one with the worshipper. The worshipper has not to seek his unity with the divine; that unity is given from the outset. The worshipper has no real existence apart from the divine, and the perpetual danger to which no pantheism hitherto has offered a sufficient resistance is that the individuality of the worshipper is lost in the divine. This is its almost necessary drawback. For the pantheistic God is impersonal, even if individual; and religion, when it has got beyond the stage of the mere recognition of what Dr. Otto in his celebrated book [1] calls the 'numinous', and lends as it must a human colouring to the numinous presence, behaves to it as if it were at least a person, responsive to man's needs as a loving father, even if also as a stern law-giver. Pantheism hardly admits this sublimation of the awful into the lovable. Spinoza's example might seem at first sight a flat contradiction of this proposition. With him the intellectual love of God takes the place of the religious passion. But the delight of the thinker in recognising his unity with the divine is a speculative and not a religious ecstasy. It only seems to be religious ecstasy because the religious passion is already alight in Spinoza's breast (the observation is not mine, but borrowed from William James), and is identified with the attitude of the imperfect creature to the perfect whole, of which he is a transitory part, a ripple on the surface of that ocean. The thinker's awareness of his participation in the universe of reality which he calls God would not be *love*, except for the enkindling efficacy of his religious desire. And so the pantheistic God is imperfectly worshipful. The same point is put in other words in the old charge against pantheism that it leaves no room for the independence of the worshipper. And hence the extreme phases of mysticism in theistic religions are almost indistinguishable from pantheism. The healthy religious impulse maintains the independence of the worshipper, and believes that man is as necessary to God as God to man — a belief which takes an extreme form in those passages of the Old Testament where God enters into covenants with his worshippers.

The transcendence of God in theism supplies this personal note to the relation. A transcendent God is

[1] *The Idea of the Holy*, English translation, Oxford, 1925.

THEISM AND PANTHEISM

palpably an individual being, and entering as he does into intercourse with men, can be the object of love, blended with religious awe. The defect of theism lies in the degree of God's externality to his world which remains in historic theisms. The separation of the divine personality and the human one is overcome in the religious act. But love is a two-sided relation, not the mere desire of the moth for the star. The theoretical problem for theism has always been to explain how the transcendent being should condescend to the relation. God does indeed need man, but not as man needs man. The unification of God and man remains artificial. The great Pauline words about God, ' In him we live and move and have our being ', declare the religious attitude and introduce the flavour of pantheism; but they describe it from the human side. Why must God, unless he be conceived with utter anthropomorphism, find his being, as it were, attain to consciousness of himself, in man? For he is transcendent and not a magnified man. Moreover, not only does he transcend his world but precedes it. How can he create beings to commune with him, as they do in religion, except either by an arbitrary act, as in deism, or by the necessity of his nature, when we are at once plunged into pantheism? We seem to be faced with the dilemma that a pantheistic God cannot be worshipped, or at least loved, by his creatures, and a transcendent God can have no creatures to worship him.

I am, with this, touching on the problem of creation, and in fact the problem of immanence and transcendence and that of creation are the same problems. Doctrines of creation form part of religious mythology. It is not their scientific insufficiency which raises any serious question — it could only do so if religious documents were thought to be infallibly inspired. Their religious significance lies in the belief that somehow God and his world are not disjoined, and that at least God, if not the cause or ground of the world, is its last and supreme meaning. Now, for pantheism, God is not strictly a creator at all; things which

THEISM AND PANTHEISM

we call creatures arise within the one reality or substance which is God. In Spinoza's language, God is their cause, much as a triangle is the cause of the equality of its angles to two right angles. They are in fact his modes or appearances. We should say they grow or evolve within the ultimate reality. Creation in the proper sense may hold as between two of these things, as when a man creates a table or a child. But there is no creation as between God and an individual thing. On the other hand, a transcendent God creates, and creates out of a pre-existent material, whether, as in crude early doctrines, he fashions the rough chaos into specific forms like an artist modelling his clay, or these forms come into being out of the chaos ('the face of the waters') by his word ('let there be light, and there was light'). When Faust rejects the words 'in the beginning was the word' and substitutes 'in the beginning was the act', he marks the passage from transcendence to immanence, from theism to pantheism. It is hardly necessary, after Kant, to labour the point that a God who creates the world out of materials which he finds is no creator but an artificer; it is more useful to add that the material upon which he works limits his power. An omnipotent God cannot create, except from himself, and he ceases then to be transcendent. And yet if he is regarded as a creator, and in some sense a person, he cannot but be transcendent. For personality or any conception which includes personality implies the existence of external beings. As we know it, personality exists in reaction upon our surroundings; we can no more be selves without the bodies of other things or persons, or at least without bodies of our own to call out the 'passions' of our minds, than we can breathe without air or grow without carbon. Whether in the body or the spirit, life depends on provocation and resistance. Thus the transcendence of a creative God limits him by something uncreated; and if truly unlimited by anything outside himself he shows himself in things, but does not create them. 'Creation out of nothing' is to speak the language of immanence while using the ideas of transcendence, to speak pantheism and think theistically.

Everywhere the attempt breaks down. And it is no answer that theologians themselves have never doubted that the union of immanence and transcendence was a mystery. What they mean, and mean rightly, is that the religious mind demands alike something which savours of pantheism and something which savours of theism. Scientifically it remains unjustifiable to maintain a mixture of oil and vinegar, so long as those ingredients will not mix. It may turn out that the composition itself has been mistaken. It appears to me vain to support our belief in any special revelation of God in man, and still less in any particular man, no matter how perfect and beautiful an exemplar he may have been of what man has it in him to become, by justifying it as the realised union of transcendence and immanence. The philosophic foundation for that belief is unsound. The belief must either be justified by a different philosophy or the realisation of its object found elsewhere. I want to suggest that immanence and transcendence can be and are unified in a God who in one respect is transcendent and in another respect immanent. But I can approach the matter only philosophically.

I call to mind in the first place a striking feature of the absolutist philosophy of the great English metaphysician, F. H. Bradley. For Bradley the things of the world are conceived quite in the spirit of Spinoza as appearances of the one ultimate reality, or absolute, compared with which they are still realities but not ultimately, or in their own right, real. Now God in this philosophy, unlike Spinoza's, is not himself the Absolute, but one of its appearances, and presumably the highest of them. Spinoza's God has become the Absolute, which is spirit. The God of religion is a being within the world of appearances, and is not ultimate reality. In this respect Bradley differed from Bosanquet, for whom God and the Absolute are one.

I am unable to accept the doctrine of an absolute spirit,

but I believe that Bradley was right in finding God among the things of the world, and therefore not identical with the world, as Spinoza thought. The ground of the obscurity which affects Bradley's conception of God, which is a theistic one (God is transcendent here as superior to all other appearances but inside the world), lies in a defect of his philosophy (I speak with all submission) which, curiously enough, is precisely the same defect which makes it impossible for the ordinary theistic God to be also immanent. Bradley's Absolute, and God as conceived in current theologies, are not subject to time or space, are timeless. I leave Bradley here, for my discourse is not about metaphysical systems, but about theological conceptions, and I confine myself to theism.

Alike in Jewish and in Christian theism the supreme being who is the creator is out of time. Time is itself a creation ; it came into being, as Plato said, along with the world. The result is that God is a perfect reality which impels from behind, sets the world going, and maybe embodies himself in some historical man. I know that God's priority to the universe he creates is not strictly a priority in time, and we may ride off upon the phrase of logical priority. But a transcendent God (I do not speak of a pantheistic God like Spinoza's) who is an individual being entering into relations with his creatures is not merely logically prior. For this destroys his transcendent individuality. True, he embraces within one finished intuition all the past and the future. But we who are entangled in the lapse of time are compelled to think of him as before us. This is the price we pay for conceiving a God for whom the whole temporal history of the world exists complete in a single moment (as we say after Kant, in a makeshift phrase). The difficulties of Bradley's Absolute are transferred to the theistic God who is creator. God is already and always has been what we may strive after as unattainable perfection. Our view is directed backwards to the past.

In Meredith's ' Thrush in February ' there occurs the

line, ' the rapture of the forward view '. I here commend in religion and theology the forward view. Time is a constituent of the very substance of reality. If so, there can be no being who already exhausts the future, for whom the world is complete and only left to timeful creatures to elaborate in time. The world is temporal in its essence, and since God, according to the suggestion I have adopted from Bradley, is within the world, God is himself a creature of time. Whereas upon the current notions man being less than God may need for his religious satisfaction a man in whom God is embodied, for the forward view man's life is preparatory to the outgrowth of the divine quality. Every man is in this notion prophetic of deity, and there are certain men of religious genius who, being prophetic in an eminent degree and with rarer insight, are distinguished by the name of prophets, of whom Jesus is one. God is not the already perfect being who for the benefit of imperfect man takes human shape, but is himself in the making, and his divine quality or deity a stage in time beyond the human quality. And as the root and leaves and sap of the plant feed its flower, so the whole world, as so far unrolled in the process of time, flowers into deity. Matter and spirit, stones, trees, and men gather together into and sustain that quality of the world. The values, truth, goodness, beauty, are not themselves divine or witnesses to divinity, but are the basis on which it is erected, or the seed from which it springs. As our human existence with its prerogatives is nurtured by everything beneath it, for we are a part of nature, so God's deity is nurtured by all that it transcends. And since this nutriment of deity is infinite, being the whole world, God's distinctive deity is infinite, since it is the expression and consummation and representative of all that conspires to its production. God's deity is thus the new quality of the universe which emerges in its forward movement in time.

In some such fashion we may with forward-directed thoughts conceive the existence of God. The union of transcendence and immanence is effected, but not in the

THEISM AND PANTHEISM

way of either theism or pantheism. Pure transcendence and pure immanence are, as we saw, irreconcilable. But in different respects God transcends and indwells. His deity, though a part of the world, within it and not without it, transcends the inferior order of developed creations, including man; but being the whole world as it tends to deity or is engaged in the production of deity, God takes in within himself the whole world and is therefore immanent in it. He is transcendent, as it were, in respect of his mind (to use a human analogy) and immanent in respect of his body. His transcendence and his immanence are united through their different functions in God's total being.

It would be easy enough to cavil at this conception. A friend of mine jested to me of the God of Abraham, Isaac, and Jacob who is to exist a million of years hence. But the jest is a misconception. For the Universe as straining towards deity is a present reality. And the Universe so conceived is God. It is only the actual existence of deity which belongs to the future.

A matter of greater importance to me is whether a God thus disclosed to the forward view does or does not satisfy the religious experience and the demands which are founded on it. That question I would submit for consideration. For in itself it is a philosophical and not in the first instance a religious conception. In other words, a God thus conceived would be consistent with the nature of the world as we know it in the guise it presents to the other sciences. He still asks aid from the pictorial imagination in order to be realised for our reflective weakness; but requires no pictures that depend on violent hypotheses. The numinous mystery still attaches to a world making for deity; and love given and returned is, as it seems to me, as conceivable towards a being, greater than ourselves, who draws us forward to himself by the force of our own aspirations, as to one who draws backward to him the creatures which he created to love him.

XIII

SPINOZA

(Separately published by the Manchester University Press, 1933. Here reprinted by permission.)

SPINOZA was born on November 24, 1632, and our commemoration of his tercentenary is a few weeks too early.[1] But we may reverse what Henry V said: nice customs curtsey to great kings. Great philosophers curtsey to the privileges of a time-table of public lectures.

The poet Heine, in the course of his lectures to the French people on German philosophers, made an epigram which I am never tired of repeating for its wit, and Heine was fond of it himself. Spinoza, in accordance with the Talmudic tradition, had acquired like other Jewish scholars a manual occupation, to earn his living. Heine says, Spinoza lived by grinding lenses, and all subsequent philosophers have seen through the glasses which Spinoza ground. He was one of the Mt. Everests of the seventeenth century, which Mr. Whitehead has called the century of genius. It was the seminal period for the intellectual life of Europe: all the great ideas which have occupied the minds of men since that time in science and philosophy and political thought had their beginnings then. It began with Galileo and Descartes and it ended with Newton and Locke and Leibniz; and these are only the greatest names among a host of great names. To think only of this country, there were Boyle and Hooke and Christopher Wren, and in Holland there was Huyghens. Locke, who was, with Newton, the maker of eighteenth-century thought, was

[1] The address in commemoration of the tercentenary of Spinoza's birth was given on October 31, 1932.

born in the same year as Spinoza, and him also we celebrate next month, this time some months *after* his date.

Spinoza's own life is more picturesque than that of most scholars and philosophers, because of the turbulent experience of his youth. He was expelled from the synagogue at Amsterdam because of his unorthodoxy; and excommunicated with what corresponds to bell, book, and candle. Apart from this incident and one or two slighter ones in later life, he lived a quiet and obscure and serene existence, corresponding with his friends about his philosophy, making lenses for optical instruments for men of science (for obscurely as he lived he had fame, so that Leibniz himself came to visit him and learn from him), preferring his undisturbed reflection to the honour and drawbacks of a chair at Heidelberg which was offered him with many honorific circumstances. Perhaps he knew that he had not long to live. At any rate he died at forty-five of consumption, a disease which could not but have been helped by his occupation with glass dust. For a century he was defamed for an infidel and atheist, this man from whose reverent lips the name of God was never absent, until Lessing taught Europe who he was, and, after Lessing, Goethe in Germany and Coleridge in England.

He has his overwhelmingly great place in the history of philosophy, where scholars have shown what he owed to his Jewish predecessors, Maimonides and Crescas (for we know the books which he had in his library), and how in the advancing thought of the world he marks the change from Descartes and the preparation for Leibniz. Of these matters I do not propose to speak, but abandoning altogether any pretence to history of him either as a man or as a philosopher, to indicate rather what light he may supply us in the problems of our own day. For he represents a type of thought which is highly relevant to our present condition.

Spinoza is at once a man of science, a philosopher, and a believer, and so far from there being dissension or discrepancy in his mind between these three things, his science and his religious faith fell naturally into their places within the scheme of his philosophy. In the seventeenth century, at least among its greater minds, this fracture so familiar to us had not occurred. It was the eighteenth century with its rationalism and the nineteenth century with its sciences which brought in doubt, till instead of accepting religion and God as part of the one world, men began to find excuses for religion, or professed indifference and uncertainty, or even denied its claims. But Spinoza is both man of science and mystic, and his mystical faith is the outcome of the same method which he applies to physics. He made, so far as I know, no distinct contribution to science as such, his concern was with the philosophy of science, the ideas at the base of it. In speaking of physical things he used the current mechanical theory, and like the other philosophers of the time was accepted as a scientific thinker. But this is not the whole of the story. Religion and the natural world are not merely juxtaposed in him without interference with one another. The study of man, or what we call psychology, is part of the whole study of things, and follows the same unprejudiced or objective method, and to understand fully what science is, is in the end to love God with what he calls in the inspired phrase ' intellectual love '.

The method of naturalism is the method of impartial description and analysis, as practised with appropriate means in the natural sciences. But the name has fallen into discredit, and to condemn a man's philosophy it is only needful nowadays to call it naturalism. That is because the naturalism of the second half of the nineteenth century practised science in respect of nature but seemed to the men of that time to lead to agnosticism and unfaith. That aloofness of science from religion is disappearing or has disappeared in our day. Science holds out to religion and the values of beauty and goodness welcoming arms. But the situation is remarkable. No longer is religion admitted as it were on sufferance, but some of the greatest thinkers about science urge that religion and beauty may supply what science cannot give. For physical science grows more and more artificial, and seems to some to be a pure construction of the mind, substituting symbols for things, while the real nature of the physical world escapes our understanding, is represented or symbolised but not known. Whereas, it is urged, in our minds themselves, and above all in our experience of goodness and beauty and religion, we have direct experience without symbols and it is reasonable to suppose that reality must be sought in something of the nature of mind. Mind, upon these views, and its experiences are a refuge from the incompetence of the sciences.

Now the reason why I said that Spinoza was so relevant to our present questions is that, instead of this half-hearted appeal to mind to help us where science has failed, we have in Spinoza the most thoroughgoing naturalism. Perhaps it is hopeless to expect that this word should smell sweet again. At any rate it is well for those who will not hear of naturalism, because it has been soiled by mistaken use, to remember that it was the method of Spinoza, who at the same time held up an exalted ideal of life and possessed the mystic vision, and held all these things together in one philosophical conception. It is quite true that for Spinoza our ordinary judgments of good and bad, beautiful and ugly, are but loose, rough and ready, and relative : we are merely comparing a given particular with our ideas of what is perfect or beautiful. But there is a definite conception of good which is set by the science of man itself. And his whole enterprise is a search for the highest good. ' After experience had taught me ', Spinoza says, in the opening of his unfinished *Treatise on the Improvement of the Understanding*, ' that all the usual surroundings of social life are vain and futile, seeing that none of the objects of my fears contained in themselves anything either good or bad, except in so far as the mind is affected by them, I finally resolved to enquire whether there might be some real good having power to communicate itself, which would affect the mind singly, to the exclusion of all else ; whether, in fact, there might be anything of which the discovery and attainment would enable me to enjoy continuous, supreme, and unending happiness.' He dismisses in turn the pursuit of riches, fame, and the pleasures of sense. All the evils that attend their pursuit ' arise ', he says, ' from the love of what is perishable. . . . But love towards a thing eternal and infinite feeds the mind wholly with joy, and is itself unmingled with any sadness, wherefore it is greatly to be desired and sought for with all our strength.'

I am to describe to you as well as I can the stages by which Spinoza conducts us from his beginning in philosophy to his end in a mystical adoration, and all within the one framework of scientific method. For he begins with God as a philosophic conception of the totality of things and ends with the love of him. It is one and the same God throughout, but as the argument proceeds the cold initial conception is warmed and enriched by the reflection upon it of our human experience, and becomes the object of a passion of religious worship. And it is scarcely possible to doubt that, as William James pointed out, the religious passion which filled Spinoza's mind, and is justified by his philosophy, determined the course of his philosophy from the outset. But at the outset ' God ' is but a name for a being which is absolutely infinite, and that there is such a being and only one such being is, though Spinoza offers a proof of the proposition, in reality only another way of saying that all this mass of finite things we are acquainted with implies a single infinite being.

Accustomed as we are to the multiplicity and variety of things, we go on to observe that they are related to one another by laws which science discovers, and then we proceed to account for this connectedness of things by a being, God, who created them. But that is not Spinoza's way, nor the way of the other philosophers of his time. What they think of first is not the separateness of things but their connectedness. Their unity comes first, and not their apparent disunity. It is very interesting to compare in this respect Locke, who closes the century and begins

SPINOZA

the new century of relative disintegration, with another of these earlier philosophers, Malebranche, who had said by way of expressing this continuity of things, that we see all things in God. Locke made mild fun of Malebranche in an essay he wrote on him. Malebranche had said that when we would think of anything in particular, we at first cast our view upon all things. ' I do not think ', says Locke, ' that my country neighbours ' (he was living then with his friends the Mashams down in Essex near Ongar) ' when they first wake in the morning, find it impossible to think of a lame horse they have, till they have run over in their minds " all beings " that are, and then pitch on dapple.' Locke was nearer to our common sense, but Malebranche and Spinoza were nearer to the facts. For the supreme fact is that somehow things are one : are organically connected is our modern phrase.

More than that. Not only are these finite things connected, but with some reflection we can realise why Spinoza, thinking of this connected whole of finite things, called that whole or God infinite. Here again we are accustomed to suppose that infinite means only something which we can never attain in our thoughts. Add as we may one finite thing to another in order to connect them together, the total eludes us. The infinite is just a negative way of describing an ideal we cannot reach. So we find it difficult to think that the infinite is something not negative but positive which precedes the finite and is superior to it, something which, though we cannot comprehend it, we do apprehend (I am using the language of Descartes) however vaguely, something which lies at the bottom of our minds even in thinking of finite things. Nowadays the mathematicians have made the notion easier for us. The series of numbers is infinite, not because merely we cannot exhaust it, though that is also true, but because it is all-inclusive, whereas a finite series of numbers is not. Add 1 to a finite series, say the numbers from 2 to 9, and the last number you get, 10, is outside the series. But add 1 to the whole series and the numbers you get are all still within the original series. Thus to say with Spinoza that there is an infinite being from which all things depend, which is prior to those things, is not so far from our thoughts as at first it seems, nor would it have seemed strange to thinking persons of his time.

The step which Spinoza took, which is distinctive of him, is that this infinite being or God is not only the origin of nature but is equated to nature, *Deus sive Natura* is his expression. He is not so much the creator of finites as that they, rightly understood, that is seen not merely in their connection with one another but with the whole which is God himself, are expressions of him, just as if they were the words he speaks which yet would have no meaning apart from the whole sentence or speech in which they are spoken. In technical phrase, they are modes of him. They flow from him by the necessity of his nature, for on the one hand they exist only in him, on the other hand he exists in them. God was not free to create the world otherwise, as if he had been some arbitrary monarch; they are his nature partially displayed. Only because we separate things from one another, and fail to see them as they are, and as God sees them, do we stumble at these ideas.

They flow, accordingly, from God's nature in virtue of the necessity under which God acts, but God himself is free because there is nothing outside him which could limit his action. We, however, and all other finite things, are not free, because we are limited by other things; and Spinoza thinks that human freedom is an illusion of ours due to our not being aware of the causes of our actions; in reality we are determined by our own characters, and the stimulations which provoke us to action from external things or our own bodies. The physics of our day inclines to believe that there is freedom even in the electrons within an atom; but whether this means that the electrons act from caprice or only incalculably (two very different things) remains to be seen, for not all physicists are agreed. At any rate the electrons are no more free than men; and

Spinoza would say that neither kind is free. On the other hand, if we choose to call men free in a relative sense (which Spinoza would not admit), because we choose what we do, in that sense the electrons also are free, but in neither case is the action capricious, but determined.

There is a further feature of Spinoza's thought which is of the last importance for understanding ourselves and other finite things. Some finites are extended, material things and some have minds. Spinoza holds that all of them are both material and have minds, and for this reason. The modes of God in his language exist under different attributes. God has attributes under which these modes exist and are apprehended. The only attributes of God that we humans apprehend are those of extension or spatiality (and this we may take as equivalent to what we call being material) and mind. God has infinite such attributes, but it is only these two that we humans can apprehend. Now as attributes of God they are infinite, and as it were cover the whole nature of God, who is fully expressed in each of them : each is coextensive with God. It follows that every mode, every finite, exists under each of the attributes of God. Every thing is extension and mind alike, though of course neither the extension nor the mind assumes in different finites the same shape. Just as my body is not the body of an electron, neither is the electron's mind my mind. But animated both are in their degree of perfection, that is, to put it roughly, in the degree to which they count in the universe of things. Our own thought, reverting as is so often pointed out to the thought of the seventeenth century, more and more tends, in its revulsion from the mechanistic ideas of the last century, to think of all things in terms of life, if not of mind. The position at which Sir Arthur Eddington and his colleagues have arrived, because they believe that in our human experience of ourselves we come into direct contact with reality, a contact which physics, according to them, never gives us, this position is taken up in a more defensible form by Spinoza as self-evident. But, as I said, in a more defensible form; for reality is not for Spinoza mind alone, as if there could be mind without body, but something which is at once mind and extension. Our puzzles about the so-called relation of mind and body are for him non-existent. Mind and body are two different sides of one and the same thing : what under one attribute of God is mind is under another attribute extension, and neither of these can be said to act upon the other. They are different expressions of the same thing.

But it is time to leave the metaphysics of Spinoza and turn to his ethics, to which his metaphysics is subordinate. Mr. Roth [1] has reminded us that he calls his book *Ethics*. How upon this foundation does Spinoza reach his ideal of the good life and of that highest condition of man in which he is face to face with the eternal and fixed things he speaks of in the passage I have quoted ? We can answer best by following him in the stages which he describes of knowledge, for to those stages there correspond the stages in our life of conduct. It is a progression in which we divest ourselves more and more of our habit of seeing things disconnectedly and more and more realise their real connection with one another and with God. In our habitual life before we begin to practise science we live, like the inhabitants of the Cave in Plato, in a world of imagination, loose images and dreams, mere opinions and hearsay evidence. The spaces occupied with things are for us then detached and almost independent, though we join them together into larger spaces or split them up into smaller ones. In truth they are but fragments of the one extension which is one aspect of the whole of nature or God. It is a world of confusion in which things tumble about and jostle one another (again to use the language of Plato, to whom in so many respects Spinoza has justly been compared). Bacon, who was an earlier contemporary of Spinoza, a forerunner of the great men of the seventeenth century who indicated but never saw the promised land, likened such knowledge to the separate twigs of a broom

[1] L. Roth, *Spinoza* (London, 1929), p. 43.

SPINOZA

before they were bound together to perform a serviceable function, and called it by the Greek name of history, mere chronicle as we should say.

From this world of dreams and hazy disconnection we are delivered first by science. That too begins at a level not far removed from mere imagination, in the formation of general ideas like horse or man or still more comprehensive generalities like substance or being, which Spinoza calls transcendental terms. Even here things cease to be regarded as perfectly distinct, for they are collated by their resemblances. It is a much higher stage when for mere descriptive accounts of things, such as that a triangle is a three-sided plane figure, we substitute some constitutive property such as that it is a figure whose interior angles are equal to two right angles, and a stage further still when we define, according to the analytical geometry discovered (I will not say invented) by Spinoza's predecessor Descartes, a straight line by a linear equation ; or instead of describing conic sections as figures derived from the section of a cone by a plane we define them by an equation of the second degree.

Besides these constitutive laws of things, science traces the interaction of things in laws of nature. Here things are still separate and affect each other, by a mode of causal determination which is entirely different from the relation of things not to one another, but to God from whom they flow — I use these words, for we can scarcely avoid metaphor in speaking of a relation of whole to part in virtue of which the whole is expressed in the part and the part retaining its imperfect reality is only perfectly real when it is, not lost, but absorbed into the whole. In tracing the relations of finite physical things Spinoza follows the ordinary conceptions of his day and talks the language of Cartesian theory, which became the foundation of scientific mechanics. The highest laws arrived at in pursuit of this physical science are the laws which pervade all physical action, the laws of ' motion and rest ', the characters which all bodies have in common with each other, and belong not only to material bodies but to organised ones as well.

In so far as science lifts its objects out of the isolation in which they remain so long as we still treat them as objects of mere imagination, in so far that is as we see their connection with one another and with the whole, science sees its objects, Spinoza says, in a manner under the form of eternity. He calls it the second grade of knowledge. But we have still to mark that he examines the life of the mind and organic life generally in the same spirit and by the same method as he has examined extended material bodies.

Obeying this principle he offers a psychology of the passions or emotions which is a miracle of scientific treatment, and was accepted as such by the great physiologist Johannes Mueller, who created modern physiology in the earlier half of the nineteenth century. His psychology of the emotions is still encumbered with philosophical presuppositions, but with that reservation it is a superb performance. But he introduces into the description of the life of mind a conception which applies more obviously to it and yet is valid of all things with proper qualifications. It is the principle that everything endeavours to persist in its being, that is to maintain the pattern or law of its nature. Whatever hinders it in that endeavour is painful, whatever helps it is pleasant, or as Spinoza puts it in technical phrase, pleasure is passage to a greater and pain to a lesser perfection. The common emotions are arrayed one after the other on this plan — love, hatred, pride, humility, and the rest. Love, for instance, to anything is pleasure which we feel when it is accompanied by the idea that the object we call loved is the cause of the pleasure; and the statement is true, as we see upon reflection, however much it may seem to us inadequate because it seems to omit the inborn bodily impulses which lead to love. Yet we have always to remember that with Spinoza the passions of the mind are also affections of the body.

But I must leave this fascinating topic and turn to the

use Spinoza makes of his analysis of the emotions for a determination of the highest good. It corresponds in the theory of conduct to science in the domain of knowledge. In a famous passage he declares that he is to examine human nature without prejudice or passion. 'That I might investigate what pertains to this science (politics) with the same freedom of mind as we are used to in mathematics, I have taken care not to laugh nor grieve at human actions, nor detest them, but to understand them; and so I have considered human emotions, such as love, hate, anger, envy, boasting, pity and the other commotions of mind, not as vices of human nature, but as properties of it, which belong to it as heat, cold, storm, thunder, and the like belong to the nature of the air, if inconvenient still necessary, with certain causes by which we seek to understand their nature; and the mind equally enjoys the true contemplation of them as it enjoys the knowledge of things which are agreeable to the senses.'

For good and evil are simply what is useful or detrimental to the mind or character in its endeavour to maintain its being. There is no preordained good; we discover what is good by finding what increases our power or virtue, virtue being, in the old Roman sense of that word, the power to be ourselves. Now subject as the mind is to the same causal determination as material things, acting as we do at the spur of the objects which excite us to action, we may act blindly or with clear ideas of our action. When we act blindly we suffer or are passive, creatures of our passions, of whatever stirs us from the outside or our own bodies. But we are active in so far as we are aware of or understand our actions, for then we are aware of ourselves and do what we do with mastery.

Consequently man approaches his highest good in proportion as through understanding his own actions he sees his actions in their relation to one another and to his whole self. Just as in science he sees things together, so in conduct he takes in the nature of his several actions and orders them in relation to a whole. Spinoza says that the aim of life is thus to subordinate passion to active life, and he describes it as acting from adequate ideas, that is with understanding of a man's self and his action, rather than from inadequate ideas, when he becomes the puppet of his passing moods. The man who knows with science is the man who knows not piecemeal but with comprehension. The man who understands himself and his actions will act from himself, and emancipating himself from the urgency of the moment will be master of his passions and of himself. Such a man Spinoza names the ' free ' man, in that positive sense of freedom, in which it does not mean dispensing with determination, for the free man remains the creature of causes, but emancipation from subjection to circumstances outside his persistent self. He is no longer slave to his passions but active controller of them, because he comprehends them and his mind is directed to what satisfies him permanently.

Moreover as science unites men, while opinion divides them, so the free man seeks the objects which he can share with others, and reason being the name we give to the mind when it recognises what unites us, he lives the life of reason, recognising the equal claims of his fellows (*homo homini deus*). Spinoza has many noble passages in which he portrays the life of a man who sees himself as one with other men, and sees each passion of himself in relation to his whole being. None is more famous than that in which he says that ' the free man thinks of nothing less than death, and his meditation is not of death but of life '. For meditation of death, we may say in a feeble commentary, impedes his activity, lessens his virtue, and depresses his endeavour. The so-called vices all depress man's life, the so-called virtues augment it ; and from this point of view Spinoza's judgment of the relative worth of virtues is not always the accepted one. The ideal may seem to be more Stoic than human average nature can attain. But it is not austere. On the contrary he pleads for a natural and healthy enjoyment of the good things of life. And himself he was no ascetic but rather a man of small needs

SPINOZA

and serene temper. The free man will 'refresh himself with moderate food and drink, with perfumes, with the soft beauty of growing plants, with dress, with music, with sports, with theatres and the like, such as every man may make use of without injury to his neighbours'.

But the life of the free man though it is the condition of the highest good is still not itself the highest condition of man. To understand this we must turn again to knowledge, the highest stage of which, knowledge of the third kind, transcends science, and sees things not ' in a manner ' under the form of eternity but completely in that light. It is not easy to explain what Spinoza means by it, for he only describes it briefly. His instance is that of seeing that 6 is the fourth proportional to 2 and 4 and 3, as if by intuition. It is like what happens when, after the labour of calculation and discovery, a man sees the solution in a single vision, sees that the angles of the triangle are equal to two right angles. It supervenes upon thinking, when the whole situation is taken in at once; and every student is familiar with the intense joy of such vision. Imagine that condition reached over the whole field of knowledge, and you will have ' intuitive science ' as something above ordinary discursive science. Such we may suppose God's own knowledge to be, for what we discover by reflection he sees in a flash. It is as if knowledge, instead of being described in sober prose, were exposed in a poetic picture, after the work of reflection was done. The relations which science sets out among things are revealed in an insight which has no need to trace the relations but has risen above them. Perhaps the artist's apprehension is the best parallel.

At any rate, in this intuition disconnection has completely vanished, and in vanishing has been replaced by direct vision of objects as in God. Now to the mind which has reached this vision corresponds in practice the highest state of man. For such a mind knows itself as in God, and, Spinoza adds in a saying which has never been completely understood, proves that it itself has a part which is eternal. This knowledge of the self as in God is no mere intellectual state but itself an emotion. We are aware of God as the cause of the joy or happiness which we feel in that submergence of ourselves in God which yet is the fulfilment of ourselves, and is therefore (according to the account given of that emotion) love. Spinoza calls it ' the intellectual love of God ' and describes it in phrases not less magnificent than the name itself. It is part of God's own love for the universe, but unlike ordinary human love it demands no return from God. This was one of the traits which so strongly recommended Spinoza to Goethe, who takes it as the highest expression of true human love : ' If I love you ', he says to Lili, ' what is that to you ? ' It is the mystic's love, absorbed in the contemplation of the highest, and though Spinoza does not call it religion, it is in fact religion, where the religious impulse has been founded upon the philosophic synthesis, and the philosophy has taken fire from the emotion which itself excites. Again it may be doubted whether it is not all the time the religious emotion which has inspired the philosophy.

It is, however, in Spinoza's eyes more than religion itself, as commonly understood. Religion in the ordinary sense is to act rightly, to do the tasks of our station in life as in the presence of God, ' as ever in the great taskmaster's eye '. Such religion corresponds to the second or scientific stage of knowledge. It is toleration itself in respect of particular religions. ' For the Turks themselves and heathens in general,' he writes in a letter, ' if they worship God by justice and charity to their neighbours, I believe that they have the spirit of Christ and are saved, whatever persuasion they may entertain through ignorance concerning Mahomet and his oracles.' He used to go downstairs in the house at the Hague to smoke a pipe in the company of the Van der Spycks, with whom he lodged. One day, the biographer records, his landlady asked him whether he believed she could be saved in the religion she professed, and he answered, ' Your religion is a good one, you need not look for another, nor doubt that you may be saved in it, provided, whilst you apply yourself to piety, you live at the same time a peaceable and quiet life '. The higher mystical religion corresponds to the third and highest stage of knowledge.

So completely is what is the supreme attainment for knowledge embodied in the highest emotional experience. For to Spinoza as to Socrates and Plato, knowledge is not bare knowledge, theoretical only, but carries with it the whole man. To Plato and Spinoza alike philosophy at its acme is love, to the one Eros, to the other the intellectual love of God. For always in reading Spinoza it must be remembered that however much he speaks in terms of cold speculation, the exercise of intellect is itself a part of the striving towards maintenance of man's being. Intellect and will are for him identical. The mere knowledge of good and evil is no corrective or controller of the passion. A passion, he says, in a principle of the last moment for understanding the moral life, can only be controlled by another passion. The free man's understanding of himself is also a condition of his body and restrains the lower passions as one passion, say of love, drives out another passion, say of envy. When the free man sees himself truly under the form of eternity, he has with that highest knowledge achieved the highest passion of which man's nature is capable. And the records of all mystics are enough to show that their vision of the divine is a state of the whole soul and of conduct. Spinoza differs from them not so much in essence as rather in the completeness with which by philosophy this state of soul has been linked up with the lower conditions and been exhibited as the consummation of man's endeavour.

With this I end where I began. I do not suggest that Spinoza's philosophy is beyond exception either as a whole or in its parts. But it is very near to our own problems, not because it raises them explicitly, but for the lessons it carries to us, as it were, by anticipation. It exhibits the science of the physical world as one part of a system whose method applied to human affairs interprets for us morals and religion not only so as to secure their value but in an exalted expression. His interpretation of morals may not please those who like to envelop the highest values with mystery, as if they contained an element which we could not hope to explain further. Nor does it seem to me surprising that Spinoza, who was certainly no theist and sate loosely not only to Judaism, from which he had revolted, but to Christianity in certain of whose adherents he found his friendships, should so long have been taken for an atheist and reviled. He was too remote from common beliefs to be regarded as what he was, a devoted servant of God. But he is at least a type of a kind of philosophy which, by pursuing the method of neutrality (I borrow the word from Bertrand Russell's ' ethical neutrality ') which is naturalism, establishes the ideals of good life, and maintains religion without excuse (it would never have occurred to his time to think it needed excuse, that was left for a later age), and at the same time without affirming that either morals or religion, as so many suppose to-day, supplies us with directer knowledge of reality than physical science. For all things alike are modes of God and have both the mind which the human sciences investigate and the extension which is the subject of the physical sciences.

XIV

SPINOZA AND TIME

(The Fourth Arthur Davis Memorial Lecture, delivered before the Jewish Historical Society at University College, May 1, 1921. Separately published, 1921, by George Allen & Unwin. Here reprinted by permission.)

I

The World of Events: Time as Intrinsic. — If I were asked to name the most characteristic feature of the thought of the last twenty-five years, I should answer, the discovery of Time. I do not mean that we have waited until to-day to become familiar with Time; I mean that we have only just begun, in our speculation to take Time seriously, and to realise that in some way or other Time is an essential ingredient in the constitution of things. Mr. Bergson, indeed, has declared Time to be the ultimate reality. The mathematicians and physicists refer things no longer to three axes of co-ordinates, but to four, the fourth being the time axis. It will take much thought between physicists and philosophers in co-operation before opinion settles down upon the exact amount of reality we are to ascribe to Time and its companion Space, whether they are in the strict sense realities at all, or only constructions of the mind, and what their relation to each other is. But there is one proposition which is vital to the understanding of the theory of relativity, and is presupposed in its finished form as put forward by Mr. Einstein, and that is the proposition that the world is a world of events. I fancy we are accustomed to think of the world as a mass of things spread out in one comprehensive Space, and somehow or other of Time as merely an interesting addition, whereby things happen and have a history. The discovery of Time means that we are to rid ourselves of this innocent habit of mind, and regard the world as through and through and intrinsically historical, and treat everything in it as events, nor merely what are obviously events, but the most permanent things also, which seem to us fixed in their repose — stones and hills and tables — which become what Mr. Whitehead calls ' chunks of events '. This is the simple meaning of the proposition of the mathematicians that we live in a four-dimensional world. It is another and purely mathematical way of saying that Time is not something which happens to extended things, but that there is no extended thing which is not temporal, that there is no reality but that of events, and that Space has no reality apart from Time, and that in truth neither has any reality in itself, but only as involved in the ultimate reality of the system of events (or Space-Time).

It is really quite a simple proposition, and though it is revolutionary enough, it is not so revolutionary as it sounds. In particular we are not to imagine that, as many people, I think, fear, Mr. Einstein and his predecessors have discovered a new kind of thing or substance. A reputable illustrated newspaper gave a picture of what a cube was like in four dimensions : it seemed to be surrounded by a kind of aura or haze. This comes from supposing that the four dimensions are all spatial, whereas the fourth is Time. Things, I may assure you, are in the four-dimensional world exactly what we are familiar with. The only difference is that we have learnt that they are four-dimensional, chunks of events. We have been living all our lives in four dimensions, but have only just come to know it, just as M. Jourdain discovered that he had been talking prose all his life without knowing it. In his book on Dickens, Mr. Chesterton observes that M. Jourdain's delight at this discovery showed that he had the freshness of the romantic spirit. And I do not know anything more romantic than that the common things which surround us, including our own selves, have all this time been in the mathematical sense four-dimensional. It will not make them different, or ourselves better, any more than when Berkeley maintained that bodies were but ideas in the mind, he maintained them to be less solid than before, though the unmetaphysical Dr. Johnson believed so. We have only gained a deeper and more satisfying insight.

Accordingly, since Time has thus stepped into the foreground of speculative interest, it seemed to me that I could best respond to the invitation of this Society to deliver the Arthur Davis Memorial Lecture by asking how far Spinoza could guide us to an understanding of Time and of the part which it plays in the reality of the world. The seventeenth century was in philosophy as well as in physical science the seminal period of European thought, and, at least in all the questions that lie on the borderland of philosophy and physics, we are nearer to the great philosophers of that time than we are to those of the nineteenth century, and our minds go back to them to get their help or make clear to ourselves how we differ from them. Spinoza is more particularly suitable to consult, apart from the interest which any Jewish society must needs take in one of the greatest of Jews. For has not Heine said of him, with as much truth as wit, alluding to Spinoza's occupation as a maker of lenses, that all subsequent philosophers have seen through glasses which Spinoza ground?

I do not, however, propose to enter minutely into Spinoza's philosophy. There are two ways of approaching a great philosopher. The one is to study his precise teaching, setting it into relation with his age and with his contemporaries and immediate predecessors. I have the greatest admiration for those who perform this work of scholarship, which is the only satisfactory and respectful method of understanding a philosopher, requiring as it does both historical research and the most sympathetic philosophical insight. But it is beyond my competence, and the only addition I shall attempt to make to the interpretation of Spinoza I shall have to omit in addressing you for want of time.[1] I shall follow the other and easier method of enquiring what a philosopher can teach us in our present problems. Relying on those who have expounded him for us with such care, I shall repeat what he has to say upon Time, and then I shall ask, in view of the new prospects opened by our present speculation, what difference it would make to Spinoza's philosophy if we assign to Time a position not allowed to it by Spinoza himself, but suggested by the difficulties and even obscurities in which he has left it.

II

Spinoza's Conception of Time. — The trouble is that there is very little to say about Spinoza's conception of Time. It stands for the general character of existence which things have: they exist for a longer or a shorter time, according as they are determined by other things. Thus the momentary closing of a current produces a flash of light; if the current remains switched on, the light endures. But when we speak thus we are, according to Spinoza, not using the language of philosophy but of imagination. We are comparing one duration of time with another in our sensible world, and we may even conceive of these bits of time as limitations of an indefinite duration. But neither the bits of duration nor the indefinite duration are true realities. We are but using relative measures of duration; because we are considering things as if they were separate from one another and had an independent existence, whereas they are but manifestations of the one reality which is God. Now just as Newton contrasts what he calls the relative measures of time with absolute Time, we might expect Spinoza to contrast these pieces of duration with Time or Duration as such. This is what he does when he considers Space or Extension. There too, when we speak of lengths and figures of things, we are not dealing with reality except in the confused

---

[1] *I.e.* in the spoken as opposed to the printed lecture. See Sect. VI. with its footnote. [Editor's note.]

manner of imagination. There are no separate lengths and figures, but only Space as such, which is God under a certain attribute, and is indivisible into lengths. But Spinoza does not contrast durations with duration as such, but with eternity, and eternity is not Time, but is timeless. When he declares that there is something eternal in the human mind, which lies at the basis of our experience that we are immortal, he does not mean that we are immortal in the sense of indefinite continuance after death. To be eternal is to be comprehended in the nature of God, and things are real in so far as they are thus comprehended and are seen in the light of eternity, *sub specie quâdam aeternitatis*. Thus times are not contrasted with Time as bits of space with Space, but with timelessness. Had he treated Time as he treats Space, Time would have been an attribute of God. As it is, Time is no more than a character of finite things. I am proposing to explain what difference it would make to Spinoza's philosophy if, to make an impossible hypothesis, he had treated Time as an attribute of God.

It is not so much to be wondered at that Spinoza has failed to conceive the relation of finite times to infinite Time with the same clearness as he has conceived that of finite spaces to infinite Space. Time is indeed thoroughly perplexing, in a way in which at first sight Space is not. For bits of Space can be kept together before our minds at once, and though we cannot imagine Space as a whole, but only an indefinitely large space, we can readily think of it. But we cannot do this with the parts of time. For Time is successive; there is no sense in a duration which is not a duration that is passing away, and when you experience a moment of time, the immediately preceding moment is gone. Otherwise Time would be a kind of Space. No doubt we do experience Time as not merely a succession but as a duration, as something that lasts: the moments of time are not discontinuous, but are as much continuous as the points of space. But how can we in our thoughts reconcile the persistence of Time which we experience, with its habit of dying from one moment to another? You will say the past is preserved for us in memory, in which the past and the present are before our minds together, just as the parts of space, distant and near, are before our eyes together. But now comes Mr. Bergson and says that when we thus conceive Time we are spatialising it, turning it into Space, and urges that the Time we thus spatialise is not real Time.

There are more ways than one of meeting these difficulties. One was the naïve answer of Descartes, to which we shall recur, that things are conserved and endure, because they are being re-created by God at each moment. This is the very *ne plus ultra* of the conception that I alluded to, that things are extended, and that Time happens to them. Another way is to show that Space and Time are not independent of each other, but as the mathematicians say, are but aspects or elements of Space-Time. Spinoza takes neither one view nor the other, yet he gives us indications which stimulate the reflecting mind to pass from the one to the other.

III

The Infinite Mode of Motion and Rest. — Let me first remind you of the main outlines of Spinoza's metaphysical doctrine. Spinoza is a pantheist, not in the superficial sense that God is a spirit which pervades all things, but in the truer sense that all things are in God and are modifications of him. There is and can be but one thing which is entirely self-dependent, needing no other being for its explanation; this being is Substance or God or Nature: it is the universe as a whole, not as an aggregate of things, not even as a whole of parts in the sense in which you and I who are organic are wholes of parts without being mere aggregates, but as a unitary being from which all its so-called parts draw their nature and in the end their existence. In themselves these parts, or as Spinoza calls them, modes, have no being except in God. Only our fancy, as I have noted, assigns them in what he calls the common order of nature a fictitious independence. God is the unity of all his modes conceived in their interrelation with one another and in their eternal, that is, ultimate and timeless, effluence from himself ; and Spinoza tries steadily to think of God as the positive comprehension of all things, though, as his commentators have pointed out, he sometimes falls into the mystical conception which defines God by the negation of all positive predicates.

For him the finite is the negation of the infinite, and not the infinite the negation of the finite, however much he may drop into the other way of thought. In truth, for Spinoza and Descartes and the men of their day the infinite was conceived positively as prior to the finite, as it is in modern mathematics, and in fact it is only by negativing the infinitude of God that we can arrive at the notion of quantity at all. To apply the idea of quantity to God were to make him not infinite but indefinitely large. Most of our modern difficulties have arisen from trying to reconcile the notion of infinity with that of quantity, and the reconciliation has been accomplished in present mathematics.

Now, Substance or God presents itself to intellect, not to our intellect alone, but to intellect of every sort, under the form of attributes. They are not constructions of the intellect nor forms of it in the Kantian sense, but what intellect discovers in the Substance, so that so far there is in Spinoza no suggestion of idealism. God as infinite possesses infinite such attributes or aspects, but only two of these are discoverable to the human intellect, namely Extension and Thought. How we are to understand the infinite other attributes is a long-standing puzzle in the interpretation of Spinoza to which I shall advert later. These attributes reveal the whole of God's nature or essence ; and the great forward step which Spinoza took in philosophy consisted in this doctrine. For it follows that since God is perceived completely either as Extension or as Thought or Thinking, Extension and Thought are not two different realities, but two forms of one and the same reality.

It follows further that since modes are modifications of God, each of them is alike extended and a thought. Hence in the first place our thoughts and our bodies are not two different things, but the same mode of God under two different attributes. This is the way Spinoza would answer the question whether brain-processes and their corresponding thought-processes accompany each other or act upon each other. For him they are the same thing twice over; there is neither correspondence nor interaction between them, but identity of essence. This he expresses by saying that an idea or thought is the idea of a certain condition of the body, which varies with the object which provokes this bodily condition. I only wish there were room for me within the limits of my subject to develop his famous proposition which really follows from this conception, that the idea which I have of the table informs me rather of the state of my body than of the table, or in other words the table reveals itself to me in so far as it induces in me a certain process of body (we should say of the brain) which is identical with what we call the thought of the table.

Next it is a consequence of the truth that every mode exists under both attributes that not only our self but every extended mode is also a thinking one, and that all things are 'in a manner animated'. The importance of this we shall see later on.

So much is simple and clear. But now I have to turn to one of the most difficult and at the same time most fascinating parts of the doctrine. Between God as perceived under the attribute of extension and the finite extended modes which are singular bodies there intervene infinite modes which as it were break the fall from Heaven to earth. Spinoza touches them only lightly, enough for his immediate purpose of explaining the constitution of our bodies, yet it is about these that what I have to say centres. The 'immediate' infinite mode of extension Spinoza calls motion and rest. The first step in breaking up the unity of God's infinite extension into multiplicity (a multiplicity still retained within the unity) is its manifestation as motion and rest. The next step is the 'mediate' infinite mode, in which God's extension is the whole system of bodies as reduced to terms of motion and rest ; and the finite modes or singular things are but the parts of this ' face of the whole universe ', when those parts are considered, as they must be for science, in their relation to the whole—as varying modifications of motion and rest. These are the gradations in the specification of God as extended. The corresponding gradations between God as a thinking being and finite thinking things or thoughts are harder to identify, and I need not refer to them further.

These immediate and mediate infinite modes of motion and rest takes us back to the doctrine of Descartes in the second part of his *Principles*. Spinoza takes it as axiomatic, speaking first of uncompounded bodies, that they are all either in motion or at rest, and move either more quickly or more slowly. Rest seems to be regarded as something positive, not the mere absence of motion, and a slower motion is as it were the blending of motion with rest, much as Goethe later regarded colour as a blending of light and darkness. Descartes apparently, perhaps only apparently, has the same notion. Compound bodies, what we ordinarily call bodies, are constituted of these simple bodies impinging on one another and communicating their motions in a certain proportion. Such an individual body remains the same when the proportion of its component motions is undisturbed, and the whole ' moves altogether if it moves at all ', and hence, though affected by other bodies in many ways, it may retain its own nature. The individual changes if this proportion is disturbed. The dissolution of our body at death is a case in point, occurring in a very composite body composed of many individual bodies which are its parts.

IV

The Transition from Extension to this Mode. — The details do not concern us so much. After all, vague as it is, the picture is but the familiar one that in the end bodies are complexes of motions. I would fain linger on its consequences for the theory of science. Motion and rest being the common characters of bodies, their laws are the ultimate and simplest conceptions for science, which Spinoza contrasts with such vague and confused conceptions as 'being', 'thing', 'something', which he calls transcendental terms. Motion and rest would be the true universals, in contrast with what are vaguely called universals, such as man, tree, etc. But I must not be tempted away from my immediate topic.

For us the question is by what right Spinoza can pass from God's attribute of extension to the infinite mode of motion and rest. That he deliberately faced the problem is clear from his attitude towards Descartes. Bodies for Spinoza are intrinsically complexes of motion and rest. For Descartes body was nothing but extension, figure, size, in three dimensions. Extension without body, that is empty space, was nothing. An empty space between two bodies or in the pores of a body meant only the presence of some other body; hence, in the famous illustration, if a vessel could be completely emptied of body, the sides of the vessel would be in contact. Motion, according to Descartes, was a mode or state of body, and it was imparted to body by God. Spinoza protests in explicit terms in two letters to his friend Tschirnhaus against the Cartesian view and denies that the variety of the universe can be deduced *a priori* from extension alone. Descartes' view that motion is imparted by God is in fact a confession that body in motion is not mere extension, if extension is conceived as by Descartes as created, not, as by Spinoza, as being an attribute of God. Matter, says Spinoza, must necessarily be explained through an attribute which expresses eternal and infinite essence. This attribute he found in Extension, which he conceived to manifest itself immediately as we have seen in the infinite mode of motion and rest.

Spinoza is thus aware of the problem; and it is a great

advance upon Descartes to see that body or matter is intrinsically motion and rest, and not bare extension into which motion is introduced by the creative act of God. But has Spinoza solved the problem ? The answer must be, I think, that he has failed because he has omitted Time. It seems to him indeed that matter is motion because extension expresses God's essence, or as Mr. Joachim puts it, expresses God's omnipotence. Substance, this admirable interpreter urges, is not lifeless, but alive, and doubtless this was at the bottom of Spinoza's mind. But life and omnipotence are undefined ideas, transferred from our experience to describe metaphorically the being of God which is held to be behind and beyond the things of experience. Life implies change and so does omnipotence ; and change implies time. Yet Time is excluded from the eternal nature of God, who comprehends Time indeed, but only, to use a paradoxical phrase, in its timelessness.

If, therefore, motion is to be the infinite mode of God's extension, it must be because Time has been slipped into Extension out of the undefined activity of God. We might be tempted to say that extension includes not only extension in space but duration in time. This would make extension a double-faced attribute. It would solve Spinoza's problem, but there is no word of it in Spinoza and could not be. On the contrary such a supposition would make existence of which Time is the general character an attribute of God, which for Spinoza it is not. God's essence and his existence are, he says, one and the same thing.

The truth appears to be that Spinoza could pass so easily from extension to motion because motion was conceived as it were statically. Nothing seems so obvious to us as the proposition that motion takes time and is unintelligible without it. But Descartes certainly, and it would seem Spinoza as well, conceives motion as change of place. Motion Descartes describes as ' the transference of a part of matter or body from the neighbourhood of those which are touching it immediately, and which we consider as at rest to the neighbourhood of some other bodies '. This conception of motion makes it something geometrical instead of physical. Consistently with this conception Descartes could think of motion only as an impulse given to matter from God. Spinoza's insight was a deeper one. Extension being an attribute of God reflected the activity of God's nature, and therefore the modes of extension were intrinsically motion, to correspond with the activity of God. He did not see that this implied Time also as an attribute. The activity of God could not translate itself into motion, when motion was conceived as more than a change of place, except if God's activity was expressed by Time. In other words, if motion and rest is the infinite mode of extension, that extension must be not Space but Space-Time. By insisting that bodies are intrinsically complexes of motion, Spinoza, though he has rather stated the problem than solved it, has put us upon the way of solution.[1]

V

Time as an Attribute of God: Consequences of this Hypothesis. — Let us ask then what changes are produced in Spinoza's doctrine if we regard Time itself as an attribute of the ultimate reality. In what remains I propose to offer these consequences as a gloss upon Spinoza's teaching, remarking explicitly that they are a gloss and not a commentary. A commentary must be historically true, but for Spinoza it was impossible to think of Time as an attribute. Slight as the change may seem verbally, it leads to a remodelling of the whole. Yet unhistorical as the procedure is, I venture upon it before an Historical Society because the real greatness and spirit of a man may often be best appreciated by asking not what he said himself but what he may lead us to say.

(1) In the first place the ultimate reality would be some-

[1] I have omitted to notice minor difficulties in Spinoza's doctrine of motion and rest, such as the question how simple bodies come to have variety of motion. (See Camerer, *Die Lehre Spinozas*, 1877, p. 61 ff.) For an admirable account of the difficulties of Descartes' treatment of motion see N. Kemp Smith, *Studies in the Cartesian Philosophy* (London, 1902), pp. 75 ff.

thing which in one aspect, under one attribute, is Space, under another, Time. It would be Space-Time or Motion itself. I dare not yet assume that Time in this conception replaces Thought as the second attribute which our intellect perceives. It might still be true that Thought is a third attribute. It will appear, however, presently that Thought is not an attribute [1] at all, but is an empirical or finite mode.

The ultimate reality or Space-Time ceases also to be Substance in Spinoza's sense, still less is it identifiable with God, which is for Spinoza the only substance. It is rather identical with the infinite immediate mode of motion and rest, or, if we rid ourselves of the perplexing idea of rest as something positive, with the infinite mode of motion. It is still infinite and self-contained and the ground of all finite modes. But it is not so much the Substance of which things are modes as the stuff of which they are pieces, the material out of which they are made. It is comparable rather to the Space which in the Platonic *Timaeus* is that which receives definite character through the ingression (I borrow the word from Mr. Whitehead) of the Forms or Ideas. The difference from Plato is that the material which thus receives form is in the *Timaeus* purely spatial, and contains intrinsically no time. For Plato Time comes into being with the creation of things and is but the shadow of eternity. In our gloss upon Spinoza the ultimate reality is full of Time, not timeless but essentially alive with Time, and the theatre of incessant change. It is only timeless in the sense that, taken as a whole, it is not particularised to any one moment or duration, but comprehends them all.

For Spinoza the ultimate reality was necessarily conceived as Substance, as the one self-dependent, self-contained or infinite, self-caused, being; this distinguished it from the finite things which were its modes. The very difference and advance which he made upon Descartes was that created things, which for Descartes were in a secondary

---

[1] *I.e.* in the technical sense of what Spinoza called 'Attribute' = what, in Alexander's terminology, is very strictly 'categorical'. [Editor's note.]

sense substances, became for Spinoza mere modes of the one Substance. And at least it is clear that if the ultimate reality is described as Substance, finite things, which in the words of Locke ' are but retainers to other parts of nature for that which they are most taken notice of by us ', cannot be substances in the same sense. But in fact substance, causality and the like are categories applicable in the first instance to finite things, and only transferred to infinite reality by a metaphor in which their meaning is changed ; and it has now become a commonplace since Kant to declare that the categories of finite things are not applicable to the ground of finite things. And when once Time is regarded as an attribute of ultimate reality, the contrast of the Spinozistic Substance and its modes falls away. Reality is Space-Time or motion itself, infinite or self-contained and having nothing outside itself ; and the vital contrast is that of this infinite or *a priori* stuff of the Universe and the empirical things or substances which are parts or modes of it. For this reason I speak of the ultimate reality of motion not as substance but as stuff.

Before passing to these empirical modes let me observe that the conception of Space-Time or Motion as the stuff of the Universe is not in all respects the same as that taken of it in the theory of relativity. That theory is a physical and not a metaphysical theory, and, properly, as a physical theory it begins with bodies. Space-Time for it is perhaps best described as an order or system of relations that subsists between bodies. Whether this is to be accepted as an ultimate statement for philosophy is just one of those matters to which I alluded at the beginning, on which discussion has yet to do its work. I may merely note in passing that one pronounced supporter of the relativity theory in this country maintains that when it is said that Space-Time is wrinkled or warped in the presence of matter this means that matter is the very wrinkle in Space-Time. From this to the proposition which I have taken as included in our gloss upon Spinoza, viz. that Space-Time is the stuff of which matter is made, is but a step.

(2) I pass to the singular things which in their totality constitute the *facies totius universi*. As with Spinoza, they are modifications of the ultimate reality which has now become Space-Time. But there is now no ditch to jump between the ultimate ground of things and things themselves; for things are, as Spinoza himself would say, but complexes of motion and made of the stuff which the ultimate or *a priori* reality is. In this way the danger is avoided which besets Spinoza's doctrine, the danger that the modes or things should be engulfed in an ultimate being which purports to be the positive ground of its modes, but always is on the point of slipping into bare indefiniteness.

This danger I have noted already, but it may be well to revert to it here by way of pointing out the source of the difficulty. The modes for Spinoza determine each other into existence within the modal system in a chain of causation. But they follow, considered in the light of eternity, from the nature of Substance or God, who is their cause or ground. This causal issuing from God is, however, not the physical relation of cause and effect, but the geometrical one of ground and consequent. The modes follow from God as the properties of a triangle follow from the nature of the triangle. This being so, the ultimate Substance being the ground of the modes must be a positive reality which accounts for them, of which they are, in modern phrase, the appearance. But then, we have to urge, the modes are not properties of Substance, but are things.

On the other hand, if we ask for the ground of these things which are modes, and are told that they follow from the ground, but that the characters which things possess in the common order of nature are the confused deliverances of our imagination, how can we conceive the ground otherwise than as something or other, we know not what except that it is their ground? The case is different if things are regarded as modes of the stuff which is Space-Time. Their relation to their ground is no longer that of the properties of a triangle to the triangle, but rather that of the two triangles which compose an oblong to the oblong. They are involved in the oblong; and in like manner the valley and the mountain are both contained in that configuration of nature which we call a valley or a mountain, but the valley does not follow from the mountain geometrically in the sense in which the properties of the triangle follow from the triangle.

But if the reality in its barest character is Space-Time, the face of the whole universe is the totality of all those configurations into which Space-Time falls through its inherent character of timefulness or restlessness. The stuff of reality is not stagnant, its soul's wings are never furled, and in virtue of this unceasing movement it strikes out fresh complexes of movements, created things.

(3) This leads us directly to a third consequence. All things as in God are alike perfect; they are what they are and cannot be other. Yet there are grades of perfection amongst things, the one has more reality than another. On this subject, as I cannot express Spinoza's sense so well myself, I will transcribe a page from Mr. Joachim's book: [1]

God, as the necessary consequent of his own free causality, is Natura Naturata — an ordered system of modes following with coherent necessity from Natura Naturans.[2] But though all things follow with the same inevitable necessity from God's nature, they differ from one another in degree of perfection or reality; and indeed the difference is one not only of degree but also of kind. 'For although a mouse and an angel, sadness and joy, depend equally on God, yet a mouse cannot be a species of angel, nor sadness a species of joy' (Ep. 23). 'The criminal expresses God's will in his own way, just as the good man does

[1] H. H. Joachim, *A Study of the Ethics of Spinoza* (Oxford, 1901), p. 73.
[2] For the distinction of 'natura naturans' and 'naturata' see *Eth.* i. 29, Sch. God as free cause is 'natura naturatans'; 'natura naturata' is all the modes of God's attributes, so far as they are considered as things which are in God and which cannot either be or be conceived without God. See Mr. Joachim's note 1, p. 65. Mr. Joachim adds that '" Natura naturata " is not the world of sense-perception, but the universe in all its articulation as a perfect understanding would grasp it, if that understanding apprehended it as the *effect* of God's causality'.

in his; but the criminal is not on that account comparable with the good man. The more perfection a thing has, the more it participates in the divine nature and the more it expresses God's perfection. The good have incalculably more perfection than the vicious; and therefore their " virtue " is not to be compared with the " virtue " of the vicious. . . .' (Ep. 19.)

It is in ' natura naturata ', the eternal system of modes, that those degrees of perfection or reality are exhibited. For there is an order in the sequence of the modes from God's nature, and on that order their degree of perfection depends. The order is not a temporal, but a logical one. There is no before and after, no temporal succession, in the relation of the modes to God; all modes are the eternal consequence of God's causality. But there is a logical priority and posteriority; and on this their degrees of reality depend. ' That effect is the most perfect which is produced by God immediately; and the more mediating causes which any effect requires, the less perfect it is.' (*Eth.* i. App.)

Now directly Time has become an attribute of the ultimate reality, this order ceases to be merely a logical one, and becomes temporal. The grades of modal perfection are no longer a ' static ' series of forms, but a hierarchy produced in the order of time. The idea of evolution is introduced, and from matter or from before matter there have grown up in time the modes of physical existence, and thence the forms of life and finally of mind. Existence is stratified, level upon level with each its distinctive quality, and the strata are not barely superposed, but each higher level is the descendant in time of the lower. Hence, for instance, living things are not merely alive, but their life is a differentiation of physico-chemical body, and that body is but a particular complexity of mere matter. Upon what particular basis bare matter depends is a question not for the philosopher but the physicist to decide. If the old doctrine of the *Timaeus* should be true, according to which solid matter is composed of elementary figures in space, we should have the notion here suggested as flowing from our gloss upon Spinoza, that the primary modes are the mere differentiations of bare Space-Time. But all the particular history of this long descent (or call it rather ascent) to higher levels of perfection amongst the modes is to be traced empirically under the guidance of science.

(4) The last level of things accessible to our senses would be that of minds, or as Spinoza would call them thinking things. Thought, therefore, upon our gloss becomes not an attribute of the ultimate reality but the distinguishing quality of the highest level of empirical things. We are left with Space and Time as the two attributes which our intellect perceives, and Time displaces Thought in the Spinozistic scheme. And yet we arrive also at a conclusion which seems to repeat Spinoza's view that thought is a universal feature of things, only with a difference. All things for him are in a sense animated, they are all in their degree thinking things. For us things which are not minds, which are merely alive or are inanimate, are no longer minds, but they do bear an aspect, or contain in themselves an element, which corresponds to the aspect or element of mind in a thinking thing. That aspect or element is Time.

We may express the relation between the orders of modes in two different ways. We may say that life is the mind of the living body, colour the mind of the coloured material body, matter or materiality the mind of the spatio-temporal substructure of a material body. In doing so, we are humoring our propensity to construe things on the pattern of what is most familiar to us, our own selves, in which mind is united with a living body; and are just comparing one set of empirical things with another. The other way penetrates more deeply into the nature of things. It starts with a piece of space-time, in which there are the bare aspects of its space and its time, and it construes thinking things after the pattern of this. One portion of the living thing, let us say its brain, is at once a peculiarly differentiated portion of space and correspondingly and inevitably a peculiarly differentiated complex of time. Were it not for the peculiar complexity of the brain, we should have the brain a merely living structure; as it is, when living matter is so differentiated as to be a brain, its time element becomes mind, or rather the character of mentality. It is as if we had a clock which not only showed the time but was the time it showed.

According, then, to the one method all things are, as Spinoza says, thinking things, and in the end, paradoxical as it sounds to say so, Time is the mind of Space. According to the other, mind is the time of its brain, life the time of the living parts of the living body and the like. On either method we realise the same truth that all the world and everything in it are constructed on the same plan, which betrays itself most plainly in our thinking bodies. But the Spinozistic method is a comparison of the modes with one another; the other method views the modes in the light of the ultimate or *a priori* reality from which they derive.

The same result is reached from a different consideration. Thinking things *know*; they have ideas. The idea of a tree which I have when I see one is for Spinoza the thought-aspect of the bodily condition into which I am thrown by the action of the tree upon my bodily senses. Or as we should say nowadays, it is the inner side of the brain-process. What is a brain-process under the attribute of extension is an idea or thinking process under the attribute of thought. To think of the tree means to have an idea or a bodily process which would be different if the tree were replaced by a table; and accordingly if for some reason or other this bodily condition recurs in the absence of the tree I still have the tree before my view as an image. Whether this is or is not a true account of the knowing process is under some discussion at the present moment among philosophers. But that does not concern us here. What does concern us is that it applies in its degree to all things alike whether minds in the empirical sense or not. The stone knows its surroundings in the same way as we know ours, though of course not to the same extent. Now, if this is so, it would seem again, that thought or knowing is a universal character of things and might claim therefore to be an attribute. Yet once more, thought as knowing is in truth merely a relation among the modes. In so far as my mind or the stone is affected by other things, it knows them. Accordingly, knowing, being an affair of modes *inter se*, is not an attribute. For an attribute is not a character which arises out of the interrelation of modes, but every mode intrinsically possesses a character in so far as it is considered under an attribute. We again arrive at the conclusion that thought is empirical, not *a priori* or ultimate ; and so far Space and Time are seen to exhaust the attributes of reality.

VI [1]

Spinoza's Infinity of Attributes. — What, then, becomes of the infinite other attributes which the ultimate reality, according to Spinoza, possesses in virtue of its infinite perfection ? The answer to this question will illustrate the tenor of the foregoing remarks. For we shall see that these supposed attributes are otiose and unnecessary ; but what is more important, we shall see that Spinoza's justification of them, to my mind successful, depends for its force not upon the view that Thought is an attribute, but on the empirical character of particular minds.

This matter is the standing unresolved puzzle of interpretation of Spinoza to which I have alluded above. For we are faced with a dilemma. All the attributes are in a metaphorical phrase coextensive, and accordingly my mind is identical not only with my body but with modes under all the other attributes — let us take one of them for short and call it the x-attribute. Why, then, do I not perceive my x-ian mode as well as my body ? I do not, and Spinoza insists that I cannot (Ep. 64). But if so, there must be thought-modes which correspond not only to body-modes, as they do, but to x-modes, that is (to quote Mr. Joachim [2]), ' there are modes of Thought which are *not* the thought-side of modes of Extension, and the

---

[1] A reader not interested in Spinoza scholarship may be recommended to pass over this section.
[2] *Op. cit.* p. 137.

"completeness" of the Attribute of Thought is more full than the "completeness" of any other Attribute', or as Tschirnhaus put it, the attribute of Thought is much wider than the other Attributes — is in fact coextensive with them all.

Even Mr. Joachim regards the difficulty as insoluble. One commentator, Sir. F. Pollock, in his excellent book,[1] reminding us that an Attribute is what intellect perceives in Substance as constituting its essence, has accepted this last result and given Spinoza's doctrine a kink in the direction of idealism. Yet exactly the same kind of reflection might with proper changes be applied to Extension, which would then be wider than all the other attributes, and Spinoza might thus receive a kink in the direction of materialism. Spinoza himself answers Tschirnhaus briefly, and perhaps a little impatiently, in a letter which I will quote (Ep. 66): ' In answer to your objection I say, that although each particular thing be expressed in infinite ways in the infinite intellect of God, yet those infinite ideas, whereby it is expressed, cannot constitute one and the same mind of a particular thing, but infinite minds; seeing that each of these infinite ideas has no connection with the rest [and he refers to *Eth.* ii. 7 and Sch. i. 10]. If you will reflect on these passages a little, you will see that all the difficulty vanishes.'

It may be doubted whether a little reflection is enough or all difficulty vanishes; but I believe that Spinoza upon his own principles is right and that his thought is clear, with a little indulgence for his language. I cannot perceive x-modes because I am a body, and I can only perceive those objects which my body enables me to apprehend. Remember that when Spinoza says that a mode of thought, my idea, has for its *ideatum* a condition of my body, he does not mean that I *perceive*[2] that condition of body. The body is expressed (objectively he says, subjectively we

---

[1] *Spinoza, His Life and Philosophy*, 2nd edition (London, 1899), p. 162.
[2] In his own copy Alexander wrote in pencil 'in the usual sense of the word' after *perceive* and altered the word 'say' in the original to the word 'mean' as printed here. [Editor's note.]

should say) as the idea, but what I perceive is the tree, whose existence is implied in my bodily condition, because that condition varies with the perceived object. We perceive extended things, and we may also perceive our body, though the perceiving of my body is of course not the same idea as corresponds to the condition of my body when I perceive the table. Thus I can be said to perceive Reality under the attribute of extension, and in like manner I may be said to perceive the attribute of Thought because I apprehend thought in my own person, although it must be admitted this statement raises certain difficulties.

Now there is an x-mode corresponding to the idea and bodily condition I am in when I perceive the table. But I cannot perceive an x-mode because my particular sort of mind which is united to a particular sort of body has no means of perceiving x-modes. My bodily organs are affected in the world of motion and rest by the extended table, but I do not perceive the x-mode of the table but only its extension-mode, and consequently though my idea has a corresponding x-mode I cannot perceive it, because I do not perceive x-objects exterior to my body.

It may be answered : granted that I do not as a matter of fact perceive the x-mode of the table, the question is still, why not ? Does not the x-mode of the table affect the x-mode of my body or mind and throw it into a condition parallel to the condition of my extended body which has for its mental correlate the idea of the table ? The answer is that interaction between a thing like the table and my body is intelligible only within the infinite mode of motion and rest ; but we cannot speak of x-modes in such terms. We cannot therefore be sure that the x-correspondent of my idea of the table gives me the perception of the x-table. It might, for instance, be possible that in order to have perception of the x-table there was needed another body composed say of half my body and half yours, or of my body and a stone. The x-correspondent of my body in perceiving the table may be only a part of the x-mode which is necessary for the perception of the x-table, which perception consequently would belong to a quite different mind from mine. In other words, a different distribution of matter or rather of motion may be required for the purpose than is afforded by that particular distribution which constitutes my human body.

I can now return more immediately to Spinoza's own words in his letter. A different kind of mind is required to apprehend things as x-modes, and so it is only such minds which can perceive x-modes, *e.g.* the x-table, and can consequently perceive themselves also as x-modes. The infinite thought-mode includes every possible empirical variety of mind, some of which may overlap ours. Such minds would of course have extended bodies, but it is easy enough to conceive that they might apprehend x-modes but fail to apprehend modes of extension, for want of the proper means. I take it that when Spinoza says that each particular thing may be expressed in infinite ways in the infinite understanding of God he means that in that infinite understanding there are minds enough to perceive the x-mode and every other mode of my body or mind ; and that he uses the word ' express ' with some looseness or inaccuracy, and does not mean that the x-mode of my mind or body has a different mind for its *correspondent*, but only a different mind for its *percipient*. This being granted, there is no further difficulty in Spinoza's reply to the question of Tschirnhaus and his modern critics than is implied in the habitual ambiguity with which he speaks of an idea sometimes as the idea of the bodily condition which is its correspondent mode of extension, sometimes as the idea of the object.

Spinoza's critics have therefore, I plead, forgotten that what we humans can perceive in the ultimate substance depends on the empirical character of our bodies, on our particular distribution of motion and rest, and correspondingly of thought.

At the same time, good as Spinoza's defence may be made, consistently with his presuppositions, the defence is only necessary because he has taken thought to be an attribute of reality instead of merely an empirical character of certain complexes of space-time or motion. Substitute Time for Thought, and the whole edifice of infinite other attributes is otiose and unverifiable. It is founded indeed on the notion that Substance being the ground of all things must not only have attributes which characterise infinite modes but an infinite number of such attributes. With our gloss, we can be content to note that mind belongs to certain things in the world and not to others. There may indeed be other minds than ours, with bodies different from or more perfect than ours. And it is legitimate enough to suppose that such minds may apprehend other characters of things than we do. Why should colour, taste, etc., be the only secondary qualities of things? But there is no reason why we should assume that the objects perceived by such minds should be other than material or quasi-material objects like ours, and like them modes of extension or rather complexes of motion. The usefulness of other minds is in probing to the full the riches and variety of the *facies totius universi*. Perfection we shall find not in the arbitrary imagination of attributes which cannot fall within our human ken, but in the hierarchy of the verifiable qualities of the real world, culminating in the quality characteristic of God.

What remains of Spinoza's doctrine upon our gloss is not that there are infinite attributes but that there are infinite levels of the modes, that there is no end to the hierarchy of qualities amongst finite things.

VII

(5) *Religion in Spinoza and the Intellectual Love of God.* — A most important, and perhaps the most interesting, question is the consequence for the conceptions of religion and God of recognising Time to be an attribute. Spinoza's official description of religion is this : ' Whatsoever we desire and do, of which we are the cause, in so far as we have the idea of God, or know God, I set down to religion' (iv. 38, Schol. 1). This describes the religious life,

and is in the spirit of the words, ' who sweeps a room as for Thy laws makes that, and the action, fine '. But when we ask what is the nature of the religious emotion and what is God who is its object, we must carry our thoughts further. God for Spinoza is identical with Substance and is the whole universe. This belief is not demonstrated, or is only formally demonstrated, it is a restatement of the definition of God. Spinoza's conception of God is none the worse for being presented in the form of a definition. The great fundamental notions of philosophers are not proved, their truth is seen. Proofs are nothing but machinery which helps others to secure the philosopher's vision. It may be doubted, I observe in passing, whether this is not also true of every scientific principle too. It is reported of the old Greek philosopher Xenophanes that he said with reference to the whole universe that the One was God. The Greek phrase which is translated ' with reference to the whole universe ' is commonly, but Mr. Burnet, the great historian of Greek philosophy, says incorrectly, translated with greater picturesqueness, ' looking up to the vault of Heaven '. At any rate Spinoza looked out upon the universe and declared it to be God : he saw it as a unity and found God there. In like manner the physicist looks out on the universe and sees it to be a system of events. The greatest truths claim but to be statements of fact which the discoverer sees by looking out upon the world and finding them there. The only question is whether his vision is pure or distorted or partial.

Our question in regard to Spinoza is whether the God which he sees is not merely a name for the universe but truly the object of worship, of the religious sentiment or emotion. If we seek in Spinoza for our experience of the religious passion, we find it in the noble and ecstatic conception of what he calls the intellectual love of God. It arises out of or along with the third or highest form of knowledge, intuitive knowledge. Science or reason, the second kind of knowledge, is the knowledge of true universals, those common properties of things which I have before alluded to as the characters of the world of motion and rest, which we would give a great deal that Spinoza had dwelt upon more fully. But intuitive knowledge is scientific knowledge seen in its connection with God. And since all knowledge of things is for Spinoza experience of ourselves, such knowledge means the experience of our own unification with God ; it enables us to realise all things in their necessary connection with God's nature as expressed by his attributes, it gives us control of our passions, for it takes us out of our isolation and gives us communion with other persons and with God, it secures us true contentment of spirit, something like the tranquillity of which Epicurus spoke, but a contentment which is not empty, but on the contrary rich in all knowledge, for it pervades the whole of our action and contemplation with the sense of the abiding reference of it to God.

It is not very easy to make clear to ourselves the nature of this intuitive knowledge and its accompanying emotion. Spinoza himself illustrates it by a simple and not very satisfying example. He takes the case of finding a fourth proportional to three given numbers. Mere science or reason would find it by multiplying the second and third numbers together and dividing the product by the first. But with simple numbers like 1, 2, 3, we recognise intuitively that the fourth proportional is 6. The notion is that of an act whereby truth is recognised without the labour of demonstration. A later philosopher of our day, Mr. Bradley, has spoken of a feeling which is above and supersedes reflection. Our simplest life is that of bare feeling ; then follows reflection in which we think of the relations of things ; then comes the feeling in which we cease to break up the unity of realities into their separate aspects or features, which our analytical reflection discloses and in which it works as in its appropriate medium, and we return to the immediacy of our original feeling, but to an immediacy which is no longer naïve and irreflective, but chastened by reflection and superior to it. Something like this is implied in the intuitive knowledge of Spinoza. And the emotional condition corresponds. It is port after stormy seas; the labour of reflection, its doubts, its strenuous pain are replaced by the passionate calm of utter conviction and satisfaction of the mind.

No conception, however exalted, suffers from homely illustrations, and a few such will help us to approximate to the condition described. I will take so simple a case as the conviction, after Euclid's demonstration with all the apparatus of geometrical construction, that the three angles of a triangle are equal to two right angles, or the angles at the base of an isosceles triangle are equal; when the result is proved the properties in question are seen and with delighted satisfaction; that 'tempest of the soul is resolved', to use a phrase of Epicurus, with which the process of reflection was attended, and the delighted spirit enjoys its vision. A still homelier example occurs to me. There is a passage of well-known difficulty in *Hamlet*, ' For if the sun breed maggots in a dead dog, being a God kissing carrion ', and so on. The original text said, ' a good kissing carrion ', but as the commentators could make no sense of it, one of them emended the text and substituted the phrase I quoted, which held its ground, although everybody felt it was too artificial even for Shakespeare in his earlier years, and certainly in his maturity when he wrote *Hamlet*. But one fine day Sir Walter Raleigh points out that the phrase ' a good kissing carrion ' is analogous to ' a good drinking water '. Our doubts disappear, and not only have we the conviction that the old text is right, but we bathe in the conviction, and go about our work for the rest of the day whistling, with the sunshine in our hearts. Everyone knows of the excitement into which Newton was thrown when, with the newly arrived corrected measurements of the distance of the moon, he discovered his theory to be verified. Mr. Einstein has not yet betrayed to us what he felt when the news reached him that the deflection of light from a star by the neighbourhood of the sun had been found in a solar eclipse to be twice what it would be if Newton's law of gravitation were accurate, and that it verified the formula which followed from the theory of relativity.

These examples may seem to be no more than mere scientific or intellectual pleasure in a limited subject. Yet they all exhibit the recognition that the limited subject fits into a whole department of our intellectual world and the pleasure pervades our whole being. They are at last approximations to the goal. Imagine that any object is conceived in its relation to God, and we have on the one side intuitive knowledge, on the other the union of ourselves with God, which is the intellectual love of God.

Spinoza does not call this intellectual love religion, but it is the emotion which, in his system, is nearest to the religious passion, and it is implied in the official account of religion which I began this section by quoting. At the same time these illustrations help us to recognise a certain defect in Spinoza's conception of intellectual love in so far as we take it to represent religious passion. It seems to describe the passion in terms of the character of its object as recognised by intelligence, to describe it by a symptom rather than intrinsically. Unless the religious passion were already lit, it is hard to see how the intellectual love would rise above a supreme intellectual satisfaction, and this is not the religious but the scientific sentiment. Suppose the passion for God, and this scientific sentiment blazes up into religion. But the religious passion must be there to begin with.

The defect must not be exaggerated. For knowing is for Spinoza an action, judgment is an exercise of will; and to that extent the intellectual recognition of the object of a passion is itself something practical. But it remains true of his whole treatment of the emotions, masterly as it admittedly is, that it defines the emotions too exclusively in intellectual terms of the knowledge involved; and is able to do so, because from the beginning emotions are considered as forms of desire. Take as typical his description of love as pleasure accompanied by the idea of an external cause, which he contrasts with the account given by some that it is the lover's will to unite himself to the beloved object, an account which he thinks expresses a property but not the essence of the emotion. The truth is rather reversed. It is rather Spinoza who is describing by a property. It is not the lover's recognition of his pleasure (which be it remembered is with Spinoza a passion and a conation) as caused by the object which makes his pleasure into love. On the contrary, it is because his pleasure has the character of love that he recognises the object as its cause. Or, in other words, the object induces a certain reaction on the part of the lover, and it is this emotional reaction, the particular form of his pleasure, which makes him recognise the object as lovely and the cause of his pleasure. Just in the same way, I do not eat an apple because I see it to be good to eat, but in so far as it excites in me the blind appetite to eat it I recognise it to be eatable. The intellectual love of God so far fails of being religious as it wants the special flavour of worship. But given the passion of worship, that passion leads us to discover and recognise God (supposing we identify God with the Spinozistic Substance) as the fountain of all our perfect knowledge. It will be seen that the question at issue, betrayed by these difficulties, is whether the ground and sum of our knowing is truly the object of our worship. For the pantheist it is.

It is outside my subject to ask whether pantheism is right in this belief. But before I pass on to my proper question I will allow myself to add two more remarks before I tear myself away from the fascination of intellectual love. It has been stigmatised as mysticism ; but to my mind that is not in itself a reproach. There is a sound and a dangerous mysticism. The sound variety is an essential ingredient in all religion ; it is not too much to say that it is the vital ingredient of religion, without which religion is a thing of forms. To say that Spinoza was a mystic is only to say that he was full of the religious passion. And in the main his mysticism in its origin from intuitive knowledge is of the sound variety, reflected in the temper of contentment, or *acquiescentia animi*, which makes all life a service of God.

The dangerous form of mysticism is that in which the worshipper is lost in the adoration of God, and God becomes an infinite abyss of negatives, an abstraction which, in purporting to be the secret of reality, is in fact attenuated into the indescribable. Spinoza's conception of God does not altogether escape this reproach, and accordingly in one of its aspects the intellectual love of God does not always leave room for the claim of the healthy individual soul, but tends towards the utter absorption of the individual in God. It asks for no answering love from God. It is but a portion of the infinite love with which God loves himself. It is not only unselfish, being intensified with the imagination that others are joined with us in this love, but it is selfless. This was the very feature which recommended Spinoza to the mind of Goethe. But it is the drawback to which the religion of Pantheism is always liable, and which Spinoza has not completely avoided. The healthy religious mind shares Spinoza's mysticism to the point of its feeling of our oneness with God ; but it asks for the fathering response, and holds that God's need of us is no less than our need of him. It saves the individual from absorption by securing his independent entry into the relation of dependence upon God, and seeks in God fulfilment of the human being and not absorption. But for Spinoza it was difficult to secure such independence because God for him, though singular, is not so much an individual as a totality, and is not a person, for personality is but a finite mode, and his eternity is not duration any more than the immortality of man is prolonged life after death.

VIII

Changes in the Conception of God and Religion : the 'Conatus' of Spinoza and the 'Nisus'. — ' But now my *gloss* proceeds.' When Time is introduced into the ultimate reality as an essential ingredient, the conception of God and of the religious passion is altered at once. If we consider Spinoza, we are at a loss to identify God as the sum of reality with the object of worship; worship, as we have seen, is with him an intellectual passion and wants the specific flavour of devotion. The difficulty is common to Spinoza with every form of Pantheism. For the pantheistic Supreme Being lacks the human note. It contains humanity and all other things indiscriminately, and it contains evil and good alike, for what from our human view is evil is not evil as in the Supreme Being. Whereas worship demands in its object something indeed greater than man, and different from him in kind, not personality, but still something in touch with personality, which therefore in our weakness of imagination we shadow forth to ourselves as a person, and something which if the predicates of good and bad are inappropriate to what is above good and evil, is yet in the lineal succession of goodness.

Now, if the ultimate reality is Space-Time, the stuff out of which by various distributions all things arise, there can be no pretence that it can be the object of worship, it can no longer be as such identified with God. We must seek accordingly for God, or let us say rather his divinity, elsewhere, as some character not coextensive with the reality but contained within it.

To find this deity or divinity let us go back to another of Spinoza's conceptions, that of the *conatus*, which, according to him, everything possesses of persisting or persevering in its being. It belongs to everything, but is best realised from considering organic creatures. In all their goings-on, various as these are with the differences of occasions which provoke them, the plant or animal maintains its single individuality of being, abandoning it only to external violence or internal decay, or perchance in rarer cases (those of divided personality) splitting for the time into two things, each of which persists in its being, though they may overlap in some respects and have common use of some portion of the one body in which they are lodged. But the description applies equally to a stone or a molecule or an atom. The atom persists in its being in so far as the motions of its planetary system of electrons moving round their central nucleus are conserved. When five alpha particles are emitted in a series, the atom of radium changes to one of lead.

Such is the illuminating conception of the conatus. In Spinoza's language we may say that within the infinite mode of motion and rest, a certain complex of motion and rest has arisen from the original Substance in which an equilibrium exists, in virtue whereof the proportions of motion and rest among the parts of the complex retain their proportion. But for him, as we have seen, these bodies which thus maintain a moving equilibrium arise by the edict of God, but do not grow from one another in the order of time, or, as we say, by evolution, but rather subsist side by side as in a museum of forms. With Time as the other aspect of Space-Time, the animating mind of the body which is Space, it is easy for us to see, vaguely perhaps and yet without doubt, that it is the restlessness of Space-Time which it owes to its temporal character, which is itself the author of this variety of forms, now no longer an array but a procession. Space-Time falls of itself under the impulse of Time into these distributions of motion, into the complexes which are bodies, and certain of them attain equilibrium and persist as such. Yet nature infected with Time, not as a disease but as its vitality, does not stop, but pushing on, evolves out of these stable forms fresh distributions and a new order of beings with their specific character and their own conatus to persevere in their type. Experience shows us this evolution and science endeavours to exhibit the methods in detail by which the evolution is effected.

This striving of Space-Time and of the world of things heretofore precipitated from that matrix, we may call, not by the Spinozistic name of conatus, but by the simpler and vague name of a *nisus*. It is not an effort of the world to go beyond itself. We cannot think of the infinite stuff widening its limits, it would in that case cease to be infinite. It goes beyond itself only by the effecting of fresh distributions of its motions into new complexes of motion. This nisus or effort of the world as a whole (which as a whole is never in moving equilibrium and therefore does not possess a conatus) is felt or shared in by the individual forms in which it has resulted, and hence out of those forms, out of one level in the hierarchy of levels of existence, a new level of existence is evolved. This is what we actually observe. The descendants of a type of beings become modified; and suiting themselves to their environment, that is, not only to other beings on their own level or on lower ones, but to all those portions of nature as well which have not yet taken the shape of individual forms of being — climate, weather, magnetic variations, everything which may be summed up as moods of the unorganised world — change their character and become new beings on a different level. They were stones, and out of that physical level arises life ; out of life, mind. Thus the nisus of the world as a whole is reflected in the transformation of types which takes place, as attested by observation and theory, out of lower to higher levels. Like a man caught in the cogs of a machine, material things are caught in the nisus, and give rise to living ones.

Moreover the nisus of the whole is shared at any moment by everything within it, though it is only in those things from which a new level not yet attained is to proceed that it is palpable. Life has been evolved and has been embodied in finite living things ; and mind in sentient things. The nisus would seem to have done its work so far as the attainment of life or mind is concerned. Yet still material and living things are caught in the nisus, in virtue of which they sustain the level above them, and without which that level would disappear, and things would shrink back to a lower stage, And within the ' minds ' of these material or living things themselves the nisus is felt as a nisus towards something unattained, and they have the analogue of what religion is for us. The ' mind ' of the stone is a dim striving towards life, which for the stone is an unattained level of existence, although we who come later know that life has taken the realised form of finite living things.

Thus the nisus of the world is not like the turning of a squirrel in a cage, a mere repetition of itself. If that were so, Space-Time would be not what it is, a stuff in which individual forms are moulded, but itself an individual; instead of an infinite mode of motion, it would be Substance, and that motion is incompatible with the essentially temporal nature of reality. It is the impulse of the world towards new levels of existence (as well as towards new kinds of being within any one level), and the guarantee that the particular distribution of motion attained shall not be permanent as a whole, but only admit those relative permanences within it which do exhibit the Spinozistic conatus.

Each of these levels in the hierarchy of beings is characterised by its distinctive quality — materiality, let us say, taking the most prominent examples, life, mind. We can now adumbrate the meaning of deity. It is the characteristic quality of the next higher level of existence prophesied by the nisus of the universe which has created mind and the finite beings endowed with it, which, observe, are not necessarily only human minds. The beings which would possess such deity would be finite gods. But when we ask what for us is God, we must answer that it is the world as a whole with this nisus towards deity. If deity were attained, there would be not infinite God but finite gods, and the world-nisus would carry the distribution of motion in turn past them. But for us, into whose experience deity attained does not enter, for whom there are not gods but infinite God, God is the being described. His body is the whole universe, his mind (or his distinctive form of temporal complex) is infinite deity. Such deity would not be coextensive with the whole world. For when we examine empirically the relation of beings of one level to existence at a lower level we find that the higher quality is not coextensive with a body of the lower level but with a portion of it. The mind, for instance, is coextensive with (Spinoza would say, is the idea of), a portion of the living body, the brain or at most the central nervous system. In like manner we must conceive deity as belonging not to the world as a whole, but to a portion of it. Only so long as we are thinking not of gods but of God, that portion is an infinite portion, which represents the whole world in the same sense as the brain is commonly believed to represent the whole body, because every affection of the body is directly or indirectly reflected in the brain. Hence, instead of a God who is identical with the whole of nature, as with Spinoza, we have to say that only God's body is so identical, but that God's deity, that which is characteristic of him, is lodged only in a part of the world. God is immanent in nature, is pantheistic, in respect of his body, but in respect of his divinity transcends us, though still remaining within nature, and is theistic.

The sentiment of religion, the emotion of worship compels an explanation upon the same lines. Sharing in the nisus of the universe ; caught as we are in the wheels of that being, which arising out of the chaos of Space-Time evolves levels of beings with their conatus, but always retains the unused chaos which allows of the emergence of new levels; we respond to that nisus in the feeling of oneness with the next higher type of quality which is to arise out of the level we or other minds have attained. As love, to go back to the old example, is in its essence a specified reaction to an individual of opposite sex, so religion is the reaction which we make to God as the whole universe with its nisus towards the new quality of deity. But whereas love is a manifestation of the conatus of the human or animal individual, religious passion is a manifestation of the nisus which the human being possesses because he is caught in the general machinery. It has therefore no specific organ though it issues in bodily movements of supplication and diffused bodily excitements. And like other emotions it leads us to the intellectual apprehension of its object. Because the whole world in its nisus to deity evokes in us the response of religion, we become aware of the world as in this tendency divine, and apprehend God, as we apprehend the object of love to be lovely. The religious passion which we find in ourselves cries out for an object which intellect then sets itself the task of describing in intellectual terms, discovering its relation to observed realities.

Thus the gap which we find in Spinoza between the speculative conception of God and the religious demand that God should be an object of worship, is filled when Time is acknowledged to be of the very life of ultimate reality. In this process, however, the idea of God suffers, in being thus brought near to the common experience of religion, a radical change, and the idea of religion, becomes in some sense, as indeed we feel it to be, a bodily passion, not merely an intellectual love.

IX

Conclusion. — Such are some, and perhaps the most important, consequences which would follow from the substitution of Time for Thought in the Spinozistic attributes. It goes without saying that no one would propose to construct a philosophy for himself in this fashion by trying upon the system of a great philosopher the effects of a hypothesis. He could in fact only make the hypothesis if he had himself reached such conclusions already, without deliberately or consciously building himself upon the philosopher in question.[1] But he may take pride in showing his affiliation to such a philosopher as Spinoza, and the more if he is himself a Jew speaking to Jews : and he may do so I think legitimately by the avowedly unhistorical method of using Spinoza to an end which the historic Spinoza would not have entertained. My hearers may think that however much I have tried to render faithfully the historic meaning of certain parts of Spinoza's doctrine, I have been more concerned with the gloss than with the text. But a great man does not exist to be followed slavishly, and may be more honoured by divergence than

[1] See the writer's *Space, Time, and Deity*, London, 1920.

by obedience. As for Spinoza himself, it is too late a day to express unbounded admiration.[1] Moreover, no courage is required to praise him, for the admirer runs no risk. The Jews will not excommunicate me for my veneration of Spinoza, neither will the Gentiles denounce this lecture as infamous. He who for a hundred years was Maledictus de Spinoza has long since recovered his proper name of Baruch or Benedictus. I have at most illustrated the commonplace that veneration is not the same thing as idolatry.

[1] In his last years Alexander often told me that the cult of Spinoza in England was being dangerously over-driven.

I have heard of vague surmises to the general effect that there may have been actual blood relationship between Alexander's forebears and Spinoza's. Alexander himself had no such dreams, but Professor J. A. Gunn writes to me from Melbourne: 'there is a belief here, shared by the Slomans, that the family were Sephardic and not Ashkenazy Jews'.

Nobody seems to know when or why Alexander's ancestors choose that surname.

Alexander used to say that the Jewish people were racially as mixed as the British; but then he was referring principally to very ancient times.

[Editor's note.]

ELENCHUS OPERUM

IN this list of published work I have intentionally omitted all obituaries, all reviews for daily newspapers, all letters and reports of speeches or lectures in the same, and some little things that seemed to me to be too unimportant for their company. I am afraid there are some other omissions, although I hope there are not very many. These are unintentional, and I have tried to trace everything of which I found any mention in Alexander's books and letters. — J. L.

ABBREVIATIONS

A.S.P. = *Aristotelian Society Proceedings.*
I.J.E. = *International Journal of Ethics.*
H.J. = *The Hibbert Journal.*
B.J.P. = *The British Journal of Psychology.*
J.P.S. = *The Journal of Philosophical Studies*, later called *Philosophy*.
B.J.R.L. = *Bulletin of the John Rylands Library* (Manchester).

1884. January 23. The *Oxford Magazine*. ' Progress, Poverty, and Logic.' (An article in pure economics on Henry George.)
May 28 and June 4. The *Oxford Magazine*. Reviews of Lotze's *System of Philosophy*, ed. B. Bosanquet.
1885. April. *Mind*. Review of O. Pfleiderer, *Religionsphilosophie auf geschichtlichen Grundlagen.*
October. *Mind*. Review of Royce, *The Religious Aspect of Philosophy.*
1886. April. *Mind*. Review of Steinthal, *Allgemeine Ethik.*
October. *Mind*. Hegel's ' Conception of Nature '.
1888. *A.S.P.* Contribution to symposium, ' Is Mind Synonymous with Consciousness ? ' (with Ritchie, Stout, and Bosanquet).
June 6. The *Oxford Magazine*. Review of A. Seth, *Hegelianism and Personality.*
1889. May 4. The *Academy*. Review of *Works of T. H. Green* (ed. R. L. Nettleship), Vol. III.
July. *Mind*. Review of St. G. Mivart, *On Truth.*
Moral Order and Progress : An Analysis of Ethical Conceptions. London, Trübner and Co.
December. *A.S.P.* Contribution to symposium, ' Is there Evidence of Design in Nature ' (along with W. L. Gildea and G. J. Romanes).

ELENCHUS OPERUM

1890. May 21. The *Oxford Magazine*. Review of Bosanquet, *Logic, or the Morphology of Knowledge*.
October. *Mind*. Review of W. C. Coupland, *The Gain of Life*.
December 27. The *Athenaeum* 'Experimental Psychology' (about Münsterberg).

1891. January. *Mind*. Review of J. S. Mackenzie, *An Introduction to Social Philosophy*.

1892. January. *Mind*. 'The Idea of Value.'
March 7. *A.S.P.* Contribution to symposium, 'Is the Distinction between "Is" and "Ought" Ultimate and Irreducible?' (with Sidgwick, Muirhead, and Stout).
April. *Mind*. Discussion, 'Dr. Münsterberg and his Critics'.
July. *I.J.E.* 'Natural Selection in Morals.'
October. The *American Journal of Psychology*. Open letter (about Oxford education).

1893. January 21. *The Speaker*. Review of J. Burnet, *Early Greek Philosophy*.
January. *Mind*. Review of H. Spencer, *Principles of Ethics*.
February 6. *A.S.P.* Contribution to symposium, 'Has the Perception of Time an Origin in Thought?' (with G. Dawes Hicks).
July. *I.J.E.* 'Character and Conduct.'

1894. January. *Mind*. Review of H. Spencer, *Principles of Ethics* (continued).
January. *I.J.E.* 'The Meaning of Motive' (2-page reply to D. G. Ritchie).
October 1. The *Journal of Education*. 'The Education of the Citizen.'

1899. January. *Mind*. Review of T. Lipps, *Raumästhetik und geometrische-optische Täuschungen*.

1900. July. *Child Life*. 'Interest' (Froebel Society Lecture).

1902. *A Plea for an Independent University in Manchester*. (Pamphlet reprinted from the *Manchester Guardian*. An article on the same subject appeared in *The Speaker* of March 1, 1902.)
March 1. *The Speaker*. 'The Disruption of the Victoria University.'

1904. June. *The Paidologist*. 'Sympathy.'

1906. July. *The Cornhill Magazine*. 'The Mind of a Dog.'

1908. June 12. *A.S.P.* Contribution to a symposium on 'Mental Activity' (with Ward, C. Read, and Stout).
Locke. London, Constable.
November. *A.S.P.* 'Mental Activity in Willing and in Ideas' (Presidential Address).

1909. October. *H.J.* 'Ptolemaic and Copernican Views of the Place of Mind in the Universe.'
November. *A.S.P.* 'On Sensations and Images' (Presidential Address).

ELENCHUS OPERUM

1910. March 12. The *Glasgow Herald*. ' Knowledge and Reality.'
November. *A.S.P.* ' Self as Subject and as Person ' (Presidential Address).
1911. December. *B.J.P.* ' Foundations and Sketch-Plan of a Conational Psychology.'
1912. January. *Mind*. ' The Method of Metaphysics and the Categories.'
May 12. *A.S.P.* Discussion contributed with reference to B. Edgell's paper on ' Images and Memory '.
July. *Mind*. ' On Relations, and in particular the Cognitive Relation.'
1913. January. *Mind*. ' Collective Willing and Truth — I.'
April. *Mind*. ' Collective Willing and Truth — II.'
1914. January 28. *Proceedings of the British Academy*. ' The Basis of Realism.'
A.S.P. ' Freedom.'
1918. *A.S.P.* ' Space-Time ' (Abstract).
1920. *Space, Time, and Deity*. 2 vols. London, Macmillan and Co.
1921. May 1. *Spinoza and Time* (Arthur Davis Memorial Lecture). Published by G. Allen and Unwin, London.
October. *Mind*. ' Some Explanations.'
1922. July. *H.J.* ' Natural Piety.'
1923. January. *Mind*. ' Sense-Perception. A Reply to Mr. Stout.'
October and November. The *Cornhill Magazine*. ' Dr. Johnson as a Philosopher.'
1924. October. The *Holborn Review*. ' Kant.'
1925. January. *H.J.* ' The Artistry of Truth.'
June. *Magazine of the Inter-University Jewish Federation*. ' The Opening of the Hebrew University.'
Art and the Material (Adamson Lecture). Manchester University Press.
1926. January. *J.P.S.* ' Art and Science.'
July. *B.J.R.L. Molière and Life*.
1927. March 13. *Spinoza: An Address*. Published by the Liberal Jewish Union.
April. *B.J.P.* ' The Creative Process in the Artist's Mind.'
May 23. *Art and Instinct* (Herbert Spencer Lecture). Oxford, Clarendon Press.
July. *B.J.R.L. Art and Nature*.
July. *H.J.* ' Theism and Pantheism.'
Lessons from Spinoza (Dissertatio ex Chronici Spinozani Tomo Quinto : The Hague).
Preface to the new impression of *Space, Time, and Deity*.
November 23. *Proceedings of the British Academy*. ' Artistic Creation and Cosmic Creation.'
1928. April. *J.P.S.* ' Morality as an Art.'
July. *B.J.R.L. The Art of Jane Austen*.

ELENCHUS OPERUM

1928. October. *The Personalist* (Los Angeles, Calif.). 'Naturalism and Value.'
1929. *Encyclopaedia Britannica*, 14th ed., Vol. XVIII. 'Qualities, Primary, Secondary, and Tertiary.'
 April. *Mind.* Note on 'Locke's Lantern'.
 April. *J.P.S.* 'Philosophy and Art.'
1930. April 28. *A.S.P.* 'Beauty and Greatness in Art.'
 July. *H.J.* 'Truth, Goodness, and Beauty.'
 July. *J.P.S.* 'Science and Art'— I.
 September. 'Truth, Goodness, and Beauty.' (*Proceedings of the VIIth International Congress of Philosophy*). Published Oxford, Clarendon Press, 1931.
 October. *J.P.S.* 'Science and Art' — II.
 December 3. *The Listener.* 'Science and Religion.' (National Broadcast, subsequently published in a volume of the same title by Gerald Howe, London.)
1931. July. *B.J.R.L. Pascal the Writer.*
 July–September. The *Political Quarterly.* 'The Purpose of a University.'
 August. *Economica.* Review of *L. T. Hobhouse: His Life and Work.*
1932. January and April. *J.P.S.* 'Poetry and Prose in the Arts.'
 T. F. Tout and the University of Manchester. In *The Collected Papers of Thomas Frederick Tout*, Vol. I. Manchester University Press, 1932.
1933. July. *B.J.R.L. Value.*
 Beauty and Other Forms of Value. London, Macmillan and Co.
 Spinoza. Manchester University Press.
1934. January 3. *The Listener.* 'Philosophy and Beauty.'
1935. *Revue de métaphysique et de morale* (No. 4, Vol. XIII). 'Valeur et Grandeur.'
1936. 'The Historicity of Things', in *Philosophy and History; Essays Presented to Ernst Cassirer.* Oxford, Clarendon Press.
1937. April. *A.S.P.* 'Form and Subject-matter in Art' (Presidential Address).
 'The Objectivity of Value.' (*IXth Congress of Philosophy*, Vol. X. Paris, Hermann et Cie.)

THE END

DATE DUE			
GAYLORD			PRINTED IN U.S.A.